Quantifying the World

To Tim,

With warm appreciation of all the great discussions and intellectual debates we have shared over the years. Your 'invisible' hand is clearly apparent in many of the observations between these covers!

Michael.

United Nations Intellectual History Project

Ahead of the Curve? UN Ideas and Global Challenges
  Louis Emmerij, Richard Jolly, and Thomas G. Weiss

Unity and Diversity in Development Ideas: Perspectives from the
UN Regional Commissions
  Edited by Yves Berthelot

UN Contributions to Development Thinking and Practice
  Richard Jolly, Louis Emmerij, Dharam Ghai, and Frédéric Lapeyre

The UN and Global Political Economy: Trade, Finance, and Development
  John Toye and Richard Toye

Quantifying the World
UN Ideas and Statistics

Michael Ward

Indiana University Press

Bloomington and Indianapolis

This book is a publication of

Indiana University Press
601 North Morton Street
Bloomington, Indiana 47404-3797 USA

http://iupress.indiana.edu

Telephone orders	800-842-6796
Fax orders	812-855-7931
Orders by e-mail	iuporder@indiana.edu

The paper used in this publication meets the minimum requirements
of American National Standard for Information Sciences—Permanence
of Paper for Printed Library Materials, ANSI Z39.48-1984.

Manufactured in the United States of America

Library of Congress Cataloging-in-Publication Data

Ward, Michael.
  Quantifying the world : UN ideas and statistics / Michael Ward.
    p. cm. — (United Nations intellectual history project)
Includes index.
  ISBN 0-253-34397-6 (cloth : alk. paper) — ISBN 0-253-
21674-5 (pbk. : alk. paper)
  1. Statistical services. 2. Statistics. 3. United Nations—
Statistical services. I. Title. II. Series.
  HA36.W37 2004
  001.4'06'01—dc22

                          2003023831

1 2 3 4 5 09 08 07 06 05 04

Contents

Boxes, Tables, Charts, and Figures

Boxes

Tables

Charts

Figures

Foreword

It is surprising that there is no comprehensive history of the United Nations family of organizations. True, a few of the UN funds and specialized agencies have or are in the process of writing their institutional histories. But this is mostly a recent endeavor and, indeed, it is no more than what should be expected of all public organizations, especially internationally accountable ones, along with enhanced efforts to organize their archives so that independent researchers can also document and analyze dispassionately their efforts and achievements. All this is an essential part of the record of international governance during the last half-century.

Faced with this major omission—which has substantial implications for the academic and policy literatures—we decided to undertake the task of beginning to write an *intellectual* history; that is, a history of the ideas launched or nurtured by the United Nations. Observers should not be put off by what may strike them as a puffed-up billing. The working assumption behind this effort is straightforward: ideas and concepts are a main driving force in human progress, and they arguably have been one of the most important contributions of the world organization.

The United Nations Intellectual History Project (UNIHP) was launched in 1999 as an independent research effort based in the Ralph Bunche Institute for International Studies at The Graduate Center of The City University of New York. The project also maintains a liaison office in Geneva. We are grateful for the enthusiastic backing from the Secretary-General and other staff and governments within the UN system. Generous financial support from five foundations and eight governments ensures total intellectual and financial independence. Details of this and other aspects of the project can be found at our Web site: www.unhistory.org.

The work of the UN can be divided into two broad categories: economic and social development, on the one hand, and peace and security, on the other. The UNIHP is committed to produce fourteen volumes on major themes in the first arena and a further three volumes if sufficient resources can be mobilized to focus on the latter. All these volumes will be published in a series by Indiana University Press. The project has also completed an oral history collection of some seventy-five lengthy interviews of persons who have played major roles in launching and nurturing UN ideas—and sometimes in hindering them! Extracts from these interviews will be published in 2004 in *UN Ideas: Voices from the Trenches and Turrets*. Authors of the project's various volumes, including this one, have drawn on these interviews to highlight substantive points in their texts. Full transcripts of the oral histories will be disseminated in electronic form at the end of the project to facilitate work by other researchers and interested persons worldwide.

There is no single way to organize research, and certainly not for such an ambitious project as this one. The way that we have structured this history is to select topics—ranging from trade and finance to human rights, from transnational corporations to development assistance, from gender to sustainability—to tease out the history of ideas under each of these topical headings. We have selected world-class experts for each topic, but each has been given freedom and responsibility to organize their own digging, analysis, and presentation. Guidance from ourselves as the project directors, as well as from peer-review groups, is provided to ensure accuracy and fairness in depicting where the ideas came from, what happened to them within the UN system, and what happened afterward.

Quantifying the World is the volume that takes on the UN's contribution to ideas, thinking, concepts, and practice in the area of statistics. As will emerge, the UN's influence in matters statistical has been greater than in most other areas of economic and social thinking, in part because for most of the period since 1945, the UN's authority in these matters has been virtually unchallenged, at least by any other institution. And in the early years, when the groundwork for international statistics and statistics on development was being laid, the UN was fortunate in securing the services of some of the world's greatest intellectual pioneers in the subject. So the strengths of the international statistical system as it developed—as well as its weaknesses and omissions—is a record of the strengths and weaknesses of the UN's own work and leadership in this area.

Michael Ward brings all this out with insight and originality. Instead of becoming immersed in the technical details of each and every UN statistical initiative and innovation, he steps back to take a broader view of the measures developed and their economic and social significance. Ward writes as both practitioner and analyst, drawing on well over forty years of experience working as a statistician and economist in more than two dozen countries all around the world. He served as a principal economist in the Data Development Group of the World Bank for fifteen years and taught and undertook research in the University of Cambridge and the Institute of Development Studies at the University of Sussex. He has contributed numerous publications on statistics and economic development and has joined countless professional meetings and discussions on matters of statistical policy.

We encouraged Ward to draw on this unique background to provide a wide-ranging perspective of the UN's contributions to ideas and thinking on statistics. As he explains in his prologue, "This book is not a technical treatise on statistics. It is an essay about the evolution of statistical ideas in response to the needs of policy. It represents an attempt to initiate a wider discussion of the political economy of numbers." Ward asks why certain data were considered important and why other data or concerns were neglected and speculates on how these decisions have influenced the ways people and policymakers round the world have come to view the world.

It was the late Dudley Seers, himself both a distinguished statistician and development economist, who so succinctly and so clearly stated why statistics and statisticians are important:

> We cannot, with our own eyes and ears, perceive more than a minute sample of human affairs, even in our own country—and a very unrandom sample at that. So we rely on statistics in order to build and maintain our own model of the world. The data that are available mould our perceptions.
>
> A statistical policy—(i.e., the policy of statistical offices)—exerts a subtle but pervasive influence on political, social and economic development: this is why the apparently dull and minor subject of statistical priorities is of crucial importance.[1]

The international significance of the subject of this historical study by Michael Ward would bring a smile of satisfaction to the lips of Dudley Seers.

We are convinced that the UN story deserves to be better documented if it is to be better understood and appreciated.[2] As UN Secretary-General Kofi Annan kindly wrote in the foreword to *Ahead of the Curve? UN Ideas and Global Challenges:* "With the publication of this first volume in the United Nations Intellectual History Project, a significant lacuna in twentieth-century scholarship and international relations begins to be filled."[3] With this present volume, a further gap in the record is filled.

We hope that readers will enjoy this journey through time.

Louis Emmerij
Richard Jolly
Thomas G. Weiss
New York

Acknowledgments

Many people have very kindly contributed their thoughts, ideas, energies, and memories to this book.

Some critical interviews of leading figures in the UN Statistics Division were conducted by Makiko Harrison at the beginning of the project. She also carried out similar interviews with four distinguished Japanese statisticians who have had a strong association with the work of the UN; Professor Y. Kurabayashi, a former Director of the UN Statistics Office; Professor Kimio Uno, who contributed particularly to UN activities in environmental accounting; Professor Kawakatsu, who was deputy director of the UN Statistical Institute for Asia and the Pacific (SIAP) and a former senior statistician at the FAO; and Dr. Saburo Kawai, chairperson of the International Development Center of Japan, who originally proposed the setting up of SIAP and a regional statistical training center in Tokyo.

At the UN itself, Hermann Habermann, when director of the UN Statistics Division, allowed me a free hand in accessing material and, through the assistance of Anna Harttmann, what little remains, sadly, of the old statistical archives. Members of his staff gave of their precious time to provide essential perspectives on the intellectual foundations, data strategies, and operational characteristics of statistical activities in their respective areas of expertise. My special thanks must go to Richard Roberts for his extensive institutional knowledge and to Robert Johnston, Mary Chamie, Alice Clague, Vladimir Drjuchin, and Alessandra Alfieri for their valuable contributions on the subjects of trade statistics, social indicators and gender statistics, classifications, demographic statistics, technical cooperation, and environmental accounts. Former members of staff who provided not only a retrospective view but also additional insight into the priorities and accomplishments of the statistical office and gave valuable advice include Professor William Seltzer, a former director of UNSO; Leo Goldstone (social statistics); Jan van Tongeren (national accounts); Parmeet Singh (household surveys); and Joann Vanek and Beverley Carlson (statistics on women). In other areas of the UN in New York, Joe Chamie, director of the Population Division; Ian Kinneburgh, director of the Development Policy Analysis Division; and Douglas Walker, a former senior economist, provided important background information about the relationship of the work of the statistical office to their own responsibilities in the UN Secretariat. Glen-Marie Lange, Asami Miketa, Alan Heston, Derek Blades, Wolf Scott, and Ramesh Chander, consultants and specialists who have been associated with UN initiatives, also kindly shared their views with me.

On the historical background and institutional connections to economic and social policy, I received great help from Professor Phyllis Deane and Sir Claus Moser, who underlined the enormous importance, especially in the early years of UN statistics, of key individuals and the influence they had in the pursuit of appropriate statistical agendas. Ralph Turvey, a former director of Statistics at the ILO who has himself made seminal contributions to questions of measurement in prices and employment, guided me in the direction of many important issues. Jacob Ryten shared with me his unique experience of the UN institutional system and the origins of the city groups.

A number of old friends and colleagues, including Anne Harrison, Andrew Brown, Tony Friend, Denis Casley, Dick Allen, Jenny Church, Gareth Jones, William White, Jon Wilmshurst, and John Eldelman, also shared with me their experiences of working with or within the international statistical system in different thematic areas and offered many helpful observations that influenced my thinking. Hans Singer, in particular, with his long and unique professional institutional involvement with the UN and its various agencies, provided a wealth of information and background context.

My most important intellectual debt, however, is to my review committee: Yves Berthelot, Richard Jolly, Oscar Altimir, Louis Emmerij, Joann Vanek, and Paulo Garonna, and, at greater arm's length, Tom Weiss and Yves Franchet. They have advised, corrected, and supported my efforts in every aspect of this work. While I thank them profusely and all the others mentioned above for their comments and criticisms, they cannot be held responsible for the approach, coverage, and emphasis adopted in this book. Some, I know, share different views from those expressed here. I have appreciated immensely their efforts and patience in explaining their positions to me and valued equally all these contributions. In the end, I am solely to blame for any inaccuracies and particular interpretations and emphasis placed in this book.

I should also like to mention the excellent assistance I received from Judi Minost, who carefully and efficiently typed one of the early drafts. But I wish to give my special thanks to Natasha Tin Mya, who, throughout the project, remained remarkably cheerful and showed an inexhaustible patience in handling the typescript, making substantive changes, and putting together this volume in such a competent, professional manner. Without her tireless efforts and unwavering loyalty to the project, this book would not have been possible. Kate Babbitt, as copyeditor, made many important contributions to the whole text, reworking points that were confusing or unclear and adding a distinctive polish that stands as a testimony to her professional skill and dedication. The final task fell to Effie MacLachlan, however, to track down and check all the references, to draw together the many remaining loose threads, and to carry out the many other often tedious and irksome editorial duties necessary to put this work into a publishable form. I am most grateful for all her hard work and unfailing dedication in bringing this volume to the submission stage.

Abbreviations

C.I.F.	carriage, insurance, and freight
CES	Conference of European Statisticians
CMEA	Council for Mutual Economic Assistance
COFOG	classification of the functions of government
Comecon	Council for Mutual Economic Cooperation
CPI	consumer price index
CSO	Central Statistics Office
DHS	demographic and health surveys
EC	European Community
ECLAC	Economic Commission for Latin America and the Caribbean
ECOSOC	Economic and Social Council
f.o.b.	free on board
FAO	Food and Agriculture Organization
FDES	Framework for the Development of Environmental Statistics
GATS	General Agreement on Trade in Services
GDDS	general data dissemination system
GDP	gross domestic product
GFS	Government Financial Statistics
GIDP	Gender in Development Program
GIS	geographic information systems

GNI	gross national income
GNP	gross national product
HDI	Human Development Index
HDR	Human Development Report
HDRO	Human Development Report Office
HIPC	heavily indebted poor countries
IAOS	International Association for Official Statistics
IARIW	International Association for Research in Income and Wealth
ICC	International Computing Center
ICP	International Comparison Program
ICRES	International Convention Relating to Economic Statistics
IDA	International Development Association
IFNS	Inter-Agency Food and Nutrition Surveillance Programme
ILO	International Labour Office
IMF	International Monetary Fund
INSEE	Institut National de la Statistique et des Études Économiques
INSTRAW	International Research and Training Institute for the Advancement of Women
IPCC	Intergovernmental Panel on Climate Change
ISI	International Statistical Institute
ISIC	International Standard Industrial Classification
ISWGNA	Inter-Secretariat Working Group on National Accounts
IUCN	International Union for the Conservation of Nature
LINK	global economic projections model
LSMS	Living Standards Measurement Studies
MICS	Multiple Indicator Cluster Survey
MNSDS	Minimum National Social Data Set
MPS	Material Product System

NAMEA	National Accounting Matrix including Environmental Accounts
NATO	North Atlantic Treaty Organization
NGO	non-governmental organization
NHSCP	National Household Survey Capability Program
NSO	national statistical office
OECD	Organisation for Economic Cooperation and Development
OEEC	Organization for European Economic Cooperation
PPP	purchasing power parity
PQLI	Physical Quality of Life Index
PSR	pressure-state-response
RMSM	revised minimum standard model
SAM	social accounting matrix
SDDS	special data dissemination standard
SEEA	System of Environmental and Economic Accounts
SIAP	Statistical Institute for Asia and the Pacific
SID	Social Indicators of Development
SITC	Standard International Trade Classification
SNA	System of National Accounts
SSDS	System of Social and Demographic Statistics
TA	technical assistance
TC	technical cooperation
UNCTAD	United Nations Conference on Trade and Development
UNDAF	UN Development Assistance Framework
UNDP	United Nations Development Program
UNEP	United Nations Environment Programme
UNESCO	United Nations Educational Scientific and Cultural Organization
UNFPA	United Nations Population Fund (originally the United Nations Fund for Population Activities)

UN-HABITAT	United Nations Human Settlement Programme
UNICEF	United Nations Children's Fund
UNIDO	United Nations Industrial Development Organization
UNRISD	UN Research Institute for Social Development
UNSD	United Nations Statistics Division
UNSO	UN Statistical Office
USAID	United States Agency for International Development
WFS	World Fertility Survey
WHA	World Health Assembly
WHO	World Health Organization
Wistat	Women's Indicators and Statistical Database
WTO	World Trade Organization
WWF	World Wildlife Fund

Quantifying the World

Prologue

How should policymakers and ordinary people look at the world? What perspective do they get when they see a conventional set of official numbers? How might their views change if they were to be presented with a different range of information relating to the same issues? This book is about the way the field of international statistics, which was developed in the postwar period, has shaped our understanding of the world. It provides contemporary answers to the above questions. In an earlier era, say, two centuries ago, when administrators were confronted with the challenge to reduce the burdens placed on society by the poor, the responses to these questions would have been quite different. In part, this difference is evidence of the fact that "progress" has been made, but it is also evidence that the problems have changed. Statistics have contributed to a continually evolving perspective of what is important and to the solution of the problems facing societies.

The United Nations has played a major role in measuring world phenomena and quantifying the importance of different human activities. This book explains how various ideas and ways of thinking within the UN organization as well as initiatives arising from outside the institution have influenced the production of statistics and guided data development. The following overview is set within the context of the broad sweep of economic history and political events that have shaped the past fifty years or more. The intention is to explore the role of the UN in the political philosophy of official statistics against a background of the attention paid by the organization to the general process of international economic, social, and environmental development.

Box 0.1. The Historical Concern with Poverty and Its Measurement

Adam Smith, who is famous for being the founding father of classical economics, is less well known for being a champion of the poor and weak and for advocating on behalf of their political rather than their economic freedom. He believed that the unbridled pursuit of self-interest would favor the rich and powerful and was not conducive to the public good. He supported free trade in corn because it made the poor less vulnerable to the incidence of local harvest failures and famine. He opposed government intervention not because of his belief in the powerful influence of "the invisible hand" but because in the late eighteenth century that hand was often arbitrary and gave authority to officials who could not be trusted to act fairly. He believed that the freedom to make decisions based on available information and the ability to exercise free will in choosing how to live were every human being's right. Smith was considered by many to be a radical and a friend of French philosophy; it is certain he knew of the reforming ideas of Turgot and Condorcet in France. Both Frenchmen were reformers: Turgot, a prominent minister before the Revolution, and Condorcet, his one-time secretary, developed public works programs to support employment of the poor and devised schemes to ameliorate the effects of famine. Turgot faded from public life with the fall of the ancien regime and Condorcet was killed in Robespierre's subsequent reign of terror, an unfitting reward for someone who had held the interests of the poor so close at heart.[1]

Only two decades later, in 1797, Sir Frederic Morton Eden produced his monumental three-volume study, *The State of the Poor,* in England and Wales. One of Eden's intentions was to provide a balance to the general optimism that he had seen in response to Smith's *Wealth of Nations.* His work influenced Sydney and Beatrice Webb as they produced their minority report to the official *Report of the Royal Commission on the Poor Laws and Relief of Distress,* and it had a major impact somewhat later in the nineteenth century on the thinking of Karl Marx, who had nothing but praise for Eden and criticism for Smith.[2]

Charles Booth, who belonged to a wealthy shipping and industrial family from England, declared that his main objective in producing his seventeen volumes on *The Life and Labour of the People in London* between 1891 and 1903 was "to show the numerical relation which poverty, misery and depravity bear to regular earnings and comparative comfort and to describe the general conditions under which each class lives."[3] His concern went beyond an analytical interest in the status of those engaged in some form of economic activity and the inadequacy of their rewards as a means of securing better living standards. The Old Age Pensions Act of 1908, which provided official support for the aged and infirm, was largely the outcome of Booth's advocacy and lobbying for this particular social reform.

An International Statistical System: A UN Success

The creation of a universally acknowledged statistical system and of a general framework guiding the collection and compilation of data according to recognized professional standards both internationally and nationally has been one of the great and mostly unsung successes of the UN organization. The global statistical community has achieved agreement on procedures through both individual and institutional cooperation and widespread consultation and associated sharing of expertise.[4] It has led to a degree of integration that should be the envy of others searching for common ground on which to build consensus. It is too simplistic to explain this harmony of understanding in terms of the intrinsic goodwill of those involved and their general desire to arrive at some shared common goals. But professional integrity; the quest for clearer understanding, if not for an elusive "truth"; and a desire to communicate were certainly strong motivating factors. This was more than the outcome of efforts by highly competent journeymen; it was the work of people with vision. The development of an international statistical system is the outcome also of an honest open interchange between the main producers and users of data.

The book suggests there have been three broad phases of UN statistical activity; the first, an original and formative period; a second, a longer period of innovation and extraterritorial organizational activity; and the third, most recent, an era characterized by data systems maintenance and methodological consolidation. The book argues that, for the most part, the UN was less an original source of new statistical thinking than it was an efficient innovator. It played an important role in developing, extending, and implementing, in different areas of the world, ideas that had been generated from various outside sources. Ideas clearly played an important part in the original setting up of the UN statistical service. They figured prominently in the discussions held to fashion the early international program of work, particularly in the areas of economic recovery and rehabilitation. Previous experience of the relative successes and failures during the interwar years of the statistical services of the League of Nations and the International Labour Organization (ILO) also played a part and provided valuable lessons about what could be achieved. The primarily innovative role the UN Statistical Office (UNSO) adopted in the practical transformation of ideas, and its subsequent organization of their wider application and implementation, influenced the way the service operated for much of its life span in promoting the development of international statistical systems.

In later years, however, UNSO lost some of its intellectual authority as a result of budgetary and real resource constraints. This undermined the capacity of UNSO to exercise due oversight of the international statistical system. It had the important consequence that, in some key data areas, UNSO ceded ground, and thus UN authority, to other international bodies. The authenticity of some critical policy numbers was also called into question by users. This may have brought about a certain caution and inertia, discouraging the pursuit of new independent initiatives. In some of its important policy committees, UNSO began to follow leads developed by other agencies. On emerging issues of statistical concern, it became guided by its member states, some of which ran powerful research divisions, and by specialist subject groups. For the first time, UNSO found itself responding to outside recommendations rather than laying down appropriate guidelines for extending the international statistical agenda. With the turn of the new millennium, UNSO has moved back to center stage to begin forging new strategies. It has been able to reassert some leadership in the defining areas of statistical standards and data quality in fields other than finance. It is promoting certain themes and topics of growing social concern, particularly where the measurement issues are "softer" and more subject to qualitative assessment. In selected fields, as where indicators can be used to strengthen macrolevel policy analysis, UNSO has made a major contribution. But some important topics in the area of human rights and security, which are fundamental to the UN Charter, are notable by their absence from the UN statistical agenda. The historical tension between what is needed and what is done remains. The limited capacity of ideas and the limited ability of professional statistical leaders to overcome the pervasive influence of established institutional politics and ideologies continue to pose a challenge.

A positive feature of UNSO is that it is not staffed predominantly by people steeped in the traditions and practice of national statistical offices. The result, however, is that it also ends up having too few staff with relevant national statistical experience. A constructive outcome of bringing in "new blood" who meet high standards of technical expertise is that UNSO is breeding a new, well-qualified professional cadre. The danger in engaging too few staff with adequate field knowledge and solid practical experience is that UNSO's ability to speak with authority on matters of some urgency to their national statistical counterparts is reduced.

UNSO has devoted much of its efforts to a statistical coordination function under its assumed mandate. It has focused on various aspects of statistical development at the expense of paying sufficient attention to matters of genuine international concern. A truly global perspective on economic and social progress and development has thus been allowed to fall by the wayside. This comes at a time when the political interest and level of debate on such questions could hardly be more intense. Having given up the crown jewels of statistical measurement and conceded control of statistical authority to institutions committed to supporting the economic and financial agenda of Western orthodoxy, UNSO has lost much of its claim to speak for the global community and provide it with required leadership to bring innovative data development into the twenty-first century.

The Scope and Audience for the Study

This book is not a technical treatise on statistics. It is an essay about the evolution of statistical ideas in response to the needs of policymakers. Some of the views expressed are normative and aim to initiate a wider discussion of the political economy of numbers. The book seeks to unravel the more uncertain but ultimately more interesting question about why certain data were considered important rather than to provide a somewhat simpler description of what data were produced. The book is designed primarily with the informed reader and those in the social sciences in mind. It is not really intended for professional statisticians working in government or the international agencies. Consequently, those looking for the revealing insights which data can provide on socioeconomic issues may be disappointed that the book contains little or no actual statistics. The concern is to explore different approaches to measurement and to identify those seminal ideas that have inspired and influenced specific choices about which data should be collected and why such a unity of interpretation was deemed important. Little in the following chapters thus will appear new to the profession. But it is to be hoped that a different light will be shed on old problems and some of the alternative perspectives presented will provoke further debate and promote a better understanding of measurement issues.[5]

An important aim is to indicate why the UN chose to follow certain directions while other avenues were not pursued. The book may help to explain why some core data series became the main province and responsibility of other organizations. These international agencies, which had different mandates than UNSO, acknowledged the crucial importance of statistics in carrying out their agendas and fulfilling their own institutional objectives. This decision proved particularly relevant to targeting policy and to laying down criteria and setting standards for constituents to follow. Conditionality leans heavily on the data required to enforce appropriate policy. The key lesson, as always, is that statistics invariably assume greater relevance and usefulness (and, consequently, are properly funded) when they are adopted in practical policy applications.

At first sight, the title of this book may seem rather presumptuous, perhaps even preposterous. But the bold objective to "quantify the world" was very close to what the founding fathers of the UN statistical system originally set out to accomplish. Several members of the initial (nuclear) Statistical Commission who attended UNSO's first meeting in 1946 at the UN's temporary headquarters at Hunter College in New York arrived with personal knowledge of the League of Nations statistical service. They could speak from direct experience of the pioneering data efforts of the ILO during the interwar period. They believed that statistical information was an essential basis for decision making.

Data were necessary for making economic policy decisions and for monitoring economic progress, conducting demographic analysis, and assessing social well-being. Statistics were also deemed crucial to the sharing and transfer of knowledge and the development of better relations between states. "Quantifying the world," if not what might now be termed "a mission statement," was certainly an important component of a shared collective vision.

But to quantify the world appropriately, it was clearly necessary to establish common standards, uniform classifications, and, above all, agreed-upon concepts to permit the UN organization to take on an international mandate to compile global statistics. Standards were essential, not only for the purpose of comparing countries and their activities through time and across the world but also for aggregating such countries into larger political and geographical entities. The newly formed UN Statistical Office determined its main tasks to be the standardization of statistical methods, the development of common classifications, and the coordination of data-collection activities between countries and agencies. The aim was to enable everyone to adopt and follow the same compilation procedures and it became incumbent on the UNSO to develop an extensive program of technical assistance to draw all countries into the fold and apprise them of their standard reporting obligations. Assistance was also required to advise member states of important methodological developments, particularly in such key areas as census organization and reporting, national accounts, and survey methods. Technical assistance played a vital role in the continuing data dialogue, underlining the intersecting interests of the UN and its member countries and reinforcing the essential interplay between the users and producers of official statistics.

Facing the Challenge of Change in International Statistics

In the early postwar period, UNSO assumed the functions of coordination, compilation, and assistance, tasks that were then more straightforward and easier to perform. At the time of founding of a statistical service, only forty-six states belonged to the UN. More than half of those represented were already established industrial countries. Many had quite sophisticated and well-developed statistical systems. This fact was to have a profound effect on the direction taken and influenced data priorities within the choice of statistical programs. As the number of UN members increased, especially through the great wave of political independence in the 1960s, balancing the different tasks and aims of policy in various parts of the world became more complex and difficult. It was no longer sufficient to share acquired knowledge and techniques that were applicable to the developed world. Other international agencies such as the Bretton Woods institutions (the International Monetary Fund and the World Bank and its affiliated organizations) and the UN specialized agencies pursued their own specific interests, sometimes independently of other institutions. Rather than refer matters to the UN, the new powers on the block engaged each new country in turn in their respective data agendas. Although the international agencies tried to observe the particular political priorities then currently confronting countries and attempted to address their respective individual domestic policy concerns, an emerging consensus soon began to drive the development debate. The concept of full employment was enshrined in the policies of all major industrial countries and the goal of creating employment was built into the mandates of both the UN and Bretton Woods institutions. For the developed industrial countries, this objective was viewed as synonymous with poverty reduction, and it accounts for the statistical preoccupation with GNP, growth, and the national accounts. However, as the number of UN members grew, the nature of the problems and the priorities changed. Employment remained an important concern, but development took on a more quantitative character. A different emphasis might have emerged if the early decision to appoint an overseeing Statistical Commission comprised of national representatives rather than of leading statistical experts to guide the collection of international statistics had been reversed. What was not recognized at the time as the crucial development priority—the alleviation of widespread poverty and reduction in the large number of poor people around the world—is the same problem and primary concern around the globe. While the issues of full employment and the restoration of stable growth assumed great prominence in postwar Europe, hunger was the overriding issue for the poorest countries. It is sad to think that had some far-seeing social scientist in the 1940s drawn attention to the devastating prevalence of grinding poverty in China, the Asian subcontinent, and Africa and the genuine threat this posed to daily human survival, the matter would probably have been dismissed, regrettably but inevitably, as "the natural human condition" in the developing countries.[6]

Why did this not happen, and what basic model of the world, therefore, drove the direction of UN statistics? In the early years, UN data emphasized the measurement of the material and essentially politically neutral aspects of economic activity—agricultural and manufacturing production, strategic commodity supplies and imports, and exports of merchandise. These were issues of core common interest to capitalist systems and centrally planned economies alike. Apart from the measurement by the Food and Agriculture Organization (FAO) of crop yields, which emphasized more ways to estimate total crop output rather than how to calculate productivity directly, there was

Box 0.2. Early Uses of Data

The use of statistics has its origins in antiquity, and its importance can be traced primarily to the exercise of power and the need for control by the prevailing authorities. The Bible recalls the significance of a decree from Caesar Augustus for all the people of Judea "to be counted." The English *Domesday Book* reflects the concern of the monarch to assess the wealth and resources of his feudal barons and to know the number of serfs and other subjects who owed allegiance to regional warlords. In this way, the king was able to ascertain the potential threats to the security of his position and identify how well he was backed by his allies. In China, the curriculum individuals studied in preparation for examinations that would enable them to become Mandarins had a numerical component. By the fifteenth century, merchants in Holland and Switzerland, supported by banking families and financiers in Italy, were regularly compiling data to support local business and international trading ventures and determine their profitability. Royal chancellors began devising new ways to tax citizens as traditional feudal relationships and their accompanying obligations began to break down. Bookkeeping became established, and dictionaries, maps, and classification schemes were devised to meet new commercial requirements linked to risk and reward. By the end of the eighteenth century, and before the industrial revolution in Europe had really begun to gain momentum, standard reporting systems were in place at the national level to collect, compile, summarize, and disseminate data. The regular monitoring in Britain of the operations of the early poor laws provides an interesting example of official "social" statistics in the eighteenth and nineteenth centuries and illustrates contemporary attitudes to a social problem (that had its roots, in essence, as an economic malaise). Even earlier, in 1795–1796, quite independently, Sir Frederick Morton Eden conducted his mammoth landmark study of *The State of the Poor* in Britain.[7] His purpose was to draw the attention of his aristocratic friends, then dominating the process of government in Parliament, to the desperate plight of the poor and to counterbalance Adam Smith's *The Wealth of Nations*.[8] The Royal Statistical Society was founded in 1834, the same year in which the Poor Law Reform Act was introduced. The International Statistical Institute (ISI) was established in 1885, but the first International Statistical Congress to derive common international standards for the comparison of observations and results was held in 1853. Politicians, however, rarely offer solutions to social problems unless they can be somehow quantified and their importance evaluated (the 1834 Poor Law Reform Act introduced standards of control and "minimum eligibility"). Unfortunately, in establishing base reference standards and measuring performance using specified indicators, governments are tempted to become more evaluative and judgmental, selectively punishing and rewarding certain actors and activities rather than using the numbers to provide a more compelling interpretation of the fundamental forces that shape people's lives and thus support arguments for improving policy.

no official agenda to compare the relative efficiencies or productivities of either system. But behind the façade of internationalism, the U.S. government began to assume an influential role in defining the course of the UN through these early years. This was far more than it has done in the recent era when, following an earlier disassociation from the ILO and the United Nations Economic, Scientific and Cultural Organization (UNESCO, which it subsequently rejoined), the U.S. delayed paying its annual dues to the UN Secretariat and then negotiated them downward. After World War II, the U.S. emerged as the economic, financial, and military leader of the Western world. Through its lend-lease policy and the Marshall Plan it pulled Western Europe back from the brink of an economic abyss and steered the struggling countries of the region through successive monetary and payments crises, ameliorating difficulties posed by the continued dollar shortage. Then, with its support of the North Atlantic Treaty Organization (NATO), the U.S. provided the crucial bulwark for the defense of Europe against what was regarded as a very real military threat from Soviet forces and their ideological ambitions. In a relatively short space of time, the U.S. switched the emphasis of its foreign policy agenda from one of extending its financial leadership of the free world to one where, prompted, if only peripherally, by the proceedings of The House Un-American Activities Committee, the defeat of Communism by economic as well as political means became its main priority.[9] The behind-the-scenes arguments at the 1946 Bretton Woods Conference illustrated the determination of the U.S. to exercise global financial direction. The U.S. position, inter alia, was informed by demands from influential industrialists representing corporate America to have the British system of imperial preferences dismantled. Imperial preferences were a privileged structure of tariffs that allowed trade between Britain and its Commonwealth partners and colonial territories in the sterling area to enjoy preferential treatment.[10] The push to have this issue placed on the agenda of discussion was interpreted as a move to get Britain "out of Asia" or "out of East of Suez." The Americans wanted better access to India in particular and wanted to establish corporate links there.[11] The pendulum had swung from universal recognition of America's technical and intellectual leadership in setting direction for production-based policies to one of guarded suspicion of its wider political motives.

By the end of the 1940s, the need to halt the rise in Soviet power and stop communist ideology from taking over the world assumed a more urgent priority. The Great March and the Communist Revolution in China toward the end of the decade brought sweeping and dramatic political change to a quarter of the world's population. The strong foothold taken at the same time by socialist ideas in a post-independence, newly self-governing India underlined the broad appeal of social concerns. The so-called defense of the free world fed into a concurrent desire, not just in America, to preserve the values of private property ownership and the merits of the free-market system at all costs. Western ideologists set their faces against state intervention and central direction, believing fervently in the market and corporate capitalism because it allowed individuals to earn a level of income that gave them the individual freedom to choose and acquire the material goods and services they cherished. The capitalist culture was considered worth preserving and expanding. And so, somewhat subtly and imperceptibly, the data system took a shift in direction that more strongly reflected a bias toward corporate capitalism and the free-market economy. In this early period, what the U.S. did and said as a leading world power and as a recognized statistical authority exerted a marked impact on UN data policy. The concepts of value added, growth, gross domestic product (GDP), and gross national product (GNP per capita) quickly became the hallmarks of economic progress. There was, likewise, strong suspicion of "social" measures and oblique criticism of any statistics that appeared to hint at some measure of social achievement or equity. The U.S., which had strengthened its stance by virtue of its membership of the Statistical Commission, was thus able to draw the attention of the international community (as it had done at Bretton Woods) to the primary importance of the domestic economic agenda and expansion of international trade for raising living standards.

Once national accounts had progressed beyond the interesting but mostly occasional and ad hoc research of early scholars (and a handful of government officials) who attempted to compile baseline estimates of the total income of the nation, they were developed into an articulated macrolevel statistical response to the operational demands of Keynesian economics. Policymakers everywhere seized on this comprehensive statistical review of the economy. For the first time, they were provided with a statistical framework that enabled them to evaluate and even model outcomes and conduct simulations of alternative scenarios and strategies. Simultaneously, however, statisticians saw quite pragmatically that the integrated data framework offered the possibility of guiding and standardizing the collection of all economic statistics according to well-established international standards and definitions.

The centralization of data functions as a fundamental responsibility of the state clearly strengthened the core role of government in policy formulation and decision making. This was sometimes at the expense of the interests of other concerned population groups. In many cases, governments entered public debates armed with official statistics but failing to remember that they also needed to use what Aristotle called prudence regarding the state's ability to identify and serve the common good. Conflict and power struggles became the order of the day. Putting control of information in the hands of government poses the danger that statistics will become one of the essential weapons in the pursuit of political agendas and special interests rather than an influential and persuasive tool to be used in the service of securing a more just society. If worth is measured uniquely in terms of material acquisitions and economic achievement, there will only be "winners" and "losers"—and all that this involves in terms of creating social cost and instability—in the world.[12]

Several more debatable measurement decisions made over the past half-century are described in the book, but questions that have been raised about the relative success or failure of such decisions have to be tempered by the clear acknowledgment that such value judgments invariably benefit from the wisdom of hindsight. Present knowledge can never take fully into account the prevailing sociopolitical conditions and contemporary circumstances that must have had a bearing on what actions were agreed upon. In many areas of statistics, whether a procedure is a success or failure depends to a large extent on the point of view analysts share about the validity and significance of the resulting findings. Statisticians recognize that the outcomes of most inquiries are closely related to the nature of the original data source; the chosen methods of investigation, including the scope and extent of coverage of the survey; and the choice of unit from which the basic information is requested. They try to approach problems in a neutral and impartial way, taking a position that is disinterested but not uninterested in the issues in question. Nevertheless, in defining appropriate methodological procedures, in setting standards, and in benchmarking data there is a danger that statisticians may appear to "set things in stone" even where the issues themselves are uncertain and subject to fundamental change.[13] Resolving the growing inherent tension over time between preserving a desired continuity and coherence in existing series and accepting the need to take account of the increasing relevance of changed circumstances remains one of the most important challenges facing official statisticians.

The issue of measurement is relevant to the question posed. People cannot simply ask "What is the answer?" until they understand "What is the question?"[14] Whether derived numbers satisfy both a technical and practical "goodness of fit" to reality—or what the Statistical Commission referred to at its inception as the "adequacy" function of data—depends on how well the initial question is framed, how correctly its conceptual basis is defined, and how well the subsequent measurement issues are formulated. It is now generally accepted that, in the absence of absolutes, the primary criterion determining the usefulness of statistics must be "fitness for purpose."[15] Fitness of purpose requires data to respond to an issue; they must not only be relevant but also potentially useful. Clearly, they must also be timely. Data should have a genuine use and actually get used to good purpose. Otherwise, no statistics can be regarded as valuable and meaningful. Many published official statistics do not fulfill even such basic criteria; they are set out in large, often incomprehensible, tables that represent "dumb" data. Such tables have little practical use because they fail to speak to people about actual content and so are unable to convey a clear message. The concern in the real world with success and failure and how this should be interpreted is thus reflected in the strengths and weakness of different statistical methodologies and data dissemination procedures. As Zvi Griliches, a distinguished econometrician, once wryly remarked about weak data, drawing on the example of an old Russian proverb, "The dogs bark, but the caravan keeps moving."[16]

Virtually nothing in the real world can be held constant; conditions are always undergoing some form of change. For better or worse, official policies inevitably get modified from one regime to the next. The important task of statisticians is to keep abreast of substantive changes, to track the evolution of new ideas and strategic thinking, and to understand the implications of these changes for statistical measurement. Statisticians follow a code of professional ethics that requires them to be fully accountable for their actions and to maintain absolute integrity in their work; they have an obligation to remain impartial and honest and detached from political pressures. Recognized constraints on an ability to be totally transparent, such as those imposed by the conditions of confidentiality, and not just anonymity, need to be made clear where they apply. A full explanation of published results plus any qualifications to the numbers produced is clearly desirable. Any fundamental limitations in the methods and instruments used (such as sample bias or significant nonresponse) should not only be stated but also clarified. Preparing good data and providing sound information takes time. Both are invariably expensive, and costs can be a serious constraint on future improvements to statistics. The alternative of not compiling the most relevant statistics, however, may be even more costly in terms of both time and money. Mistakes arising from omission and oversight or procrastination in policymaking because good data are not available can be extremely wasteful. The independent collection of statistics provides a necessary but not always sufficient protection against the arbitrary exercise of individual political whim and ideological authority. It supports the preferred and usually more democratic option of making policy based on evidence because that process is more transparent and objective. Data clearly matter to people's lives, and efforts to improve their relevance and adjust for any acknowledged deficiencies need to continue. Statistics also improve communication and span disciplines. Outside their own immediate realm of expertise, experts often soon find themselves out of their depth. Statistics span the differences between cultures and their respective knowledge capital. They help bridge gaps in understanding through their common numerical language.

The evolution of the emerging interface between development ideas, policy concerns, and statistics and how they have coalesced over time, in particular within the United Nations organization, is thus highly relevant. As in any ideological debate, it is the ideas and not the actions that continue to arouse most interest and controversy. UNSO has thus sought to achieve the maximum positive feedback between ideas, knowledge, methodology, and policy advice in pursuing its programs. The UN has made no apology for focusing primarily on the socioeconomic aspects of data development. The adoption of particular concepts, the compilation of specific statistical series, and the generation of different statistical initiatives are seen as part of the package of UN responses to policy concerns, the emphasis of which has changed over the years. These actions can be set against a background of international political events and policy thinking and of UN involvement in global debates about such issues.

The policies implemented by the main international development agencies to address various concerns also need to be described. The development agencies have had access to a significant share of the available resources, which has enabled them, if sometimes by default, to become the main driving force dispensing funds, determining thereby particular programs of action. Yet despite their regular interaction with academics and awareness of current development thinking, neither the UN nor the Bretton Woods institutions have shown much willingness over the years to entertain ideas that may have appeared inimical to a follower of liberal market ideology and Benthamite philosophy[17] or that seemed to challenge the existing world order and international power matrix. Such points of view have been founded on both the moral and economic basis of growing imbalances and inequity. Other critiques of free-market capitalism over the years, including theories about structural dependency, core and (or center and) periphery, multinationalism, marginalization and polarization, intermediate- and appropriate-technology approaches, mixed economic management, human capital, and the "greening" of economic activity, have received relatively short shrift in international policy review despite the apparent relevance of such viewpoints to economic engagement, trade patterns, terms of trade, distributional inequality, international and internal migration (especially labor movements), rural development, project appraisal criteria, and program implementation guided by alternative performance indicators. Table 0.1 provides a list, beginning from the original signing of the UN

Charter, of the various events and ideas that have influenced international development debate. The corresponding UN contribution and reaction to these phenomena and the independent line of thinking it took about data is also presented. The table illustrates some of the main statistical responses of UNSO and the various UN specialized agencies.

A quite different set of factors that influenced development thinking and how the UN operated, especially in the earlier period of its existence, can be related to the particular geographical focus at the time. An initial concern with India and the Asian subcontinent and the assumed importance of heavy industry in creating the desired "big push" spilled over into a somewhat different approach to the economic policy problems then confronting various countries in Latin America, particularly Argentina, Brazil, and Chile. Many analysts believed that these economies would soon catch up with Europe. In Latin America, as a direct result of concerns about deteriorating trends in their terms of trade, countries placed a strong emphasis on policies of rapid and diversified industrialization. This was closely linked to a strategy of import substitution, which was promoted by Raúl Prebisch, the executive director of the Economic Commission for Latin America (ECLA).[18] The wider interest in development policy (as opposed to pure political concern with independence) came later with the emergence of the newly independent postcolonial African nations. This drew attention to the problems of economies based on monoculture and resources (both agricultural and mineral) with large rural subsistence sectors. These economies included the Pacific and Caribbean islands as well as African states. All relied heavily on the export of a single primary commodity. Five-year development plans with a heavy emphasis on economic growth through investment in infrastructure, "manpower" planning, and the promotion of export potential and diversification of markets then moved into vogue as former colonial powers began to grapple with the questions of how to achieve an independent sustainability for their former territories and, by the same process, secure their own early release from lingering financial commitments to these former dependencies. Other important cross-cutting problems, such as the alleviation of poverty, food sufficiency and nutritional deficiency, property ownership rights, and public control, received remarkably little attention from either the colonial powers or the new national governments.

The institutional context and historical circumstances in which economic strategies and social policies evolved to deal with these problems, and for which corresponding statistical initiatives were implemented, are clearly important. These events show how policies have shifted the relative emphasis among economic, social, and environmental issues. They help set the scene for determining the priorities and possible direction of future data work in the UN system and identifying where any new emphasis might need to be placed.

Table 0.1. The Changing Socioeconomic Policy and International Development Agenda

Policy Era	Objectives and Strategy	Policy Instruments	Statistical Events	UN Initiatives and Involvement
Mid- to Late 1940s Rebuilding, Reconstruction, and Restoration	Physical reconstruction, institutional rebuilding, human rehabilitation, alleviation of hunger and improvement of nutrition, refugee control, conservation of foreign exchange, initial phase of decolonization (Indian subcontinent)	Marshall Plan, emergency house building, plant construction and basic (energy and transport) infrastructure development, industrial estates and factory parks, agricultural expansion, travel regulation, rationing, capital controls, trade restrictions and import substitution, UN Charter full employment policy, direct taxes, wage boards, rationalization	Agricultural crops and industrial production series, house-building counts, Central Bank foreign-exchange certificates, reserve values, quantity measures (miles of road, length of rail, telephone connections, etc.)	Nuclear Statistical Commission, UNSO set up, SITC, ISIC, UN World Economic Report, FAO crop output volumes and food supply tables introduced
1950s Rehabilitation and Reinstatement of National Identity and Institutions	Continued reconstruction, production rehabilitation, securing supplies of essential raw materials, agricultural development, raising living standards and removal of rationing, skills training, independence and decolonization, fixed exchange rates, exchange control, commodity destabilization	Marshall Plan, international technical assistance, engineering projects, power development (electricity), schools building, high taxes (direct and indirect), "colonial" development and welfare loans (and budget grants), farm collectives and cooperatives, extension services, extension of state control of strategic industries	System of National Accounts (SNA), index numbers (prices and industrial production), population censuses, household budget surveys, census of industrial production, balance of payments manual, government finance statistics, crop surveys	UN Report on the World Social Situation, SNA, ILO price reports on basic goods, FAO food balance sheets, FAO crop sampling methodology, setting up statistical offices in developing countries, laying down population census guidelines, providing technical assistance

(continued)

Table 0.1. The Changing Socioeconomic Policy and International Development Agenda (*continued*)

Policy Era	Objectives and Strategy	Policy Instruments	Statistical Events	UN Initiatives and Involvement
1960s "Big Push" and Development (economic growth, investment, replacing traditional technologies and institutions)	Economic growth and industrialization, enhancing standards of living, freeing local markets, international investment, "manpower" development, tertiary education, infant industry support, political independence and further decolonization	Development plans, major infrastructure projects, business investment incentives and tax support, tariff protection, indirect taxes, "manpower" planning, development aid, direct investment, incomes policy, exchange rate management (devaluation), denationalization	Input-output tables, Seers model for developing countries, agricultural censuses, education statistics, production functions and long-term growth models	First Development Decade, International Standard Classification of Occupations, revised SNA, WFP set up, UNCTAD set up, UN Broad Economic End-Use Classification, UNIDO set up, UNESCO data on education enrollments
1970s Stagnation and Inflation (foreign investment and issues of dependency)	Exchange rate liberalization, energy-saving fuel (especially oil) conservation and search for alternatives, price and incomes control, employment creation, regional development, meeting basic needs, income redistribution, economic diversification	Interest rates, money supply, price and incomes boards, development plans, relaxation of licensing and registration, health and safety legislation, development of local markets, sector programs, rural development	New price index methodology, national and global models, satellite accounts, World Fertility Survey, Social Accounting Matrices, social indicators	Second Development Decade, ILO informal sector, environmental statistics, UN-HABITAT set up, transnational corporations surveillance set up, UN takes over ICP, SSDS, UNRISD
1980s Preeminence of Markets and Structural Adjustment (the so-called lost decade)	Removal of price controls, liberalizing markets, freer trade, direct investment, rural development, minimization of debt crises, restoration of financial stability, improving the role and status of women, improving the environment, reduction in aid dependency, the Washington Consensus	Integrated rural development schemes, reducing government expenditures and state control of enterprises, adjustment loans, privatization and "getting prices right" (the Washington Consensus)	Composite social indicators, gender statistics, health and nutrition, labor participation, trade in services, measurement of capital, leading indicators	UNICEF basic health monitors, NHSCP, UN Social Indicators Manual, Manual on Distribution Statistics, INSTRAW and Report on World's Women, UNDP Human Development Report, HDI, Women's Summit (Cairo), Social Panorama (ECLAC)

Policy Era	Objectives and Strategy	Policy Instruments	Statistical Events	UN Initiatives and Involvement
1990s Institutional and Policy Reform	Policy reform (transition from central planning), institutional development, better governance, overcoming corruption, free trade, privatization, global environmental issues, human development	Country assistance strategies, decentralization and local participation, small enterprise development, improving productivity and competitiveness, expanding education, developing the "new economy"	Green GDP, environmental accounts, government statistics and performance measures, debt statistics services output	ICP manual, revision of SNA, SEEA, Beijing Summit, Copenhagen Summit, Education for All and Health for All initiatives, Minimum National Social Data Set
Current Period Global Initiatives	Poverty reduction, international integration, globalization and global inequality, human rights, global climate change, sustainability	Provision of public goods, global performance, policy surveillance, debt forgiveness, international agreements and protocols (e.g., Kyoto and Monterey initiatives), Millennium Development Goals	Shaping the Twenty-First Century initiative, human rights indicators, "freedom" and "corruption" measures, global distribution statistics	Millennium development targets, UNDP development assistance framework indicators

The substance of this volume thus addresses some of the less glamorous, but on the whole more successful, behind-the-scenes data-compilation activities of the UN. Despite some oversights that few could have envisaged at the time, a handful of backroom UN technocrats, their national counterparts, and other acknowledged data experts together laid the foundations of an efficient and workable international statistical system. The role of the UN in bringing statistical ideas to fruition in the context of more fundamental notions about policy functions and the creation of information has been significant. The organization has tried to avoid debates about the philosophy of numbers, but it has encouraged a view that information should serve not only as the basis for developing new knowledge and improving general wisdom and insight but also as the basis for treating policy issues fairly and objectively. Statistics have been rapidly accepted as an everyday part of life. Indeed, it is easy to become overwhelmed by the constant stream of numbers coming from all directions on every subject. Pollsters, politicians, market researchers, the news media, and all manner of soothsayers use statistics to profile markets, determine strategies, balance investment options, project images, and strengthen their "sales" messages. Good data serve to enhance a perception about life and deepen an understanding of reality. Public expressions that refer to specific measures such as GNP, GDP per capita, infant mortality, and life expectancy have slipped into common parlance. Everyone understands, in some general sense, what these statistical artifacts mean, but many remain unaware of the pitfalls behind the estimates.

The Structure of the Book

The book begins with a brief description of the nature of statistics and their contribution to knowledge. Statistics are not just concerned with describing events and phenomena; they are also the way to test the validity of whatever model has been adopted, to collate information, and to understand the dynamics of the system. The book identifies the special functions of official statistics, particularly international statistics, in providing a standard basis for compiling, aggregating, and comparing data collected under different political statistical regimes across the globe in a uniform manner. It describes the framework of the international statistical system and the authoritative role and central position of the UN Statistical Office in this context. In the more than half a century since UNSO was first established in 1946, the world has changed and grown far more complex. The international statistical system has similarly developed into something more involved, interconnected, and sophisticated to reflect that growing complexity and to meet the continually expanding demands of managers and policymakers.

The chapters that follow outline some of the important instruments and pathbreaking methodological procedures that the UN adopted to compile information and the limitations of these instruments and procedures. Sometimes national statistical agencies have had few choices other than to adopt accepted conventional procedures to provide whatever information is required to fulfill assumed national data needs and meet externally determined international obligations. But issues of cost and the relevance of chosen international methodologies to domestic development goals also drive decisions about how data are compiled. These issues may affect coverage and the possible interpretation of published data.

The book reviews in more detail those subject areas that are considered to be important to people's lives and human behavior. Reflecting, chronologically, the topic areas that have been extensively dealt with by UNSO since its inception, the book covers three principal domains: the economic, the social, and the environmental. While other issues are perhaps of equal political importance, the various interactions between these core subject areas, such as the pressure of economic activity on the environment, the effects of growth on social well-being, and the interactive impact of the environment on social conditions and economic choices, are believed to play the most dominant role in affecting people's daily lives.[19] The evolving interest among officials and government leaders in monitoring the social situation and evaluating environmental matters represents the growing political unease with GNP as a bellwether and a recognition that economic growth should not be regarded as the be-all and end-all of strategy and development. Time has shown that growth, while necessary and important, does not provide an automatic panacea for the world's problems.[20] Therefore, increasing attention has been paid to the more qualitative, and not just the quantitative and material, aspects of life and to the significant role of government as an agent of progress. This wider perspective is also reflected in a more balanced official emphasis between ends and means in assessing human well-being. It has been accompanied by a move to a statistical system that is not solely based on objective quantification but implies a degree of dependency on broader value judgments and the need to distinguish, subjectively, between individual, collective, and other social notions of well-being. Beyond these overall defining frameworks, the book considers aspects of the dimensions of each core domain, particularly the need for appropriate conceptual foundations, relevant classifications, gender distinctions, and other primary breakdowns involving people and their activities.

The economic dimension, first, deals mainly with the issues of production and trade. It focuses on goods and services and the nature of markets and how economic characteristics are measured. It is concerned with incomes rather than wealth and with price formation rather than plan allocations of resources. Historically, the emphasis on physical or reported output has tended to preclude an all-important and more fundamental debate about agency involvement and who controls these activities and outcomes. It has led to the neglect of questions relating to the appropriate trade-off between social efficacy and economic efficiency in determining resource allocations and the satisfaction of people's needs. Such a key issue should have been high on the agenda of the newly formed United Nations if its leaders were going to act pragmatically according to the guiding principles laid down in the UN Charter. In the early years, however, concerns about "equity" and instituting the basis for a fairer global society were mostly identified ideologically and hence, politically, with communism. In the climate of postwar reconstruction and realignment in Europe and the emergence of Cold War politics, such issues tended to be dismissed out of hand. The race was on to demonstrate who had the best production system, capitalists or socialists.

UNSO's adoption of an approach to statistics that was essentially based on market output was led as much by reasons of practicality as by political influence. The drawback was that this approach did not give the office enough flexibility to adapt its basic data structures to look at different systems from an alternative perspective. Nor did it allow the statistical service to explore the data implications of new concepts and ideas (such as structural dependence) that were emerging as other countries developed and the international economy changed. In fact, data-compilation procedures became embedded in a specific institutional view of the world. Everything was judged to be implicitly black or white and "good" or "evil" in terms of economic efficiency and productivity. The hegemony of Western ideas and their bearing on statistics allowed for few compromises. With hindsight, this period can be judged as an era of missed opportunity; a time when the UN perhaps shirked one of its first major challenges in establishing the principles of measurement and a responsibility to examine and test alternative ideological viewpoints. The UN decided not to exercise the moral authority and independent leadership required to weigh these economic and social scales in balance. It also saw no reason to distinguish between need and demand (as represented by need that was backed up by the ability and willingness to pay) and the consequences this lack of understanding might have for people's well-being and ways to achieve it. In doing so, the organization acquiesced to Western ideas about what determined real economic power. The reasons for overlooking other dimensions of development at the time, however, were understandable and were linked to the enormous success of postwar macroeconomic policies in Europe and the emphasis both the West and East placed on production. Thus, there was no reason to examine how alternative systems might have allocated resources more fairly and alleviated distress. Nor was there any opportunity to examine at the institutional level how agencies, companies, governments, and labor—as forces for change—determined the structure of economic relationships.[21]

The social dimension of statistical research was pursued quite separately and fairly late by UNSO and then, perhaps, only reluctantly. Social policy emerged as an important issue only around 1970, when it became increasingly obvious to politicians that social progress—which resulted in an improvement in social well-being for the majority in the population—was not being evenly achieved by means of economic progress alone. This inability to appreciate the real nature of social problems was, in effect, the guiding influence behind UNSO's subsequent approach to social measurement. UNSO felt that the pattern of social development and social progress should be monitored separately from the measuring stick of GNP but that GNP was still important in helping to define "development." While specific aspects of social well-being such as education and health are important in this respect, the overview in this book addresses some broader political and methodological tensions surrounding conflicting approaches to social quantification. The issue of social progress is thus treated as a whole rather than as it may have applied to any particular social sector. Welfare advances in many social sectors may be driven as much by human endeavor and personal effort, combined with the visionary zeal and insights of special people, as they are the inevitable outcome of some defined policy, such as a decision to raise the school-leaving age or the treatment of the elderly.

The economic and social milieus in which economic and social activity takes place, and the various interconnections between these major domains, combine to have a marked but not always desirable or easily identifiable impact on the surrounding natural environment. The UN came late to an understanding of the importance of measuring these issues in a consistent way. Quantifying the environmental dimension of the world and its relevant dynamics is a complex and elusive task that is technically even more demanding than the task of evaluating individual socioeconomic circumstances. The need to identify the conflicting environmental forces at work constitutes a multifaceted problem that continues to test the ingenuity of both the scientific and statistical community alike. The environment and its sustainability[22] is an overarching issue that embraces what C. P. Snow has elsewhere referred to as "the polar cultures" of science and the humanities.[23] It is an area where external global climatic and geological forces, or "nature," and people's activities independently combine to exert a significant influence on individual patterns of life. Even more remote extraterrestrial galactic events within the solar system may exert a profound ecological impact on the earth's environment.[24] A wide range of factors may contribute to confound the interpretation of observed phenomena that may be viewed more generally as "environmental degradation."[25]

Beyond these essentially systemic and conceptual dimensions lies the more difficult problem of measuring the culturally and ideologically determined status of individuals who live within a particular framework of government or under a perceived authority in society. Such issues emerged toward the end of the 1980s; they include the role of women in the world and issues of human rights, freedom, and civil society. The concern with social exclusion and giving people the ability to have a say in the decisions that affect them is similarly elusive of easy quantification. Ideological and cultural circumstances, taken in their broadest meaning, influence how people react to different stimuli, both positive and negative, and are embedded in the various economic, social, and environmental dimensions that are conventionally identified. Ideas about how features of governance, political participation, access to public goods, and social inclusion should be measured have only just begun to evolve but are obviously of key importance to the emerging directions being taken at present by the United Nations. The UN has declared its intention to bring about a less socially contentious and economically divided world in order to secure lasting peace and stability and individual security for its members.

The main conclusion of this book is that the UN's role in the international harmonization of statistical concepts and classifications has been impressive and invaluable. Equally indispensable to international discourse and understanding has been the integration and coordination of statistical methodologies and data-compilation procedures. Nevertheless, some fundamental questions remain unanswered about the nature and validity of the underlying concepts assumed in standard frameworks. In addition, in a dynamic and expanding international system, the fixed structure of standard statistical procedures needs to be held up to more regular scrutiny to assess how up-to-date and relevant they are. Perhaps these data problems are generic and inevitable. It is in the essential nature of any statistical compilation that no matter when quantification takes place, the resulting data will represent a blend of conventional practice and contemporary thinking.

Bringing a Keynesian perspective to economic statistics delivered untold benefits, but it also transformed the primary focus of data away from the individual and his or her respective role and status in the economy, as well as in society, toward an overriding focus on government and its control of the economy. It reinstated the traditional functions of official statistics as primarily the tools of the tax collectors and as information for those anxious to establish a more secure power base. Macroeconomic data reinforced the self-serving policy interest of governments while sometimes ignoring the plight of those left behind by the process of economic growth. Nevertheless, the increased availability of statistics has encouraged more open and eclectic debate and expanded the policy dialogue. It has provided opportunities for disadvantaged groups to present their respective cases. Questions about whether established frameworks determine how data are generated remain valid. Whether the established frameworks allow people to challenge the cultural and moral basis of values on which the present edifice of international statistics is constructed, however, continues to be the subject of controversy.

1

Ideas and Statistics: An Introduction

- **Statistics and Measures**
- **Statistics and Facts**
- **Statistics and Method**
- **Statistics and Information**
- **The Establishment of the Statistical Commission**
- **The United Nations Statistical Office**
- **Statistical Standards and Systems**
- **Ends and Means: Economic Progress and Social Outcomes**
- **Data through the Looking Glass**

Claude Monet, the nineteenth-century grand master of French impressionist painting, stunned the art world on more than one occasion with his interpretations of the unfolding relationship between events and physical objects as he saw them. His pictures expressed an urge to represent a truer understanding of reality. Unlike any other artist before him, he often painted the same scene many times. Most famously, he painted the imposing stone façade of Rouen Cathedral twenty-six times. Each of these paintings exquisitely expresses the mood, light, and time that were unique to the occasion. His idea was to emphasize that the building did not stay the same, even though it possessed the same dimensions and material characteristics each time he painted it. The paintings, of course, are not essentially about the building, its stones and mortar, or the physical reality of the cathedral as a masterpiece of ecclesiastical architecture. They concern the nature of the moment, the actual time and place, and the special contextual reality that affects everything under observation. This was not the first or only occasion the artist painted this way. Monet carried out a number of "series" pictures of a similar nature, including his famous paintings of haystacks through the seasons, lilies on the pond in his garden at Giverney, and ethereal landscapes of the Thames and Hungerford Bridge seen alongside the embankment in London.

Statistics and Measures

Statisticians, by contrast, are rarely presented with such an opportunity to indulge in artistic experimentation and license. They may sometimes measure the same phenomena or variable more than once, or from a different perspective and angle, but only if (as with unemployment) they have good reason to believe that the reality they seek is likely to look different or change over time. The limited availability of resources does not allow them to duplicate measurements (although replicability is a fundamental criterion of statistical methodology). Little is served if statisticians indulge in repeatedly measuring the same features or distance between two fixed points. Nevertheless, in some areas they might well—as in employment—measure the circumstances of the same (or a similar) human being in different ways in various places and at different moments of time. The statistician's problem is that the object of attention and the observation of that object sometimes does not change independently or randomly. As a rule, the statistician must first formulate, either implicitly or explicitly, a certain hypothesis about how the variable being observed might behave under alternative conditions. Analysts can then "measure" the issue by collecting information in a specific way that enables these different assumptions to be reviewed and the resulting counterfactual hypotheses to be tested. The fundamental driving force behind statistical analysis is inference—the determination of assumed truths on the basis of deduction from observed characteristics, either through scientific survey procedures or through induction and descriptive methods.

To be effective—as has been made demonstrably clear in recent years—the legal regulation of economic behavior (particularly of the activities of companies) requires current evidence in an unambiguous and quantifiable form that can be set against benchmarks and established standards. Over time, governments have passed laws about weights and measures; they have introduced regulations on hours worked, wages paid, the age and sex of employed persons, and prices; and they have enforced product descriptions and quality standards. These actions have allowed statisticians to generate information that permits governments to assess the degree of conformity with their regulations.[1] Some of these laws are now becoming less relevant to countries where services have risen in relative importance and where the costs of observing and administering these laws outweigh any economic gain.

Statistics and Facts

Strangely, the public seems generally unaware of the dilemmas and problems statisticians face in deciding how to remain independent and thus depict reality or describe behavior as they see it and need to interpret it. To many an untrained eye, figures convey a form of truth that is uncontestable and incontrovertible. People regard data as facts and assume that statistics represent reality. They view statistics as a neutral, sanitized, and objective expression of an unseen truth. Statistics are "matters of fact," seemingly devoid of emotional content, at least until they are personalized and internalized. As Stalin is quoted as once saying, "A single death is a tragedy; a million deaths is just another statistic." But just as people have come to accept the triumph of objective information over political rhetoric and concerted propaganda, the principle of evidence-based policy has encountered some recent high-profile setbacks in both the corporate and political sectors that have undermined public trust in data. The public has come to recognize that, in the media, the synthesis and packaging of some political decisions often reflects a particular interpretation and understanding that decision makers wish to project. The desire for an independent perspective is a manifestation of a wider appeal for objectivity in reporting. The widespread use of statistics is part of the search for informed insight that will enhance better understanding. How far moral persuasion enters into the formulation of policy and can be enhanced by actual evidence of living conditions and thus existing ideologies can be guided by the empirical authority of numbers ought not to be left to chance or to any conjecture about the true nature of such evidence.

In the field of statistics, there appears to be a gaping chasm between the scientific physiocrats (the measurers) on the one hand, who have their feet firmly planted on the ground and quantify what can be physically observed, and the philosophers (or abstract theorists) on the other, who have their heads in the air and desire to identify influences. It has contributed to a long-standing debate about means and outcomes and about the difference between description and interpretation and, hence, to the extent of the statistician's direct engagement in economic and social policy issues. At a pragmatic level, it was once thought that statistics could replace the more traditional metaphysical and epistemological speculations about the nature of reality. Data were a prime source of information, it was argued. Statistics were able to open up the threshold through which people could gain access to previously untapped knowledge and thereby acquire wisdom and understand certain facets of truth. Numbers provided the appropriate meaning to apparently meaningless, random, and disconnected events. They set the right stage and context by establishing the relevant benchmarks against which progress and change could be monitored, magnitudes could be measured, trends could be evaluated, and performance could be assessed. In other words, statistics helped ordinary people "figure things out." Statistics cannot only explain things directly; they can also be used as elements in an analytical model to describe another reality that is less readily identifiable and quantifiable.

In statistics, the search for a rational basis for ideas has depended as much on formal data mechanisms as it has on actual measured outcomes. Data hold up a mirror to contemporary culture as reflected, for example, in the relative importance of the public and private sectors in providing goods and services for individual household use. Statistics are instrumental in making sense of the world whose path has been partially predetermined by a pattern of behavior dictated by the nature of individual societies and their social structure. It is the mission and responsibility of the statistician to fill in critical gaps in information (and thus knowledge). In the area of data compilation, it is sometimes difficult to determine the proper chronology of events and identify the key documents that can illuminate the defining moments of a past half-century's analysis of statistics, especially UN international statistics.[2] But some events, reports, and papers stand out, and it is crucial to be able to place this material in context. Statistics have played a dominant role in the crucible of public affairs, particularly at the national level, and the lessons of statistics have often been applied successfully in an international context. It is gratifying that, with perhaps some recent exceptions, most statistics produced by governments have been used objectively. They have been used more genuinely for policy than for political advocacy. In both the national and international scheme of things, however, numbers often seem to take on an iconographic significance rather than being seen as allegorical evidence that has been hitched to a particular political or social perspective. Increasingly, data are being used in a selective and biased way to provide the appropriate justification or supporting "spin" for a particular political or official viewpoint. This has given rise to important and independent moves in the profession to lay down universally acknowledged codes of conduct that set clear ethical standards for statistical practices.[3] It has increased the need for quality assurance and observance of standards.[4] For this reason also, statistical offices in many countries are now established outside the immediate structure of government to ensure their greater independence from political influence.

As explicitly enshrined in its founding principles, the basic mandate of the UN organization is no less than to change the world, although the organization no longer pursues the role of a "global government."[5] But to change the world it is first necessary to understand it, and an important element of that understanding springs from the information gathered in compiling statistics. Data must be compiled in a way that enables the statistics thus derived to serve as an independent arbiter and provide a common, agreed-upon universal language. Statistics must constitute an acceptable channel for imparting knowledge, sharing information, and improving communication. This condition imposes on statistics an even greater requirement than that demanded of any language. A language can serve as a means of communication if it can be understood by at least one other person. Although numbers can move readily across linguistic boundaries, the use of statistics requires that, around the world, the associated "vocabulary" of numbers is unambiguous and can be uniquely understood (even if their actual interpretation may be a source of contention) by all who defer to data.

In the task of quantifying the world, it follows that there must be a common set of definitions of recognized units and interrelated classification systems that can credibly structure global activity and its many elements in a standard way. Statistics must be prepared in a form that enables compilers and users alike to come to exactly the same understanding of phenomena; they must know how and what things are and how and why they behave as they do.

In this sense, most UN statistics represent not just public goods but international public goods. This is a remarkable achievement for UN data. Even the most fleeting tour of the history of international relations over the period since the UN was first established would clearly suggest the world has been divided by unceasing political dissent. International statistics are public goods because there is little or no rivalry in either their production or their potential use. Similarly, the actual use of statistics does not preclude any similar use of the same data by another person or agency. Although many agencies now levy a charge for official data, statistics are still made available for the common good. They are readily transferable and, in almost all cases, users can download data instantaneously in electronic form. The consumption of official statistics does not reduce their value; it may even enhance their importance since everyone is similarly informed and can benefit from sharing the same data.

Nevertheless, history and culture as well as theory (which, in itself, may well be shaped by prevailing culture and available data) play an important part in determining by which rules data are collected and the procedures whereby they are converted into the array of statistics that go into guiding decisions and informing policy. At the very simplest level of basic number systems, the laws governing the scales of measurement and the arithmetic of commutation and aggregation are universally acknowledged. Many of the units to which such numbers are attached are also readily understood; kilograms and kilometers mean the same thing wherever they are found and to whatever characteristics and phenomena they may be applied. But other units and measures, especially composite items and aggregates, such as import quantities, personal consumption and energy equivalents, or even dollar values, are more difficult to understand. They demand more explicit definition. Moreover, to avoid any possible ambiguity and confusion, a condition or phenomenon must be defined in a mutually exclusive sense; it cannot be one thing while simultaneously being something else within the same overall classification framework, except with respect to its source and use. In addition, not all scales used in the measurement process (across their whole range) mean the same thing.

The implications of a reported change in measurement units can be quite different. This is reasonably clear in the context of comparing industrial production and carbon dioxide emissions where, beyond a certain level, the emissions become progressively more damaging, or in using the Richter scale, which measures an exponential increase in earthquake force that is well defined and understood. But it is less well recognized that a five-year change in life expectancy from 45 to 50 years compared with a similar five-year improvement from 70 to 75 years implies quite a different set of circumstances. Moreover, when statistics move into the vaguer area of indicators that are designed as proxy measures to represent phenomena that are not directly observable (such as in interpreting carbon dioxide emissions as greenhouse gas effects and using measurements of these emissions to determine their contribution to global warming), officials find themselves on less safe ground in drawing conclusions about scaling differences and making judgment calls about levels of acceptability. Many of these vague "units" are defined not so much by what they are or by what can be observed about them as they are by a model or specific understanding about how the world works.

When quantifying the world, statisticians must be careful, therefore, not to become too enmeshed in any particular fashionable wisdom and avoid the circularity of meaning arising from the adoption of certain descriptive terms and data constructs. They must be driven as much by standards of fitness for use as by more theoretical conditions of goodness of fit to make sure that users can claim the maximum possible information from a set of statistics. At higher levels of use, statisticians may also be called upon to provide various additional subjective and objective assessments concerning the accuracy, integrity, reliability, and overall quality of public data. This is particularly pertinent when using a sample set of observations to pronounce upon the universe to which these observations are thought to refer. It applies to estimating correspondence points, presenting projections about future events, and making forecasts of crop production or investment trends.

Box 1.1. The Divination of History: Facts and Methods

Filling the Gaps and Prejudicing Outcomes

Extrapolation and interpolation methodologies based on simple trends or the joining of two points that are not necessarily endpoints in either space or time may ignore less-quantitative evidence that might indicate an alternative perspective. Some straight-line interpolations between not necessarily consistent benchmarks will compound any bias that is inherent in the baseline values. Data built upon a premise of an artificial and more or less exact gradualism, whether they project forward or backward to reported economic events, are not very helpful for understanding and explaining long-term processes of change.[6] Further, data assumptions that imply a smooth process of change also suggest that such change is positively transformative and readily manageable, and this can be quite misleading. Pressure thus mounts to supplement such historical data with other observations (that are often also incomplete) about the pattern of change in economic activity. The danger then exists that these assumptions will get embedded within the numbers, ascribing to them a degree of authenticity that is essentially unsubstantiatable. In addition, this apparent authenticity tends to reinforce prevailing explanations based, in all probability, on the most casual of observations that are usually taken from one specific social viewpoint.[7] The data stand only as numerical metaphors; they restate in quantitative terms a particular perception of historical events.[8] They can thus portray a spurious impression of accuracy that has all the appearance of a neutral expression of actual evidence when, in reality, they are merely a manifestation of traditional economic and social folklore.

Essentially endogenous features such as factor prices, innovations, and new production technologies as well as distributional effectiveness all combine to play an important role in altering proportions of labor and capital that lead to a reengineering of the processes of the management of production. Other, primarily exogenous, influences that can play havoc with the continuity of any statistical series include changes in administrations and political boundaries. Over even the short period of the past half-century, new countries have been created and many important boundaries have shifted. The distinction between urban and rural regions remains arbitrary and opaque. Differences in institutional arrangements give rise to different sources of data and different procedures for reporting that data. The extent of coverage of official data reflects both the strength of purpose and degree of control governments can exercise over their realm of interest.

For these reasons, the defining criterion must be that like should be compared with like when analyzing data, giving due recognition to the inherent biases and other known inadequacies in the data such as undercoverage but assuming these faults to be reasonably constant—at least over relatively short periods of time. When comparing countries, it may be more difficult to preserve such an approach, since it is unlikely that there will be such consistency in data sources. Where much of the data are largely conjectural, assumptions fundamentally compromise the explanatory and potential analytical power of official series. They also affect the ability of researchers to formulate alternative independent hypotheses.

Algorithms and Repetitive Processes

Algorithms consist of a defined sequence of steps that govern how information is processed; the steps are repeated in the same way each time. An idea originally attributable to the famous seventeenth-century mathematician Gottfried Leibnitz, algorithms were taken up and their logic developed in computer applications by people such as Alan Turing.

Scientific theory describes an ordered, uniformly symmetrical process, and statistical theory sits comfortably in this framework by bringing order out of the seeming debris of chaos and observed randomness. Through the properties of the central limit theorem and the ability of predetermined taxonomies and classifications to establish a form and structure with which to process disparate information from which descriptive measures can be derived, statistical method is able to distill the essence of a situation and clarify the main issues at stake. The application of statistics can exert a profound influence on how the central elements of a problem are teased out through scientific methods of investigation and a logical approach that uses the basics of probabilistic reasoning.[9] The only danger is that any structure that continually filters raw information through a standard format can become progressively inappropriate as real circumstances change.

Statistics and Method

The place of ideas in revealing development progress through statistics is an important concern. Ideas rarely develop spontaneously, especially in a topic such as statistics. This is not only because the subject is intrinsically technical and complex but also because statistics are essentially just an investigative tool. Ideas in statistics are methodological; ideas about statistics are interpretative. They shape the way people look at a given question. Statistics are both a means to convey information and a means to obtain information to help people understand issues. Consequently, they form an integral part of the process of generating ideas. But the ideas themselves are generally formed elsewhere. In statistics, the search for a rational basis for ideas has depended as much on data mechanisms as it has on actual measured outcomes. Data hold up a mirror to contemporary culture as reflected, for example, in the relative importance of the public and private sectors in providing goods and services for individual household use. They are instrumental in making sense of the world whose path has been partially predetermined by a pattern of behavior dictated by the institutional context and structure of society.

The science of statistics merely provides the appropriate methodology to explore the question, provide the necessary tools to help unravel the meaning of events, and describe observed phenomena in the world. The expansion of knowledge springs from this better understanding of how things work and how phenomena interrelate with each other. Statistics thus serve as an important guide to the underlying interactive dynamics of human economic and social behavior. They constitute the essential creative plasma out of which ideas emerge, thoughts develop, and beliefs are formulated. They are the instruments through which such ideas are transformed into knowledge.

If the field of statistics is to be one of the critical mediums with which to transform ideas and beliefs into new social and political action, it must be increasingly proactive instead of merely empiricist in its approach. Statistics generally provide an evidence-based methodology to clothe existing paradigms and represent the world as it is perceived in contemporary terms. Even in the West, the paradigms have changed significantly over the past decades, in the area of development thinking in particular. The latest paradigm, as expounded at the UN Conference on Financing for Development,[10] which focused on global partnership and local ownership as the context for action, is just a way of tackling development concerns in a more holistic way. The paradigm cannot make a strong claim that it offers a different conceptual approach to development. To have an impact, statistics need to move beyond the immediate requirements of description, assessment, and evaluation of existing paradigms and reach toward situations and procedures. Somehow, statistics must become more than response tools that react to situations and go beyond recognized levels of superficiality to reconsider and reconstitute basic principles and ethics of behavior.

Statistics and Theory

Official statistics are produced mainly to inform the policymaking process. Initially, any approach to the measurement of economic and social phenomena must be driven by a particular hypothesis, or some notion or theory about events. Such theories pinpoint priorities and attempt to explain the nature of the sequences, actions, and behavior patterns that investigators believe take place or that they actually observe. In turn, the related hypotheses that underlie theory must be set within the context of known institutional processes because these processes, in part, govern what transpires in the real world. The theories and associated explicit and implicit institutional rules of the game help explain events, but generally they lie outside the specific subject matter of statistics. However, they play an essential role in determining the methodology and system of data collection that governments and other investigators have decided to adopt to describe their administrative operations. Effective statistical measures must conform with the terms, concepts, definitions, and categories that are deemed relevant to the issue under investigation. These may not necessarily be the same as those administrators use. Terms that are conventionally recognized by users should be applied, although these, too, like "investment" or "saving" may mean something quite different and require specification.

The generation of ideas, the drive for creativity, and the quest for understanding are characterized by a slow but steady and progressive accretion of knowledge. Each new piece of information improves the quality of the data by building on what is known and strengthens the foundation for ongoing inquiry. Before they are refined and become part of established thinking and are embodied into the acknowledged way of doing things, ideas are linked to a growing awareness of issues. This awareness is facilitated by careful numerical descriptions that generate better perceptions about the importance and relevance of all issues. The objective of statistics is first to identify the issues and then to provide explanations and answers to the questions under investigation.

Creativity and the Generation of Ideas

The pursuit of knowledge demands an appropriate congruence of concepts and information driven by ideas and different, but generally contemporary, currents of thought. Concepts are framed by a combination of theory, philosophy, and understanding gained from observation and experience. Infor-

---

Box 1.2. Ideas and Statistics

Ideas have always been important in moving forward a particular agenda. In statistics, as in scientific method, the essential methodology applies inferential and analytical procedures to raw data based on agreed-upon methods of description and data collection. Recognized tests of inductive and deductive logic are then centered on a null hypothesis. The process of linking ideas with evidence-based information flows interactively in each direction. The ideas give insight into different hypotheses and data construction, and the resulting information, in turn, provides the necessary substance to generate new ideas and identify significant relationships. Such ideas are fundamental to statistical estimation because they relate to how data should be coded and structured and guide how raw data can be appropriately mined and analyzed. They influence the way data are drawn into particular statistical systems and are modeled in specific ways to mirror reality and promote greater understanding. The choice of appropriate methodology for and the design of these frameworks is crucial.

Ideas also emerge from a better understanding of data. These come from well-chosen ways to present statistics to describe situations. All numbers need to be placed into an appropriate and meaningful context to make them useful as information. The guiding principle in producing relevant, useful, and meaningful statistics must be a theoretical model or uniform understanding of behavior linked to an appropriate conceptual framework. This framework needs to be constructed using recognized axioms, agreed-upon premises, and assumed (i.e., not yet proven) hypotheses. The data emerging from these systems and structures provide the main basis for understanding and informing actions and creating knowledge.

mation assumes its rightful usefulness only when it is accompanied by a proper understanding of how the world works. Ideas and notions are critically important in defining this process.

The ancient Greeks, who have bequeathed to posterity an unparalleled legacy of thought, recognized the basic dilemmas involved in investigating the conditions and possibilities of understanding that lead to the progressive acquisition of knowledge. Philosophers and scientists in those days would have posed first the question "Under what intellectual and moral conditions is it possible to produce meaningful statistics, particularly relating to the economy?" Plato emphasized the importance of establishing the meaning of concepts. For him, the academy was the proper forum where such questions could be discussed and argued in abstract. Aristotle, opposing what he would have perceived as an inconclusive process for reaching solutions to real issues, felt that experience and practice could serve as appropriate means of discovery. Indeed, his lyceum of intellectuals, thinkers, artists, and historians existed to help people such as architects and scientists grasp the nature of their subjects better. Aristotle underlined the importance of proceeding from a more empirical foundation that relied on lessons drawn from life, production, action, and existing knowledge rather than pursuing some ephemeral objective of conceptual purity. In this he would be aligned with the earlier Pythagoreans and contemporary theorists who believed in the harmony of numbers.

The unquenchable thirst for knowledge formed the core of Greek civilization, and its pursuit was considered (in a society where slaves performed all necessary tasks for daily existence) a natural, universal, and essential characteristic of human activity. Few now, given the urgency of the moment, can devote time to contemplation about the nature and direction of their work and the principles underlying it. But those who guided and advised during the setting up of the new UN Statistics Office, although they did not necessarily acknowledge the basic moral imperatives overtly, had to give serious thought to data priorities and to choosing the strategic path to follow.

In their proposals for the Statistical Commission, the team of advisors began in 1946 with the idea of a "lyceum" represented by an expert body to whom official practitioners could appeal for guidance and advice. The commission was conceived as providing the highest level of technical expertise and professionalism. The intention was that it should give direction on policy and make judgments on relevance and quality. At the outset, the nuclear group felt that a complete command of the mathematical mechanisms of statistics, and of sampling techniques in particular, was an essential qualification for the commission's members.

As will be described in more detail later, the initial discussions held in New York in 1946 about the nature and role of the UN Statistics Office and the functions of the UN Statistical Commission centered around whether the commission should be set up as this elitist panel of independent technical experts with an internationally recognized authority to advise and deliberate on global statistical questions or whether it should be a representative body that reflected the different and often divergent political positions of the various national and international organizations that belonged to the statistical community.[11] In the end, the latter force won over, and surprisingly—perhaps because there was a higher shared intention to come to common agreement on terms, methodologies, and systems or because such a group of national experts was more in touch with the policy needs of governments—the process has worked well.

At the conceptual level, ideas and probabilities—which provide theoretical underpinnings for much work that is done under the rubric of statistical method and inference—are clearly interrelated. They are aligned particularly closely at certain points where what begins as a vague or simple possibility merges into a testable reality or virtual certainty. Governments tend to take a broad view of how the needs for policy actions should drive the statistical agenda and how, in response, the various data constructs have influenced subsequent policy decisions. This perspective places the UN, as an agent of these governments, in the role of an institution that is continually absorbing, refining, disseminating, and applying ideas that, in general, emerged elsewhere. The studies of individual researchers and academics as much as the work of official agencies have influenced this process. While UNSO has been quick to absorb and implement many initiatives and act as an innovator, it has rarely been responsible for originating any fundamentally new ideas itself. In part, this is because UNSO has been a victim of the unavoidable legacy left by previous statistical administrations, and in part, it is because of only lukewarm interest in the UN Secretariat itself. Sadly, it reflects the low status of statistics in the UN system. Institutionally, most organizations such as UNSO find their programs subject to the inexorable forces of social, economic, and political power and the influence of historical and budgetary priorities.

At the outset, when the UN consisted of only forty-six member countries, it inherited the priorities and agendas of the politically powerful and industrially advanced countries. It took time to shake off some of this influence and to turn more attention to providing statistical support to countries with weaker data capabilities.

Statistics and Information

It is hard to envisage statistics as one of the great moral challenges of modern times. Yet data pose intellectual and political questions that reach beyond purely technical questions.[12] The publication of official data arouses both interest and concern about how societies are run. Data tap into the root of people's consciousness and the nature of their existence. Official statistics draw attention to special influences and can reveal information about control, direction, discrimination, and exploitation by both the private and public sectors if agencies are allowed a measure of dependence in disseminating data. Such data can help expose administrative inefficiency and ineffectiveness and reveal other social irregularities and inequalities. Statistics have also encouraged positive action and have guided policymakers in devising suitable actions to address social needs and identify priorities. The existence of statistics and their ready availability to the public encourages social progress and more informed democratic attitudes.

Yet before World War II, in the absence of any recognized central need or authority, most official data at the national level were not collected in a coherent, coordinated, and centralized way. Nor were statistics routinely disseminated to the public. Many statistical units were simply the adjunct of some individual department or ministry charged with a specific administrative task. While fairly strong and well-established registration offices existed to undertake censuses and monitor population and demographic characteristics, little of the current range of information was made available; few states had the truly national coverage that is now considered essential for policymaking. Price information tended to be haphazard and selective and was mostly related to working-class families and urban living conditions. Information about inflation was linked primarily to medieval notions of a "just" wage and appears to have been designed to ensure minimally adequate living conditions. Unemployment data were inconsistent and lacked comprehensive coverage, especially of women. Wages information outside the government sector in industrial countries referred mostly to a handful of recognized occupations or key strategic industries such as coal mining or the railways. Like officials and civil servants, employees and their conditions of labor in these sectors were usually governed by statutory regulation and their remuneration was subject to criteria determined by wages boards. This legal requirement was the only reason why data were collected about them. Other administrative data generally consisted of routinely collected statistics that manifested a combination of policies in place and decisions taken and established bureaucratic procedures and institutional rules of the game that were observed by the authorities in power.

Indeed, most administrative data at the time tended to be developed in house to satisfy financial regulations, facilitate reporting to public auditors about money spent, and justify actions taken under assigned budgets. They were thus limited to more general information about how institutions or entities function, except about how officialdom operated. Consequently, much data remained uncoordinated and was founded on definitions that were not comparable across datasets. Questions of research, analysis, and diagnostic inquiry relating to socioeconomic conditions were left mainly to academics and outside observers. The stories are legion about how investigators had to piece together data from different sources.[13] Sampling methods for large-scale economic and social inquiries were still in their infancy and were practiced only in a handful of countries.

Within these narrow compartmentalized structures, there was little concern about identifying the weaknesses of capitalist, socialist, or communist ideology in a review of strategic policy options. Official attempts to evaluate the success or otherwise of the respective policies such regimes implemented seem few and far between.[14] It is not until after World War II that many governments assumed some broader central responsibility for official reporting and data dissemination. This coincided with the greater government control of the economy associated with the implementation of macroeconomic policies and was often driven by the immediate and urgent need for reconstruction. In some countries, rationing (of both consumption and investment resources), the control of external balances, and the management of fixed exchange rates all required regular surveillance as well. Policies reflected an impassioned political desire to avoid the massive unemployment of the interwar depression years. As they emerged from this unsettled period, most governments' deeper involvement in a wide range of economic activities was increasingly accompanied by the means to accomplish their aims.

All this coincided with the emergence of what turned out to be the most important and expedient macroeconomic policy instrument so far devised— the national accounts. The national accounts reinforced those paths of action that required central authority. The accounts helped to define not only the direction of policy at the national level but also how it should be implemented. In establishing a coherent structure for the collection of economic statistics, the adoption of this system entrenched government power and widened its scope of control.

The Establishment of the Statistical Commission

The postwar period witnessed a strange interregnum in international data organization. There was an embryonic statistical office in place, a relic of the disbanded League of Nations, and a recognized legal status for an international statistical system and secretariat under the terms of the 1928 International Convention Relating to Economic Statistics (ICRES). The League had also set up a Committee of Statistical Experts that included such distinguished statisticians as Oskar Morgenstern (Austria), R. H. Coats (Canada), Sir Alfred Flux (Great Britain), and Dana Durand (U.S.). It also included Dr. G. Jahn of Norway, who, by virtue of the indefinite tenure accorded to the League's Committee, became the only member to sit on the new Statistical Commission after the war. But one of the first major tasks of the commission was to acknowledge, implicitly, its own temporary incumbency of a defining and founding role for international statistical organization. It had to recommend the nature and structure of a permanent commission to succeed it and serve the needs of international statistical policy. The group agreed that the permanent commission should have an authoritative role that allowed it to arbitrate on matters of contention. The main debate, however, was whether the commission should exercise such authority by virtue of the professional integrity and intellectual standing of its appointed members or whether its authority should be vested in official technocrats and thus wielded less independently by a political cross-section of the world's governments.

Box 1.3. The Nuclear Commission

The forerunner of the present Statistical Commission, the nuclear commission was comprised of a small group of distinguished but transitory members. It first met in 1946 at Hunter College in New York City. Its objective was to agree on a broad program of statistical development and to define a set of objectives for pursuing the mandate under which it had assumed the responsibility of international data production. In this, it had to guide the direction of work of the embryonic UN Statistical Office. The basic concern, namely, to promote the worldwide compilation and coordinated development of key statistics, particularly relating to the economies of each country, and to make such information as comparable as possible, has changed little since that date.

Members of the Nuclear Statistical Commission
Meeting at Hunter College, 1–14 May 1946

Stuart Rice (U.S.), Chairman
Harry Campion (UK)
P. C. Mahalanobis (India)
A. Sauvy (France)
D. K. Lieu (China)
G. Jahn (Norway)

A. Rosenberg, head of the League of Nations Mission in the U.S., served as a technical consultant, and H. Venneman of the Division of Statistical Standards of the U.S. Bureau of the Budget acted as secretary.

P. I. Fedesimov of the USSR was also invited to join the meeting as a temporary member. Foreign Minister Gromyko's assistant announced on 3 May that Mr. Chernikov would attend the meeting and that he had left Moscow on 21 April. However, Mr. Fedesimov turned up late on the seventh day and close to the end of the meeting. Mr. Lieu also turned up late and could attend only the last two days of the meeting. (Problems of travel and restrictions on travel, visas, etc., were particularly acute at this time.)

Teixeira de Freitas from Brazil declined appointment on the grounds of ill health but promised to comment on items on the agenda.

The U.S. influence and, specifically, that of the Office of Management and Budget, as it is now called, appears to have been strong, particularly as the first commission report was drafted by the chairman (Rice) and secretary (Venneman).

The nuclear Commission thought it should "confine itself to general principles" and lay down standards of adequacy and comparability and also advise on solutions to statistical problems. It saw the principal role of the commission as a technical one to develop and improve statistics around the world.

On the fifth day, the meeting declared that the International Statistical Institute had only a "precarious foothold on the collection of statistics" (the emphasis was, it seems, on the *collection* aspect and not on any other aspects of statistical expertise) and that it should not serve as "a court of last resort."

The commission recommended that a central statistical unit of the UN Secretariat should be established to become an international repository of statistical information. UNSO was established shortly after and was charged with coordinating international activities in statistics. Successive refinements introduced over the years have been designed to ensure that official statistics produced by national governments become increasingly relevant to national objectives and to shared policy strategies, particularly in the areas of economic progress and social development. In more recent years, successive global summits on critical issues of international concern have introduced other specific measures and indicators that have needed to be added to the common statistical agenda.

The majority of members of the first commission (with the exception of the Russian and Chinese representatives) favored the former approach, not surprisingly because the group itself was comprised of a collection of highly distinguished statisticians. They wanted independent experts who could readily speak with acknowledged international authority on policy. They recommended that the permanent commission take over the functions of the former League of Nations Committee on Statistics.

All members of the nuclear commission were professional enough to realize that they would not know all the answers. They also wanted, therefore, to see the International Statistical Institute (ISI) vested with some special authority to serve in the role of international overseer. The ISI, supported mostly by government contributions and established by that time for around 100 years, was the only professional agency in existence that explicitly embodied in its statutes the coordination and promotion of the development of world statistics. During the interwar period, however, the ISI's data role had been largely displaced by the international statistical activities of the League of Nations. Nevertheless, it was felt that the ISI, as in the American Statistical Association's intercession with the U.S. government over the validity of a cost of living index, could exercise a presiding role in arbitration.

A few felt that if any already established body could be called upon for advice and direction on the types of economic problems then facing the post-war world, it should be the Conference, later renamed the International Association, on Research in Income and Wealth (IARIW), rather than the ISI. The IARIW was deeply involved in the development of national accounts and the members of the conference constituted a cross-section of leading academics, government statisticians, and official policymakers working in macroeconomics. The IARIW seemed to be the more relevant body to recommend the statistical priorities appropriate to the economic policy initiatives being taken. In a sense, the dilemma this posed for the Statistical Commission acted as the thin end of the wedge. In suggesting a potentially neutral source of external expertise, the proposal opened the door to the formal representation of national views on the commission—the position consistently propounded by the Soviet and Chinese delegates to the nuclear body. What these debates also reflect, however, is the primacy of economic issues in the postwar data agenda to the virtual exclusion of other concerns in the international community.

It was agreed that the commission would be made up of representatives from countries, not individual experts. Reluctant to concede the need for independent professional oversight, the early commission decreed that the persons designated by countries should be responsible officials in the national statistical service. It was further proposed their qualifications should be submitted to the UN Economic and Social Council (ECOSOC). In practice, this criterion was never officially applied and it is unlikely it would have worked, but it was clearly designed to avoid the "stuffing" of positions by political appointees, which was quite common at the time. The commission acknowledged the distinct statistical responsibilities of the United Nations and those of the specialized agencies, and the division of their respective activities was left an agreed-upon understanding. The role of the ISI in the new global statistical system seemed to be a more controversial topic than the relationship between the infant UNSO and the statistical services of the old and new specialized agencies. The latter continued to exert a strong influence over the issues and priorities taken up by the UN office, in part because UNSO inherited an agenda left over from the interwar period.

The early years of the commission were particularly important in providing a recognized international authority to validate a number of new and revolutionary developments in official statistics. Two examples should have special mention: sampling and national accounts. In both cases, important pioneers in these fields, P. C. Mahalanobis and Richard Stone, took the lead on behalf of the commission. Prior to World War II, both probability sampling and national accounting were viewed as somewhat untried and questionable endeavors. Doubts about their relevance and reliability persisted even after the war, despite the successful uses of both approaches by governments in the intervening period. Among the first substantive actions taken by the commission was (a) the approval of the publication under United Nations auspices of a report prepared under the direction of Richard Stone for the League of Nations on national income and social accounting;[15] and (b) the establishment of a Sub-Commission on Sampling under the chairmanship of P. C. Mahalanobis.

Box 1.4. Issues Faced by the Statistical Commission

The members of the first Statistical Commission who met in 1946 faced several important choices that would determine how the world would be quantified for the next fifty years. The two defining issues were:

- Whether a UN statistical office should primarily serve the needs of the new UN organization and its own strategic agenda for world development or whether it should be a broad-based body that served international needs, particularly the coordination and standardization of statistics produced by countries

- Whether the programs of the office should be guided and approved by an extended and independent body of experts who would advise and oversee progress or whether the evaluation and monitoring of its programs should be carried out by a representative body of national officials appointed by their respective governments

In addition, in related discussions in the Economic and Social Council, the statisticians involved in creating the commission and the diplomats they interacted with faced several other crucial questions:

- What would be the relation between the Statistical Commission and the United Nations Statistical Office, on the one hand, and the specialized agencies with their own statistical services on the other?

- What would be the relationship between the Statistical Commission and nongovernmental organizations that were active in the field, particularly the International Statistics Institute?

- Would the standards, recommendations, and classifications adopted by the Statistical Commission be mandatory or voluntary by nature?

Few were prepared, at the time, to let an international statistical body set mandatory standards or classifications for member states. Nevertheless, it was agreed the commission should lay down guidelines and recommend their observance internationally.

From the outset, in addition to this work on methodology, the commission addressed many of the other main categories of work that still concern it, but which often now take different forms:

- Establishment of a publication program for UNSO, including the monthly bulletin of statistics

- Coordination, including a review of basic interagency agreements

- Preparations for the 1950 Population Census Program, including both methodological and technical cooperation

It is of particular interest to note that the first official meeting of the commission in 1946 had, as the first item on its substantive agenda, "the establishment of a special information and statistical service on 'the status of women.'"[16] Evidence suggests this was in no small part due to the special interest of Eleanor Roosevelt, who was then chairperson of the UN Human Rights Committee and who maintained a strong personal involvement in women's issues.

The United Nations Statistical Office

As outlined in the UN Charter, ECOSOC was intended to have a profile of importance that ranked alongside that of the UN Security Council. It was at first planned that the new statistical office would serve ECOSOC, but a wider mandate was soon envisaged. Peace had recently been restored, and the main priorities were seen to be economic reconstruction and development. There was a universal desire to raise standards of living around the world. It was fervently hoped that political confrontations, international brinkmanship, and military threats to national identity and security would no longer be the overriding issues dominating the UN agenda as they had that of its predecessor, the League of Nations. But in the subsequent prolonged Cold War period and unsettled era of decolonization, all these problems rapidly reemerged and became the overriding concerns of the organization to the virtual exclusion of most other issues. ECOSOC's early decline and the loss of any real strategic

Chart 1.1. Organizational Relationship of the Statistics Division in the UN

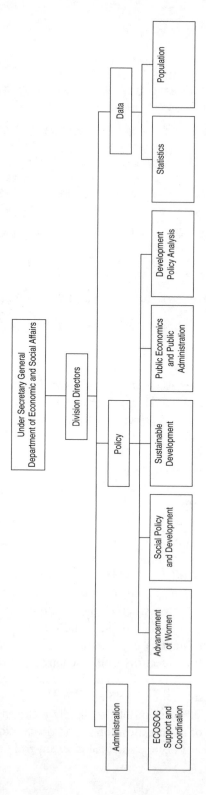

Mirroring the political organizational structure of the UN under the umbrella of the General Assembly and functions of the Economic and Social Council (ECOSOC), an administrative subdivision of responsibilities falls under the authority of the under-secretary-general in charge of the Department of Economic and Social Affairs.

At the technical level, the Statistics Division has direct links with the Population Division through its demographic statistics section. It also regularly interacts with those divisions concerned with the Advancement of Women, Social Policy Development, Development Policy Analysis, and Sustainable Development, particularly in the areas of national accounts, social indicators and environmental measurement. The directions of policy emphasis for the Statistics Division originate from three main sources:

1. Data recommendations handed down from different global summits reporting to the UN General Assembly
2. Proposals adopted by the Statistical Commission
3. Recommendations made by various inter-secretariat committees and intergovernmental working groups

Despite the ever-expanding scope and coverage of the various constituencies attending (as "representatives" or "observers") at what have recently become annual rather than biennial meetings of the Statistical Commission, gaps in the process of policy feedback and delays in implementing initiatives have caused growing frustration among some national agencies. The acknowledged difficulty of working through the UN bureaucracy is frequently cited as the primary reason why the separate city groups of technical experts were independently convened under the auspices of national statistical offices to deal with increasingly problematic critical statistical issues.

or operational role for UN headquarters in the development process in the decades immediately following left little or no rationale for UNSO to be an internal data unit with such a limited function and scope.

As a result, UNSO became an international agency in its own right. But it was one whose policies could be potentially circumscribed by more powerful national political agendas. To its credit, the office—despite the early influence on the Statistical Commission of representatives drawn overwhelmingly from the advanced industrial (and mostly Western) countries—adopted a genuinely international policy perspective. That perspective, nevertheless, often represented an agreed-upon compromise between states on how an international methodology or classification should be applied. In particular, it reflected a distinct unidimensional and linear view of development that rested on a belief that sooner or later, the poorer and less advanced countries would catch up with the industrial nations and go through much the same processes as the more mature economies had passed through up to a century before then. This theory implied that growth was the priority and that the faster it took place, the quicker countries would catch up in the development race. It also suggested that the richer countries had the right answers that should be applied to the economic problems of the rest of the world.

Box 1.5. Successive Directors of the UN Statistical Division, 1945–2003

Harry Campion, UK (temporary)
William R. Leonard, U.S.
Pat Loftus, UK
Simon Goldberg, Canada
Sven Norbotten, Norway
Y. Kurabayashi, Japan
William Seltzer, U.S.
Herman Habermann, U.S.
Willem deVries, The Netherlands (acting)

Setting UNSO's Initial Agenda

The commission believed that it was important to lay down the best practices (despite their complexity and sophistication) for others to follow. A decade later, Walt Rostow's thesis, which he outlined in *Stages of Economic Growth*, reinforced this perspective, which was to hold sway among most political thinkers for many years.[17] Rostow's book was referred to equally often by its subtitle, *A Non-Communist Manifesto,* because it reinforced a belief in liberal market democracies. But the thesis was nonrevolutionary rather than non-Communist, partly because the processes described were slowly evolutionary and chronological and partly because both the Soviet system and Chinese socialism also embraced rapid industrialization as a means to achieve a higher level of economic growth and development. Countries firmly believed that industrialization enhanced their power and status on the global political platform. Industrialization, it was widely thought, would win higher living standards for the working classes by raising the level of aggregate demand, increasing the total flow of output, and improving people's well-being through an enhancement of their command over an expanded supply of material goods and services. There was heated debate, however, about whether nations should focus on producing investment goods or consumption goods to raise people's living standards.[18]

In the final analysis, despite a respectful acknowledgment in the direction of socialist statistical systems and some limited technical recognition of the formal structure of the system of material balances (and the "normal" standardized pricing procedures that went along with it for quantity audit and accounting purposes), UNSO embraced the system of trade and production statistics adopted by the developed Western industrial nations. This approach had been laid down already by the League of Nations and was reinforced by the postwar adoption of national accounts.

The League of Nations had earlier taken some initiatives to develop trade statistics and to compile population data. It was on the point of launching an international information system for the collection of industrial data related to trade flows when World War II broke out. The coverage of such data, however, was limited to the reasonably well-developed world and to the developed enclaves of poorer communities. Immediately after the war, the focus of thinking among UN officials and their advisors remained Eurocentric and continued to be strongly influenced by Western ideas about ways of doing things. Many felt that statistical information about Russia could not be separated from political propaganda. China was a former feudal economy that remained essentially divided until after 1949, when it became a closed system and it became difficult to determine which data represented actual numbers and which represented propaganda. Central Asia, Tibet, and Mongolia were mostly a mystery to outside interests and were formally incorporated into the USSR. Many other regions of the world were ruled by colonial powers or fell under other forms of jurisdictional control from the West. Few indigenous authorities had any say in defining statistical priorities.

After the war there was an explosion in the demand for data in the developed and industrializing countries of the world. The requirements of the new economic policy framework and national planning were data intensive. Information on incomes, employment, and the conditions of labor assumed a political importance that had previously gone unrecognized, and the statistical work of the ILO and the League of Nations during the previous era became revitalized. Statistics were needed not only for physical reconstruction but also for social rebuilding programs. They helped to define the requirements for housing, schools, health and nutrition policies, and all other matters pertaining to the responsibilities of the new welfare states in Europe and elsewhere.

The priority attached to developing a system of national accounts drove the early UN agenda in statistics. It was expected that these would be implemented by every country and thus provide each government with the essential standard tools to allow their decision makers to formulate integrated rational macroeconomic policies. It was assumed these tools would enable countries to avoid the major pitfalls of the past. They supported the role of government in exercising its new socioeconomic authority. The System of National Accounts (SNA), was first developed internationally by Richard Stone at the Organization for European Economic Cooperation (OEEC) in 1952 and was published a year later by the UN.[19] It was issued originally as a slim but pathbreaking methodological manual based on Stone's earlier work with James Meade for the British government.

This pioneering work was to have far-reaching implications for international statistics. It not only laid the foundation for more rigorous policy analysis but it also set out a comprehensive framework that established the appropriate standard format for collecting and compiling all economic statistics. It created an interrelated network of concepts and definitions that remain more or less unchanged to the present day. Indeed, although they pay some lip service to the subsequent revisions and changed emphasis of approach introduced in the 1968 and 1993 versions of the SNA, many countries still adhere to the basic system and its corresponding accounting foundations as first set out. Around the world, the core concepts of gross domestic product (GDP) and gross national product (GNP) and their associated macroeconomic balances are universally recognized and understood in this context. (The key notion of GNP, for example, essentially disappeared in 1968 only to reemerge, in a slightly different guise, as "gross national income" in the 1993 revision).[20]

In addition to this core interest in the SNA, the main concerns and themes of UNSO until the late 1980s as determined or endorsed by the Statistical Commission were:[21]

- The comparability of data across nations
- The establishment of international standards to achieve this end
- Technical cooperation, which was viewed primarily as exporting "best-practice" (and sometimes inapplicable) Western/North American solutions. (This could be justified, of course, under the legitimate rubric of international standardization and comparability.)
- Data compilation for statistical yearbooks
- The development of strong national statistical systems to serve national statistical needs (with international comparability as a by-product)
- Giving greater emphasis to methodological work and implementation of uniform statistical processes, instead of defining their exact content, to meet national needs. (In so doing, the promotion of a single uniform standard to achieve international comparability was placed to one side.)
- Technical cooperation which focused on capacity building and paid attention to local conditions and resource limitations
- Data compilation and dissemination involving the gradual introduction of special-purpose publications containing more analytical and user-friendly elements and machine-readable outputs, in addition to the more traditional publications

Since the mid-1990s there has been a renewed emphasis on improving the international comparability of data. Methodological work has attempted to address both national uses and concerns about international comparability. Through technical cooperation, UNSO has concentrated mainly on specific problems rather than systemic issues, except in the special case of the transition economies. With the rapid technological advances in computing and the like, data compilation has moved strongly in the direction of more standard procedures and electronic dissemination.

The focus on coordination has also shifted emphasis over the decades. After the problem of the respective authority of UNSO and the role of the specialized agencies had been sorted out, there followed a period of concern in the 1970s over the World Fertility Survey.[22] This was carried out by national agencies and their consultants under the auspices of the International Statistical Institute. The survey touched on many issues and was seen in some quarters to be in competition with the UN activities and, despite the ISI's international authority, thwarting UNSO's international statistical mandate. Later, coordination of the traditional United Nations agencies with the Bretton Woods institutions (which are nominally part of the UN family) proved to be increasingly difficult. The World Bank and the IMF began early to exert their global influence and produce policy-relevant statistics that were more current and more extensive than those UNSO was producing. The World Bank never had a defined data mandate, but the IMF needed to collect statistics about finance in several important areas in order to fulfill its particular surveillance functions and supervisory role in maintaining monetary stability. The coordination of the activities of the Statistical Office of the European Communities (Eurostat) and the Organisation for Economic Cooperation and Development (OECD) with those of the UN and the rest of the global statistical system also became more contentious, although relations between the UN's Economic Commission for Europe (ECE) and these two agencies—particularly in the Conference of European Statisticians—remained good. In general, intraorganizational problems have been resolved by dividing different statistical responsibilities by topic within the UN system (e.g., assigning prices, wages, and employment to the ILO; services to the World Trade Organization [WTO]; tariffs to UNCTAD, etc.).[23] The same tacit agreement has been made with those agencies that have a specific international mandate and policy agenda. Thus, the IMF produces international data on the balance of payments, government financial systems and public accounts, and money and banking statistics, while the World Bank concentrates on compiling GDP and poverty data and collects loan-by-loan debt statistics. Elsewhere, issues have been divided geographically as, for example, in the case of the OECD and Eurostat and the various regional development banks, which each have their own distinct political imperatives and national constituencies.

To understand the position of the UN in this period and its role in the promotion of statistical ideas, particularly those based on the use of sound statistics, it is also necessary to look at the philosophies of the UN in general and at the direction given by the Statistical Commission. The way the commission was first set up and operated influenced not only the way countries positioned their statistical offices in the organization of government but also how they devised their statistical programs and determined data priorities. Ultimately, it also affected the pattern of development itself. On the positive side, the commission maintained a consistent emphasis on data that was designed to guide policy to improve general material well-being. On the negative side, it shuffled its feet and moved slowly—but not indecisively—on social questions. It took an ultra-conservative stance on issues related to individual social status, assigning the implicit responsibility for most concerns to the respective specialized agencies and their governing authorities or simply allowing them to drop.

Early on, it was decided that the declared goals for data harmonization could be best achieved through giving priority to statistical coordination, international cooperation, and the general dissemination of information according to agreed-upon codes. Different committees were set up, expert groups were convened, and special advisors were hired under UN auspices to guide this process. But tucked away in a hidden agenda, there have almost always lurked some unwritten objectives. Implicit pressure was exerted on the official data producers of member countries to comply with the commission's decisions and to support its endorsement of certain international statistical mandates. The commission assumed—through the UN Statistical Office as its secretariat and implementing (or coordinating) agency—the highest powers of statistical authority. In practice, for many years, it was the Statistical Office itself that assumed this leadership until, as was inevitable in a global society subject to rapid economic and social change, strict adherence to rigid data structures and definitions in the interest of consistency and uniformity began to expose a fundamental weakness in the UNSO approach. As a result, other institutions which seemed politically and strategically better placed to respond to policy changes took over some of UNSO's functions. The IMF, the World Bank and, later, the various so-called city groups have thus assumed leadership in the production of some key development data. (The city groups are discussed in Chapter 5.)

UNSO Leadership in Setting Statistical Priorities

The role of the United Nations and, more specifically, of UNSO in increasing global awareness of fundamental economic and social issues and in helping policymakers address them is a main concern of the international organization. It is evident that not all of the ideas to have come out of UNSO over the past half-century have borne fruit. The main ones, however, are now an integral part of most countries' data-compilation procedures. They are also applied in the operations and strategic planning of all international agencies. Some of the UN's ideas are still being tested in the crucible of practical policy application. Eventually, UNSO's methods may become the commonly adopted way of calibrating the relevant issues concerned. The major early achievements of UNSO in the field of international statistics in laying the foundation for a common understanding represent an accomplishment that is equivalent to the accomplishments that earned the UN its glittering prizes in the area of international cooperation. Particular contributions such as the national accounts and demographic statistics represent some of the crowning glories of professional achievement and technical integrity. Indeed it is significant to note that in pursuing its avenues of statistical inquiry, UNSO has been associated with the award of one Nobel Prize (to Sir Richard Stone) in the field of economics. It has also been closely associated with the activities of at least two other Nobel laureates—Lawrence Klein and Amartya Sen. Many others who have had close links with UN data initiatives have received international professional and academic recognition for their distinguished contributions to international statistical inquiry.

Ideas that have worked and are now commonplace include data standardization in all its complex and multidimensional aspects, the national accounts system, trade statistics and, not least, population and demographic statistics. To this should be added the significant early initiative the UN took in promoting gender distinction as an important data characteristic. Other UNSO ideas, though scientifically sound and conceptually innovative, never went very far. For example, at the time of their introduction, the System of Social and Demographic Statistics (SSDS) and the early formulation of social indicators to provide policy guidelines on issues that were not regarded as directly measurable were deemed inappropriate or conceptually inapplicable. Statistics on the distribution of income, consumption, and accumulation, where, perhaps surprisingly, there has been a distinct lack of global leadership by the UN, were not pursued.

There are other areas where the jury is still out or where the trial period continues to be extensive. These relate to real international comparisons of economic phenomena that were originally expressed in terms of domestic value (and the corresponding determination of purchasing-power parities), satellite accounts, human resource accounting, national household sample survey methodology and general survey organization, and environmental accounts (which are bedeviled, in part, by an associated political pressure to produce estimates of "green GDP"). Progress in these fields has been mixed. UNSO has performed a very useful service by drawing the attention of data users to the important methodological distinction between, for example, the System of National Accounts (SNA) and the system of material balance accounts (also known as the Material Product System) and the distinction between national accounts and business accounts. At a mostly theoretical level, UNSO has detailed the relative merits of different sampling procedures, but it has yet to produce a manual to describe how and when to use various survey methods. Despite the fact that some moderate success has been achieved in many of these subjects, the fact that they have not been universally adopted and that they are not widely understood implies that, as ideas, they have not yet come to fruition or become commonly accepted method and practice.

Beyond this, however, lie a number of special topics—some of which, admittedly, remain conceptually tricky and politically sensitive and elusive—where the UN has yet to make a mark. These include areas where leadership from UNSO has been less assertive and slow to take effect. Such topics include poverty measurement; the global characteristics of important variables such as inflation and growth; the nature of deprivation, inequality, and wealth; and the measurement of overall resource depletion. Other evident and emerging global problems—which appear as urgent concerns at UN global summits—include climate change and global warming, the determinants of good governance (and the identification of corruption), and the participation of civil society in decision making. Human-rights indicators are not on the agenda. The nature of the production of services and assessments of the contribution of the informal and unobserved sectors to the economy have yet to be tackled comprehensively. No corresponding UN statistical recommendations, manuals, or guidelines have been issued on these topics. A number of these subjects, in consequence, have been taken up independently by one or another of the so-called city groups. (These are associations of interested international, government, and academic experts in these respective statistical areas of concern; some UN staff members may also be involved.)

Immediately after World War II, UNSO had a clearly perceived data mission, and it maintained a well-defined vision of its leadership role in statistics. UNSO set out to make methodological advances, implement new data frameworks, and coordinate statistical procedures. It assumed the responsibility for these tasks and continues to fulfill these roles today as the UN Statistical Division (UNSD).[24] It took upon itself the duty to reflect, through suitable monitoring and surveillance techniques, all the key developments in policy analysis that had occurred before, during, and immediately after its establishment; especially relevant were macroeconomic policy and the monitoring of production and trade flows. Through a consultative process, UNSO laid down definitions and classification schemes to allow every country to compile the data required to drive policies in key fields. The emerging political independence of many new nations added urgency to this imperative. At the same time, because of the differences between the two distinct political ideologies pursued by the West and the Communist bloc, the UN structure demanded that attention be paid to both statistical systems. UNSO set out to describe the underlying data that supported the frameworks each required, while paying perhaps less attention, presumably for reasons of international politics, to the different philosophies and implicit objective functions the respective systems and their supporting ideologies implied.

The broader emphasis continued to be on the coordination, comparability, and consistency of statistical methods. There was a desire to ensure that, as far as possible, everything the UN published followed a well-recognized set of rules. UNSO provided a transparent framework, the System of National Accounts, that could lead easily to the replication of similar sets of information in every country. This system made countries more readily accountable for their official data. While the SNA was perhaps the most significant achievement, there was also the system of material balances, the direction of trade reports (responsibility for which was subsequently taken over by the IMF), the UN *Short Manual on Sampling,* and other manuals providing guidelines on the compilation of statistics.[25] These manuals dealt with a variety of topics, including the composition of trade; the classification of imports of commodities and broad economic end use of those commodities; codes for industry, employment, and the functions of government; and the population handbooks.[26] In its early stages, the work of the office reflected the enormous influence and intellectual standing of P. C. Mahalanobis, although Chernikov, the USSR representative, raised objections to having a subcommittee on sampling. Later, UNSO devoted a great deal of effort to preparing guidelines for choosing appropriate sampling methods. It thought that surveys would be more widely adopted in government inquiry, but in countries where they were most needed because of resource constraints, the absence of appropriate frameworks restricted the effectiveness of the sampling methods that were used. In the final analysis, UNSO made only brief forays into the area of sampling and resorted mainly to recruiting expert technical assistance and providing funding to the consultants it identified to help countries undertake national projects and manage inquiries.

In the early days, in practice, the commission did not have to make up a statistical program or assign any particular priority ranking to certain subjects. In effect, UNSO inherited certain prior established commitments to produce trade and industry data. It took on new responsibilities to compile national income statistics and to widen the scope of surveys and sampling applications. There was a sense that UNSO could and should rely less on conventional administrative records, including tax data. National offices in particular wanted to avoid using data from those ministries and government departments that were notorious for hiding the full facts in order to paint a good image of their performance. Data about selected industries such as tourism and public works and their employment characteristics sometimes made their economies look brighter than they really were.

There was also a huge and unavoidable data agenda linked closely to the needs of postwar reconstruction and development. The primary limitations facing most data agencies—and the UN was no exception—related to the substantial data start-up costs in member countries in an era that was characterized by highly constrained national budgets and serious resource problems, including a scarcity of trained and skilled personnel. In addition, at this early stage, the commission saw itself as the spiritual heir to the League of Nations Committee of Statistical Experts. As such, it believed that one of its major roles was to ratify or amend the statistical legacy bequeathed to it from the interwar period. High on the League's original work program (and hence on the new commission's agenda) was the preparation of the essential ground rules for establishing an international standard industrial classification. Constructing a comprehensive list of goods involved in international trade, as always, was a crucial item on the policy agenda because specialization and exchange was seen even then as a major means to increase wealth and raise living standards. These programs were to become the central linchpins of economic analysis and emerged in the shape of the International Standard Industrial Classification (ISIC) and the Standard International Trade Classification (SITC). Along with the standard methods of compiling census of population and related demographic statistics recommended by the UN Population Division, which was essentially another arm of the statistical wing of the UN, these classifications formed the core of UNSO's standardization activities. The classifications became established as the cornerstones for a more general and integrated system of economic statistics. But they focused exclusively on exchange and the production and trade of goods and not on which agents were instrumental in these activities. As time wore on and societies and their behavior became more complex, the weaknesses of these systems and their declining relevance and limited ability to provide comprehensive results grew more apparent.

At the beginning, statistical priorities were driven primarily by the policy needs of the more advanced industrial nations. At that time, trade and output classifications served their main economic purposes well. Indeed, they went on to form the main foundations for the System of National Accounts. But as social structures and their influence on economic performance became more important, an exclusive concentration on an establishment-based categorization of industry and a product approach without an understanding of the interrelated dynamics was called into question.

The Role and Influence of UNSO

In reviewing the raison d'être for UNSO and its original objectives, terms of reference, and perceived role, it is important to assess how much it contributed to providing meaningful policy direction. UNSO established common definitions, classifications, and frameworks that have contributed to a more consistent, coherent, comprehensive, and internally and externally harmonized (if not fully comparable) international statistical system. It took an essential lead in drawing all the pieces together. However, was its role really to provide national guidance or was it intended to be essentially global (or at least international) in its scope? To be successful at both, UNSO had to establish a uniformity that ensured cross-country comparability and a corresponding facility with regional aggregation.

Some observers felt that the main purpose of UNSO was to serve the UN organization and its interests. The UN has never assigned to itself any mandate forcing compliance with its views in promoting or implementing policies in its member states, although it might well have wanted to assume an advocacy role. But it has encouraged particular courses of action. UNSO tried, quite successfully in the earlier years, to lead by example and move forward by mutual agreement. Perhaps only the IMF and the World Bank, as independent international stabilization and development agencies, have been able (through their resource transfer functions) to exercise any similar authority in laying down international data-reporting requirements for overall monitoring purposes. They have been able to establish certain guidelines for strategic action that have been politically endorsed and sometimes legally buttressed by agreed-upon terms of association and conditionality. These conditions relate to economic performance goals and the acceptance of acknowledged regimes of policy. They contain obligations to produce certain economic and financial data. But were such issues and concerns of development (vis-à-vis economic progress in traditional spheres of influence) part of the original thinking and agenda of the UN statisticians? Even in the postwar period, it seems evident that social concerns as an everyday issue (as opposed to crisis circumstances) were assigned a lower level of importance in the statistical modus operandi of UNSO, at least until the emergence in the late 1960s of the social indicator movement. UNSO essentially bypassed this early initiative in social measurement and relegated it to an area of research. Even today, few attempts are made to cross-analyze economic status with social conditions with respect to opportunities, conditions of deprivation, and equity of access, especially to nonmarket goods and services such as health, education, and community welfare services that are provided by the public sector. Recent initiatives, such as the OECD's Shaping the Twenty-First Century and the UN's Millennium Development Goals,[27] however, have specified the production of particular statistics by calling for the adoption of a minimum core set of indicators. These are intended to monitor social progress in developing countries toward the achievement of certain basic standards of health, education, and welfare. The need for such measures is further reinforced by the multilateral initiative to forgive the debts of heavily indebted poor countries (HIPC), a process that is designed to trade the outstanding official debt of the poorest countries for new programs designed to alleviate the plight of the poor and provide improved access to health and education services.

Statistical Standards and Systems

The establishment and universal acceptance of standard international classifications, common statistical definitions, and recognized data frameworks around the world is perhaps one of the most important achievements of

UNSO. It is what has helped make international statistics, in general, international public goods. When analysts, policymakers, researchers, and even the ordinary public see a reference to birth rates, fertility, GNP, or growth or read a newspaper article about the value of exports and average life expectancy with respect to a given country, they have a common understanding of what these numbers and concepts mean. They know that, subject to certain limitations (as when values in domestic prices need to be converted into a common international currency numeraire), the world can legitimately compare the statistics of one country with those of another. For the most part, it is possible to add together national figures that use the same classification schemes to provide some other meaningful higher aggregate or regional total.

However, this success in achieving standardization has all the warning signs of becoming the UN's nemesis in statistics. For years, successive UN data administrations have worked hard to preserve formal data structures and procedures to maintain standards with the goal of ensuring historical and cross-country consistency and continuity. Coordination and cooperation (which some may see as euphemisms for preserving overall UN control of the international data regime) have figured prominently in the statistical agenda. Where it has proved difficult to bring about agreement, appropriate concordances and other agreed-upon harmonization rules concerning the preferred approach to be followed have been worked out. But the world is rapidly changing, and new concepts and theories based on other premises have begun to emerge. New techniques, products, and production organizations have evolved. At the same time, different priorities have become important to policymakers and certain conventional data structures are sometimes considered less relevant and meaningful to contemporary analytical thinking. The awareness of governments of the need to adapt to these changes and to introduce amendments has sometimes been slow, as has been indicated by recent work on measuring productivity.[28] The importance of new approaches and the need for flexibility have been recognized only at a late stage by both national and international data agencies.

UNSO was the first organization to set statistical standards and examine them as a set of tools in their own right. It looked at the background and purposes of statistical standards and the main factors influencing them, noticing the way they evolved over time. But along with some of the essential classification schemes that accompany them, these procedures have become the international commandments which have become set in stone in their core structures and characteristics.[29] The evolution of national and international statistical standards has not always proceeded according to agreed-upon principles that place a priority on policy use. While issues of politics and national (and international) bureaucratic rivalry and pride have influenced the process of data organization over the past 150 years, the problem has other fundamental roots. It is often difficult to agree on a single statistical standard in particular fields because suppliers, users, and potential users of any given standard may, quite legitimately, have sharply different views and requirements.

The term "statistical standards" can be taken as referring to three somewhat related requirements: 1) international agreement on the concepts, definitions, and classifications that underlie the collection, compilation, and dissemination of official statistics; 2) the common acceptance of norms to guide the operations of collection, compilation, aggregation, and eventual dissemination of data. These might include estimation and gap-filling techniques for missing data; and 3) observed principles of analysis and use of recognized methodologies in the assessment of the data themselves. Statistical standards sometimes need to serve interests other than those of immediate data users. They are relevant to questions raised in the sciences, public policy administration, law, and other disciplines. Economists and sociologists may wish to define social class differently, labor economists and labor exchange officials may have different ways of grouping occupations or measuring employment, the laws of different jurisdictions may define residence or crime quite differently, and so on. Issues of practicality vary across populations, regions, enterprises, and methods of data collection. The respective data-compilation processes and the extent of their coverage may occasionally imply that, superficially, similar statistics are related to something quite different than their descriptions suggest. When data sources extend beyond administrative records to censuses and household surveys, data that seem to pertain to the same phenomena can be seriously at variance with each other.

Statistics is primarily a science of order and classification. It is evident that any classification procedure that brings together like features into similar groups, such as diseases that tend to occur in particular parts of the human body, or that distinguishes between medical conditions that are similar but not the same is likely to improve understanding. In the above example, the accurate classification of diseases may help researchers and physicians deduce general principles about medical conditions. But classification is simply a method of generalization. There is no unique classification structure that serves all conceivable purposes equally well. Several classifications may be used to suit more than one purpose; for example, the physician, the pathologist, or the jurist, each from their own point of view, may legitimately classify the diseases and the causes of death in the way that he or she thinks best suits their own inquiries and yet still come up with results of general interest to all.

An important concern, however, is whether the classification used in the processing and presentation of statistics can still properly exhibit the heterogeneity that is present in the raw data. The various dimensions and locations of this heterogeneity are not known a priori in some cases; they may then remain hidden if the data are stored and then published according to a grouping that has not previously identified these basic characteristics. In other cases, the sources of the heterogeneity are known but the classifications being used may not be fully adequate. This could blur a good deal of the disparities that are of potential socioeconomic significance and interest.

Another goal of statistical standards is to facilitate and promote the fundamental scientific requirement of replicability. Seen from this perspective, statistical standards are an essential element of any robust scientific assessment. The scientific relevance of statistical standards is related to how well official statistics advance research in one field or another. Many issues and priorities are shaped by how closely the standard corresponds to the model or hypothesis being tested. Statistical standards need to conform to established notions about scientific theory. For example, in the discussions leading up to the development of a new industrial classification system, Jacob Ryten argued that the principles of classification for economic data must be grounded in economic theory; this supports the fundamental principle that economic measurement must be designed to serve the purpose for which the data are going to be used.

The two scientific principles of replicability and established consistent theory, however, sometimes work in opposite directions. The desire for replicability, taken by itself, argues for standards that do not vary, while the need to test models or hypotheses, again taken by itself, calls for fluid concepts, definitions, and classifications that respond quickly to developments and controversies in subject-matter theory. Even if the goal is the more modest one that a statistical classification and the units being classified be derived from a consistent perception of reality, the need for the standard to respond to the evolution of the theory on which it is based must be faced. A further complicating factor is that the same standards may be used in relation to quite different kinds of things (for example, people, establishments, and events) where different bodies of theory are seen as relevant.[30]

While scientific researchers may be looking for truth, public policy makers and administrators are simply looking for solutions. As a result, they tend to see statistical standards quite differently. For the former, the choice is often between the right or wrong standard, while for the latter it is between a better or worse standard. The researcher, at least in principle, can reserve judgment, while the policymaker or administrator generally has little alternative but to take a decision and make it operational.

Without independently laid down standards and methodologies, policymakers and administrators have enormous power to influence how data-gathering procedures are applied. They often have direct authority over the development of specific standards in their areas of responsibility. Indeed, the policymaking and administrative uses of information, defined and classified in accordance with statistical standards, probably represent the widest use of these standards. Users often disagree over the perceived wisdom and advantages of relatively stable standards that, for example, permit long-term monitoring of program performance. Some prefer to see relatively flexible standards that can more readily conform to current policy concerns and emphases. The problem is that structures are continually changing and benchmarks, along with associated points of reference, need to be regularly updated.

Fortunately, perhaps, the desire for statistical uniformity and need to establish a common base of reference for discussion and evaluation within an integrated international economic system has transcended narrow political and state interest. Until recently, the statistical community espoused the qualities of professional integrity, honesty, neutrality, and objectivity and rose above petty national rivalry. Through the commission and other conferences, statisticians have reached across political boundaries to establish a truly "united nations" approach to conducting statistical tasks embracing a wide range of policy issues. Now, however, some agencies are selectively disseminating official data and are running into political opposition not only from users but also from the public at large.

Ends and Means: Economic Progress and Social Outcomes

This postwar emphasis on macroeconomic strategy and materialism did not form part of what some now regard as the "great tradition" in statistics. The more dominant historical concern of statisticians in previous centuries had been with social reform and individual well-being. During the nineteenth and early twentieth centuries, the personal research activities of leading statisticians were connected with inquiries into the sufferings of the poor and their inability to obtain their basic needs. These microlevel studies revealed how the lives of low-income workers were linked to the lack of fundamental human rights both at home and in the workplace. In England, these early heroes of empirical research played an important part in influencing Parliament to adopt pioneering health and safety codes and factory legislation. Nineteenth-century statisticians went beyond government files and collected data at the household or institutional level. Their primary objective was to draw public attention to the plight of those who found themselves incapable of acquiring the basic wherewithal to feed their families. Their work made the public aware of the inability of the poor to shake themselves free from the daily burden of appallingly long hours, laboring under nonexistent or unsatisfactory employment laws, and physically arduous working conditions. Even though they worked twelve hours a day and six days a week, the working poor did not, in many cases, provide a sufficient wage to give their families enough to live on. Employers vehemently opposed legislation that restricted the hours an individual could work each day, contending (untruthfully) that they made their profits only in the last hour of work put in each day by their workers.

The post–World War II drive for material well-being and prosperity, however, overshadowed the need to focus on the plight of the poor. In Europe, the poor were dealt with through official "altruism" in the form of statutory social transfer provisions and the allocation of benefits of the welfare state. Benefits in money and kind in amounts that officials thought necessary to ameliorate a social problem (e.g., unemployment, old age, additional children) were distributed to low-income families to enable them to function socially at an adequate level. This reduced the pressure on companies to provide a satisfactory living wage. In practice, it was only the periods of prolonged economic progress and low unemployment (which also significantly funded the existing welfare provisions) that ultimately helped the poor escape from the permanent shackles of poverty in post-war industrial Europe.

Postwar economic and social recovery was inevitably overshadowed by the bitter memories most adults throughout the world retained about the interwar depression. Most wanted to escape the demoralizing impact of unemployment and deprivation that had been universally inflicted on the collective psyche irrespective of a person's background and occupation. Few families with roots in certain locations and industries were left untouched by this experience. Governments were blamed for the interwar chaos, emptiness, and disillusion. To many, the governments of the capitalist industrial world had shown themselves incapable of stimulating economic progress and generating employment. They had demonstrated an unwillingness to reach any international agreement, particularly with respect to trade, that might have improved national prospects. Western governments seemed bereft of any ideas about how to resolve the problem of inadequate aggregate demand and nurture economic resurgence until the process of rearmament began to take effect. The situation seemed poised for political change and possible upheaval.

Only in the U.S., where Roosevelt's New Deal in the 1930s helped legitimize the notion of public planning of a market environment, did the idea of direct government intervention in the economic system gain ground. The New Deal programs involved widespread public spending on major investment projects such as the Tennessee Valley Authority. The government proved that it had the potential to act effectively on a large scale. These actions sowed the early seeds of government planning in general. Public investment strategy began to assume great significance in a wide range of countries. Many governments were figuratively (and literally) digging themselves out of a hole, and this process was to last for many decades after the war. The official way of thinking about and of organizing national efforts affected how countries' statistical systems were structured and developed. Governments emphasized commodities over actions, transactions over transactors, and identifying types of units instead of who owned and controlled them. There was great concern with flows at the expense of the issues of stocks and balances that had interested previous generations.

Data through the Looking Glass

The world is thus measured according to a particular way of looking at things, and any changes in the world over time have had to be looked at through the same instrument and perspective, even if the actual situation being observed and measured may have changed fundamentally. This poses even greater difficulties, clearly, when trying to predict a pattern of future change. Changes usually require the application of a different measuring instrument if they are to be depicted accurately. A concrete example may serve to illustrate this issue and the dilemma it poses for statisticians. Some social scientists are engaged in trying to compare the economic performance of China and India over the past 100 years; others are looking at progress in Russia over the twentieth century and comparing it with progress in the U.S. or Africa. To do this, researchers need to determine an appropriate instrument that standardizes comparisons not only between countries but also over time. Invariably they choose the Western GNP model (and related productivity measures) not only to measure change but also to help them understand the dynamics of that change.

Box 1.6. The Nature of Prediction and Theory

There are two types of prediction in science: one in which claims are deduced from a theory in order to test it and another that seeks to foretell future behavior. The former type concerns forecasts, while the latter fits more comfortably in the area of prophecy. When there are no irrefutable natural laws (such as Newton's law of gravity) to assure an outcome, results are more dependent on probabilities that tend to change over time and according to circumstance.

There may be a need to distinguish between failures of prediction that call for the unqualified rejection of a theory and mistaken assertions that demand further fine-tuning or the need to adopt a different perspective to have validity. The difference hinges on whether the overall pattern of predictive behavior indicates that further modification and extension of assumed theory offers more promise than abandoning the theory completely. Experiments and observations are thus required to make sure alternative theories are incorrect.

A phenomenon must be not only observable and observed but must also be measurable before such analysis can be conducted. The evidence of strongly correlated links is only supportive; it is widely acknowledged that such links are not proof positive of a causal connection. Indeed, such a positive outcome may well deflect attention from other relevant avenues of research.[31] Karl Popper argued that empirical observations can never truly confirm a theory; they can only falsify (or fail to falsify) it. However, every theory may have its antithesis—its direct opposite. If so, then a theory can perhaps be confirmed by the falsification of its antithesis. This may seem quite a reasonable approach to apply where the case of reverse correlation or causation is assumed to hold. But large and complex multifactor systems with different interactive characteristics are difficult to test in this way, mostly because they cannot be comprehensively modeled or put in a "laboratory" where certain conditions that might exert an influence can be held constant. In addition, other unidentified factors may be at work to confound the outcome.

Data gathering in the social sciences, then, becomes a different procedure and a considerably more difficult affair. It is subject to uncontrollable and unalterable social and environmental circumstances that are in a continual state of flux. These have to be taken as givens because they are impossible to isolate. Social researchers must pay attention to initial conditions and to tracking their possible influence. In addition, they can attempt to control for variability in circumstantial factors by introducing dummy variables to track or separate contextual features.

Actual economic behavior and rational reaction to economic circumstances often deviates—for quite logical and unsurprising reasons—from standard views about the precepts of accepted theory. The primary purpose of such theory should be to explain and not just describe the relationship between phenomena and events. In traditional economics, the role of the unit—the individual, household, or firm—and its rational reaction to the task of making ends meet or balancing complex choices to obtain the best outcome (value for money) assumes overriding significance. The theory is built upon an elaborate edifice of premises about behavior that lead, ultimately, to an amalgam of equilibrium positions. The evidence of observation has long challenged these tenets of faith and has indicated that increasing disparities and discrepancies in socio-economic actions (leading to growing instability) is the more likely outcome of individual behavior, but no corresponding theory concerning the chaos in complexity has yet been developed.

Such a model subsumes many heroic economic premises; its values necessarily include the idea that prices reflect the interaction of supply and demand. For example, it assumes that a true price is one that clears the market and that demand is the expression of need (backed up by a willingness—or, increasingly, ability—to pay). In addition, the statistician must make an assumption about which benchmark prices should be used; the choice hinges on the particular standpoint—the beginning, the end, or somewhere in between—from which such an assessment is to be made. Ordinary index numbers cannot deal with substantial change satisfactorily, particularly in absolute and relative prices, over long periods.[32] By contrast, the socialist production system was driven by other criteria and signals in which nominal prices served only as accounting tools and statistical "tabs" to facilitate aggregation requirements for different physical commodities. The performance of socialist production units, particularly with respect to the provision of nonmarket goods and services, would not be accurately assessed using a conventional Western national accounts and pricing procedure. The problem with the national accounts as a statistical instrument is that it attributes little or no weight to distributive justice in the economic system. It thus falls short as an index of individual economic well-being because it subsumes questions of equity and effectively conceals any notion of welfare.

Although GNP provides an important means of quantifying the world, it provides essentially a singular dimension that relates to production and to net, not gross, output and to a gross, and not more economically meaningful, concept of net value added. The Soviet Material Product System (MPS), though similarly linked to a detailed structure of production balances generated from the establishment level within their respective industry sectors, automatically generates measures of gross material output. These have the virtuous property that, at the industry and enterprise level, they can be associated directly and perhaps more meaningfully to employment and overall productivity and to statistics about occupational status. Each of the two systems has value. They are intimately related because both focus primary attention on the production account, which is gross in one case (the MPS) and net (i.e., adjusted for intermediate consumption) in the other (the SNA). The national accounts go farther, because in emphasizing values and not physical quantities, the system reflects the essential viability of resource use in sustaining the production process since it draws attention to (market) efficiency and operating surplus. The accounts extend the notion of output to embrace the important part that "nonproductive" services play in their role as both outputs and inputs associated with overall economic activity. Even so, the MPS underlines technological efficiency and labor productivity in the production of goods.

A different perspective of the world, and of world income, would be obtained if national data systems were to concentrate instead on building up measures of gross income directly from enterprises and from individuals (and the household) or were to emphasize the identification of final expenditures from the final demand side. The consumption-based notion of disposable income comes closer to common ideas about well-being and individual concerns about personal economic security, sufficiency, and sustainability. In primitive farming and hunter-gatherer communities, production "work" is a matter of personal volition and is directly related to individual reward and well-being. Those who don't work don't eat unless they can rely on the generosity of others. In more advanced societies, decisions about production and employment very much lie with the entrepreneurial class, though individuals can still exercise some choice about where they work. So, to an important extent, an individual or household's well-being is dependent on those factors which influence business decisions and the respective ownership of assets. This creates tension between production income and individual income and is reflected in the relative returns accruing to capital and labor across a wide swath of sectoral economic activity.

In all these approaches, however, the global element of quantifying the world does not really emerge. Instead, because the data-collection process at each separate country level has such an impact on statistical results, the results continue to be more polystatist than international. They can be rarely described as global. This distinction has to do with the choice of the basic institutional unit on which the aggregation is performed. If it is at the country level (and is already subject to a given form of aggregation), then the outcome of adding all the data together is, at best, "international," assuming that similar data-processing methods have been followed and the same sources tapped in all countries. If it is not at the country level, then the resulting total constitutes a somewhat indeterminate amalgam of information. When the issue under investigation is, say, global income inequality or global inflation, the relevant aggregate will correspond to a global concept only if its elements are aggregated at the primary level of the unit of inquiry; for example, incomes of individuals or prices of items. Even then there may be certain interactive features that will make it difficult to clearly determine the measure desired.

2

The Economic Dimension

- **The UN and World Data**
- **National Accounts and GNP**
- **The Measurement of Trade**
- **The Measurement of Labor and Output**
- **Employment and Labor Issues**
- **The Measurement of Agriculture**
- **International Comparisons**

Behind any attempt to measure the world in a particular way lies a decision that reflects a particular paradigm. This paradigm pursued the need for certain definitions and classifications. Whatever perspective is taken, it needs to be located within an internationally accepted data framework. The framework must be rooted in a recognized conceptual model of socioeconomic dynamics if it is to be readily understood and serve as a practical, meaningful tool for policymaking. The associated data system can be just a sequential or hierarchical way of grouping similar things for the sake of simplicity and coherence; for example, as in the conventional categorizing of goods and services and the sequencing of goods before services in UN classifications designed to quantify commodities and production activities.

An alternative schematic approach, for example, the Material Product System, may prioritize or sequence other things. In ordering primary production and agriculture (and the production of basic raw or unprocessed products such as fish and forests) before mining (extraction) and ordering manufacturing (the secondary transformation of primary and produced goods into other produced goods) before construction and utilities, the structure of the material goods output system appeals to an intrinsic logic.

A classification scheme may also be institutional and thus reflect an inherently convenient accounting or administrative structure. Separating current accounts from capital accounts in the general government financial system and when recording the external transactions of the balance of payments, however, lends more economic meaning to a conventional accounting rationale. A data system defined by a conceptual model demands that a more rigorous theoretical structure underpin its basis. While theories of behavior change over time, often because the surrounding circumstances change, theories related to the more axiomatic dynamics of economic relations and the basic incentive systems of society tend to change very little as time passes. Some of these theories then become embedded in the collective consciousness of the population and policymakers. When a certain paradigm appears no longer to hold true, it is because the professional analysts have adopted new beliefs about reality and have rejected existing symbolic generalizations about how things operate.[1] Once established, however, the data frameworks are more difficult to change.

In the beginning, UNSO stood at the crossroads between adopting the traditional methodologies that were familiar to policymakers who maintained a conservative vision of international stability or following a handful of prophets who were pedaling relatively untried ideas about economic management. UNSO grasped the enormous possibilities the latter seemed to offer in their recognition of the importance of Keynesian ideas as a dynamic new theory of macroeconomic behavior that was quite separate from the conventional perspective of an aggregation of microequilibrium positions. UNSO established very early on the extensive and intricate data foundations for implementing and evaluating policies pursued in this mode. For better or worse, new ideas generate excitement, and UNSO enthusiastically embraced Keynesian thinking. Dudley Seers later pointed out that Keynesian macroeconomic policy represented only the economics of the special case.[2] It was not really applicable to poor, open, and undiversified economies, particularly those based on agriculture. At the time when many interrelated data-collection programs were being implemented across the "free" world to support the new emphasis of policy, something in the order of three-quarters of the world's population survived on very low incomes in cash or in kind, and most of those people lived in rural areas. Today, the world's rural inhabitants still constitute the overwhelming proportion of people in low-income countries. The new theory was not, therefore, the global panacea everyone had hoped for, but the political and bureaucratic process, the education system, and institutionalized procedures of data gathering that UNSO had established in implementing the model actively discouraged the search for new knowledge and alternative models of the world. Although the economic "Reformation" had begun, it was geographically defined; symbolically, Keynesian economic thought resembled a Protestant critique of traditional Rome. It did not constitute a fundamentally different religion or a new way of economic thinking that challenged the central universal role of the market, but it did re-align the emphasis.

If the main socioeconomic problems of the world can be described as those suffered by the majority of its people, then it is abundantly clear that Keynesian economics and the market system have failed to deliver on their promise of secure strategies to improve the living conditions and opportunities for the poor. This is evident from the more or less unchanged overall structure of income distribution in the world. Since 1945, the same rich minority has continued to absorb the greatest share of global income while the overwhelming proportion of the world's population has had to settle for the scraps left over (see Figure 2.1 and Table 2.1). The same global structure will continue to apply, unless there are some major changes in political thinking, for the next generations. The persistence of poverty is perhaps the most serious indictment of the UN. It was an agency that initially set out to change the world, but it seems to have settled over the years for the comfortable assurance of dealing with known conditions governed by a predetermined set of rules.

The real test of the validity of policies that have become enshrined in conventional wisdom is not whether they work (as measured by some indicator of economic performance), but whether they have had any desirable impact on living standards and the process of securing sustained development. It is easier, of course, to assess the success or failure of different approaches in hindsight. It is perhaps also unfair to level criticism at the founders of the UN statistical system, with the knowledge on hand, for failing to see that poverty and global inequality, and not the postwar reconstruction of Europe, were the most important economic and social evils confronting the international community.

High-profile decisions about direction and strategic philosophy tend to be driven by national or, more specifically, party political interests rather than by a chosen ideology or contemporary modes of thought. The line between the political and the analytical approach is often gray and blurred, and it sometimes obscures the more fundamental issues at stake and the real concerns that need to be addressed. To think through this question, it is usually necessary to have an overarching vision which sets out the means to achieve the objectives implied in taking a chosen perspective. This may mean adopting a path of action quite different from one suggested by a traditional policy approach passed down through the inherited legacy of conventional wisdom. Had the UN identified poverty as the key issue and thus given some thought, in its early years, to the question of how to reduce, alleviate, and eventually eliminate poverty rather than how to raise production levels and eradicate formal unemployment in industrialized countries, then the direction and agenda of its statistics organization might have been quite different.

Figure 2.1. World Income Distribution, 1999

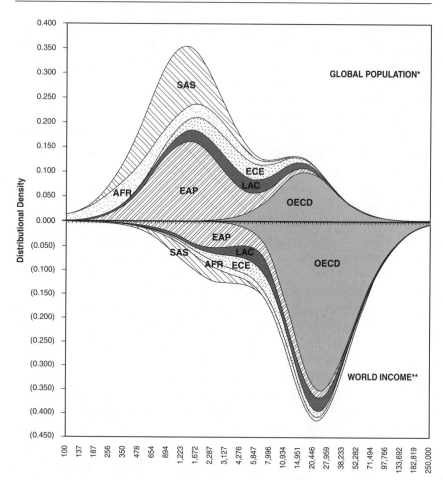

*In this graph, the areas under the outer "global" curve above the *x* axis (population) and below the *x* axis (income) are both equal to 1.000. The respective shares are defined by positions of the other curves.

**Average income per head (logarithm) in international dollars.

Key: AFR = Africa, SAS = South Asia, EAP = East Asia and the Pacific (including China), ECE = Former Soviet Union and East and Central Europe, LAC = Latin America and the Caribbean, OECD = Organisation for Economic Cooperation and Development countries

Source: Y. Dikhanov and M. Ward, "Evolution of the Global Distribution of Income, 1970–1999," paper presented to the fifty-third session of the International Statistics Institute, Seoul, Korea, 22–29 August 2001.

Figure 2.2. Evolution of Global Income Distribution, 1970–1999, Trace for Each Percentile*

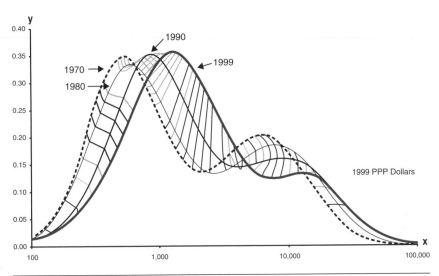

* The trace for each percentile shows how the income levels of the bottom 1 percent, 2 percent, and so forth in 1970 are transformed into their corresponding percentile groupings in 1999. As might be expected, over the succeeding decades between 1970 and 1999, the global distribution shifts to the right to reflect the overall growth in incomes over this period.

Key:
   y axis = relative distributional density of global income
   x axis = average income per capita in PPP international dollars on a logarithmic scale

Source: Y. Dikhanov and M. Ward, "Evolution of the Global Distribution of Income, 1970–1999," paper presented to the fifty-third session of the International Statistics Institute, Seoul, Korea, 22–29 August 2001.

Table 2.1. Estimated Global Income Levels by Decile, 1970–1999 (in 1999 PPP dollars)

	1970	1980	1990	1999
Decile 1	205	209	261	281
Decile 2	343	364	478	561
Decile 3	470	510	673	816
Decile 4	630	694	901	1,105
Decile 5	878	964	1,213	1,468
Decile 6	1,404	1,496	1,723	1,984
Decile 7	2,778	2,929	2,879	2,861
Decile 8	4,999	5,683	5,676	4,927
Decile 9	8,348	9,964	10,800	10,526
Decile 10	18,895	22,808	27,057	29,183
Mean Income	3,895	4,562	5,166	5,371
Median Income	1,061	1,157	1,418	1,690

Source: Y. Dikhanov and M. Ward, "Evolution of the Global Distribution of Income, 1970–1999," paper presented to the fifty-third session of the International Statistics Institute, Seoul, Korea, 22–29 August 2001

The perceived challenge facing the founding member states in 1945 was to overcome the big social and economic ills that had afflicted the prewar industrial world and ensure full employment. The original powers decided to resolve these problems not by offering temporary palliatives but by adopting an entirely different philosophy regarding macroeconomic behavior. The new theory allowed governments to discard some well-worn "cost-saving" supply-side economic strategies. These had not worked. But the new measures, which emphasized aggregate economic demand, mainly provided evidence of immediate and superficial short-term success; they did not see the need to test the overall validity of the assumptions underlying the approach.[3]

In the setting up of the United Nations, the original forty-six founding members—which included England, France, Holland, and Portugal and their extensive overseas territories—exercised a dominant influence over the prevailing philosophy. That philosophy, at least in the areas of economics and development thinking, was rooted in classical economic axioms, modified by the fresh perspective added to theory by the evolving influence of Keynesian economics. The conflicting ideas of Friedrich Hayek and John Maynard Keynes[4] were born in the context of an emerging but uneasy "free world" alliance to determine the approach to economic expansion. Polices about infrastructure development, the operations of private firms, the definition and scope of public enterprise, the role of nationalized concerns, and the control of the market were hotly debated. In the aligned field of development and projecting progress, an early 1930s Soviet idea linking capital investment to economic growth was embraced by Evsey D. Domar and Roy R. Harrod and embodied into the Keynesian framework. This theory divided the world into that component driven by private decisions and actions (the private sector) and that controlled more centrally, on account of its general strategic importance to the nation, by government authority (the public sector).

The institutions and the data systems that supported policy reflected the importance of a commodity culture and the behavior of individuals in response to the market. The enormous success of the "mixed economy" strategy, particularly in postwar Europe, reinforced the importance of a technocratically managed approach to policy. After long periods of debilitating unemployment and apparent labor surplus in the prewar period, countries in Western Europe such as England and France were having to draw in immigrant labor to keep their systems running.

A core component of the underlying philosophy of these approaches could be traced back to the individualism embodied in the Western Protestant ethic espoused by Max Weber and Richard Tawney.[5] If the founding members of the UN system had been drawn from, say, East Asia, then perhaps a different philosophical approach to people's existence and their interactions might have been adopted. In such a case, the motivation of policy would presumably have taken account of the cultural and spiritual quality of life and emphasized a more compassionate and socially engaged sense of community. A greater emphasis on the stability of society as a unit rather than on a philosophy of individual self-advancement and material gain would have been brought to bear on issues of ownership and private possession, possibly introducing constraints on the more ruthless zeal to accumulate personal property. All that capitalism entails with respect to economic philosophy would thus have assumed less importance.

But that is not what happened. The new approach depended heavily on obtaining measures of total effective demand. Determining GNP and its associated macroeconomic subaggregates and constructing supporting national accounts tables has reigned supreme in the priorities and core functions of national statistical offices. This was not always so; from 1920 onward, the development of an alternative political and economic system with different goals, priorities, and means of conducting policy ran quite counter to the existing ways of doing things. Communism or socialism established an apparently viable, more centralized, and distributionally fairer socioeconomic model. The socialist approach mandated proactive official strategies and deliberate state interventions to allocate and redistribute resources and output more equitably. The general strike in Britain in 1926, hyperinflation in Germany, the great crash in 1929, and the Great Depression of the 1930s, with its sweeping unemployment, were among the highly visible events that disabused some people of the merits of capitalism and influenced public support for a socialist way of thinking.[6] Economists in the Western world had until then relied heavily on the assumption that the market was efficient and that price signals worked automatically to indicate need and channel resources. Even under the subsequent Keynesian rules, policy analysts adhered to the classical notion of a "liberal" market system. Western economics focused on processes of exchange and efficiency and on ways to facilitate transactions (inter alia, "fair" competition) to the neglect of specific targeted outcomes. During the interwar period, this focus fundamentally affected the approach of industrial countries to such crucial policy concerns as unemployment, prices, and the determination of wage levels, interest rates, and currency values. It was only in the postwar environment of reconstruction that the collective public social and political conscience about prewar economic failure was pricked. The Western world set full employment and growth as its primary objective and embraced the more holistic approach of macroeconomics. In particular, it adopted a Keynesian understanding of aggregate economic behavior. Policymakers thus finally rejected Say's Law ("supply creates its own demand") and with it a disproportionate and unhealthy interest in driving down wages to lower production costs and increase efficiency, which they had seen as the only way to stimulate economic activity. Instead, they embraced policies to create and maintain aggregate demand, including both public investment and private household consumption.

The Keynesian model provided a coherent framework with which to understand both international economic relationships and the role of the public sector in overall economic management. By establishing and reinforcing the role of government in the running of the nation's affairs, Keynesian ideas appealed to political interests and breathed new life into sectarian party debate. Social theory and models of social behavior have not matured in the same way and this line of approach has been far less successful in gaining recognition and acceptance at the operational level, even though social policy deals directly with social disadvantage and exclusion. Indeed, it remains difficult—without referring to existing socioeconomic status and prior conditions—to define the interrelationships between education, health, housing, criminality, and so forth and their respective links to economic change. In practice, the dynamics of their significance to economic progress works in both directions.

The world and its laws, institutions, conventions, and technologies are constantly changing, sometimes dramatically. This continually affects how data are collected and compiled and influences the nature of evidence. Changes in accountancy conventions, auditing procedures, corporate law, valuation methods, taxation, malpractice laws, and so forth have all had a major impact on how appropriate information on output, value added, net profit, net worth, liabilities, and asset values is assembled and understood. In recent years, moreover, there have been some serious questions about the integrity of both public and corporate financial reporting. The increasing complexity of societies and their activities, transactions, and financial settlements as well as accompanying changes in fundamental incentives exert a significant influence on how the world is measured.[7] The sophistication of modern society demands the use of meaningful and reliable numbers to help organize life and ensure that available scarce resources are allocated fairly, efficiently, and to good effect. Even at the microlevel, every derived "statistic" reflects some implicit assumptions about the way the world is structured and the way that societies, institutions, and corporations operate.[8] Thus, the basis for making judgments, including the judgment that determines the choice of the empirical method itself, is influenced strongly by the value systems held by society and its related institutional arrangements, a reality that Douglass North has well recognized.[9]

The current socioeconomic model that underlines the policy framework of most countries around the world is that of the market and its price system. The degree to which markets are controlled ranges from selective administrative regulation and official sectoral and corporate monopoly surveillance to more liberal and open (but not necessarily "free") transactions between consenting parties. The existence of the price mechanism, whatever its imperfections and however much it is subject to the limitations of information and other special conditions, regulations, and forces, facilitates the development of a theoretical framework. In the pragmatic context in which individual choices are made and observed in actual transactions, a data-reporting system can be readily generated. Statisticians can measure the size and volume of an exchange and its value simultaneously. The number of choices that are based on these various price signals can be captured in aggregate. All activity is manifested collectively in the myriad of reported economic transactions that contribute to the measurement of GNP. The quantification appears to be complete, but this is not entirely the case because nonpriced and nonmarket transactions are rarely recorded and must be estimated using different means.

In a market economy in which enterprises that control production units endeavor to cover their full long-term costs of production, including what it takes to stay in business,[10] it is convenient and appropriate to quantify the size of these enterprises—that is, their economic significance—in terms of some measure of output or turnover. This measure can be assessed in relation to the overall economic size of the country or to the industrial sector in which the firms operate. The relative importance of enterprises can be expressed by reference to their contribution to total output, their value added to the economy (that is, the net output value of the flow of new goods and services they help to generate), net operating profits, and their asset value. The measurement of net worth is also important, especially in relation to the respective numbers each firm employs. Many such concepts closely correspond to conventional business and financial accounting procedures that firms themselves adopt to evaluate the economic standing of their enterprise and to assess the profitability of the various lines of activity in which they are engaged.

The system of national accounts, analogously, attempts to build up a picture of economic activity for the whole country on the basis of such detailed microlevel data. UNSO has made important efforts to blend the concepts and methods of corporate business accounting with those used in the national accounts system.[11] The latter, however, utilizes a broader conceptual definition of productive transactions than an auditor or commercial accountant might typically use for reporting a company's financial position. What the national accounts framework does is to allow analysts to reflect logically on the revealed overall demand and supply for goods and services within a given price mechanism. This is determined by known market structures and existing market conditions, including situations where goods and services are produced by families and exchanged between them. The system of national accounts incorporates a series of transaction balances to help identify gaps and fill in the missing economic data. The framework also enables analysts to review how the allocation process between capital and labor has functioned.

In the market system, need is revealed through demand, which is expressed in terms of exchange transactions. Scarce resources are thus absorbed, both directly and indirectly, by those who are able and willing to pay (in cash or in kind) for them. Unfortunately, the market approach creates important lacunae in the social system. People question the efficacy of the distributive process because it treats everyone in the same way under the price mechanism. This point is fundamental to the discussion of poverty and its eradication, particularly in the poorer and economically "weak" developing countries, where many basic needs remain unsatisfied because "wants" are only loosely linked to price "signals."

The UN and World Data

What people know about the world in which they live and the activities they are engaged in is in no small measure due to the fundamental role the UN has played in standardizing economic definitions, codes, classifications, and aggregation procedures in compiling national statistics. This extends to information about the social, economic, and political environment in which actions take place, activities are performed, and transactions occur. Knowing which people and what institutions participate in these processes is important to an understanding of the nature and impact of the processes.

Thanks to the work of UNSO, while the world remains divided by race, language, ideology, religion, climate, terrain, and currencies and is otherwise extraordinarily diverse, its inhabitants are nevertheless able to communicate in the same numerical language. The observed differences between countries (and their regions) represent distinctive cultures and beliefs that give rise to values that have a great deal to do with the way in which individuals, communities, and other social groups behave and interact. These features determine the nature and pattern of survival in every society and may even, at times, constitute a source of conflict. A country's inherent culture of values also assigns a certain significance or priority to various aspects of individual economic activity and commercial existence. The voluntary adoption by countries and organizations worldwide of common procedures, agreed-upon standards, recognized conventions, established methodologies, and other acknowledged scientific measures is truly remarkable.

Furthermore, an implicit cultural weighting structure emerges from a population's age and sex composition. This, too, affects the value system, money metrics, and other measuring standards adopted in daily commerce. For example, through changing consumption patterns, aging and long-term declines in average family size exert a not-insignificant impact on reported prices and expenditures. Consequently, indices of inflation and of real-quantity outlays derived from deflating spending by prices will be affected. Demographic characteristics thus influence the meaning of comparative per capita consumption data and hence growth rates over time.

The availability of worldwide data is a relatively modern phenomenon. Even in the industrialized countries, apart from basic statistics on population and demography and records of international trade in goods, little official information was disseminated before World War II.[12] Only incomplete survey data on manufacturing and agricultural production and employment information were made available to the public. These were often confined to certain key products and strategic sectors such as coal mining and the railways. Thinking during the interwar period was dominated by the specter of unemployment, incipient labor troubles, and social unease. Political concern about the potential for social and political unrest, and even revolution, was rampant in most Western countries. The failure of capitalist economic policies at that time was abundantly evident. Keynes's *General Theory of Employment, Interest, and Money,* which was published in the mid-1930s, represented a fundamental shift in thinking.[13] But it took some time to combat widespread opposition to his views and ignite the enthusiasm of policymakers for a new approach. Only the comparative success of these ideas in wartime strategic planning persuaded many policymakers of their merits. Until the theory could establish its rightful place in the history of ideas, however, there was a general belief that capitalist ideology had failed and that national economic policy in the West was bankrupt.

Although existing strategies had failed to produce any workable macroeconomic solution in the Great Depression period, Keynesian ideas still did not gain immediate public appeal. They were not generally embraced, not least because of their socialist flavor and the cogent criticisms of other highly respected thinkers and theorists such as A. C. Pigou. Pigou propounded arguments about employment creation that proved popular with traditionalists. These were strongly favored by cost-conscious businessmen and conservative officials, who believed that wage cuts would spur economic recovery.[14] Companies were fond of citing corporate priorities and the evident decline in profits as the primary cause of their problems. They argued that these accounted for the absence of entrepreneurial enterprise and the general economic malaise. Businesspeople failed to recognize the importance of deficiencies in aggregate effective demand and routinely alluded to the need to cut costs, especially wages, as the obvious and only solution to the problem of how to raise output and thus create the jobs to combat rising unemployment. Many thus continued to support the supply-side policymakers. The incongruity and illogicality of such beggar-thy-neighbor competitiveness for the economy as a whole passed unnoticed.

At the time, there was no macroeconomic policy panacea that could be effectively and universally applied by governments. But by the time World War II had ended, Keynesian policy had demonstrated its effectiveness and taken a firm hold on the political imagination. Keynes underlined the relevance of his theories with his treatise on *How to Pay for the War*, and the new economics embarked on its postwar march of triumph.[15] Returning military personnel were rapidly absorbed into the labor force (unlike in the post–World War I period), and the problem of reconstruction in the context of enormous resource constraints became the primary task facing all governments of Europe, including Russia. U.S. Marshall Plan aid, which was (perhaps unconsciously) Keynesian in character, helped come to the rescue to support postwar adjustment.

The implementation of the 1948 Marshall Plan by the U.S. was a major force in European reconstruction. The plan required, at least up until 1952, the establishment and regular monitoring of detailed quantitative goals related not only to overall economic performance but also to levels of output in key industrial sectors, the agricultural sector, and the energy sector. A number of senior American economists, including Milton Gilbert and Richard Ruggles, both of whom played such a significant part in launching the International Association for Research in Income and Wealth, which provided an independent forum and authority on matters relating to the national accounts, were appointed to supervise the process.[16] The focus was on rebuilding the core infrastructure, so little attention was paid to social reconstruction and rehabilitation. The success of this initiative raises one interesting question: Why did the American government think it was acceptable to adopt planning techniques and thus lay the foundations of future strategic approaches along these lines in Europe and yet not deem this process to be relevant to the U.S., at least on a similar scale? Was it simply because the U.S. saw the problem as an issue of physical reconstruction necessitated by the devastation caused by a prolonged war, or was the failure of the U.S. to apply economic planning so extensively to its own economy more ideological? It could be argued that the Americans would have seen no reason for such a massive investment in productive capital in their own economy because it was seen to be on the forefront of technology and was left virtually unscathed by the hostilities. Certainly, the U.S. member on the group of economic experts, Arthur Burns of the Council of Economic Advisors, pushed the U.S. government away from active Keynesian policy in favor of price stability and budget balancing. These two fundamental principles of sound stewardship are now much in vogue in the European Community and that formed the foundations of British financial administration for many years. On the other hand, the methods followed to lay down benchmarks and standards to monitor the programs under the plan could be found in corporate planning in American industry. Parallel work on control of the quality of products and the management of production was also initiated by American statisticians and was closely linked to the efforts of W. Edwards Deming.[17]

A major actor behind the implementation of the Marshall Plan was Robert Marjolin, the secretary-general of the OEEC (the organization originally set up to implement the program). Marjolin was deputy commissioner-general under Monnet in France who had spent much of his time in Washington during the latter part of the war. He has been described by those associated with him as a person of luminous intelligence who believed in the force of ideas to change the world by pragmatic action. He later played an enthusiastic part in the efforts Monnet spearheaded to bring about a European Customs Union.

After the Marshall Plan, a new emphasis was placed on strategies to create full employment. Statistics on resource supplies and production levels, nevertheless, still assumed the highest priority in national data-collection agendas. Except in England (where rationing continued into the mid-1950s), there was little information collected on living levels and household budgets. Moreover, other than the handful of pioneering national income statisticians, several of whom embarked on their careers as backroom assistants to Keynes during the war or had worked with Simon Kuznets in the U.S. and Colin Clark in England, few others knew or took much notice of (much less made the connection between) the scope and scale of production activities, output capacity, and the corresponding need to house, feed, and clothe families.[18] Censuses and surveys of production and (particularly) of manufacturing, which, at the time, was a sector that was undergoing a major transition from a mobilized war machine to peacetime production, began to assume increasing importance. Official statistics moved in the same direction, often putting goods before people in the widely held belief that increased output would result in rapidly improved living standards.

The longstanding attention economists have paid to the importance of scarcity has emphasized the significance of resources and how they should be used in the most efficacious manner. In ascribing to economic growth the virtue of securing general improvements in living standards, less attention has been paid to the isolation and alienation that has come about as a consequence of such material gains being unfairly spread among potential recipients. In playing on the basic human characteristics of envy and covetousness, those who manipulate the economic system influence the whole social context in which individual incentives are promulgated and encouraged. The core reliance of policy on fast economic growth and on the assumption that, under a market system, the benefits will be equally shared across society, has to a large extent precluded any proper consideration of alternative policies of community sharing in solving social problems.

National Accounts and GNP

The System of National Accounts (SNA) is a fully articulated statistical system that corresponds with a well-defined conceptual and theoretical understanding of macroeconomic behavior. While the conceptual macroeconomic basis of the national accounts is clear, the formal relationship of the accounts with a longer-standing traditional theory of economic value is more controversial and less evident. Reich, for example, argues that the theory of value embodied in the national accounts is different from the traditional macroeconomic model. The matter turns on how a set of descriptive accounting balances described in monetary terms should be interpreted as representing an economic value system in some more dynamic interrelated micro sense. Observed values in the national accounts depend on a multiplicity of revealed intersections of prices with quantities (and qualities) in the market that may not necessarily reflect utilities viewed overall. In part this is because the fundamental emphasis in the accounts is on production and on the incomes such economic activity generates and not on expenditures and the preferences these outlays represent.[19]

The SNA provides a data structure that attempts to describe and explain how an economy works and how its sectors interconnect. Embedded in the tables are a set of standard parameters, variables, and assumed relationships that lend substance to the dynamics of observed economic change. As in a conventional accounting structure, every economic flow or transaction in the system can be represented as both a payment (an outgoing resource) and a receipt (an incoming resource), whether the transaction is conducted in cash or not. When the data are aggregated, all identified receipts and payments corresponding to these transactions between various economic agents must balance. The system is articulated and comprehensive in the sense that in principle, all transactions (monetary or otherwise) are interlinked and accounted for, even if they are not formally reported by an identified institution.

The SNA, with its focus on the interrelationship between production, consumption, and investment and its identification of a defining role for government, represents the most important statistical achievement of the UN system. This is because the system draws attention to the choices that must be made to achieve growth and progress. Economic progress is an important component of the goal of the UN organization to enhance universal welfare. The SNA has thus come to underpin economic policy decisions at all levels in every country throughout the world. While the ideas for a macroeconomic policy framework were floating around Cambridge and official sources in England even before the war,[20] the origins of this seminal contribution to statistics and policy understanding can be traced back to the 1940s and early 1950s. UNSO took on board the national accounts as its primary activity from the very outset in 1945. At the time, this was uncharted territory and UNSO's decision represented a significant leap of faith.

It is useful to look back to see how the process developed and how this single but complex approach has come to dominate everything in the economic policy field. Through the type of statistics it generates, the SNA has influenced directly not only stabilization policies and short-term policy decisions but also longer-term development strategy, structural transformation, and initiatives to reduce poverty. In a way, because the idea has so often presented the appropriate quantitative framework to resolve many difficult questions of development, other ideas and approaches have been somewhat overshadowed. The essential idea behind the SNA is that it is necessary to resolve the question of how countries can make more goods and services available with the resources at their disposal, through both the private and public sectors, to their expanding populations.

Many of the alternative viewpoints on policy have taken a more social stance in their perspective. These are regarded as supplementary frameworks that provide "softer" and more eclectic but less certain options to achieving human progress. They are not directly linked, at least dynamically, to policy. The social indicators movement of the late 1960s and early 1970s, with which the UN became only half-heartedly engaged, falls into this category. In the context of growing resource constraints, work in this area was largely eclipsed by the focus on development plans and on ways to strengthen economic conditions. Economic progress was believed by rich and poor governments alike to be the prime engine of social progress and the solution to better household living conditions.[21]

The Successive Development of the SNA

The benchmark dates for the UN System of the National Accounts (SNA) are 1953, 1968, and 1993.[22] The first SNA in 1953 was based on the accounting system Richard Stone had produced originally for the Organization for European Economic Cooperation (now the OECD) the previous year.[23] This, in turn, was developed from the work he and James Meade[24] had started in the war years in Britain, which formed the main statistical basis of postwar economic policy. This system defined the statistical relationships between the aggregates of national income, represented, on the one hand, by production and factor incomes earned in generating output and, on the other, by private and public consumption and investment outlays (and, consequently, savings), within the Keynesian macroeconomic conceptual framework. The core income, production, and expenditure accounts continue to serve as the primary statistical basis that guides government monetary and fiscal policy and public investment strategy in rich and poor countries alike.[25]

The first revision of the SNA in 1968 is also attributable to Stone who, for some years previously, had worked hand in hand with Abe Aidenoff in UNSO to produce a comprehensive system that represented a quantum leap forward. The precursor of the 1968 system can be traced to the seminal work conducted from 1960 onward by the Cambridge Growth Project led by Stone himself at the Department of Applied Economics at Cambridge University. The 1968 version advanced the national accounts into a full-fledged input-output system that included associated price vectors relevant to producers and purchasers. In embracing a structure that defined the relationships between industries and commodities within separate submatrices, it went well beyond the more familiar and conventional interindustry input-output tables that had been earlier championed and developed by Wassily Leontief.[26] The 1968 system also incorporated a "final use" matrix that showed how the total supply of final goods and services produced by the various industries (including the service sector) in the economy were allocated to private use, government consumption, capital formation, and exports. The framework embraced the traditional value-added matrix that showed how the value added (wages and salaries, gross operating surpluses of enterprises, etc.) generated by different industries as they produced final goods and services for current distribution in the economy could be broken down into the more distinct rewards accruing to the factors of production, labor, and capital (and indirect taxes) that were paid by firms. While the 1968 system made some changes in nomenclature and structure and made the respective valuation bases more distinct and appropriate at the institutional and industrial sector level, the

Table 2.2. UN National Accounts Developments

Year	Authority	Title/Outcome	Contents
1939	League of Nations	*World Economic Survey*	Estimates for all or part of the period 1929–1938 for 26 countries (about half "official" estimates, the rest academic and private studies).
1944–1945	Meeting of national representatives of U.S., Canada, and UK	First international agreement on the conceptual methods and presentation of national estimates	Review of problems of comparability.
1945	Subcommittee on National Income Statistics of the League of Nations Committee of Statistical Experts	*Definition and Measurement of the National Income and Related Totals* (published 1947)	Memorandum prepared by Richard Stone. Showed how national income could be obtained by combining the elementary transactions of an economic system. Revealed their interdependence. First use of social accounting instead of single total estimation approach and adoption of specific accounts and district institutional sectoring of the economy.
1950	UNSO	National Income Statistics, 1938–1948	Data from 41 countries for several years with 13 countries using the social accounting approach
1950	OEEC (OECD)	A simplified system of national accounts	Established national accounts as a basic data framework for country studies and demonstrated their use for policy analysis.

(continued)

Table 2.2. UN National Accounts Developments (*continued*)

Year	Authority	Title/Outcome	Contents
1952	OEEC (OECD)	A standardized system of national accounts	Showed in more detail the relevance of accounts for economic policy prescription and presented an articulated set of accounts with defined entries and classifications, e.g., of consumers' expenditures.
1953	UN	Meeting of Expert Group appointed by Secretary-General held under auspices of the UNSO director of statistics and chaired by Richard Stone	Recommended uniform reporting basis for UN member countries and set out to formulate a standard system of national accounting for countries to follow.
1953	UNSO	*A System of National Accounts and Supporting Tables* (the 1953 SNA)	Six standard accounts depicting production, appropriation, capital formation, and external transactions for three main institutional sectors: enterprises, households, and nonprofit institutions taken together and government. Took needs of developing countries into account, especially the rural sector and nonmonetary transactions.
1956	OEEC (OECD)	*Quality and Price Indexes in National Accounts*	Report by Richard Stone paving the way for measurement of national accounts aggregates in constant prices and the derivation and use of compound GNP deflators.

Year	Authority	Title/Outcome	Contents
1957	UNSO for UN Statistical Commission	*A System of Price and Quantity Indexes for National Accounts*	Surveyed country-level practices of constant price measurement and defined a system of quantity indexes, including ones for measuring noncommodity flows.
1960, 1964	UNSO	Revised editions of 1953 SNA	Sought closer harmonization with IMF and OEEC, especially with the Fund's Balance of Payments Manual.
1968	UNSO	*A System of National Accounts* (1968 SNA)	Expert Group chaired by Richard Stone elaborated the existing system to include commodity by industry input-output tables and flow of funds; provided a rigorous treatment of values decomposed into their respective price and quantity components to provide more robust procedures for estimating constant prices.*
1971	UNSO for UN Statistical Commission	*Basic Principles of the System of Balances of the National Economy*	A step designed to bring the Material Product System of the Council for Mutual Economic Assistance (the standard used by the Soviet Union and socialist countries of East and Central Europe) into closer alignment with UN principles and the SNA.

*It also added a special supply and disposition table for developing countries.

(continued)

Table 2.2. UN National Accounts Developments (*continued*)

Year	Authority	Title/Outcome	Contents
1970 (rev. 1980)	Statistical Office of the European Communities	*European System of Integrated Economic Accounts*	Provided information on production and finance and the distribution and redistribution of income beyond that in the 1968 SNA; provided more precise and rigorous definitions.
1993	UNSO, IMF, Eurostat, OECD, World Bank	*System of National Accounts 1993* (SNA 1993)	Developed SNA as a framework for statistical systems as a whole and as a definitive point of reference in establishing standards for related economic statistics (that rank ahead of standards developed for particular fields such as government statistics). Introduced balance sheets and more detailed institutional sectoring of the accounts.

Notes

1. Supporting all the methodological work was the development of national accounts questionnaires which, from 1972, were jointly prepared by the UNSO and OECD and distributed to all countries.
2. The first *Yearbook of National Accounts Statistics,* covering 70 countries, was published in 1958 and was subsequently issued annually. In 1982 it was renamed *National Accounts Statistics: Main Aggregates and Detailed Tables.*
3. Related national accounts manuals dealing with data compilation methods (1955) and components of the system such as national and sectoral balance sheet and reconciliation accounts (1977); guidelines on the distribution of income, consumption, and the accumulation of households (1977); and national accounts at constant prices (1979) were all produced to strengthen the core system and extend its usefulness.

system contained the relevant accounting balances to facilitate a direct link with the original 1953 SNA. The combined square matrix that depicted these various transactions and their structural components produced, in aggregate, the summary balance of Total Supply = Total Demand for the whole nation. In this respect, the 1968 revision reflected some of the notions behind the Soviet system of material balances, at least insofar as the Material Product System referred specifically to the output of goods.[27]

The 1968 SNA recommended a different approach to output valuation, consistent with input-output methodology, that distinguished between basic prices, approximate basic prices, producer prices, and purchaser prices at their appropriate levels of production and distribution. This was all very logical when taxes on commodities, transport and distribution costs, and implicit sales margins had to be taken into account in an input-output structure, but it was often confusing to compilers and users. Furthermore, the level of so-phistication seemed less relevant to economies dominated by one or two main industries and (in terms of numbers) by household own-account activities and "one-man" businesses. Many household enterprises and farms carried out their own transportation and marketing arrangements and rarely paid (direct) taxes. Much of their production was destined for their own consumption rather than for the market. Subsistence and survival rather than entre-preneurial risk-taking formed the prime rationale for economic decisions in these cases.

Only a few years after the 1968 SNA was published, statisticians were al-ready beginning to discuss possible revisions. Those working in developing countries who were using the system talked about the need for simplification and the desirability of consolidating certain tables to concentrate on core fea-tures of the basic accounts. Within UNSO, Nancy Ruggles, as chief of the Division of National Accounts, pushed for a fairly quick and simple revision. Richard Ruggles, as an advisor and consultant to UNSO, took a similar posi-tion but urged that microdata (particularly that relating to households) be integrated directly into the compilation process. He believed that this would have an advantageous reverse feedback effect because the consistency of defi-nitions and classifications adopted in the national accounts would improve the reliability and intrinsic comparability of the detailed microdata and en-courage their more widespread use. National disposable income, in principle, could then also be disaggregated to provide a more detailed picture of the distribution of individual income.

As the process moved forward, the divergent views aligned more clearly on two sides. One position, taken by the Ruggleses, favored a simple version and the consolidation of microlevel and macrolevel approaches. Others supported the adoption of what were referred to then as the system of traditional T-accounts (which was associated with the Netherlands), in which data were arrayed either as incomes and outlays or as supply and demand measures.[28] These accounts could be disaggregated by sectors and activities. But they were generally limited to the recording of observable monetary transactions, which, apart from government, were compiled on an accrual rather than cash payment/transfer basis. Such accounts usually excluded all imputations and estimates of unrealized gains and losses from current transactions other than those for stocks. Supporters of this system strongly argued that the approach was more compatible with actual policy requirements because T-accounts underpinned the way governments normally worked in framing their decisions.[29]

The alternative position belonged to those who preferred to take the view that the establishment of a comprehensive conceptual framework that integrally linked prices and quantities to appropriate actual or estimated values was essential. They expressed unhappiness with the untidy nature of the reconciliation accounts developed for the 1968 SNA. This broader conceptual approach meant that the framework would need to be expanded and that certain elements, including the depreciation of government assets and the value of national monuments such as statues and works of art, and individual wealth holdings, would have to be taken back into consideration. The latter group won the debate, arguing that it was necessary to set a proper "gold standard" to serve as the correct conceptual basis for reference. To have a comprehensive structure that defined the binding economic logic of all the interrelationships and boundaries of production was clearly important for the purpose of guiding compilers of national accounts faced with tricky issues of allocating raw data and for determining relevant imputations. It was also crucial to the separation of value changes (price effects) from other volume changes and to the relevant matching of beginning- and end-period asset values and their corresponding economic flows over a predetermined accounting period.

By 1993, in contrast, the SNA revision process no longer represented the outcome of the efforts of one person or institution but had become the work of an international committee, the Inter-Secretariat Working Group on National Accounts (ISWGNA). The ISWGNA, while retaining the capability to draw on external expertise, is drawn up from statisticians representing the major international agencies. Apart from UNSO, the primary sponsors of the 1993 SNA were the IMF, the World Bank, the OECD, and Eurostat. Though it was originally instructed only to consider relatively minor adjustments and revisions, the committee undertook a sweeping historical, conceptual, and practical review of the system of national accounts and its component structures. In their revision, the committee came up with a comprehensive ac-

counting system of market and nonmarket activities that incorporated observed and imputed economic transactions. The committee applied an accounting basis of valuation that measured exchange at the time of the reported
change of ownership of the assets, goods, and services concerned; that is, it
adopted through an accrual rather than cash basis of valuation.

The 1993 SNA continued to develop further the separate institutional sec-
toring (by households, nonprofit institutions, government, etc.) that had been
introduced into the 1968 SNA. More significant, it moved the whole system
into an integrated stock-flow framework that is no longer concerned exclusively with cash flows and transactions between transactors in the economy.
The structure now allows (in principle) for all transactions taking place within
a given accounting period to be related appropriately to a comprehensive set
of opening and closing balance sheets as in any other enterprise engaged in
economic activities within a country. These balance sheets record the value of
the financial and nonfinancial assets and liabilities of every sector at the end
(or beginning) of each accounting period. Since the basis of the system is
current market prices, such balance sheets are affected by whatever quality
changes and price (valuation) differences, as well as timing questions, occur
over a particular accounting period. This matters a lot more when countries
are experiencing rapid inflation, and further adjustments must be made to
take into account changes in timing and volume and price and differentiate
between them when recording movements in values.

Many people from different institutional and national backgrounds participated in the production of the 1993 SNA, including consultants and advisors who attended a series of special expert group meetings, and contributed
to the final version of the text. When it approved the manual, the Statistical
Commission paid particular tribute to Peter Hill and André Vanoli[30] as the
primary authors of this benchmark reference study and accorded due recognition to Carol Carson for her invaluable management of the revision.

Beyond this strengthening of the internal coherence of the national accounts,
there were major complementary efforts to harmonize the definitions, classifications, and methodologies of other integrated and closely linked systems with
the SNA. In particular, the IMF did extensive work to ensure that the new system of government financial statistics (GFS), whose structure depicted the functional allocation of current expenditures by both central and local (including
municipal) governments, as well as the revised *Balance of Payments Manual*
were completely compatible with the national accounts.[31] For the government
accounts, this meant switching from reported cash outlays to a commonly accepted accrual basis of accounting. For the balance of payments, similar adjustments in procedures were needed to distinguish between income and transfers.

More attention had to be paid to the timing and valuation of transactions relating to the change of ownership of assets, especially if, like software and intellectual capital, they were deemed intangible.

In the new SNA, other distinctions are made related to the extension of the production boundary. A clearer separation is drawn between the specific individual's (or household's) use and collective use of government services. This is essential for a better understanding of the relative importance of nonmarket goods and services to household well-being. There is also a further disaggregation of the primary institutional sectors and an important distinction is made between households and nonprofit institutions serving households. A more precise definition of financial service and a broader and more consistent perspective of the composition of gross fixed capital formation and the consumption of government fixed capital are introduced. All these adjustments have an impact on extending (slightly) the coverage of GDP and result in some changes to the relative magnitudes of various aggregates and their respective sectors. The resulting expanded notion of GNP is redefined as gross national income (GNI).

Significant Aspects of the 1993 SNA Revision Process

The switch in emphasis in national accounting between 1968 and 1993 reflected a continuing evolution of thinking that gradually shifted macrolevel policy formulation from an ex post evaluative approach, or learning from doing and avoiding the major mistakes of the past, to an approach that looked ahead to desired policy outcomes. It focused on the need to put in place the right mechanisms to ensure that the engine of the economy would deliver the appropriate growth performance to allow social goals to become a reality. Whereas the 1968 SNA provided the comprehensive framework that could contribute to an intellectual meshing of the free-market ideas of Hayek with the macrolevel emphasis propounded by Keynes and his disciples (a debate that dominated much of the postwar academic thinking about policy), the 1993 SNA represented an attempt to implement an all-encompassing system that combined a conceptual perspective about economic activity with the basic precepts of economic theory.

The 1993 review also took account of developments in information technology and the importance of simulation procedures based on microdata both for building up a comprehensive view of economic behavior and for facilitating and enhancing the data-compilation process. The review acknowledged that in monitoring "progress," the system had to embrace economic activities that, although they were hidden, underrecorded, or unrecognized as such, clearly contributed to human welfare. The review still failed to appreciate, however, that activities that are conventionally regarded as personally profitable might not necessarily benefit society or the environment, as traditional economic orthodoxy had suggested they would. Long-standing general concerns about the need for corresponding welfare monitoring would still have to wait.

Between 1968 and 1993, a lot of water flowed under the bridge in the international economy; many structural changes took place throughout the world, and attitudes toward policy were affected. The 1968 SNA was a landmark data structure, but despite the importance of the innovative and pathbreaking systemic approach it brought to bear on all dynamic issues of broader socioeconomic concern, it was essentially a stand-alone national data construct. It was viewed by some policy critics as a closed economic model of unreconstructed Keynesianism and, at worst, a framework for making transparent the inexorable force of Marxist presumptions about the implications of what he would argue were institutionally reinforced factor relations in production. The 1968 SNA made some provision for "the rest of the world," but only as an adjunct to the core operations of the domestic economy. The explicit external transactions implicitly assumed that fixed official exchange rates would apply. This seemed acceptable at the time within a system that assumed the general homogeneity of prices. But by 1973, the Bretton Woods mechanism of fixed exchange rates had broken down. Furthermore, the oil crisis had given rise to unexpected fluctuations in the prices of international commodities and had contributed to serious inflation in a number of countries.

The apparent operational faults of the 1968 SNA were not of its own making. The 1968 system used an implicit fixed-technology interindustry framework of the conventional Leontief type (although in an admittedly sophisticated form; its separate "make" and "absorption" matrices distinguished between industries and commodities). This allowed analysts to look at quantity and output responses to different patterns of increase in final demand and explore the implications of those responses for the intermediate purchases of industry inputs. Although the development of associated modeling techniques in places such as the Department of Applied Economics in Cambridge, where the essentials of the 1968 SNA had been created, were well advanced, most agencies that used the 1968 framework for planning purposes did not attach the same significance to the crucial questions about endogeneity and substitution that are implicit in the practice of projecting changes in price and output.[32] Nevertheless, the framework did permit further elaboration to allow the more sophisticated analysis of absolute and relative price changes and to examine the implications of input and output substitution as a result of both price and technological change.

Because it combined an interindustry table and the standard national accounts relationships within the same structure, the 1968 SNA had an unintended positive effect of setting off some macrostatistical research into a separate input-output direction that included a partial focus on social issues. Some of this work, such as the social accounting matrix (SAM) work pioneered by Eric Thorbecke, on the one hand, and by Graham Pyatt and his colleagues at the University of Warwick on the other (which was later taken up by the World Bank) was easily linked into the SNA structure.[33] Even though the framework these researchers proposed was more sophisticated, its development from the SNA was logical and its background economic model was simple to understand. They demonstrated this by conducting a number of practical case studies in Indonesia, Sri Lanka, Malaysia, and Botswana that showed that their system was operationally feasible. Their framework was very data intensive, though, because of the need to elaborate the different patterns of household demand according to certain significant distinguishing socioeconomic characteristics, such as income level or employment status. It is significant that the SAM compilers drew attention to the fact that low incomes (and hence conditions of poverty) could not be adequately analyzed without reference to the nature of individual economic engagement and the related institutional conditions surrounding such personal economic involvement. The researchers also recognized that the observed prices at which expenditures took place constituted three distinct elements in the case of most commodities: that main part attributable to the intrinsic (physical) nature of the item in question, a transport and distribution margin, and the respective product taxes that were applicable to different goods and services. Their primary aim in developing these more elaborate data structures for simpler economies was to keep the SNA as a whole relevant to the policy needs and objectives of developing countries. Against the background of the debate originating in the late 1950s and prompted, inter alia, by the writings of W. Arthur Lewis, Hans Singer, Gerald Meier, Hla Myint, Dudley Seers, and others about the existence of a separate discipline that could be described as "development economics," this approach reflected a belief in the essential universality and coherence of economic laws. But it also recognized that institutional circumstances could exert sometimes perverse effects on behavior.

Another high-profile group branched off in a separate direction that extended the logic and mechanics of the integral input-output analysis in a somewhat different way. In a sense, their independent pursuit of solutions to input-output questions echoed the early schisms between Keynes and Jan Tinbergen regarding the relevance of modeling and of projections and forecasting to basic national accounts work. The so-called Tinbergen approach was favored by Lawrence Klein[34] and others such as Edmond Malinvaud, director of INSEE in France,[35] because it could be adapted directly to the simulation of various policy scenarios that were relevant to the mixed-planning approach of governments such as France, Holland, and Austria that were popular in the 1960s and early 1970s. In particular, it lent itself to the parallel development of general-equilibrium models and met a desire to provide full endogeneity, that is, an interactive price and quantity logic, to the evaluation process.

The introduction of satellite accounts was a similarly important initiative; it was a spin-off that linked economic inputs expressed in value terms, in most cases, to social outputs expressed in quantitative terms. These accounts took the form of macrosectoral frameworks that were grafted onto the SNA. The satellite accounts were an important and useful tool that was invented and developed by the French. They were devised as a way to bring into data analysis desired social outcomes, expressed often only in physical terms such as "patients cured," "pupils qualified," or "calories consumed." These outcomes needed to be related, through the national accounts, to resource requirements and inputs that are typically expressed in terms of financial cost. Initially, satellite accounts were most commonly developed for the health and education sectors because it was in these areas that they could be most useful in linking inputs to observed outcomes and government budgetary outlays. This had genuine practical value in guiding operational policy decisions. Satellite accounts also provided a way to assess alternatives when determining strategic development choices. Later, satellite accounts were extended to embrace other topics that cut across sectors. They were also used to address concerns of economic and cultural interest such as the environment and the tourism industry, two areas with widely overlapping interests where the standard conventional classification schemes could not be applied in a unique and meaningful way. Their unique industry characteristics related to categories that could not be found in the national accounts without partial aggregations across many sectors. Consequently, different accounting procedures had to be introduced, mostly under the direction of UNSO, to deal with these and other industries that cut across sectors such as communications, transportation, services, and distribution.

Social accounting matrices (SAMs), by comparison, offered a more holistic and integrated perspective because they extended the basic national accounts framework by incorporating social dimensions and human behavior into the central input-output structure. They allowed evaluation of the impact on production of different patterns of household demand associated with households of different demographic, income level, and socioeconomic status. The profile groupings could be directly related to different output responses. Policy analysis could be more detailed and precise; it could take into account the level of, say, employee compensation, certain corresponding economic parameters, such as elasticities in income and demand, and marginal propensities to consume and import goods and services. SAMs could capture other significant or distinctive social characteristics (including the location of habitation, ethnicity, and the occupational and employment status of household members) that might cause people to react to market conditions with a quite different impact on the structure of consumer demand. Hence, the system could also review the influence of these variables on production and growth.

Both the SAMs and satellite accounts create new demands for information, sometimes from nontraditional sources. They also require high-quality demographic and vital statistics data and detailed socioeconomic statistics in order to establish the essential numeraires, linkages, and benchmark reference points. Such frameworks are expensive when prepared *ab initio* and must necessarily draw on related social statistics extracted from administrative working files that serve other purposes. In recent years, however, governments have recognized the merits of compiling social data from special subject surveys, especially general household surveys. The SAMs and other SNA extensions are rich statistical frameworks that combine macrolevel and microlevel distributional data in an analytically useful way that has significantly broadened the outreach of operational policy.

Box 2.1. The Planning Era and Keynesian Policy

The idea of the centrally coordinated national plan and its importance in supporting and guiding the desired big push for socioeconomic progress emanated initially from the socialist command-and-control states. In these countries, the plan was crucial to the programming and coordination, from the supply side, of the economy's production, investment, and infrastructure targets. In resource-constrained developing countries that contend daily with serious choices in prioritizing policies to meet declared objectives, the notion of a plan was a process that was intended not only to get everyone involved but also to get things moving organizationally in an efficient and effective way. Many of these countries had new governments and were setting out to formulate policy strategies for the first time. They continually faced questions of what was an appropriate, if not always necessarily economically optimal, way to allocate resources. Sadly, often because of unpredicted external volatility, especially associated with climate and fluctuating commodity market prices, the early development decades were littered with failed plans, even when they were indicative and normative rather than command programs with enforceable directives.

On the other hand, the less-rigid macroeconomic approach of the Keynesian system, which allowed for the operation of market forces, focused more on the manipulation of aggregate effective demand as a policy instrument. Supply-side questions and capacity considerations also received recognition as part of the same coherent approach. In practical policy terms, Keynesian analysis implied paying close attention to the coordination of public investment plans, budgeted current government expenditure with private-sector capital spending, and anticipated household consumption. For much of the period until the end of the 1970s, therefore, many countries in Europe embraced some form of national planning as a framework for setting goals and priorities, evaluating alternative policy paths, balancing trade-offs, and establishing a sound basis for deciding on suitable medium-term investment strategies. The corresponding statistical requirements blended descriptive methods and analytic modeling. This was essential to endowing the systems with dynamic properties in their functional format. More important, the combination paved the way for the extension of traditional Leontief models based on fixed parameters derived from corresponding input-output tables and subsequent adoption of more endogenized systems. The earlier postwar consensus on matters of macroeconomic statistics branched out into three interdependent directions: the Tinbergen approach (modeling), input-output statistics (interindustry analysis and later social accounting matrices), and national accounts. This development was significantly facilitated and enhanced by the introduction of the 1968 SNA.

There was another and perhaps more fundamental break with the original draft proposal for revising the first SNA. The 1968 system, as it initially stood, did not serve well the policy requirements of developing countries that relied on one or two crops or mineral exports. An addendum, which represented a significant modification to the core system, was thus devised to be attached to the main set of tables. Most of the problems of the developing countries arose because their domestic economies were heavily concentrated on the public (nonmarket) sector while they were inextricably linked, although far from integrated, into an uneven international trading system. In this situation, the activities of multinational corporate enterprise were frequently supported (usually indirectly but sometimes explicitly) by policies and agreements that were pursued by the governments of the mostly richer nations, where the headquarters of these companies were based. Integration into the international economy for the poorer undiversified economies was thus often one-sided, taking place on usually disadvantageous terms that left them vulnerable and potentially exposed to external market risks over which they had little or no control. At the same time, these countries needed to satisfy a constant and undiminished demand for funds to support the current operations of their governments. In these circumstances, a highly developed interindustry data framework, which UNSO advocated for general adoption by the international community, served little or no purpose.

As a consequence, and effectively as an afterthought, an additional chapter to meet the needs of the many developing countries in this situation was introduced into the final document. The simplified format developed in Chapter 9 of the 1968 SNA followed very closely the structure of the national accounting framework that had been adopted by the French authorities in their overseas territories. It conformed to what was generally recognized in the international statistical community as the Courcier system. This approach was much favored by critics of the UN 1968 SNA such as Dudley Seers, who had earlier given considerable thought to how best to portray and monitor the economic fortunes and policies of such less-sophisticated economies.[36] The reduced form of the proposed framework of supply and disposition presented in this last chapter also better suited the evaluation of the various policy goals of simple agricultural economies that had large, mostly subsistence rural household sectors. It is thus significant that the revised 1993 SNA later attached considerable importance to the proper independent statistical elaboration of the household sector.

Launched toward the end of what was to become only the first of a sequence of UN development decades, the 1968 SNA reflected the virtually unanimous view that a high rate of economic growth was the secret to the achievement of social progress. By 1993, and thus at the beginning of the fourth development decade and against the background of the failure to reduce international poverty, the UN's "State of the World Economy" reports had successively upped the required rates of growth in global production from 5 percent per annum in 1960–1969 to 6 percent in 1970–1979, and then up again from 7 percent in 1980–1989 to 10 percent in 1990–1999. Throughout the four decades, the assumed growth rate for the component of agricultural output remained at 4 percent, although by the fourth decade this had been translated into a more specific target for the annual increase in food production.

For most economists over the past few centuries, and even before the pioneering treatise by Adam Smith (1776) that gave birth to modern economics, the defining issue of economic science was not only to explain the "wealth of nations" but also why some people become rich while others remain poor.[37] Nevertheless, when it defined the terms of economic reference to construct the SNA, the UN did not take the additional crucial step of creating a supporting data system that would allow analysts to explore the relationship between long-term economic growth and the persistent inequality that is found uniformly across nations. Before it is possible to explain why growth differs in both its structure and pace of progress, it is first necessary to collect at the national level credible and comparable evidence about the historical pattern of economic performance. The national accounts represent the most important statistical artifact available for understanding economic and structural change, but an important group of centrally planned countries existed that had achieved considerable success in expanding their production systems that could not be compared on the same basis. Their own more conceptually limited and statistically truncated form of social accounts left out, for primarily ideological reasons (since the raw data were often available), important sections of the economy.

Some Implications of the Emphasis on National Accounts

The national accounts provide a comprehensive and integrated framework for evaluating the performance of an economy. But until more recent extensions and revisions helped circumvent some recognized problems and weaknesses in the system and its component categorization, the system contained several important limitations.

First, the structure and very comprehensiveness of the accounts has tended to place increased power over the areas of data compilation and dissemination, as well as of policy implementation, more strongly into the hands of central government. The national accounts provide the basic economic atlas, and many decisions, both local and national, including decisions to alter taxes, are based upon them. This allows less scope for ordinary people and private enterprises to have a direct say in the decisions about allocations of resources that immediately affect them.

Second, the accounts relate primarily to commodity (goods and services) flows, and have far less to say about the nature of the ownership of resources, the control of productive assets, and the location and concentration of economic power. As constructed, they may thus limit analysis of the more fundamental institutional decisions that drive economies. In the past, this specific focus has tended to constrain a proper evaluation of alternative theories of economic behavior.

Third, given the integrated nature of the accounts that embraces both the government sector and the balance of payments and defines them within a country-specific value system (of price and external exchange rates), the emphasis on commodity balances—for example, with respect to international trade—has led to misunderstandings about the nature of derived imbalances, particularly deficits facing countries. It is misleading to refer universally to the implicit morality of a country's balance-of-payments deficit without further examining the nature of this "overdraft." The world remains in overall balance. Countries themselves do not trade; it is their resident enterprises that carry out economic activities and conduct overseas transactions with other agents. No transaction will be effected unless there is some private agreement, guarantee, and contractual assurance that payment will be made for any goods (or services) transferred and delivered across national borders. In many cases, the trading entities involved in foreign transactions will have operations and accounts in more than one country. This makes it difficult to argue confidently about "national" accountability and overseas payments obligations or to assess a country's real financial standing in the international economy.

Fourth, GDP or GNI (GNP) as an aggregate when measured over time reflects overall changes in an economy's *net* position. Changes in overall GDP measure net growth and give little indication of underlying economic change in a country. To understand structural progress, it is necessary to examine in far more detail the different sector-by-sector changes. These need to be investigated from both a production and expenditure point of view. GDP is merely the aggregate outcome of all the separate increases and decreases in the various industry and expenditure subcomponents of the economy. Even if relative prices remain unaffected, the same GDP growth does not measure the same economic performance or economic capability of a country. There is a significant difference between growth that has been determined by the combination of spectacular progress in a small but dynamic and innovative technology sector and much slower change in large traditional industries compared with growth that has been achieved because of an even pace of development across the whole economy (agriculture, industry, and services). This argues for some form of aggregate indicator to describe the degree and nature of economic change to supplement existing statistics that conventionally measure only the overall magnitude of that change from one period to another. As a statistic, GDP or GNI conveys little hint of the extent to which much of what is consumed today is different from what was consumed in the past. The commodity categorization and aggregation procedures in place do not necessarily permit such detailed analysis to be undertaken.

Fifth, it is generally not easy to find out whether the "growth" observed represents increased incomes that accrue disproportionately to the already wealthy or if it arises from increased employment and wage earnings for the poor and those below the mean or median income. What is known is that a significant share of low incomes is paid in kind and is imputed in the national accounts only on the basis of price movements and population change related to an assumed fixed basket of consumption by those living at a subsistence level.

Finally, there is some latitude, or degree of freedom, about how equivalent marginal row and column balances in the accounts are calculated. While these balances, which are integral to the accounting framework, provide an inherent assessment of the internal numerical integrity of the reported data in the accounts, they cannot provide a foolproof check on their actual accuracy or intrinsic validity. One of the merits of the national accounts that was clearly advocated by its proponents was that it provided a coherent framework for co-coordinating and cross-checking the integrity of economic statistics in general because all such data, in one form or another, would eventually become incorporated into this macrostatistical data system. The system, nevertheless, has little capacity to highlight inconsistencies introduced when firms report misleading information about their financial position and then back it up with audited figures that creatively match identified end-of-period asset values with declared income flows.

In the two decades following the publication of the first UN handbook on national accounts in 1953, UNSO and its extensive technical assistance (TA) arrangements led the way in the adoption, implementation, and development of good national accounting practices around the world. It spread knowledge about the system through its own experts and consultants, who worked closely with local officials. This assistance not only determined what statistics were collected but it also strongly influenced the whole structure of national statistical organizations. Over time, these TA experts adapted the standard estimation procedures to the variety of local conditions they encountered in developing countries—large unreported rural subsistence sectors, extensive unregistered urban informal activities, large foreign-controlled mining and plantation operations, and so forth. UNSO backed up local in-house statistical expertise and competence in this area in such countries with its own regular field advisory staff and technical assistance service. With the help of donors, it hired recognized international experts in national accounts to support its efforts. The UN also funded training centers in Asia, Africa, and the Middle East to enhance statistical capacity and raise the level of technical competence, especially in national accounts.

Although the national accounts system is basically Keynesian in its construction as a macrostatistical framework, it has worked quite well both in theory and in practice for many different policy requirements.[38] The system represents a core model around which alternative policy scenarios and longer-term strategizing can be carried out. This says much for the strength of the original 1953 SNA system, which was so elegant in its simplicity and logical in the symmetry of its hierarchically sequenced structure of integrated accounting balances that more than a few developing countries still, in principle, adhere to this basic methodology and overall framework. The methods of data collection and tabular compilation were so well founded and institutionalized in many countries that—without subsequent UN technical assistance in this area, much of which dried up in the 1980s, or extensive overseas training—the basic system remains intact. The conventional methods of piecing together the national accounts using specific enterprise and household surveys and population censuses as well as annual administrative reports, tax returns, and other official records, have undergone very little change over the years. If anything, with budget constraints that restrict the conduct of essential surveys, the national accounts of some countries may have even become rather worse instead of better over time. Some countries that were industrially less complex and economically less sophisticated thus saw little reason to implement the revised 1968 System of National Accounts, which maintained, at its core, a well-defined two-dimensional input-output structure, and some policymakers restricted budgets to the national statistical offices for such an exercise. Although the 1968 system proved invaluable for analysis of policy simulations, many developing countries felt it had little application to their own undiversified economies.

In response to what was perceived as a need for a macrostatistical framework that was designed for poorer countries, Seers proposed a simple supply-and-use accounting framework for countries that produce and export a single primary commodity (such as mineral extraction or a plantation crop).[39] This model was successfully applied by Seers himself in Trinidad (1963), by Eric Esaieson in successive UN economic development missions to Zambia that followed independence (1965), by Edward Dommen for the Commonwealth Secretariat in Fiji (1969), and for the National Economic Development Authority in Oman (1976).[40] The Seers method blended techniques borrowed from the French Courcier system of national accounts with the Material Product System (MPS) approach used in the former Soviet and Council for Mutual Economic Assistance (CMEA) countries. Like the MPS, the Seers method relied heavily on the detailed construction of individual commodity balances that were indispensable to the assessment of centralized planning and performance. It was, in effect, an extended "supply and disposition" model that took as its starting point a highly aggregated framework similar to that subsequently prescribed for developing countries in Chapter 9 of the 1968 SNA.[41] The Seers model also fully incorporated services (particularly those related to tourism) as both intermediate inputs and outputs in a comprehensive market-oriented system. It altered the rules, especially in the logical way it combined vertically and horizontally integrated industrial activities into coherent minisectors, but it also demonstrated the inherent flexibility of the SNA commodity-flow approach.[42]

The UN's Loss of Leadership in National Accounts

UNSO proved very good at benchmarking and getting the economic structures right, but particularly after the oil crises of 1973 and 1978, the practical

work on national accounts both in UNSO and in member countries got farther and farther behind. Increasingly, other international agencies and the
major donors began to express their frustration at the poor quality and time-
liness of the national accounts data of their client countries, for which they
held the UN partially responsible. UNSO, however, had its hands tied. The
regular publication of the most current national accounts tables became more
and more delayed, and many countries lagged behind and were slow in updating their estimates. To users, the errors and inconsistencies in these estimates appeared progressively more glaring. UNSO could do little about the
quality of the national data. It tried initially to get countries to revise those
numbers that were clearly wrong without much effect. Within the UN, the
word was passed down that such numbers were to be regarded as the official
series because they were the same figures the governments themselves adhered to in UN negotiations and they represented the figures used internally
in the formulation of domestic policies.

The World Bank was the first institution to become frustrated by the poor
quality of what it perceived as the "UN national accounts estimates" for low-
income countries. While the UN generated fairly comprehensive tables that
depicted the economic structure portrayed by the national accounts, this took
time and the World Bank was more interested in current performance. It needed
up-to-date information to analyze processes of change and, in particular, to
assess the impact of investment on growth in appraising proposed development projects. Its main concern was with determining how much aid and loan
support would be needed to fill the identified investment gap that existed in
each of its different member countries applying for finances for development
projects. At the same time, in order to determine appropriate lending criteria
for its operational guidelines, the Bank also compiled current GNP estimates
expressed in a standard currency (in practice, the U.S. dollar) to define a country's
approximate development status.[43] More exactly, the Bank found it necessary
to produce a current estimate—for all its member countries—of annual income (GNP) per capita in U.S. dollar terms. The Bank also devised its own U.S.
dollar conversion factors. Because official exchange rates change from one year
to the next when countries adopt different exchange-rate regimes and when,
deliberately or involuntarily, they allow their currencies to find their appropriate level in the foreign-exchange market, the Bank developed its Atlas methodology and calculated what it considered to be effective exchange rates.[44] This
Atlas method was intended to even out any extremes of volatility in individual
exchange rates that might have seriously undermined year-to-year assessments.
It was believed, incorrectly, that the method also improved inter-country comparability. The Atlas method determined the conversion factors to be applied to

bring all GNP figures to a common but not strictly comparable currency basis (see discussion below on the International Comparisons Project). In those extreme cases where exchange rates were believed to be egregiously out of line (and some inevitable formal correction to the official exchange rate was anticipated), a different basis of estimation was applied. This happened regularly in the case of certain countries in Latin America and Africa. Later, the Bank determined the conversion factors for corrections to the exchange rates for countries belonging to the former Soviet Union and parts of Central and Eastern Europe, Burma (Myanmar), Indochina, and mainland China.

Other complications arose where multiple exchange rates were officially recognized in several countries, such as Syria or Turkey, and where unofficial parallel rates and black market rates were common. The Bank introduced certain statistical adjustments to these exchange rates. These were usually based on a range of factors linked to a country's history of inflation, past growth, and pattern of external trade relations. Trade value data were also used to appropriately weight the different primary, secondary, and other exchange rates to determine a single principal exchange rate that could be used in preparing data used in policy negotiations.

In due course, the Atlas GNP per capita figures became widely accepted, even by the UN system itself. They were frequently quoted by politicians and journalists, even though in many instances the Bank's per capita numbers were at variance, especially historically, with the U.S. dollar series prepared by UNSO, which continued to use reported date and unadjusted official exchange rates for the year in question. But even the Atlas procedure gave rise to contradictory results in a number of high-profile cases such as Nigeria and China, as a perusal of past World Development Reports and World Bank Atlas publications reveals. Because they appeared more current and consistent, however, the Bank's per capita income figures were universally adopted even to the extent of advising and, in some cases, defining policy and deciding priorities in the UN Secretariat, the United Nations Development Programme (UNDP), UNICEF, and certain other UN specialized agencies.

This is surprising because the Bank never had a mandate to compile statistics and was never involved in actual basic data collection for the national accounts. (Quite independently, in the 1980s, it became involved in household survey activities that were separately implemented under the Living Standards Measurement Studies Program; see Chapter 3.) The Bank's so-called field missions to compile national accounts statistics were concerned primarily with overall data reviews and simple data correction, repair, and maintenance activities. These were far more in the nature of quick fixes to improve GNP and growth-rate numbers that were clearly out of line than substantive exercises in data evaluation. (Later there were some notable exceptions: the early work on China's statistical system and on the national accounts for the new Russian Federation and other former Soviet Union countries carried out in cooperation with the national offices concerned.) One reason the Bank could forge ahead across a wide front with its GNP estimates was because of a regular policy interface with senior officials in its member countries about the implementation of Bank-supported projects and development programs. These invariably involved specific data requirements and routine monitoring activities. The Bank's interactions with governments at the highest level ensured that its officials were granted access to data that others did not have. It also meant that numbers were subsequently generated that were, in some political sense, endorsed by those in authority. Through their involvement with high-level government officials, the World Bank and IMF could always obtain the latest internal figures; even the UN, despite its prime contact with national statistical offices (but, much less so, with the central banks) often had no recourse to such unreleased figures. In addition, regular visits by teams of experts from the Bretton Woods institutions always received strong backup from their own permanent missions in the various countries. Such offices were far more focused on economic policy issues than their politically more diversified counterpart, the UNDP resident missions, which tended to address a wider range of social and economic issues.

Perhaps even more relevant to the production of its current macrolevel numbers and evaluations, the Bank adopted a specific model and resorted to a particular tool, the revised minimum standard model (or RMSM) that allowed the statistical practitioners, in association with the Bank's country economists, to come up with the latest consistent (in an accounting sense) estimates of a country's GNP and its major economic aggregates.[45] These current numbers were, of course, essentially modeled projections. They were based on a reasonably acceptable benchmark to which various assumed growth rates and the latest government estimates about price changes, imports, exports, construction activity, and so on were applied. Sometimes the GNP growth measures were consistent with anticipated investment targets, and sometimes they were related to the estimated growth performance in the country's three major sectors: agriculture, industry, and services. (The share of services, however, was often derived as a residual and was not calculated individually.) This occasionally gave rise to inexplicable inconsistencies in the size and growth rate of sectors, especially the service sector. Given all the relevant data inputs and assumptions about elasticities, however, the RMSM model automatically produced consistent estimates of GNP and capital formation and consumption and their respective rates of growth.

The reasons that were given for the adoption of these more fragile but "up to date" figures prepared by the Bank were similar to the reasons that had been advanced earlier to defend the use of the unadjusted national estimates countries submitted to the UN. The Bank's data, right or wrong, represented the "agreed-upon" numbers that were accepted by both the Bank and its respective country members as the basis for their policy dialogue. The Bank's numbers were heavily biased toward the production measure of GDP. These were rarely reviewed independently or cross-checked in any formally structured way against alternative expenditure or income estimates. Consequently, it was always necessary to revise economic history. For its part, the IMF focused its statistical attention on GDP expenditure measures; its policy interest was in government expenditures, investment outlays, and the external balance between the import and export of goods and services (and how spending in these areas was associated with borrowing and the accumulation of debt). However, this focus often implied acknowledging the status of the Bank's original GDP (or GNP) aggregate, since without it there was no way, in most cases, to generate any estimate of the largest expenditure component of final household consumption.

In effect, to many statisticians working "at the coal face," this development of data artifacts, which replaced more robust but time-consuming procedures in some countries, seemed dangerous because it rolled assumptions and hypotheses into official numbers. Genuine measurement took a back seat. In reality, there were no recent official GNP estimates based on actual detailed source data in many countries, especially the poorest. The Bank's procedures demonstrated that key numbers could be generated by institutional pressures and constraints and equally could be arrived at using models influenced by particular policy objectives, assumptions, and institutional imperatives. The critical ordering of countries according to their development status and whether they constituted "low-income developing countries"[46] that were eligible, in particular, for International Development Association (IDA) lending and assistance became dependent on the Bank's Atlas U.S. dollar denominated estimates of income per capita. The GNP per capita figures were an essential component of the Bank's operational guidelines. The Atlas numbers could be significantly affected by in-house adjustments to GNP, by Bank-determined conversion factors where official exchange rates were considered "egregiously" out of line, or by revisions of internal estimates of the midyear population of a country when, from local evidence, the demographic reality was believed to be at variance with the UN's global intercensus estimates. Other calculations, for example with respect to unrecorded transactions, could also be used to amend the measures of income per capita.

Unlike UNSO, the Bank—except (peripherally) in its de facto management over the last decade or so of the International Comparison Program (ICP)—did little or nothing to provide technical assistance or offer training to developing countries to help improve the quality of their national income statistics and help make them more current. This may change as the agency uses the newly created statistical capacity-building fund to strengthen data reporting. The Bank consistently argued in the past that statistics are solely a UN responsibility and that its own primary interest is not in the national accounts per se but in the GNP aggregates and the growth performance of its member countries. More recently, Bank interest has been extended to include concerns about poverty for which income-distribution information as well as GNP estimates and purchasing power parity (PPP) measures are required. Gaps in the national accounts clearly remain; unfortunately, these gaps are not value neutral. They occur because there is a conceptual, managerial, budgetary, or political reason why some national data are simply not collected.

Box 2.2. Growth and Investment

After Walt Rostow published his *Stages of Economic Growth* in 1960, it became the accepted wisdom that capital was important to modern industrialization and to emerging middle-income developing countries that were embarking on new, mostly import-substituting manufacturing ventures. This idea became a sine qua non in the evaluation and selection of development projects in the World Bank. In the 1990s, the relative importance of the technologies made possible by capital imported from the advanced industrial countries was recognized, reinforcing the value of the presumed importance of investment in the growth process. In situations that seemed ripe for the introduction of modern industrial plants and machinery, policymakers simply accepted without question the idea that new investment in capital would lead to improved economic performance and growth of incomes. But in countries that lack the necessary capacity, experienced labor, and knowledge to operate such equipment and to regularly maintain and repair its capital, there is no guarantee that this investment will lead to faster growth.

In recent years, it has been left mostly to the IMF to strengthen national statistics, in part in pursuit of its interest in getting countries to subscribe to the SDDS (special data dissemination standard) and GDDS (general data dissemination system) and to use recognized procedures that improve the quality of the data that is collected. As a result of the fallout from recent financial crises, the IMF is now required by its management board to provide better national data, to implement quality-assurance procedures, and to establish improved data reliability and dissemination in key policy areas.[47] The Fund took the initiative to secure a more consistent foundation for monetary, real economy, external sector, and government statistics at the country level. The Fund has also begun to develop a basis for national accounts estimates that is more sound, especially in countries where, for one reason or another, a weak tradition of statistical capability exists. Much of the training it has sponsored over the past five years has been conducted by specialists with direct operational experience and professional expertise in the compilation of national accounts in developing countries. Where this work has been carried out, the effects are noticeable; there have been palpable improvements in the structure and timelines of all economic data entering the national accounts. Considerable attention has been paid to establishing the regular reporting of quarterly national accounts. Despite the obvious problems in commodity-based economies that are subject to seasonal influences and harvests, high-frequency short-term measures are seen to be key to the improved formulation and monitoring of current economic policy. Importance must still be attached, however, to long-term trends and economic sustainability.

By contrast, at the turn of the twenty-first century, the Bank was giving little or no statistical attention to national accounts problems, either to concepts or national practices, and no attention to the development of quarterly reporting. The Bank's overriding operational concern with current GNP rather than with the overall structure of the accounts has had important negative implications. The widespread desire of politicians to have "a number," whatever its credentials, has undermined more substantive statistical inquiry in general. It also affected the Bank's own data work on poverty and the measurement of income distribution. International cross-section analysis of the critical role of investment in the development process, which is conventionally based on capital-output measures and national rates of growth, remain precarious; often such figures have been manipulated and the truth may be quite different.[48] The main weakness of these intercountry economic comparisons lies in the failure to adjust data that is expressed in national prices into purchasing-power-parity terms that reflect differentials in price levels.

Recently, the agencies concerned with improving the quality of national accounts estimates have turned their attention to standardizing compilation methodologies and practices. UNSO, in particular, has tried to secure greater consistency across countries in the way data steps are sequenced and the basic macroeconomic information is initially gathered and then put together. Simply having an internationally agreed-upon framework and classification structure—however detailed, comprehensive, and complex they might be—does not guarantee that the numbers corresponding to different variables and aggregates will be consistently measured and comparable across countries. Comparability depends a great deal on the sources of information and their continuity; how raw data have been collected; what aggregation formulae have been adopted, including the summation sequence that was followed in putting the numbers together; and upon agreed definitions. The introduction of standard procedures is not so much a novel idea as it is a logical step in compiling estimates that reflect a more profound practical insight into what makes any given number more relevant and reliable in the language of statistical communication.

The Measurement of Trade

Trade between countries consists of both movements of goods and transactions in services. The essential character of these two exchanges may be quite different, although they are motivated by the same economic forces.

Merchandise Trade

As economies develop and economic diversity accompanies increasing production specialization and sophistication, simple production for own use across a range of subsistence products, accompanied by occasional barter, gives way to more extensive market transactions and international trade. Trade is the inevitable consequence of the geographical concentration and specialization of production and the differential distribution of the world's resources across different countries. An important element of quantifying the world must relate, therefore, to the sheer magnitude of trade flows. The problem of measuring how many different goods and services are transacted between nations and the associated value of this trade to each country is one of the oldest in official statistics. In principle, in the case of physical goods (merchandise trade), these flows are observable and relatively easy to measure, other than when smuggling occurs.[49] But for services, it is much more difficult. There are also some difficult problems of valuation and pricing to be resolved.

One of the major accomplishments of UNSO over years has been the development of an extensive and detailed system of trade statistics. Along with population figures, this has proved to be perhaps the most widely used database extant. UNSO was among the first of the modern systems to standardize data across countries and to do so through the coordination of different official agencies. Even in the countries themselves, statisticians are not the primary collectors of trade data. Nevertheless, the producers, exporters, importing agencies, and franchising firms engaged in trade transactions interact with customs officials, who deal daily with this information. All responsible for re-cording trade properly have adopted the same international trade-reporting system, which the statisticians in consultation with customs authorities have devised. When it was first introduced, the software system driving the current information process was one of the most innovative then put into operation. Without it, given the volume of data resulting from the regular reporting of the rapidly expanding daily volume of trade transactions taking place in the inter-national economy, which must be measured by commodity and by country, the current array of trade statistics would not have been possible.[50]

Trade (along with population) was one of the first phenomena to be moni-tored on a regular basis by governments. For the mercantilists, it was a mani-festation of a country's wealth and power and it was a means of creating income for those involved. Trade, through customs duties, also provided, of course, a primary source of revenue for the realm and for the authorities that con-trolled it. International trade and its classification was one of the more im-portant issues the League of Nations was able to monitor effectively in the interwar period. It became one of the first and most immediate tasks taken over by the newly formed UNSO in 1946.

Initially, trade data were compiled manually by a small branch of UNSO, which was first based in New York and then in Geneva. In the early 1970s, trade data were processed through the International Computing Center (ICC) in Geneva using punch cards and an IBM mainframe. In 1979, a new mag-netic tape–based system for handling the enormous amounts of data involved was developed that was known as Comtrade.[51] This produced consolidated information that was held on magnetic tapes that had been entered first through a conventional batched-card process. The cards, in turn, served as the means by which values and volumes of imports and exports of merchan-dise trade conducted by all countries, originally recorded on paper documents, were transformed and uniformly compiled from the tapes. Detailed data were then generated relating to the specific commodities traded by countries.

The system permitted aggregations to be performed both by countries (and regions) and by commodity descriptions. The respective volumes could be distinguished by two different quantity fields, either by the number of units or pieces (e.g., number of motor vehicles) or by their actual volume amounts. Specifically, goods were classified by their net weight or some similar quan-tum metric (such as tons of wheat, liters of alcohol, barrels of oil, etc.).

The creators of the system recognized that because of the value and vol-ume of the data, it was possible to collate information on the various tariffs and duties applicable to the traded goods in question. Comtrade itself, how-ever, had nothing to do with providing such customs information. Information on tariffs was separately collected by the United Nations Conference on Trade and Development (UNCTAD) in Geneva. But this proved easier said than done, and the links to the detailed trade flows were quite tenuous in places. Items identified in the trade classification used a six-digit coding scheme whereas tariffs might sometimes apply, in a harmonized classification, to 8-digit categories. This greater detail was usually introduced to allow for the reporting and notification of special preferential trading arrangements concerning particular goods or between certain countries. The absence of a clear overlap and correspondence—and the difficulties of identifying and quantifying barriers unrelated to tariffs such as licenses, quotas, and quarantine restrictions; health controls and endangered species lists; and so forth—has tended to hinder robust economic analysis and more exact testing of trade theory.

Comtrade also allowed statistics to be compiled that showed the changing patterns in the all-important direction of trade flows between countries. The magnitude of these commodity flows demonstrates not only comparative competitiveness and market openings but also the nature of political relations between countries. Summaries of "direction of trade" data, at a fairly aggregated level, were for a while produced and disseminated in regular annual reports issued by the IMF. This was because trade flows were deemed important to an understanding of overall economic performance. In addition, agencies could check observance of various international trade agreements (including sanctions) and other contractual trade arrangements. Originally, it was thought that the flows impacted on the assumed equilibrium relationship between foreign-exchange rates and a country's current balance of trade and payments and financial position. The IMF, however, disbanded the mechanism of fixed-exchange rates after 1973, and the progressive adoption by countries around the globe of more flexible exchange-rate regimes that were anchored to various different currency baskets made such close monitoring of intercountry bilateral trade flows less relevant from an economic policy perspective.

In 1989, against the wishes of some users as well as producers of trade data, Comtrade was moved to New York and the special UNSO trade statistics unit in Geneva was closed down. Some staff in UNCTAD and the newly established World Trade Organization (WTO) were reluctant to see the trade files move out because they believed this might jeopardize their own access to detailed trade data and the priority they were given in the use of that data. The move, however, did not have the effect some had feared; improved technology allowed the database itself to be based in Geneva while the staff worked from New York.

Trade data are kept as current as possible. UNSO at first asks countries for provisional data; after that it incorporates any reported revisions and updates on a regular (mostly weekly) rolling basis. While at one time such data were collected and issued quarterly, all information is now produced and disseminated only on an annual basis. Access to UNCTAD data on tariffs (national collections and rates) at the detailed level is still regarded as privileged, but otherwise, since its inception, trade data—provided they cannot be linked to individual suppliers or buyers of traded goods—have been regularly provided (at a charge) to outside sources. Recent developments have included the recording of trade values with greater precision to avoid cumulative rounding errors, the grouping of re-exports with exports both in total and as distinct groups, and to improve the separation of reusable and returnable containers (of all types) from trade totals. Problems of how to distinguish between the reported countries of original consignment from those of final destination are still being debated.[52]

Yet despite the attention paid to these issues, an extensive range of trade is conducted on a global basis that still goes unrecorded. Some of this is deliberately ignored, as in the case of interpersonal gifts and merchandise transfers as samples. But the big-ticket items that are missing, such as drugs, illicit gem-smuggling, the illegal logging trade, the unreported transfer in kind of gold and cigarettes, and bootlegging often make up an important part of the wealth of local businessmen and of specific government regimes and their civil servants. These problems are more acute where national boundaries are difficult to police. Thus, the official story on international trade as it has unfolded over history is incomplete, and information about the direction of certain trade flows remains (perhaps in some cases deliberately) opaque. These issues have more to do with internal social and economic politics, international legal agreements, and the absence of any surveillance systems that might control the "undesirable" trade in substances than they do with statistical practice.[53]

Box 2.3. Terms of Trade

Economists have always been interested in analyzing the effects of international terms of trade and their impact on development. Separate price data that refer to specific trade transactions are essential to determine real changes in the terms of trade. Terms of trade refer to changes from a chosen base date in the relative prices that exporters receive in relationship to the prices they must pay, on average, for imported merchandise goods. Following ECLA's *Economic Survey of Latin America* of 1949 and the pioneering studies of Raúl Prebisch and Hans Singer, when the issue was given its first political airing, this problem became an important topic in economic policy debate. It was soon realized that a deterioration in a country's terms-of-trade position could seriously damage its economic stability.

Despite the fact that trade data were originally recorded separately by value and volume, it is difficult in many cases to assign an appropriate "price" to most import and export trade transactions that is in some sense both meaningful and comparable over time and across countries.

In the first place, for any given country, the basis for recording exports, on the one hand, and imports, on the other, is different. This is because the border of the country assumes critical significance in defining the principle evaluation of trade transactions. Goods exported are valued at the final point of dispatch, such as the airport, land crossing, or port. This is conventionally referred to as the free on board (f.o.b.) value. While some goods are priced "ex factory," the f.o.b. basis for evaluation is intended to cover all the local costs incurred by the producer in shipping manufactured items from the factory to the point of domestic departure. For imports into a country, the equivalent valuation basis for the purpose of external trade (but not balance of payments) relates to all the costs incurred, including those of international trade, up to the point of arrival of the goods in the country. Thus, the costs of freight, packaging, international transportation, and insurance involved in shipping goods from their point of origin to the border of their country of consignment are included in the carriage, insurance, and freight (C.I.F.) values used for imported goods.

Second, even where a corresponding quantity is specified in relation to the volume of imports or exports, it does not necessarily enable analysts to determine an appropriate price relevant to the goods in question. In some cases, the volume will refer to a mixed batch of goods in a consignment. In others, the specification of units may be vague and the consignment will be described broadly in terms of "cartons," "boxes," or even "containers." The word "units" itself is ambiguous in this context because the items they relate to can be quite different and may vary in quality; for example, shirts, dresses, and so forth. An exact weight measure for a consignment may also be misleading because it relates not to a particular item but to a bundle of goods. At best, all that can be derived from such value and quantity measures is an implicit "unit value" rather than a specific price. Unit-value statistics are rarely robust in comparisons over time or between countries because the composition of the bundle will vary. The more detailed the commodity classification, the more confidence can usually be placed in a unit-value estimate; that is, the observed volatility in the derived statistic will tend to show a lower degree of variation.

Third, particularly in the case of values reported on an export manifest, where it might be reasonably supposed that the information in the country of origin is more accessible, the actual realized final value of goods exported by a local supplier may turn out to be quite different from the value that was initially recorded. This is because the conditions of sale in the international market may change between the date when the product is shipped and the time of arrival of the consignment at its point of destination, or the time it is purchased by the foreign customer. In a few cases, the product may be resold to another customer while still on the high seas.

It is significant that many recorded trade transactions do not report the corresponding quantities involved, even though they show the values of imports or exports that are required to satisfy taxation regulations. Items are identified by the respective purchaser or shipper according to its invoice or customs code number. Where the national tariff code applies a specific rate (applicable to trade volumes) instead of an ad valorem rate (applicable to trade values), a quantity must be clearly specified for customs purposes. In such cases, it is more feasible to match a unit value with a relevant corresponding price for certain products.

The derived unit values simply represent the closest proxy to the required specific price information. For the most part, countries have had to be satisfied with measurements of terms of trade based, historically, on unit-value indices of imports and exports that have been calculated at an aggregate level. In practice, it often proves easier to identify the respective prices for export goods than it does to identify import prices; it is more difficult to obtain, through existing price mechanisms, the prices charged for specific imports from overseas suppliers. In addition, when there is a need to express these prices in corresponding domestic terms, a problem of defining an appropriate exchange rate has to be taken into account. For any particular group of imported products that is classified by an SITC heading, there is likely to be a range of different international sources of supply, each of which uses a different currency.[54]

For the most part, the poorer, less integrated, and less economically complex developing countries export goods for which the level of processing is relatively limited. By contrast, most of the goods they import, an important part of which is machinery and equipment, are more sophisticated. Such imports tend to come from the more industrially advanced countries. In principle, when they import these goods, developing countries acquire all the new and sophisticated technologies that these goods offer. This has a double impact. First, if such high-tech goods represent better quality and create an improvement in productivity, then observed changes in unit values might make it look like the country in question has experienced a deterioration in the terms of trade. Such a conclusion would be incorrect. In reality, changes in unit values mean that the terms of trade for many developing countries could be much better. Second, assuming the ready availability of the necessary human capital to operate such goods, the installation of more-advanced machinery and equipment by many countries could lead to a general improvement in productivity and the efficiency of the production process. In turn, this might also lead to a weaker demand for basic raw materials and for lower-technology intermediate goods and hence reinforce any general downward trend in the terms of trade.

This brings out another important question about the extent to which services have become increasingly embedded in the products traded and whether, in the present age, some parallel calculations should be made to adjust for changes in the terms of trade in services. Such a calculation would be fraught with difficulty and would reflect not just responses to price movements but also changes in the international institutional and political environment.

All these factors clearly make the proper determination of a country's terms of trade, viewed in the broadest sense, a difficult and contentious exercise. Analysts continue to make such calculations on the assumption that the errors that are believed to lurk within unit values across a wide range of traded goods will tend to cancel each other out as more aggregative indices at the country level are constructed.

Trade in Services

Recent debate about international trade policy and globalization has drawn attention to the incomplete coverage and lack of comprehensiveness of data about trade in services.[55] The paucity of information relating to this rapidly growing area of economic activity was noted in the 1994 Uruguay Round negotiations and discussions surrounding the General Agreement on Trade in Services (GATS).[56] The traditional notion of trade in services as perceived and defined in successive IMF balance of payments manuals is now regarded as unsatisfactory for the purposes of transactions analysis.[57] The conventional scope of the IMF's guidelines does not sufficiently reflect some of the important changes that have been occurring in the service sector in recent years. Many of these are associated not only with the growth of income but with the organizational transformation that has accompanied the sweeping technological innovations in information exchange and computer systems since 1995. The dramatic escalation in electronic communications, software use, information transfer, and shifts in management operations that has accompanied what is widely (but perhaps misleadingly) referred to as "the new economy" has rapidly extended the boundaries of what constitutes "service." The IMF definition in the balance of payments manual is more limited because it is restricted to identifiable cross-border trade in services tied to traditional concepts of residency. The OECD was one of the first organizations outside the embryonic WTO and UNCTAD to recognize the emerging policy significance of this issue.[58] In the early 1990s, it established a special policy unit to look into the question of measuring the output of services, particularly trade in services. Shortly thereafter, in 1993, the Voorburg Group—the first of the independent special-subject city groups—was set up to consider from a general perspective how to measure trade in services more appropriately.

Discussions of (merchandise) trade liberalization and of the extent and effects of globalization are clearly incomplete without some clear understanding of what constitutes "services" and what role services and other non-merchandise trans-actions that represent a wider notion of what used to be referred to as "in-visibles" play in trade. An increasing component of the service sector is now physically embodied in reported trade in merchandise that is quite different from those service activities such as insurance, storage, transport, and so forth that are traditionally associated with and are essential to the physical trans-shipment of goods. The removal of barriers that impede trade in services is now viewed as an important component of policies to speed the process of development, raise incomes, and improve the distribution of global income.[59] As in the case of normal export and import trade, many of these barriers are not directly associated with explicit tariffs but reflect legal and licensing pro-visions and intellectual property rights. Most barriers appear to relate to pre-ventive measures that, at least superficially, may not be overtly designed for the specific purposes of economic protection. Nevertheless, they have the same effect of restricting the free movement of trade.

In recent years it has been observed that the average share of services in national output is closely correlated with the increase in people's incomes, a premise that was first advanced some fifty years ago by Rostow.[60] There is strong evidence to show that the demand for services in the areas of educa-tion, health, recreation, tourism, real estate, and finance expands much faster than the demand for goods as countries and their inhabitants become richer. This applies across the board to both intermediate expenditure and the final consumption of services. It is illustrated in the observed structural change in employment and the substantial growth of service jobs and profusion of new occupational categories in the service sector. Recent data produced by the OECD[61] indicate that in the advanced industrial countries, overall labor pro-ductivity in the service sector outperforms that in most manufacturing in-dustries. Inevitably, however, such estimates must remain fragile because of the difficulty of measuring accurately the true scope of service output under existing conditions. Such conclusions probably apply most convincingly to particular sectors, such as finance, communications, business, and informa-tion services, where growth has recently been most dramatic. All these areas possess the unique features that characterize services. The transactions in which they are engaged are essentially intangible and often invisible. They often can-not be stored and require one-to-one encounters. These factors do not neces-sarily mean that such services are unrecognizable or that they cannot be replicated, but it does make service trade more difficult to measure reliably.

The very nature of trade in services requires close or direct contact between producers and consumers. The rapidly expanding availability across global and domestic markets of instant electronic access and telecommunications increasingly obviates the need for direct personal contact in many service transactions. For certain activities and situations, however, it is necessary for the producer and consumer to meet in order to close a deal and effect a trade in a service. This means that proximity is necessary and that either the supplier must move to the consumer, as in the case of a specialist who is a consultant, or the consumer must travel to the producer's location to satisfy their needs. This is clear in the cases of tourism, obtaining specialized medical care, overseas college education, and so forth. The four distinct modes of trade in services defined by GATS are described below. It should be noted that "quality," although it is not separately identified, is a further aspect of service that overlays all four modes. It is clearly a dynamic force that is related to superior efficiency and productivity, but it exerts an unknown influence on the value and volume of services trade.

1. Cross-border trade:
   This refers to the situation where the services are applied to merchandise goods directly and are transferred along with them without any corresponding movement of either the supplier or the consumer. Examples are the transport and insurance of merchandise trade, the supply of services embedded in CD-ROMs, diskettes, legal documents, and engineering and architectural blueprints.

2. Consumption abroad:
   This occurs when customers move to the supplier's country to acquire a service directly for the purposes of pleasure, leisure, health, education, entertainment, sport, and so forth.

3. Commercial presence:
   This relates to situations where a service supplier establishes a presence overseas in order to produce services for a foreign local market. Sometimes that presence may serve a broader constituency and purpose and be drawn, perhaps, by considerations of cost, tax, capital, and human resources to relocate activity in the country of choice.

4. Presence of natural persons:
   This is often temporary; it applies to situations where individual service suppliers such as entertainers, carpenters, doctors, university teachers, and so forth, travel to foreign countries to deliver their particular skills and work directly for their clients (or act) and as hired consultants.

It is evident from the above distinctions that how services are traded is as important as what those services are, although the latter helps to explain why they have grown in importance internationally.

The Measurement of Labor and Output

Economists analyze the patterns and processes of production through the ways in which land, labor, and capital are combined to generate output.[62] When the ILO was set up in 1919, the post–World War I political and economic environment was being subjected to previously unimagined tensions. Two strongly conflicting ideologies had emerged, one from grassroots revolution, the other from feudal capitalism. Each believed it had the answer to the question of how economies and their societies should be organized. One favored a central authority that directed the use of a country's scarce resources of land, labor, and capital to ensure that they were most effectively organized and collectively used for the greater good of the society at large. The other put its faith in the efficacy of the market and price signals to guide individual choice and household autonomy and to allocate resources efficiently. It relied heavily on the ability of the "invisible hand" to deliver to people the goods and services they believed were valuable and useful. Proponents of the market mostly rejected its regulation and continue to object to any extensive official intervention in the economic system.[63] This ideological confrontation raised important questions not only about equity but also about cost efficiency and economic effectiveness; that is, the question of whether each system had the ability to use available resources to their fullest capacity. It also drew attention to related issues of productivity.[64] Key to the debate was the role of investment in relation to society's time preferences (the choice between "jam today" or "more jam tomorrow") and who should decide these. Equity and need were clearly fundamental issues that were part of the debate; one system tried to deal with such concerns directly, while the other assumed that they would be satisfactorily addressed through the achievement of faster economic progress.

During the interwar period, on the basis of production effort, all evidence suggested the socialist central-planning model would win hands down in this contest. The West felt, however, that this success had been achieved only at the cost of untold and perhaps unacceptable suffering in the form of social disruption, human misery, family dislocation, cost to communities, and sweeping cultural destruction. After the end of World War II and the fall of the Iron Curtain, there were genuine fears in the West that the socialist production system would again prevail because of its apparent economic superiority and assumed greater fairness in its rewards structure. Some Western politicians feared that communism would eventually rule the world, both economically and militarily. The onset of socialism in Europe, they felt, would automatically spawn the spread of communist ideas and thereby fundamentally transform the traditional structure of Western society. Many believed that the democratic processes would be overturned, traditional institutions would be demolished, and personal freedom would be destroyed. This seemed too great a price to pay, and such fears forestalled an evenhanded evaluation of alternative ideas and systems by the UN.

As it happened, the unchecked advance of communism did not take place. In part this was because most Western countries introduced their own peculiar model of socialist organization in the form of Keynesian economics and paid greater homage to the ideals of mixed economic systems. In its own way, Keynesian economics enhanced the role of government in many aspects of policymaking, quite aside from economics. This process was reinforced by the coincident establishment of the welfare state in much of Europe and a general recognition (and social acceptance) of the need for more extensive social protection and redistributive transfers through existing taxation mechanisms.[65] In postwar Europe, it was the law that the production system allow labor to have a greater say in the process of determining output levels and on respective allocations of factor rewards such as wages and dividends. However, this was not participation in production decisions on the same order as that of the Soviet and Chinese cooperatives, collectives, communes, and factory workers' organizations.[66] Nevertheless, European trade unions played an important role in strengthening the position of labor and making sure that workers received adequate rewards for their efforts and that their conditions of labor were considerably improved.

Employment and Labor Issues

The ILO Statistical Section, which has become an independent technical department called the Bureau of Statistics, has been in operation for a much longer period than UNSO. Set up in 1919 under Article 396 of the Versailles Treaty and Article 10(1) of the Constitution of the ILO, statistical activities have formed an integral part of ILO operations from the outset.[67] Unique among the UN agencies, however, the ILO is governed by a tripartite structure of representatives of employers, workers' organizations, and governments whose aim is to unite in the cause of social justice and the improvement in living conditions.[68]

For more than eighty years, the Bureau of Statistics has had to adapt to dramatically changing conditions in production technology and economic activity and the impact of those changes on labor engagement. The ILO has also had to keep under review the disparities in types of labor engagement across the globe, including changes in attitudes toward social security and protection and the effects of stricter factory regulations regarding the health and safety of workers. The management structure, in bringing together three (sometimes conflicting) perspectives has through the years illustrated the value of ideas contributed from different sources to the determination of policy paths and labor resolutions.

Over the period since the ILO's inception, the population of the world has more than tripled, creating conditions that continually demand flexible, adaptive, and innovative approaches to carrying out the ILO's basic mandate of the collection and distribution of information relating to the conditions of international life and labor. The ILO's coverage of data extends beyond employment numbers to include living conditions, prices, and the determination of real wages. The mandate of the Bureau of Statistics was later expanded to include the monitoring of occupational hazards and industrial accidents. In this connection, the bureau has had to consider questions not only of concept and coverage but also of statistical methods, measurement, and classification. This broad mandate has had important implications for the development of appropriate data sources, including surveys of enterprises (industries), households, and individuals. The potential data outcomes can be affected both socially and politically by the choice of sources and the adoption of different concepts. For example, it is likely that the employers' side of business operations would be most concerned with the concept of gross wages and, specifically, the total wage bill. This, to firms, is the most relevant consideration in managing production, controlling costs, and determining profits. Such information is readily collected in surveys of establishments and enterprises. On the other hand, a firm's employees are generally more interested in their individual net wages, that is, their take-home pay packets. Such data are best collected from household surveys. Some household members may also have a second job. If the ILO (or its country members) carries out labor surveys based on establishments, then the information compiled will provide an ambiguous interpretation of the numbers in employment. The approach will also favor employers' interest and will emphasize macro production concerns. However, if similar information is collected from household surveys, a more human perspective will be given. The former survey approach is better able to map data about cost outlays, whereas the latter is more useful for recording individual receipts and activities. Household surveys are able to capture workers' wage and employment characteristics, such as hours worked, and identify them by the age, gender, occupation, and industry of workers; they may even categorize them according to their education and level of skill. In principle, well-designed official reporting files could serve both purposes, but in practice, the various departments that are usually involved in this area of bureaucratic reporting—tax, registration and licensing, health and social security, training, and so forth—are often not well coordinated or are prevented by law from sharing their data. If this is the case, then a coherent, integrated, and comprehensive core database cannot be readily established, despite the fact that the departments use the same codes, identifiers, and classifications.

At an early stage of its existence, the ILO recognized the need for statistics that could compare data about labor between countries and monitor conditions of work and thus help establish clear international employment standards. The approach the ILO took was to consolidate and redefine essentially what was already being done in the relatively rich advanced Western industrial nations. Many had "considerable experience in this domain."[69] But this was not enough. This method of setting statistical standards was increasingly called into question in the 1970s as newly independent countries began implementing their own development strategies, which focused on infant industry and import substitution. Serious gaps in economic data coverage were appearing, and the problems that arose around the issue of how to identify unorganized urban labor and street-peddling activity were becoming increasingly apparent. Analysts were aware that company registers or lists of business licenses provided little information that was relevant to the type of informal economic activity in which many people, particularly poor and uneducated families and their children, were regularly engaged. In a break with both UNSO and UNIDO and their respective adherence to the International Standard Industrial Classification and national accounts structures, the ILO—following missions to Colombia, Kenya, and Sri Lanka to review their employment situations—began to develop new approaches to defining the labor force. The pathbreaking concept of the informal sector emerged during the Kenya mission.[70] The informal sector represented a loosely defined structure of unorganized, often mobile, diverse, and flexible economic activity that, in the absence of adequate formal employment opportunities, allowed casual workers to interact on an occasional basis with the market. The importance of the informal economy was the gap it revealed in conventional thinking about economic progress and the linearity of development. It demonstrated that creating formal employment opportunities did not work in countries with unbalanced and undiversified economies. This was because these economies housed large enclaves that were either not well integrated into the international market or, at the other extreme, were intimately linked with the market but only through selected, relatively advanced, and mutually exclusive niche sectors that were mostly isolated from the mainstream of economic activity. The existence of such enclaves focused increasing attention on structuralism and served to enhance the validity of the arguments of the dependency theorists, who saw this concentration of economic power as a threat to political sovereignty and evenhanded policy. It also underlined the fact that distributional imbalances were not necessarily associated with geographically located cores and peripheries but were linked to economic nodes and institutional arrangements that were sometimes grafted onto society.

When the ILO was set up, attitudes toward workers in the early 1920s were very different than they are today, both in private corporations and in most hierarchically structured governments. It was an exemplary achievement of the ILO, therefore, to organize the collection and dissemination of statistics about the working population, conditions of work, and living standards in the interwar period. From 1935 to 1936, the ILO published labor data on a regular basis in the form of annual series. In the postwar period, some of these series became monthly or quarterly. The bureau also launched its annual "October Enquiry" of occupational wages and hours of work that also covered retail prices of selected food items. During its early days, the bureau gathered data in only twenty-three industrial countries; by the early 1970s, it was computing information from some 200 countries. Accompanying the standard statistical material disseminated through the *Yearbook of Labour Statistics* and the monthly *Bulletin of Labour Statistics,* the ILO has produced a series of source volumes and technical guides dealing with consumer prices, employment, hours of work, and wages (from establishment surveys). These also contain definitions of the terms "economically active population," "employment," "unemployment," and "hours of work" when such information is taken from administrative records and related sources. The ILO has also produced descriptions of the total and economically active population, employment, and unemployment (from population censuses). Over the years, it has published various accompanying supplements or clarifying amendments. Additional volumes have covered the cost of labor, occupational injuries, strikes and lockouts, and household income and expenditures.

Apart from supporting the ILO's broad initial mandate to resolve the fundamental problem of unemployment through an understanding of how it was associated with the business-cycle phenomenon of industrial market economies,[71] the bureau received more specific guidelines for developing its data strategy. These came either in the form of resolutions adopted by the International Conference of Labor Statisticians (which started meeting in 1923) or, very occasionally, through specific conventions, resolutions, and recommendations adopted by the General Conference of the ILO. The bureau's preparation of manuals was designed to translate such recommendations into practical terms and to provide guidance on the aspects of statistics covered by these international labor standards. The manuals invariably established concepts and definitions, and they usually included some discussion of the details of survey and questionnaire design, fieldwork, data processing, and estimation methods.

One important impact of this data activity to monitor labor standards was to unite international labor interests with national employment concerns. The ILO provided the technical backup to allow countries to develop their own statistical programs in these important and interrelated areas of labor organization and to do so along a broad common front. The ILO's authority rested, however, in the ten states of "chief industrial importance in Europe, Japan, and North America," so it was some time before most observers and data users recognized that certain ILO statistical "standards" did not adequately or appropriately serve the economic and social planning needs of most member countries. These standards did not fit well to the specific conditions existing in an economy that was predominantly agricultural or one that was based on resource extraction. Nor were they very relevant in other countries where self-employment and household enterprises formed the primary economic activity. Furthermore, the ILO's tripartite organization made it difficult for the organization to come to terms with important emerging but ill-defined concepts, such as the informal sector.[72] It is interesting to note that by the end of 1990, only twenty-some countries had signed up for the Labor Statistics Convention (No. 160)[73] adopted five years earlier by the General Conference of the ILO. This convention set out, through a supplementary Recommendation (No. 170), the minimum requirements for the regular publication of data and classification of (mainly formal) labor activities.

The important matter of labor productivity did not figure very highly on the agenda of the ILO or in the work of its Bureau of Statistics. Nevertheless, in the late 1980s, the organization did acknowledge the importance of multifactor productivity indices and the relevance of PPP measures to the international comparison of real output and expenditure.[74] Efficiency, even in its narrow labor context, was another key question to which the ILO paid little attention. All three issues have become of increasing concern in a modern electronic age when invention, productivity, efficiency, economy, and quality have become embedded in new technology and significantly affect prices.

A number of concepts, definitions, and classifications are relevant to the measurement of progress and development in which the ILO has played an important role. These include the identification of the boundary of economic activity and the engagement of people within that production boundary. The notion of labor cost (as opposed to the notion of the compensation of employees), the coding of occupations and industries, and the identification of people's status in employment have all come from the ILO. Related aspects of this conceptual work have embraced the question of the distinction between paid and unpaid work, the nature of female labor-force participation (particularly in developing countries), the measurement of unemployment, and the associated matters of underemployment and inadequate employment, where this includes the underutilization of labor capacity and the mismatching of skill and tasks. Many of these aspects came under the purview of "manpower planning" during the 1965–1975 era, when several studies with this rubric were sponsored by the ILO, especially in Africa. In more recent years, the ILO has taken an interest in panel surveys and has pursued inquiries into time use. (Some of these issues are taken up later in the discussion of the gender dimension in statistics.)

A clear understanding of the notion of production and the boundary of economic activity is a requirement if one is to correctly use the concepts of employment, unemployment, and economically active population in a statistical study. According to the ILO framework, all production of goods and services should be counted whether the output is for sale, barter, or own consumption, and the count should include any household construction for own use. The production boundary also includes the provision of nonmarket (mostly public, but also some nonprofit) goods and services that are made available to households on both an individual and collective basis. However, because unpaid domestic activities and volunteer community services are not included in this definition, many of the activities of women are still largely ignored in the process, even though women produce output and contribute significantly to the greater welfare of human society.[75] Women's economic activities and their engagement in work are also disproportionately underrepresented when data are compiled on numbers actively seeking work.

Apart from additionally collecting data on unpaid work performed by women in and for the household (and specifically on the land belonging to the household), the ILO has contributed to a better understanding of individual "engagement in economic activity" in at least two other important ways. The first is in its definition of employment and the second is its support of time-use surveys.

The ILO's definition of employment distinguishes between paid employment and self-employment and uses a short reference period. Employed persons are those over the age of 15 who perform at least one hour of work for a wage or salary in cash or kind during the reference period (on the previous day, week, or month but sometimes over a longer period). Analysts sometimes struggle with this "minimalist" definition and complain that unless employment is also categorized by hours of work, the numbers can be quite misleading. The intention of this criterion is simply to make the definition as comprehensive as possible. It is used to make sure that the whole extent and nature of work is covered; "work" should include casual, standby, and other types of temporary and regular employment that are common features of many poorer and less industrially developed countries. More specifically, the ILO definition sees employment as the obverse of unemployment, which should be unequivocally defined as the total lack of work. However, a person's employment status may change or they may go to other parts of the world to find work; this mobility introduces ambiguity into any concept of aggregate national employment under this definition. In practice, this definition may make it more difficult for various branches of industry to establish the appropriate match between total production and the corresponding level of labor input, one of the primary intentions for adopting the definition. Comparative labor productivity and efficiency measures clearly cannot be compiled on such an eclectic basis of variable labor inputs.

It is perhaps worthy of note that in the former Soviet Union and other centrally planned economies where labor was historically defined within the macroconcept of the balance sheet of labor resources, the notion of "unemployed" labor did not even exist. "Unemployed" workers formed part of the able-bodied population of working age. Indeed, a main concern of planners in certain regions in the Soviet Union was to mobilize employment in the so-called labor reserves of urban and rural inhabitants of working age who were engaged in "personal" subsidiary agriculture and/or performing household duties.[76] The overwhelming proportion of "unemployed" people—who were mostly women—were engaged in both lines of unpaid work. The primary aim of policy was to place everyone into "properly supervised" full-time employment.

Another important and related statistical contribution made by ILO has involved the development of time-use surveys. These have been introduced to better capture the real nature of labor inputs and the structure of the labor market. Sometimes people take two jobs and sometimes they move between personal labor and household activities and occasional engagement in the "gray" or "black" economy. This latter sector makes or sells things or provides services, some of which may be quite sophisticated, as in situations where these units circumvent franchise and cartel arrangements and bypass or infringe intellectual property rights. None of this kind of work is adequately picked up in conventional single-purpose surveys of the labor force, which usually define a job or occupation in a mutually exclusive sense. Furthermore, in completing their survey questionnaires, some respondents make a distinction between "unpaid" and "unremunerated" (in cash) work when deciding whether they should consider themselves economically active.

Certain activities in underdeveloped market economies and their associated methods of payment create ambiguity in resolving the work/nonwork dichotomy. When work is remunerated in kind or conducted on a casual, noncontractual, and ad hoc basis or is perceived as fulfilling or creating a reciprocal obligation on the part of the labor provider, it is usually not regarded as real work or employment. Time-use surveys are designed to get around this problem and to capture how individuals allocate their time to different activities during the day. These surveys generate work profiles that are independent of the type of work and amount of remuneration. They reveal that people can work when they are traveling or in the evening at home, especially since the advent of the mobile phone and laptop computers. These surveys are particularly important because they can pick up unpaid activities such as child care, food preparation, animal minding, household management, voluntary support, and community service that are economically and socially significant. Work that is commonly performed by women is notoriously downplayed in more conventional data-collection processes because they use mutually exclusive categorization methods when describing labor activity. In part, this is a cognitive problem, and it emerges clearly when female rather than male enumerators are used. This statistical bias is a reflection not only of the sociocultural status of women but also their own perceived roles in the economy. The problem has been aggravated by an associated lack of comprehension of the technical terms used in survey work compared with their "conventional" usage. The inadequate understanding of the real contribution women make to economic activity has led, over many years, to an underestimation of the importance of their work and its undervaluation in the national accounts.

Despite what looks like a rather traditional bureaucratic attitude to what constitutes "work," the bureau and ILO staff have made some significant breakthroughs in the approach to labor-related issues. It has also introduced a number of important ideas about how labor markets operate. The ILO's surveys of the economically active population and labor-participation rates are fundamental to understanding how labor markets function around the globe and how these impact, in turn, on the age and gender composition of the labor force. In tandem with the pathbreaking work on the informal economy,[77] the bureau and its consultants have carried out research on the nature of domestic activities and have measured the importance of much unpaid work conducted by women.[78] This research has been expanded to cover subsistence activities more generally and now embraces many other aspects of regular work that are not typically rewarded in cash. In recent years, this interest has increasingly involved the need to refine the design and conduct of time-use surveys. The ILO's role in defining and identifying unemployment, measuring the internal geographical and occupational mobility of labor, assessing the economic consequences of absence from work and the impact of strikes, identifying child labor practices, and defining the scope and meaning of job vacancies represents an important contribution to a better understanding of labor engagement. These inquiries reflect both the emergence of different ideas about work and a delicate balancing between economic principles, cultural preferences, and social and political interests.

Information collected on occupations and education outputs assumed critical importance in the construction of "manpower" plans in the 1970s in the West, and a decade or so later in those developing countries that had embraced central planning or were pursuing "indicative" development plans. Manpower plans were used extensively in the guidance of official training and employment policy. Although manpower planning was not to become a core interest of the central ILO unit in Geneva, it represented a national-level technical cooperation activity that was common across many countries. Manpower (and hence educational) planning eventually fell out of fashion, although efforts are still made through scholarship schemes and special placements to encourage young people to follow particular courses at school, acquire particular skills, and take up science-based technical and vocational training.

Beyond this, in compliance with the ILO's more general concern with living conditions, the bureau provided leadership in the compilation of consumer price indices (CPI). The ILO considered this a natural duty that was fundamental to the organization's basic terms of reference and longstanding concern with real wages and living standards. Privately, some expressed the opinion that the UN could not be trusted with this task and was not the appropriate body to produce information that could be so politically sensitive as the CPI. Some people also felt UNSO was already overextended in its primary data-collection activities and that it could not contemplate taking on the compilation of monthly CPI information. UNSO devoted its attention instead to identifying a system of price and quantity indices compatible with the national accounts. UNSO thus concentrated on the derivation of appropriate (annual) deflators that could be used to adjust current macroeconomic values into constant price volume series. Similar price measures could be used to convert observed quantities and reported physical series into current values. The CPI became the first volume in the bureau's *Statistical Sources and Methods* series; this manual was to serve as a standard on price-measurement procedures (and the relevant computational choices to be made) for the next fifteen years. The methodology was later expanded and has recently been the subject of a more comprehensive review by the Ottawa Group on Prices, a city group whose mandate also covers the much-neglected area of producer prices. Historically, these have been mixed up with commodity prices, raw material prices, and wholesale prices.

Finally, the bureau played a major role in helping the former centrally planned socialist economies transform their labor data to conform with recognized international standards during the period of transition. This required much more than the simple adjustment of definitions and a rearrangement of classifications. Some critical conceptual misunderstandings concerning the definition of the nature of work and of total employee rewards had to be resolved before the data could satisfactorily comply with accepted ILO conventions.

An important step toward improving labor statistics and their relevance occurred in 1993 when the bureau launched its ideas for a labor accounting system. Statistics relating to the labor market are normally fragmented because they come from different sources and have thus been collected for different reasons, usually to meet certain specific and often legislated objectives. As a consequence, the coverage of labor data is occasionally inconsistent and irregular. The use of different definitions and classifications for closely related concepts adds to the problem. Across countries, this lack of uniformity exists within topics such as employment, unemployment, wage and income measures, and other aspects of labor market statistics. A clear understanding of the main concepts used in the description of labor stocks, changes in labor markets, and the interrelationship of labor with the economy is needed to overcome this situation. To meet this challenge, a labor accounting system was devised by the bureau that extended the conventional labor matrix to include education and training activities and the characteristics of migrant labor. The structure provided a mainly supply-side focus on the labor market. For such a system to be truly comprehensive, it was necessary to pay attention to the question of vacancies and the earmarking of those economic sectors and skill and occupational categories where employment gaps tend to occur. The intention was to allow analysts to look simultaneously at the wider scope of annual earnings and labor costs within the context of individual labor rewards while relating these to actual working hours and people's jobs—that is, to "real" labor inputs.

Investigation in this important area has not progressed very far, although UNSO has independently taken up the broader question of human resource accounting. Key inputs have been provided for this initiative by Nobel laureate Lawrence Klein.[79] Klein, who has long been associated with the UN, has also assisted staff in the preparation of the UN's global economic projections model (LINK).

The Measurement of Agriculture

At the end of World War II, the overwhelming proportion of the world's population still lived in rural areas. One of the overriding concerns of almost all countries, both rich and poor, was whether there would be sufficient food produced globally to avert widespread hunger. Hunger and starvation was, and still is, the most evident price of poverty. The extent of hunger and malnutrition is a measure of inadequate economic opportunity that impacts on the ability of individuals and households to function satisfactorily. Many countries want to know, therefore, if enough can be grown locally to nourish the population and support development and industrialization. In some countries, such as India and China, there was even greater anxiety because famine was a proven reality and national leaders feared that large numbers might die of hunger. This was not idle speculation; in the immediate prewar years as many as 17 million had died from starvation in the Soviet Union (the Ukraine especially) as a result of disastrous industrial and collective farming policies. In China and in the Horn of Africa, starvation was endemic. The threat of widespread malnutrition, even in Europe, was very evident in the immediate postwar period. During this time, famine continued to ravage China, causing the deaths of millions more. Political leaders blamed it on the inability of farmers to produce sufficient staple products, particularly grain crops. But it was also a problem of allocating surpluses to deficit areas and of getting out of official contractual commitments to supply external markets. China's difficulties were especially compounded by inefficient storage and distribution of food resources (especially of perishables) and inadequate transportation systems. Early ideas about development and aid were strongly influenced by threats of starvation and a humanitarian concern to feed the poor.[80] Priority was given, consequently, to the preparation of food balances for every country at risk.

The difficulties faced by local populations were aggravated in some countries by the political desire, for nationalistic or strategic reasons, to be self-sufficient in food production, especially basic staples (mainly cereals). Other countries that faced desperate foreign-exchange shortages were committed either to exporting a significant share of their staple crops or to replacing food imports. Most could not afford to buy the food supplies they needed on the international market at existing exchange rates. The U.S. and a handful of other countries gave generously in providing food aid, perhaps most conspicuously in the case of the PL480 program of shipments of grain to countries such as India. However, there was often a wider political and commercial agenda behind this food aid. Unfortunately, whether unknowingly and unwittingly, such transfers may have also contributed to the undermining of domestic production efforts and farming capacity by weakening local market arrangements. Some have further suggested that the type of grain provided was not appropriate to the local area and that people found it difficult to digest because it was not an item in their regular daily diet.

One of the Food and Agricultural Association's (FAO) immediate concerns was thus to initiate the first serious attempt to quantify agricultural production globally, particularly the international output of food crops. The FAO's work on the collection and dissemination of statistical information on food and agriculture represents a core element of the organization's mandate. Article I of its constitution requires the organization to collect, analyze, interpret, and disseminate information relating to nutrition, food, and agriculture (where the term "agriculture" and its derivatives include fisheries, marine products, forestry, and primary forestry products). The first session of the FAO Conference in 1945 provided the rationale: "If FAO is to carry out its work successfully it will need to know where and why hunger and malnutrition exist, what forms they take, and how widespread they are. Such data will serve as a basis for making plans, determining the efficacy of measures used, and measuring progress from time to time."[81]

The statistical system established and maintained by the FAO is characterized by global coverage based on national statistical data compiled by its member countries (supplemented by data from other sources). The FAO provides intercountry comparability based on common definitions and standards. The database is comprehensive in scope, covering key aspects of the production, trade, and consumption of primary food and agricultural commodities of each member country. Because national official statistics are the main source of information, data quality depends substantially on the capacity of countries' statistical systems. The FAO's statistical work benefits, however, from integration with the organization's other information and data activities and from networks of contacts with a range of technical and statistical institutions dealing with crop research, climate changes, and so forth.

To pursue its goals, the agency launched a large-scale program in the 1960s to conduct agricultural censuses in all member countries. The focus was primarily on crop production, but many countries also tried to collect data on livestock holdings.[82] The potential scope of these studies was huge, wide ranging, time specific, and time-consuming (because of the need to encompass seasonal harvests), and it called for sampling procedures. But some very costly benchmark surveys still were undertaken. Sampling methods were generally applied at two levels: first, in the selection of farm holdings, and second, in choosing the plots and crops to be sampled on those farms. In addition, decisions had to be made about the nature of the experiment's crop-cutting to be applied to different plots with different standing crops and more permanent tree crops. The basic equation linked crop yield per acre to plot size to give estimates of gross output (before losses). These various survey approaches involved quite different sampling procedures; each designed with independently distinct objectives in mind. The approaches to both random plot selection and crop-cutting measurement raised new issues about the estimation of areas and yields and the required precision and level of reliability deemed acceptable in the results. Precision was an important concern in the cumulative preparation of national, regional, and global estimates of total crop output. There were also questions about the choice of aggregation procedure and weighting methods. The FAO became a focus of new methodological sampling and national survey work. In the formative years of the organization, this was due largely to the appointment of P. V. Sukhatme, a universally recognized authority on sample survey methodology, as director of statistics. Dr. Sukhatme held this position at the FAO for some twenty years.

The importance of the FAO's agricultural census work was that it made international agencies, aid organizations, politicians, and civil servants aware of the serious plight of the malnourished and encouraged them to think in terms of strengthening policies to meet national and global food needs. This humanitarian concern gave direction to food support and in many ways it marked the beginning of international development aid. It also played an important part in supporting the burgeoning development movement more generally.

Parallel work on personal nutritional needs and calorie intake emerged that was closely linked to this question of food production. Both were defined at an individual level but were determined from a macrolevel perspective. Attempts were made to associate adult (working male) calorie requirements with total available food supply. The latter was assumed to consist of annual production, which was adjusted for stock changes and retentions for seed and animal feed, minus wastage and spoilage plus imports minus exports of unprocessed food. The work was carried out, commodity by commodity, in terms of physical quantity (weight and volume), and the estimates were compiled on a per capita basis, although food consumption and distribution is very much a household concern. Some of these assessments were related only to staple crops, but others were more comprehensive, covering a range of items consumed in the normal average diet. Judgments about sufficiency required some corresponding estimate of a characteristic, or representative, diet, which was usually obtained from special surveys. In principle, adjustments to individual calorie intakes to account for the age and sex composition of the household were also required. Similar adjustment procedures were adopted to estimate poor people's diets when the U.S. poverty line was calculated.[83] In the early postwar period, there is no record of any other adjustments being made in the FAO for the concept of adult equivalence or to account for the fact that a high percentage of people lived in households of more than one person or that the age and sex composition of each household was important. Some people also lived in compounds or in communes. Cohabitation clearly permitted economies of scale in feeding that correlated closely with the size of the family. While the WHO was later to introduce such refinements in their own nutritional surveys, no further adjustments were made at the household level for the inevitable wastage at the cooking (and eating) stage in the FAO work. Crop losses, nevertheless, were taken into account at the macrolevel in preparing national accounts estimates.

The FAO's broad approach encountered many problems. The weights (quantities) of traded goods were not always available; processed, partially processed, and canned food goods were sometimes not taken into account; crop retention for own use, animal feed and seed, and food waste at the household level was difficult to estimate; and alcohol consumption (produced by the household using local sorghum, corn, and barley) was often assigned a production value (and corresponding calorie consumption value) of zero. This was particularly the case if the alcohol was not only produced but also consumed within the household. The resulting measures of individual calorie intake and estimated undernutrition were thus deficient in several respects. The publication of some of these basic series, however, has regularly continued through to the twenty-first century. The estimates have served only as conservative ballpark national averages. They frequently conceal significant local and regional variations. The FAO's calorie norms and their actual estimates of consumption were regularly disputed by the WHO.

Some of the complex sampling methodology that was applied was also criticized by outside observers. It was seen as technically flawed, particularly at the crop-cutting level, because it led inevitably to overestimates of harvested output. Nevertheless, the procedure and the results that the FAO generated drew direct attention to those countries and areas where there appeared to be a deficiency in food supply and demonstrated a need to address this pressing concern. Later, from about the mid-1970s, the FAO developed its own early warning system of crop forecasts, which combined assessments of rainfall and climatic conditions with appraisals of local policy and other available indicators to give some better indication of whether the output of major crops could be expected to increase or decline in the current period. This activity still continues for countries with limited external contact and overseas markets and those that regularly face serious crop production problems such as North Korea, Somalia, Sudan, and other similarly poor agriculturally based economies.

The work on food supply and nutrition was logically expanded by the FAO to generate estimates of poverty and indigence.[84] The definition of poverty was the percentage of people considered to be undernourished. The problem was to link poverty to hunger and thus hunger to undernutrition as defined by an assumed minimum food intake norm expressed in calories. While the percentage of food in daily consumption (invariably measured at a household level) is widely recognized as being highly correlated with total income level—with the very poorest spending what meager incomes they receive both in cash and in kind almost entirely on food (and with the rural poor mostly relying on their own subsistence production to do this)—such simple standards ignored other important nutrient requirements for adequate survival, particularly proteins. Nevertheless, the "legitimacy" of this work was recognized when Dr. Sukhatme was awarded the silver medal of The Royal Statistical Society in 1962. It is noticeable, however, that the World Bank no longer publishes the FAO estimates of either calorie intake or the percentage of population undernourished in each country in its annual *World Development Indicators*. The FAO continues, nevertheless, to produce the core-food balance sheets upon which such estimates are based, and these balances are used to develop detailed estimates of household expenditures on food.

The FAO also initiated, and encouraged at the individual country level, studies designed to assess the overall economic importance of the agricultural sector. The intention was to measure efficiency and value added at the farm level. This was a significant departure from the approach based on single-crop–production taken earlier. It recognized the farm as the economic unit that takes decisions and probably makes the biggest contribution to productivity. Institutionally, it is the farm that transforms agricultural output into potential well-being. These FAO studies took the form of farm economic surveys, and their results were considered to be directly relevant to the generation of more accurate national accounts estimates. While the detail these surveys provided was still important for deriving demand and supply balances, the approach was no longer based solely on commodities. It treated the farm as an integrated economic unit that carries out different activities and produces a variety of crops and livestock by converting a range of inputs into outputs using labor and land. Agricultural production was looked at from an organizational and management point of view rather than from a more detached and dispassionate perspective of deriving total output by aggregating individual holdings and plots of specific crops. Plot-sampling studies, nevertheless, remained relevant to estimates of total quantities produced and aggregate yields in physical units. The FAO farm surveys were important because they related effective resource use by economic units to efficient farm management and productivity in a value rather than a purely physical sense.

During the process of collecting data according to both crop-level and pro-duction-unit methods, it became apparent to some observers that, in the case of homogenous single-crop stands, farmers were generally better at estimat-ing available post-harvest output than statisticians who relied on scientific crop-sampling procedures.[85] While the FAO has never accepted this conten-tion, farmers' estimates have some relevance to assessments of household well-being, not least because they tend to be universally lower than those generated statistically. This is partly because the traditional sampling procedures of sur-veys rarely took into account the more barren areas around the edges of fields and so probably overestimated plot yields.

In recent years, the focus on the household has also become more impor-tant with the introduction of separate household-sector production and con-sumption accounts in the 1993 SNA. As with the conduct and support of agricultural censuses and the large-scale crop-cutting and livestock surveys in the 1960s, much of this work on farm statistics was significantly curtailed through the 1980s as the FAO, in line with other UN agencies, suffered severe budget constraints and ran into serious funding problems. It was thus forced to close down many of its regional offices and country-based data-gathering field operations. This has given rise to gaps in data, and now many country estimates are generated from historical information, observed benchmark parameters, and assumed output relationships and ratios to other variables.

With the emerging current international concern and donor interest in levels of household well-being, the FAO has begun to look at agricultural ac-tivities from a household rather than the conventional area-holding perspec-tive. The questions countries and analysts are now asking are concerned not only with finding out how far farm output provides what is enough for house-hold members to reach a satisfactory nutritional standard (either directly or via market sales) but also whether household-based agricultural activities provide an adequate standard of living for every person in the family. These issues have been combined with global positioning data and household in-come and expenditure survey information to give a more clearly defined pic-ture of differences in living standards across regions that can be associated with distinct geographical locations and topographical features. Alternative crop cultures, farm size, soil properties, patterns of agricultural activity, and labor use also need to be explored.

Probably the most important and far-reaching example of this different approach, in which the FAO played a significant role, was the First National Census of Agriculture in China in 1997/1998.[86] This was a mammoth under-taking and the first of its kind in the country. The inquiry moved from the FAO's traditional farm holding and plot approach to a household-based survey that covered the whole of China. It employed in the process 7 million enumerators and their supervisors. China's census of agriculture examined the relationship between rural household living standards and agricultural activities. It took particular note of the engagement of other household members in rural enterprises and off-farm employment and assessed the value of their contribution to overall household well-being and more effective farming operations.

This represented an important break from the traditional method of conducting an agricultural census in developing countries. One of the main aims of the early studies was to produce comparable estimates of yields. Using simultaneously determined estimates of areas under cultivation, it was possible to generate measures of total crop output by country. This was the FAO's primary interest. It also wanted to gain some idea of productivity levels for major crops by country. The main concern of international policymakers was to improve total output levels and enhance yields and thus to make the use of land and inputs more efficient. They sought to identify those areas where fertilizer, pesticides, and so forth were needed to raise output. As a further objective, the outcomes were expected to help policymakers identify market shortfalls and production gaps at the macrolevel and thereby determine appropriate farm and crop support and compensation strategies. Commodity prices, and the volatility of those prices, was another important question that troubled producers and users of raw materials alike, but it was an issue that was tackled mostly outside this survey mechanism. This concern, nevertheless, gave rise to a number of preferential agreements and special contractual arrangements that were both international and bilateral in nature and that included establishing production quotas and price agreements for certain key tropical crops such as bananas, sugar, coffee, and copra. The holding of farm crops and stockpiling of strategic commodities also emerged as relevant concerns. These measures, the creation of "buffers" and issues related to aid support in kind and subsidies to farmers in the rich countries, have had important and often contradictory downstream implications for the well-being and sustainability of small-scale farmers, itinerant crop-cutters, and other casual farm laborers in the developing countries.

Statistically speaking, the downside of the traditional FAO census approach was that its adoption of common goals gave rise to an assumed parallel requirement to apply and replicate standard methodologies. Some survey procedures and associated data were forced into uniform predefined boxes, irrespective of the level of development, social organization, or unique topography of the countries involved. This issue emerged dramatically when census personnel were confronted, quite early on, with the problem of how to appropriately handle, from a statistical sampling perspective (and hence from an analytical viewpoint), multiple cropping on the same plot and interplanted tree crops and ground crops. Boundaries in these cases are often difficult to demarcate, plots are shaped irregularly and are not always equally planted, and it is sometimes not clear who owns which plots. Many plots vary in size and are scattered around both individual holdings and communal village areas. Different types of farm activity and crop-tending work are spread over the year unequally. The social relationships between landlords, "plot owners," and the persons who actually cultivate the crops have an important bearing on how much is planted, cultivated, and then actually harvested by the farmer as both cultivator and landlord. Nonspecific use of communal grazing grounds poses other measurement problems. Although some of the survey approaches and sampling procedures advocated by the FAO have been criticized as being flawed, unnecessarily expensive, or too complicated and full of errors (which has led in some cases to the abandonment of the surveys), the studies have forced politicians to think seriously about agricultural policies and improving food supplies. This has led them also to address issues that were endemic and perhaps were contributing to stagnant yields and output in their countries. The country studies drew attention to the precarious nature of local food supplies, nutrition levels, and calorie deficiencies, and, ultimately, they underlined the scope of the poverty question and its particular depth of incidence in the rural areas.

The FAO's global concerns became more readily apparent in the area of forestry and fishing in the 1980s, when new ecological problems were beginning to be recognized. In the decade that followed, apparent issues of deforestation, structural changes in species diversity, overgrazing, and overfishing raised urgent global questions and sounded important environmental alarm bells around the world. Thus, while there may have been a certain latitude in the validity of some global agricultural statistics, there is little doubt that the FAO continued to play a significant role over the years in pointing out some important socioeconomic issues and environmental concerns. It is perhaps worth noting that questions of rainforest depletion in the Amazonian basin in Brazil and the extensive rural development project work carried out by the World Bank in northern Nigeria in the 1980s adopted what was considered to be well-tried FAO scientific methodology as the basis for gathering information. In due course, however, the Bank developed its own distinct monitoring and evaluation techniques to test the effectiveness of various agricultural-based development programs and projects it sponsored.[87] The Bank also implemented a separate multipurpose household survey program (the Living Standards Measurement Study Program) for both urban and rural areas to determine living conditions, employment activities, and those factors that contribute to people's well-being.

International Comparisons

For more than two decades after the war, international comparisons of economic values could be made only in terms of some standardized numeraire currency (usually the U.S. dollar). Even today, in the twenty-first century, important economic comparisons are still being made inappropriately on this basis both in the UN Secretariat and at the World Bank.[88] Exchange rates are volatile and are subject to a range of speculative financial and political factors as well as real economic forces that influence capital movements. Exchange rates reflect neither relative price levels between countries nor, with any consistency, movements in national prices over time. In other words, exchange rates do not behave according to an assumed purchasing-power-parity theory expressed either in its strong absolute form (actual differences) or weaker relative form (change over time). This means that when various economic aggregates such as GDP are expressed on a uniform currency basis such as U.S. dollars using existing exchange rates, the results are not comparable across countries. Very often, the reported dollar values represent quite different bundles or quantities of goods and services. This problem arises because the respective price levels vary significantly among the countries in the comparison. Poor countries, generally, have much lower price levels than rich ones, and this does not come out in comparisons of exchange rates. The problem is analogous to that of measuring comparative changes in real economic magnitudes over time where adjustments have to be made to account for the differential price change between any two (or more) reference dates in question. Policy decisions need to relate, in principle, to volumes that are free of price distortions if the concern is to assess the significance of real changes and differences in economic magnitudes.

The absence of a common valuation standard across countries obfuscates important economic questions such as the significance of investment (gross fixed-capital formation) and capital stocks to development, the role and size of government in the economy, or the degree of poverty in the world. This problem was first recognized in the late 1950s by Milton Gilbert and Irving Kravis at the OEEC (now OECD) in Paris. (Gilbert, it has been suggested, originally moved to Paris, in part fearing possible victimization in the McCarthy purges in the U.S. against alleged Communist sympathizers.[89] But, along with Richard Ruggles, he was mainly charged with monitoring the implementation of the Marshall Plan in Europe.) Gilbert and Kravis set out to demonstrate that real international comparisons should always be made in PPP equivalent terms if they were to make any economic sense. In the late 1960s, Irving Kravis, who headed a team of distinguished colleagues at the University of Pennsylvania to pursue this research, took up this work in earnest. The

International Comparisons Project (ICP) was established in 1968 as a joint venture of the UN, the World Bank, and the University of Pennsylvania. It also received substantial external funding from the Ford Foundation and other private-sector organizations.

Over a series of four phases in 1970, 1975, 1980, and 1985, the ICP conducted price and expenditure surveys in a range of countries for different components of final expenditure. The group initially included 10 countries, then 34, then 60, and eventually 64 countries in each of these respective years. By 1980, however, much of the work in the developed world (Europe and OECD countries) had been taken over by the Eurostat in Luxembourg. The OECD then built on the foundations established by Eurostat to compile its own set of estimates.[90] The international program was regionalized (broadly organized by continent or by UN regional commission groupings) in the 1980s, and the central coordination was moved first from the University of Pennsylvania to the United Nations and then, eventually, toward the end of the decade, from the UN to the World Bank. The University of Pennsylvania continued to compile its own set of results in the form of the well-known Penn World Tables. During the early period of this transfer, one of the ICP authors, Professor Alan Heston, transferred to UNSO in New York for two years. His role was to strengthen the basis of UN coordination and help firmly establish the ICP internationally. Some of the others who had worked on the team in Philadelphia also moved to different prices data and international salary comparisons posts at the UN in New York, and one of the early researchers went to the World Bank. The Bank had always shown a special interest in the work and had helped finance the initial studies. It later put together estimates for both the developed and developing countries of the world.

From the mid-1980s onward, using regression-based econometric estimates for countries not directly covered by the ICP surveys, and by making price- and growth-based extrapolations to nonbenchmark years, both the University of Pennsylvania and the World Bank began publishing time series of PPP estimates for most countries in the world.[91] These organizations also generated estimates of the various macroeconomic subcomponents of GDP such as final household consumption (that separately showed, for example, food outlays and household durables), investment expenditures, and government outlays. Some fiscal outlays by governments to individual consumers (for services such as health and education) were added to private consumption to add a use rather than a cost or payment perspective to the comparisons to allow a truer comparison between countries pursuing different public policy regimes.

UNSO maintained an interest in this work from a distance. It was less than enthusiastic about investing its own scarce time, budget, and staff in such a resource-hungry program, especially in the financially constrained period of the 1990s. UNSO retained a presiding but not always very well-informed role in the program; the real knowledge and expertise about the program resided mostly in the OECD and Eurostat. It is at this time that the global oversight of the ICP was shifted, almost by default, to the World Bank.

Nevertheless, with the support of outside consultants (who were partially funded by the World Bank), the UN did eventually publish a UN handbook on the International Comparison Program in 1992.[92] This helped guide some of the subsequent work in this area, especially in informing the developing countries of the aims and raison d'être of the ICP. The manual, in fact, had been produced several years earlier but it was not made widely available at the country level early enough to help support much of the ICP fieldwork in the next major wave of inquiries in the developing world the following year. Although the handbook contains detailed lists of the standard final expenditure categories (referred to as "basic headings") relating to household consumption, government expenditure, and capital formation and an extensive list of the items to be priced, the available documentation does not provide sufficient guidance about several important aspects of item selection. It does not clearly define the process for computing the annual national average prices for each of these items. This procedure is quite complex, and methods differ depending on the nature of the product and type of item to be priced; for example, a kilo of apples, a chair, a postage stamp, a haircut, housing rent, a telephone call, a railway journey, or a farm tractor. In some cases, such as motor vehicle and housing space prices, hedonic methods rather than direct price observations are adopted.

Organizationally and statistically, the ICP is a large and complicated exercise to manage and implement. Over the years, the world has become a much more complex and sophisticated place than it was when Gilbert and Kravis first embarked on this work almost fifty years ago. The program has run into a lot of criticism, particularly over the past few years, and the quality of the reported PPP estimates has been seriously questioned.[93] It was one of the few programs to be reviewed formally by the Statistical Commission. Its irregular and inadequate financing has been a major problem in efforts to get the program properly established and supervised. The preoccupation of UNSO with the 1993 revision of the System of National Accounts meant that its overview of the ICP program tended to get sidelined. Nevertheless, all critics have joined in one voice with researchers and analysts in underlining the importance of the PPP estimates and accompanying price and expenditure data for policymaking. These figures are essential to a proper understanding of the scope of inequality, the extent of poverty and the dynamics of real economic change. Analysts have also stressed that without the ICP, the national accounts remain incomplete. Yet it is only recently, with an enormous new effort by the World Bank to put the program onto a safer financial and operational footing, that there has been any full international endorsement of this essential exercise.

While the World Bank contributed significantly to the early financing of the ICP (and has recently taken on the global coordination of the latest round of inquiries), the Bretton Woods organizations never fully embraced the concept the program presented. They preferred to see the exercise as a piece of research. In large part this was because the initial emphasis of these studies seemed to suggest that the calculation of PPPs, in line with the writings of Gustav Cassel, would enable policymakers to explore the extent of observed deviations in countries' official exchange rates from the derived PPPs, which some assumed reflected a notion of an "equilibrium" rate of exchange. Such a line of approach challenged the IMF's basic mandate on exchange-rate maintenance and was fundamentally inconsistent with the institutional management imperatives of the Bank, which applied the exchange-rate methodology of the Atlas method to help determine its operational guidelines in devising its lending programs to member countries. That the ICP is essentially the spatial analogue to well-established temporal price index measurement and analysis and is thus about the determination of differences in price levels across countries and between major expenditure categories was less well recognized.

In efforts to get international support and build new coalitions, one of the problems has thus been the fact that policy management and aid decision processes in the leading international agencies have been thoroughly institutionalized and remain entrenched in conventional exchange-rate–based numbers. It has suited management not to have to rethink its methods and priorities and perhaps change historical and current perspectives.

But if there is one international statistical task that clearly falls under the responsibility of an international statistical agency, such as UNSO, it is the ICP. Yet UNSO, possibly because it was facing severe budgetary pressures and freezes on established posts at the time, shirked this responsibility and failed to take a proper intellectual and organizational lead either directly or through the Statistical Commission. At the same time, a number of highly influential national statistical offices—already burdened with their own heavy national work programs and data obligations—were clearly pressuring the UN to back away from the ICP. They exerted some pressure on UNSO not to ask countries to take on any "new" international statistical commitments, particularly programs that were as data intensive as the ICP. But in the area of international statistics, nations have a duty to contribute to international data collection. That is part of the responsibility of being part of the UN community.

Although UNSO was only peripherally involved in the ICP and the countries concerned really needed to take their case to the OECD or Eurostat authorities, these national statistical offices realized that UNSO, indirectly through the Statistical Commission on which one or more of them also served, could possibly do more to block the program than it could to influence its wider adoption. UNSO would have preferred to see the whole problem go away. In the eyes of many of those in organizations committed to working with PPPs in a policy context, UNSO did not exercise the necessary leadership expected of the UN in this critical area of data collection. At the most fundamental level, the outcomes of these studies have to do with informing policy about the more efficient and equitable distribution of global resources and keeping differences in price levels as well as price changes under some control.

In terms of internationally comparable measures of relative economic progress, especially because the relevant metrics refer to final expenditures and, specifically, personal consumption, the ICP provides the only basis for determining whether the gaps between countries are widening or narrowing. It quantifies the extent to which the economic relations between countries have become more or less equal and where differences are occurring. The results of the program provide an important and consistent perspective on how far people are better or worse off than they were ten, twenty, or thirty years ago. These are, surely, vital elements of the UN mandate and thus of the highest importance to the implementation of its operational agenda.

Box 2.4. Stone and Seers: Merlin and the Mariner

Richard Stone and Dudley Seers each made very different but important contributions to statistical thinking. Both abhorred any suggestion that facts be fit to theory and spent their lives building theory around observed facts and creating frameworks that more usefully depicted how the real world worked. Equally charismatic, flamboyant, and intellectually persuasive in their individually distinct, but almost opposite, ways, they both gathered an influential following that was to have a major impact on the development of official statistics.

In personal demeanor and appearance Stone was the complete gentleman. He always dressed impeccably, cutting a very elegant and majestic figure. Attired in his smart charcoal-gray and black velvet–collared Edwardian frock coat, bow tie, and black felt hat to match, he could have been easily mistaken for the archetypal stage magician as he strolled along the corridors of the Department of Applied Economics in Cambridge with his silver-handled cane swinging gently in his hand. Time after time in the area of economic statistics, Stone revealed his magical touch. A wizard more than a conjurer, he was the master of the alchemy that transformed the base metal of raw data into statistical gold. From such materials, he fashioned the finest numerical artifacts with which the most relevant analysis could be wrought. He did not have to resort to deft sleights of hand or rely on tricks hidden up his sleeve. He never had to pull any rabbits from the hat or dazzle with stardust to impress people with his skills and foresight. Stone's wizardry with statistics came from long-standing practical experience, profound knowledge of the subject, and a meticulous attention to detail. To every question he applied a singular concentrated effort and penetrating insight. He possessed a unique gift of wisdom and a vision that enabled him to unify preconceived notions about how different pieces of information could fit together in a larger, more complex scheme of things. To this foresight he added a sense of order, composure, and direction that was simply a wider reflection of his personal style. Above all, he generously shared his ideas, knowledge, and individual approach with a politeness, patience, and understanding that is the hallmark of all truly great people.

Seers, too, possessed the same remarkable understanding and a clear perception of what was relevant and important. More casual and cavalier than Stone, Seers was no less precise or exacting. He was extremely pragmatic in his quest for "truth" and search for knowledge to improve the effectiveness of development policies. When dressed in his chunky woolen sweater, his appearance epitomized the many weekend sailors who "mucked about in boats" back home in New Zealand. He was, in fact, a seasoned mariner used to unraveling knots. He also learned and applied his statistical craft in New Zealand. Not surprisingly, therefore, once embarked on a new voyage of discovery, he could not only be an explorer and navigator but also a potentially mutinous seadog and formidable pirate. His sense of adventure was fired by an impatience to map uncharted shores, to dig up hidden treasure, and to uncover buried gold in unexplored and unknown territory. True to his calling, after returning from a long voyage, he would recount tales of adventure about how the charts were poorly drafted and could not be trusted or how they had been tampered with deliberately in order to mislead. He would describe how officials were fond of repeating standard mantras and of flirting with economic folklore and foreign ideas. He was worried about how many politicians had a penchant for courting local superstitions rather than accept what they could readily observe around them. He waged long and lonely campaigns with both messianic passion and personal bravado with the sole intention of plundering the existing store of conventional wisdom. Throughout his life, he retained an urgent sense of mission to uncover any possibly concealed traces of gold, however minute. Seers was no mean statistician. His established reputation drew on a strong practical and methodological background acquired under the discipline of the government statistical service and as a researcher at the Oxford Institute of Economics and Statistics. He would nevertheless scuttle and capsize with enthusiasm any vessel that purported to be carrying valuable new goods if, in fact, he believed it to be bringing in damaged cargo.

Both were held in enormous respect.

Table 2.3. Economic Time Line

Era	Event	Ideas and Issues
1945–1949	Beveridge Report and Plan (1944)	Goal of full employment
	Rationing and regulation (prices, investment controls)	Welfare state established
		Nationalization of the means of production
	Housing shortage	
		Prioritizing resource allocations
	Dollar shortage	
		Postwar scarcities of materials
	Marshall Plan (June 1947)	
		"Factory" housing; apartment blocks
	Indian independence (and partition)	
		Exchange controls; devaluation
	Economic Survey of Latin America (1949)	
		Rebuilding of national infrastructure in Europe
	Winding up of UN Relief and Rehabilitation Administration (UNRRA) in 1949	Socialist planning introduced in developing countries
		Terms of trade trends (Prebisch)
		Center-periphery model
		Ending of emergency humanitarian first aid support
1950–1959	Challenge of social market economy alternative	Apparent better performance of centrally planned states
	Cold War and military buildup	Resource allocation distortion
	Energy crisis	European Coal and Steel Community (1951)
	Early decolonization	
		Secure access to raw materials threatened
	Industrialization and import-substitution strategies	Tariff protection
	European Economic Committee (1957)	"Dependentista" theory

(continued)

Table 2.3. Economic Time Line (*continued*)

Era	Event	Ideas and Issues
1960–1969	(First) UN Development Decade	Growth rates set at 5 percent per annum
	Era of "The Plan"	Transformation of agriculture
	OAU (1963)	Investment and capital: output priorities
	Emergence of Japan	Nationalization in developing countries
	Intermediate technology	Enhance productivity, improve export performance
	Kennedy Round	"Manpower" planning
	Pearson Report (1968)	Promote international trade
	ILO World Employment Program (1969)	Strengthen aid
		Widespread devaluation of major currencies against U.S. dollar
1970–1979	Second Development Decade	Growth rates set at 6 percent per annum
	New International Economic Order (NIEO)	Pressure for decolonization
	U.S. suspension of the official gold standard (1971)	Foreign reserve values
	ILO Employment Mission to Kenya (1972)	Identification of the informal sector
	Collapse of Bretton Woods fixed exchange-rate system (1973)	Floating exchange rates and currency baskets
	Tokyo Round	Tariff reduction
	Decline in "Plan" approach	Focus on monetary policy and prices and incomes policies
	OPEC and first oil crisis (1973)	International Energy Agency
	Second oil crisis (1978	Pressure to conserve fuel reserves and raise efficiency

Era	Event	Ideas and Issues
1980–1989	Third Development Decade	Growth rates set at 7 percent per annum
	UN Conference on the Least Developed Countries (1981)	LDC growth rate set at over 7.2 percent per annum
	Uruguay Round	Expansion of scope of international trade
	Debt crisis	Institutional reform
	Washington Consensus	Liberalize markets; nonintervention by the state
	Structural adjustment	Privatization; "getting prices right"
	Emergence of "Asian Tigers"	Pressures to compete in international market
	Rapid inflation in Europe	Tightened monetary policy and higher interest rates
	Fall of Berlin Wall (1989)	Collapse of communist command-and-control mechanisms
1990–1999	Fourth Development Decade	10 percent industrial growth target
	Issues of transition	Structural transformation
	Promotion of foreign direct investment	Modernization of the "new economy"
	Technology transfer	Inflation control
	Trade liberalization	Performance indicators
	Monetary management	Corporate influence and power as a challenge to state authority
	OECD initiative: Shaping the Twenty-First Century	
	Globalization	
2000–	Millennium Development Goals	Establishing targets for poverty reduction, health education, and the environment
	Creation of a single currency in Europe (2002)	

3

The Social Dimension

- Measuring Social Change and Progress
- Directions of Social Measurement
- Social Indicators
- Tools of Inquiry: Surveys and Sampling
- Statistics on Women
- The Measurement of Population
- The Measurement of Education
- The Measurement of Health
- UNDP Human Development Index

Measuring Social Change and Progress

The debt society and culture owes the field of statistics for its work in unifying ideas about the human condition is incalculable. Many aspects of life that affect its quality, however, are not directly measurable and their significance remains difficult to assess. Statistics make an important contribution to the essential structural framework around which the building blocks of modern society and the fabric of local culture are constructed. They influence how social institutions evolve and mold the way ideas are progressively shaped. Data which raise issues about systems of education, the role of women, the security of conurbations, and so forth, have an undeniable impact on the political landscape. They affect the policies of those countries whose governments seek guidance about the appropriate social route to follow and how it can be financed.

If life is a quest for values, reason, or purpose or merely a search for greater security, then it cannot be governed solely by individual responsibility. A harmonious social existence will inevitably require a balanced oversight and contribution from a higher responsible authority which is able to see the wider picture and promote and secure commonly held goals. Societies are too complex and the scale of the problems confronting individuals in society often too extensive to allow some social issues to be tackled solely through the exercise of free personal choice. To help better understand the nature and quality of life, an individual's own place in society, and the importance of an economy that supports such a status and other attributes that are desirable but not directly quantifiable, such as freedom of speech, certain sector-specific socioeconomic indicators are needed. It is not just a question of performance evaluation but one of being able to add to the ability of individuals and households to exercise the essential freedom of choice (which they can do mostly by virtue of the incomes they receive) the value of the individual and collective nonmarket goods and services that governments make available to their citizens.

Box 3.1. The Ideological Influences on Social Thinking

It is possible to underestimate the influence of national ways of thinking and firmly held political ideologies on the early formulation of UN policy and procedures. In the social domain, certain U.S. politicians believed, probably for quite irrational reasons, that capitalism could be undermined and that the American way of life could be threatened if ideas were espoused that extolled the merits of adding a social dimension to policy. Some were deeply perturbed by the use of the terms "socialism," "the welfare state," and "collective" or "state" production and viewed the ideas with a mixture of suspicion and skepticism.[1] The leaders of industry had created an ideological edifice around entrepreneurship, individualism, and material well-being that prominent politicians were prepared to defend and protect. Some, such as Senator Joseph McCarthy, the chairman of the Permanent Sub-Committee on Investigations of the Senate Committee on Government Operations, even set out deliberately to pursue "the enemy from within." This committee, which was set up in 1952, had the power to identify and isolate from the community anyone who had shown (or had been reported by his or her "neighbors" to have shown) even the remotest connections or sympathies with communism or socialist ideas. The committee particularly hounded those who had visited the countries that supported socialist ideas. There is no doubt that such thinking infiltrated the U.S. State Department, affecting its relations with foreign countries and its basic approach to the UN. Socialism, collectivism, and cooperation were not part of the accepted language in the U.S. Social ideas threatened the traditional puritanical view that an individual's welfare was primarily of their own making and was solely dependent on their personal work ethic, a philosophy that was rejected by most of postwar Europe. The perception was growing in the rest of the world, especially among the poorer members of societies, that social status and minimal well-being were not the automatic rewards for hard work. But in the early years of the UN, the U.S. remained skeptical about the need for, even the desirability of, any social measurement. This directly influenced the attitude of the Statistical Commission, which opposed for some years any work on social statistics other than in the area of population and demography.

The relationship between individual autonomy and integrity, on the one hand, and social and political authority, on the other, needs to be formalized. It falls to governments to make judgments about the personal and social need for public goods. For the most part, the social choices and priorities governments must consider defy easy quantification. The decisions states actually make when faced by constrained resources and different, difficult-to-assess social circumstances require the construction and use of a range of social measures and other general proxy indicators to guide their policy choices. In this area, the variety of criteria is bewildering.

In life, only one thing is definite and that is death. If the postponement of death were the only goal that mattered in life, then all of GDP would be spent on this objective. Preserving people's health would be the sole concern. If life is more a question of daily survival, however, other things such as food would be a priority.[2] People also value the future differently. Some attach greater importance to a known present than to an uncertain future. Many believe that the quality of life matters, not just its length.[3] The question of time preference, taking things now instead of sometime in the future, is fundamental to choice and crucial to economic understanding and individual behavior in seeking desired outcomes. Social indicators, which represent proxies for various aspects of personal well-being, are thus essential to an understanding of the achievement of certain social objectives as well as civil progress in general. But they hold up imperfect mirrors to society for both conceptual and practical measurement reasons.

In most of Europe in the immediate postwar period, the weekly wage of the average working man was barely sufficient to keep ends together and to meet the ordinary needs of the family. Education and health services, however, were primarily the state's responsibility. Later, the postwar reconstruction effort and the period of expansion during the late 1950s and early 1960s was accompanied by a boom in commodity prices in most developing countries. Many people experienced a significant improvement in their material living standards. Politicians could claim that people had "never had it so good."[4] In some countries, however, concern was growing that the benefits of economic prosperity were not being spread among the whole community and that some segments of society remained vulnerable. Some families continued to suffer and remained excluded or neglected. People also began to worry about the environment and depletion of resources. The specter of Malthus loomed large in the debate about food and energy supplies. Those concerned about enhancing social well-being began to focus attention on the government's direct role in introducing a more effective redistribution that went beyond the provision of welfare benefits. They began to pay attention to how social objectives could be achieved by the more equitable provision of nonmarket goods and services to the public. "Equality of opportunity," by itself, it was felt, might not be enough.

Since its inception, the United Nations has been concerned with issues of national development, levels of living, and related social, economic, and environment questions. These have always been considered key elements of national culture and identity, reflecting a country's independence and sovereignty. Enshrined in the UN Charter is the requirement to promote "higher standards of living, full employment, and conditions of economic and social progress and development" (Article 55), but the Charter also prohibits the direct interference of the organization in the internal affairs of its member states. This poses a difficult dilemma for the UN in influencing the direction of social policy. In the context of the UN's work in macroeconomic policy and statistics, however, the Charter's edict eventually began to drive the parallel development of social reporting. But it is only since the mid-1960s that the UN has supported national, regional, and other international initiatives to compile social indicators on levels of living. The importance of distinguishing age, gender, and other key characteristics relating to the social and economic circumstances and physical conditions that affect people's lives was not recognized until recently. Initially, there was some tension and debate about whether any office of the UN Secretariat should be involved in making social assessments of member countries. The UN feared that any attempt at social measurement might be seen as the Secretariat making political "judgments" about member governments, especially because an early intention was to quantify "development" and create an ordinal listing of countries along relevant common scales appropriate to selected social indicators. Indeed, it is understood that, unofficially, some governments, and not just those of the developing countries, tried to block what was considered as potential trespass into their political affairs. They were worried the indicators might hint at the establishment of "targets" and might thus define approved goals for governments.

The idea within UNSO, however, was simply to build up a new database containing a variety of social measures and gender-specific indicators. To aid this process, Bob Johnston, an official who had been involved in some of the pioneering work on indicators that had been earlier carried out in the U.S. by its Department of Health and Social Administration, was brought in for this purpose. (Previously Johnston had been transferred from the U.S. to the OECD in Paris to cooperate in similar work being conducted there.) But UNSO could make very little headway in this field because the initiative was not endorsed by the Statistical Commission. A portion of this indicator work was subsequently outsourced because it was believed it could be conducted more appropriately and effectively as a research exercise. Thus, a significant part of this activity was transferred to the UN Research Institute for Social Development (UNRISD), which was established in Geneva in 1963. Some felt, consequently, that UNRISD would become bogged down in an essentially academic exercise to compile synthetic and composite indicators. Rather than highlighting specific social concerns, the indicators produced by UNRISD were mainly designed to identify the underlying factors that determine development "progress" and to provide an alternative to the GNP per capita statistic. The agency conducted some technically interesting studies but most were not directly useful in helping governments make decisions about social programs and priorities.

After the war, governments became interested in the dynamics of the relationship between social conditions and economic change only slowly. An understanding of this relationship offered two different routes to social progress: one, through changing society directly, and two, by bringing about improvements indirectly via the economy. How a strong economic performance—by creating larger incomes, new capabilities, and a broader tax base—could contribute across the social spectrum to enhanced human well-being became a primary concern of officials and a priority for many countries.[5]

The debate over the need to measure social development directly began to emerge in the 1960s, when it became evident that economic progress on its own would not secure the many social objectives governments had identified. The desire to measure social progress sprang, at least in part, from a fundamentally humanistic idealism that was prevalent throughout Europe in the postwar period. The populations of wartorn societies yearned, perhaps romantically, for a new social and political utopia. This ideal was seen as the ultimate rationale of life, as a yardstick for establishing the goals and assessment of all human action. Philosophers such as Bertrand Russell fueled these feelings and lent intellectual substance to their validity.[6] Influenced, inter alia, by Jean-Jacques Rousseau's theory of human nature and society, Robert Owen's nineteenth-century vision of a model civilized industrial society, and even, perhaps, by Karl Marx's critique of unbridled capitalism and the human exploitation he believed it entailed, people began to develop their own ideas about social progress. Each of these philosophers offered different visions of society that captured people's imaginations. This clearly had an impact on the political scene, affecting the thinking and culture behind the approach to social development. But most social thinkers felt that the main job of the democratic state was to exercise its moral authority and decide on priorities for society. It had to accept overall responsibility for improving social conditions.

Social measurement has had a checkered history in the UN system. Some important statistical initiatives stumbled at the first hurdle (endorsement by the UN Statistical Commission), while others never even left the starting gate. In the case of social indicators, confusion reigned at the point when the proposals went forward to the stage of formal international review. The reasons for this were primarily political and were related to the UN philosophy of not interfering in (or inquiring into) the internal affairs of its member states. But the worries were partly technical in the sense that the statistical system that was initially contemplated as the standard framework for social data seemed too complex, yet it was not designed in a sufficiently flexible manner to accommodate many of the proposed thematic indicators. The system also seemed to require too many resources for many countries to consider as an operational model for guiding the collection of social information. The poorer developing countries, which had weaker statistical organizations, argued they did not have the capacity and resources to implement the sophisticated models and procedures that were being proposed. Above all, in the first few decades of its existence, the whole emphasis of UNSO strategy had been on trying to persuade countries to adopt a common statistical approach that would yield uniformity and comparability in key economic policy variables, leaving specific domestic social concerns as an internal matter for the countries themselves.

Outside UNSO and the direct influence of the Statistical Commission, the UN specialized agencies such as UNESCO, UNICEF, the WHO, the FAO, and the ILO were all developing their own statistical ideas and systems in the social arena. The data systems they developed in the social area were designed to fulfill their respective organizational mandates and focused primarily on questions of education facilities and status, health and nutrition, the condition of women and children, employment, and working conditions and occupational hazards. Agencies such as the FAO and, later, the United Nations Environment Programme (UNEP), UNICEF, UN-HABITAT, and the UNDP introduced a strong social focus into their databases. In this early period, however, UNRISD was assigned the task of producing social statistics and giving some sense of direction to data compilation in the social area (even if it never actually initiated practical guidelines). Unique among UN agencies, UNRISD apparently had no specific policy responsibilities and could develop its own agenda and research program, subject to the approval of its governing board.

In a way, given the heavy political emphasis in the General Assembly on the freedom of peoples, particularly in the context of decolonization and the UN body's support for independence movements (which reemerged, only much later, as concerns about human rights), the early lack of interest in social development is surprising. It was a reflection, in part, of the lack of operational contact between the central UN Secretariat, its affiliated offices, and

UN specialized agencies. The UN Secretariat was not a user of the data UNSO routinely produced. Neither the Secretariat nor UNSO fully recognized the needs of other users for internationally comparable social data. While regular consultations by UNSO with official data producers continue, it is unfortunate that there has never been much direct communication between the ultimate users of UN social data and UNSO itself. Certainly what little information-sharing has gone on has rarely been in the same spirit as that between the UNDP (and specifically the Human Development Report Office), UNICEF, the UN regional commissions, and the wide constituency of users of national and international human development data. Policy-relevant social information cannot be properly and systematically compiled in the same way as economic data, at least in a form that provides regular built-in checks on data reliability. The desired statistical coherence does not have quite the same conceptual integrity as cross-tabulations of economic data that can be balanced and articulated (as receipts and payments) in row and column margins that give identical totals corresponding to theory.

Although the first *Report on the World Social Situation* was published in 1957 under UN auspices, the work made little impact and had weak political momentum. The primary interest of policymakers was in economic progress. Development was understood almost universally to be an economic issue and it was loosely (but mistakenly) interpreted in many countries as industrialization. In any case, UNSO did not see itself as centrally responsible for social statistics and it did not pursue any special mandate in this area during this period. There was no functional directive or organizational arrangement within the UN system to empower UNSO to collect or compile social information from member countries.

In the beginning, therefore, the UN placed less emphasis on the social area. Subsequently, however, a comprehensive framework was created under UNSO auspices to integrate social, demographic, and related economic and other statistics. This idea was originally devised by Stone in the mid-1960s with the goal of providing an appropriate organizational and conceptual structure to guide the collection and analysis of social data.[7] The framework drew on concepts and methods developed for the 1968 System of National Accounts and integrated them with basic statistical data-collection activities in social administrations such as health and education. It provided a coherent, systemic, and integrated approach to evaluating social change. Although it was never formally adopted by the Statistical Commission, the model still plays an important role in determining how sectoral social issues are approached from a longer-term perspective. It serves the interests of future planning for social facilities and human capital well, but it does not measure social status, relative deprivation, or individual well-being effectively.

The aim at the time was simply to link social statistics and social policy scenarios to an SNA-type economic framework to carry out an integrated macrolevel analysis. The approach was designed to allow different modeling and simulation procedures to be linked to projected population and related demographic accounts through cohort analysis. The system provided the foundation for developing a sequence of transitional matrices for evaluating social conditions that was especially suited to tracking educational status, achievement, and the performance of a nation's education system. There was an automatic chronological link between age sequence and grade progression. Many saw what was referred to as the System of Social and Demographic Statistics (SSDS) as an important adjunct to "manpower" planning that also tracked the provision of human capital back into the economic mechanism. At the bottom line, "the economy" determined what social alternatives were financially feasible, and the human resource development that took place as a result then strengthened the capacity of the economy to grow over the longer term. As a statistical system, the SSDS was elegant and sophisticated. It was internally coherent, and it formed an integral part of an even wider and more comprehensive institutional structure. Embedded in the core of what appeared, superficially, to be just a descriptive data framework was a system of interconnected transitional matrices and Markov chains that gave theoretical statistical substance to the model's properties. This encouraged the desired dynamic analysis and facilitated the preparation of projected social outcomes based on known parameters and alternative simulations for different social sectors and activities. Within the planning mode that was in vogue at the time, the system delivered information that had immediate policy relevance because it relied directly on the observed operational features of the economy and the prevailing national, social, and demographic characteristics.

Undoubtedly innovative and important though this work was, and quite brilliant in its conception, the SSDS was not put into operational use by the UN statistical system. This was more for practical reasons than it was because of concerns about its basic philosophy. Quite literally, the SSDS was ahead of its time. It facilitated links between analysis of the social sector and economic capacity. Where it failed was in its inability to describe social disadvantage. The SSDS was more a model for fortifying resource needs than a social data structure. It helped to identify which social sectors required support and where governments needed to allocate more resources and invest in new facilities. It was essentially an aid to central policy and the formulation of medium-term sectoral planning scenarios rather than a true social framework. The features of the SDSS enabled governments to think strategically and plan ahead for education, health, and social protection in a rational and robust way. It helped them determine priorities and decide, for example, how many teachers were needed at different education levels in the years ahead and what new types of school buildings would be required. All this, in principle, could be broken down regionally. The SDSS was, potentially, a powerful policy tool for medium- and longer-term planning for the social sector. But it was not suitable for social planning in a personal sense or for analyzing social deprivation and need. It did not identify or attribute any significance to poverty, and it did not characterize the socioeconomic status of those who had less access to the social and communal provisions of government such as public health and education services. It was not a tool, therefore, for identifying the socially disadvantaged. The SSDS was simply a macrolevel modeling system, a policy framework for organizing and resourcing sector programs.

Box 3.2. The UN Debate on Social Statistics

The archives of the UN Statistical Office are remarkably silent on the important debate that informed the decision taken in the early 1970s to develop social statistics. The documents do not speak about why there was such protracted discussion on this issue and why, as a consequence, it took so long to implement a recommended program of data compilation in the general area of social inquiry. The decision not to formally adopt Richard Stone's original proposal in 1972 for a system of social and demographic accounts, in particular, is shrouded in mystery. The decision seems to have reflected more a feeling about what the international statistical community did not want more than it did a belief that something else that might be simpler and potentially more useful could be developed. Stone's social framework linked directly into the 1968 SNA, which depicted the nature of the economy. It thus seemed, at the time, especially relevant in an era when policymakers shared a considerable enthusiasm for comprehensive development planning. The proposed framework, although it was not officially approved, was nevertheless issued as a technical UN publication, *Towards a System of Social and Demographic Statistics.*[8]

The decision, while essentially sensible and correct in an international context, represented a compromise between potential users and producers. What does seem to be generally understood is that Simon Goldberg, then director of statistics at UNSO, invited Claus Moser to be the rapporteur of the UN Expert Advisory Committee on Social Statistics, which was chaired by Stone. Moser, himself a distinguished former professor of social statistics at the University of London, had been appointed in 1967—in a significant break from British civil service tradition—as the director of the UK Central Statistics Office (CSO). Under clear direction from the Labour government of the time, Moser had been given a specific mandate to develop social statistics. The requirements included a directive to "find out what was happening in society," especially in the areas of education, employment, housing, health, and crime, and to search for links between these social phenomena. (One suspects that Moser had a significant hand in framing his own technical terms of reference.) The Office of Population and Census

Statistics was merged under the umbrella of the CSO in order to help perform this task. New surveys were planned and the existing Family Expenditure Survey was expanded.

Moser undoubtedly saw the virtue of applying the SSDS to some of these issues because it offered the chance to explore, in a technical way, the analytical links between social status and societal structures at different points in time. He also realized that despite the comprehensive nature of the SSDS approach, the system did not correspond to any known equivalent body of social theory. But even if it did not reflect an appropriate conceptual social construct, the SSDS clearly provided the critical connection between empiricism and statistical method and had the potential to reveal some of the important social interlinkages of interest to researchers. Moser's thinking appears to have been aligned more with that of his French counterparts at INSEE, who focused directly on specific themes of social investigation. It is not surprising that the UN expert committee, while acknowledging the pathbreaking importance of Stone's work, took the view that the time was not yet ripe for its formal adoption as a UN manual. The committee believed that national statistical offices, many of which were still struggling with the complexities of implementing the somewhat unfamiliar framework of the 1968 revised SNA, would face considerable difficulty in introducing another intricate and sophisticated data system that also required the development of yet more new data sources. But the UN encouraged further research, and it is interesting to note that the SSDS was taken up by Timothy King, a former member of the Faculty of Economics at Cambridge, in his work at the World Bank on analyzing demographic changes and social development programs. Similarly, the SSDS stimulated Seers's own reinterpretation of Stone's social life profiles and led to his construction of a conceptually similar approach that had the merits of indicating how individual life chances and the probability of experiencing different situations were often conditional upon a person's prior social status. Most significant, perhaps, the methodological procedures the SDSS used were applied to the first OECD *Yearbook of Education Statistics,* which was published in 1974. This volume was prepared under the initiative and direction of Angus Maddison, who viewed the OECD's effort as a contribution to the understanding of the role of social phenomena in growth, employment, and redistribution. The presentation adopted was designed to show the flow of pupils by age and sex through different levels of formal education within a framework of demographic accounts that was relevant to various cohorts of children. The data were then linked to comparable information on public expenditures on education and, in a few select cases, by level of education. By 1975, however, with much higher inflation and considerably slower economic growth in the OECD countries, there was a reexamination of the size and structure of government and of social spending in general. Several social transfers as well as work on producing statistics about the supply of educated persons were later dropped.[9]

In a special interview conducted in June 2000 for the UNIHP, Moser declared how impressed he and many of his contemporaries were with the elegant coherence and dynamic structure of the SSDS. He admired Stone's seminal contributions to statistics and to an improved general understanding of economic reality. He expressed these feelings at a moving eulogy at Stone's memorial service in King's College Chapel in December 1991.

Two related social modeling developments, which occurred later, belong to the same family. They were also centered on the SNA. These were the Social Accounting Matrix (SAM) and satellite accounts. Both approaches have experienced mixed success and are still being developed in various contexts. Even without formal UN backing or endorsement, SAMs have proved very popular in a handful of countries that are both developed and developing. They are used as an aid to medium-term planning and for evaluating the distributional significance and impact of certain policy decisions. As such, both move the SSDS forward because they better characterize the types of benefits persons or households of different socioeconomic status receive. SAMs have been used to assess the interrelated social and economic effects of such varied decisions as increasing electricity and fuel prices, conceding to a major wage demand from the public sector, and raising the school-leaving age. While the use of SAMs has been discussed extensively at international conferences and continues to be on the agenda of some UN statistical meetings, they have never been formally acknowledged or endorsed by UNSO or the UN Statistical Commission. Despite their name, SAMs remain essentially economic in character.[10] Their basic dynamics are driven primarily by macrolevel monetary and financial policy and the distribution of the means of production. They depend heavily on the different feedback mechanisms that come from distinguishing the various responses people (or households) of different socioeconomic status and income levels make to economic stimuli. Most recently, SAMs have been used to good effect in assessing the impact of selected environmental policy changes.

Satellite accounts deal more directly and specifically with developments in the social sector. The idea of satellite accounting was first promoted by the French, who had a long tradition in strategic sector-level planning. It has had somewhat greater success than other macrolevel approaches, although no particular format or structure of satellite accounts was ever approved by the Statistical Commission (except, recently, for the tourism sector accounts). The approach has the merit of matching physical inputs and outcomes to defined costs and other inputs. It has been used effectively in France and its administrations, but in most applications, the methodology has had more to do with evaluating real performance and the costing and valuing of outputs across interconnected sectors in society (such as health and education) than with identifying areas of social concern. They seem less useful in determining social priorities related to the poor and economically weak.

In the mid-1970s, UNSO set out to provide a universal orientation to social indicators. It was intended the proposals would be drawn up regardless of the statistical experience and level of development of a country and irrespective of the different social and economic circumstances and policy interests each country faced. In the actual presentation of the series, as well as in drawing up classifications for indicators, UNSO decided, however, to distinguish between specific sets that were considered more relevant and practicable for countries at various stages of development. The categories of countries suggested were "least developed," "developing," and "developed." This procedure was deliberately chosen over a "lowest common denominator" approach that defined a standard set of social measures that was appropriate to all countries. The stratified approach posed fewer practical problems for those poor countries faced with limited resources and a constrained range of possibilities for collecting data and for pursuing alternatives for planning appropriate policy and social programs. The strategy thus initially moved the UN away from the idea of a unified social theory based on the assumption of a common social scale toward a social appraisal method that was more practical, country specific, and related to progress already achieved.

The first UN *Handbook on Social Indicators* clearly shied away from presenting recommendations on social indicators. The Statistical Commission frequently reiterated the importance of an indicative and nondirective approach to social measurement. It focused on possibilities and alternatives to suit particular circumstances instead of advocating a fixed set of universally valid indicators that might prove inapplicable to a number of situations and countries. The commission set its face against any suggestion of "targets" and social achievement goals. It is interesting that in recent years the identification of indicators to track progress has nevertheless leaned heavily toward defining objectives and achieving universally agreed-upon global development targets such as the UN Millennium Development Goals.[11] This "policy direction" approach has been taken because donors and international agencies have become increasingly concerned about the lack of attention paid by governments of developing countries to social strategy. The international community is thus urging improved monitoring of policy and program performance and the adoption of common assessment standards by all countries that receive aid.

The development of social measures is a wide-ranging, multifaceted process. It brings together basic statistics from many different fields, drawing on various sources and data-collection programs, including censuses, surveys, and administrative records, all dealing with a variety of topics. The UNSO approach is designed to identify measures to provide broad indications of social change and to suggest measures that can meet a variety of user needs. At the same time, the indicators should keep track of evolving social concerns and of policies intended to resolve them.

Preliminary guidelines for social measurement (particularly for social indicators) were accepted by the Statistical Commission at its nineteenth session in 1976, and these were subsequently issued in 1978.[12] The commission decided that the guidelines should be published and widely circulated; it recognized the various purposes social indicators might serve in planning, policymaking, and social research. The monitoring and analysis of social change related to levels of living and circumstances of life as a whole became a primary interest. The commission also noted that the series described were intended to provide a useful inventory of social information that could be consulted by interested producers and users of statistics in the process of identifying and defining indicators that would be useful for a number of different purposes.[13] The handbook provided a detailed presentation on the concept and relevance of social indicators to measure levels of living and a discussion of the social and economic factors and areas of social concern that were believed to influence levels of human development. This was similar to the approach taken by the OECD, considered at the time to be the lead agency in this area, in its own social-indicator initiatives. The guidelines emphasized that traditional basic data sources for social, demographic, and related economic statistics could be developed and used to compile these indicators. They also reinforced the need for the harmonization of the underlying statistical concepts, classifications, and definitions rather than the development of parallel ad hoc data sources and concepts, many of which already existed in one-off research studies and specially commissioned surveys. In practice, as analysts and policymakers began to use these various social measures, they realized that some of the fundamental criteria and conditions proposed were basically incompatible with defined social goals. The use of existing data sources clearly predetermined the nature of the indicators because the available raw data reflected the social structures, concepts, and procedures that underlay them. New information had to be gathered, particularly to highlight possible social interrelationships.

Both the general methodological work and actual compilation of social indicators was undertaken by several units of the United Nations system. Some of these, such as UNICEF and the United National Population Fund (UNFPA), had a clear thematic and subject interest in the data. Other non-UN international organizations such as the OECD and, later, Eurostat had their own specific mandates. From the outset there was considerable political interest in indicators dealing with special international activities and events. These included the United Nations Decade for Women, The Decade of Disabled Persons, Health for All by the Year 2000, and The World Program of Action for Agrarian Reform and Rural Development. These programs contained a number of explicit and implicit directives that necessitated the development of indicators. Hence, they stimulated a considerable amount of conceptual and operational work, which undoubtedly strengthened the international reporting systems for particular indicators. Suggested lists of indicators for national and international use were also issued by the FAO, specifically for monitoring progress in agrarian reform and rural development; the WHO, for monitoring Health for All by the Year 2000; and UNCTAD, to assess basic social and economic progress in the least developed countries.

Lists of indicators were also prepared for general national and international use by the Council for Mutual Economic Assistance (CMEA), which represented the former socialist countries of Eastern and Central Europe and the Soviet Union. These lists were based on an extensive array of measures that were developed for reporting regularly on social production and related matters in these countries. In practice, some of these measures had a strong economic focus. From the early 1970s, the Economic Commission for Europe (ECE) in Geneva regularly convened working group meetings that were concerned with both the reintegration of social, demographic, and related economic statistics and with making actual comparisons of social conditions among its member states using social indicators. The ECE was particularly keen to monitor the relative pace of progress between the CMEA countries and Western Europe and used indicators to estimate GDP, national income per capita, and economic growth for the centrally planned economies. Paradoxically, therefore, while the West was at last beginning to look at how social progress was related to economic development, the CMEA was combining indicators to estimate economic progress in its countries.

In 1985, UNRISD published a comprehensive methodological study on indicators for the measurement and analysis of socioeconomic development. UNRISD's most valuable and lasting contribution in this area was the establishment of a comprehensive worldwide *Research Databank of Development Indicators*.[14] The United Nations University also published a general review of indicators methods, but it never played a significant role in the development of working measures.[15]

The annual UK publication *Social Trends*, which regularly included analytical articles that appeared separately from the more detailed statistical tables, was one of the first national official documents to report routinely on social progress.[16] It set a precedent for subsequent social review work, in particular, by combining analysis with data and focusing on levels of living and the different circumstances that influence various levels of well-being among com-.munities, their households, and individuals. INSEE also favored this approach. Other countries adopted this model of interpreting social data, but, UNSO could not do the same for political reasons.[17] The crucial importance of this detailed social measurement work was to bring data activities back down to the level of people's lives. National indicators, though they are normalized by population counts to provide an "individual" perspective, do not do this. Most indicators are too generalized and aggregative to serve as useful measures of the discriminatory effects of location, education, and class. This has since forced policymakers to reexamine people's socioeconomic status and the prospects for progress in society. Before this time, little statistical work went beyond the normal bounds defined by GNP and average income levels.

Box 3.3. UK *Social Trends* Report

The UK's pioneering *Social Trends* report, published annually from 1970, provided more narrowly defined but useful examples of social interconnection. The publication set out to analyze various observed phenomena against the context of location and other socioeconomic circumstances and societal influences. Thus, for example, the prevalence of different types of crime against property or persons and the assessment of some narrower notion of human security might be approached in terms of social status, housing conditions, population density, unemployment, access to welfare benefits, community facilities (such as street lighting), and so on. The UK developed this capacity to report on small areas (or neighborhoods) from its census and survey work, and the Central Statistical Office (now the Office of National Statistics) felt it was important to introduce some guiding and interpretative notion of the socioeconomic status of individuals and households—what some might refer to as a statistical definition of the class structure. This subclassification of people into classes is now more widely accepted as a means to understand better the social relationships associated with, for example, health status (and related medical provisioning), occupation, or education. Predefining groups under study according to their socioeconomic status—such as occupation and income—is now widely seen as essential in guiding policy toward delivering social services efficiently and prioritizing community needs. Social differences could also be superimposed on geographical groupings of population characteristics using GIS (geographic information systems) points of reference. From a practical policy perspective, *Social Trends* provides guidelines for an approach to administration that, within the normal framework of ministerial responsibility and authority for social programs, helps authorities at various levels tackle and resolve some critical resource-related social problems. The approach is integrated in the sense that it brings into play things that appear to matter to people's well-being and that have a bearing on social outcomes.

Directions of Social Measurement

Since the beginning, the domain of social measurement in the UN has been one where the tensions between the physiocrats and policy pragmatists, on the one hand, and the philosophers and social thinkers, on the other, have come to the fore. At one extreme were those practitioners who wanted simply to track, at the microlevel, what progress could be observed in attempts to achieve specific social goals in such fields as education and health. At the other extreme stood the more abstract modelers and social theorists, who demanded that a holistic perspective should be taken in order to understand society and social progress. At the root of this debate lay the contention that it was just as important to understand the behavioral elements that determine *why* people decide to follow a certain course of action as it is to assess the status they have achieved. It was also necessary to record *how* they had reacted to different social conditions. Above this debate lurked the potential confrontation with party politicians about social priorities and the resolution of conflicts surrounding their choices between economic and social needs (and the need for taxes to be levied to meet them).

Nevertheless, there was basic agreement that an interlinking data framework of some kind was important. The idealists wanted the framework to be fully integrated—much in the same way the national accounts were integrated through an explicit articulation of the social gains and losses the system identified. They argued that such a framework should allow for the analysis of social stress and reactions to that stress as well as more general pressure-state-response mechanisms involved in social interaction. Early reaction of statistical offices was to produce tables of indicators depicting inputs, outputs, and impact, separately listing the relationships between them across society. Thus, in an education table, the data might refer to number of teachers as inputs, pupil-teacher ratios and average class size as outputs, and examinations passed or grade reached as an impact.

If a social framework was to provide suitable guidelines for policymakers, it would need to be comprehensive, touching particularly on the weakest and most disadvantaged members of society. But very early on, it was recognized that a comprehensive framework that described changes in society as well as their causes would be impossible to formalize in an overarching sense. This did not stop staff in UNRISD and other outside researchers in academic circles such as Seers, Lucas, and others at the Institute of Development Studies (IDS) and Cole at the Science Policy Research Unit (SPRU) at the University of Sussex, for example, from attempting to identify different horizontal and vertical and even chronologically linked systems using some common coherent theme such as life expectancy to explain social patterns. Interacting with different UN and international agencies, these research initiatives (such as the "social life cycle" approach) were launched in an attempt to develop what were considered to be more meaningful and dynamic frameworks for social analysis.[18]

These proposed frameworks went way beyond the more conservative and conventional "area of social concern" classification logic that was originally used at the OECD and subsequently adopted in the UNSO approach.

In part, the differences in perspective on social issues within the UN system, including those related to the issue of gender, reflected the nature and relative strengths of different UN governing bodies. The work of UNSO came under the regular oversight (but not supervision) of the Statistical Commission. In practice, the commission was primarily an endorsing rather than a regulatory body at the time. While it maintained a conservative stance, the Statistical Commission nevertheless exercised a somewhat more powerful influence over UNSO than that wielded by the Social Commission in its own oversight of the research activities of UNRISD.[19]

In its first five years or so, UNRISD set out to define an appropriate methodology for measuring the social elements of development and the relationship of social change to economic variables. The problem the UN faced was how to give a clearer social orientation to development planning which, until then, had concentrated solely on economic progress. Policy at the time concentrated heavily on the need to allocate scarce resources (particularly investment funds) as efficiently as possible and how to determine national investment plans. UNRISD, uniquely, allowed and encouraged its staff to express their own views. Papers were published under the respective authors' own names, with the usual caveats that their views might not represent the official policy of the organization. Most researchers in academia recognize this but view such independence as an enormous strength in any institution because it encourages people, data producers and users alike, to expand the limits of their conventional thinking, challenge prescribed research horizons, and think outside the box. But ideas expressed in this way can give rise to serious internal conflict and disagreement, especially when budgets are constrained and programs come under the scrutiny of an external oversight body. Before leaving UNRISD in 1969 for the Institute of Social Studies in The Hague, Jan Drewnowski, a widely acclaimed international authority on social measurement who developed the Level of Living Index, declared: "It is probably fair to say, in respect of the papers that I prepared, that the discrepancy between my views and those guiding UNRISD research policies was quite considerable."[20]

Drewnowski's ideas were controversial (some might have even argued that they were abstract or impractical), but he did lay down some general principles to guide the approach to social measurement that still serves as a basis for debate. Generally, the principles he enunciated were sensible and incontrovertible, but applying these principles in a practical way was difficult. In the field, therefore, it was left to his colleagues such as Wolf Scott, who had done pioneering studies in Kerala, India, to set the more pragmatic standards for social policy guidance. Drewnowski's first contention—which is now widely accepted at all levels—was that what people want is not more national product but better social conditions so they can secure increased well-being and a higher quality of life. This perspective goes beyond the pure accumulation of material goods and services. His views were very similar to those earlier propounded by Gunnar Myrdal in his *Asian Drama*.[21] But governments were not yet ready to acknowledge the validity of this point of view. Their argument went like this: Higher incomes enabled people to enjoy increased consumption which, in turn, led to improved nutrition levels and better health. Higher incomes expanded opportunities for individuals and brought not only better lifestyles but also greater capability to acquire their needs and less vulnerability to social risks for households. Higher incomes allowed individuals to enjoy more sovereignty of choice over what they wanted and how their lives were run. The resulting increase in consumption endowed households with greater security and personal well-being, providing self-sufficiency on a more sustained basis. Many benefits to society were directly attributable to higher real incomes. An increased food intake combined with a more varied and better-quality diet improved the health of families and individuals. They could spend more on housing and the comforts of the home, including acquiring the convenience of immediate access to a safe water supply and internal plumbing. The resulting higher taxes could be used to support improved public services and social amenities and allow the greater distribution of benefits to those who were less well placed in society. The problem with this argument was that it was becoming clear to many observers that the higher incomes mostly accrued to those who were already better off than the average and a large part of the population was being left behind.

Drewnowski argued that "facts" that were reflected in the variables of national accounts surveys were not the same as those which constitute "social conditions" or which could stand as a proxy quality of life. It is doubtful whether he would have even been prepared to accept some of these economic variables as belonging to a subset of any measure of well-being because he called for the creation of new analytical tools and a data framework that would be better able to deal with the social side of development.

Drewnowski argued that what is measured in terms of economic variables is observable and readily quantifiable, but those measures do not convey everything that decision-makers desire to know about social conditions. He set out to identify methods to give quantitative expression to various phenomena that, by general consensus, constituted the main aspects of the social conditions that represent gains in human welfare. His ultimate goal was to get social variables explicitly embedded into national planning, both as desired outcomes and as factors that contribute to the implementation of a development plan's goals.

The problem Drewnowski and many others since have faced in measuring social conditions is how to begin thinking about social status and social changes in quantitative terms. This requires a conceptual leap of faith because, practically speaking, most social phenomena cannot be considered as "quantities"; they need to be replaced by some quantifiable near-equivalents and qualitative assessments. He pointed out that unlike, say, real output or prices, a given social phenomenon might have several quantifiable aspects; schooling, poverty, and communications are just a few examples. Nevertheless, Drewnowski did not mean to imply that any of the phenomena could be readily quantified in an overall meaningful way. Instead, he argued that social phenomena are representative complexes of correlated facts. He argued that conceptually, although some of those facts may overlap, they can still be aggregated in a composite, synthetic sense using either equal weights or relevant population measures (such as specific age-sex groupings) or some other implicit value weights.

UNRISD developed not only an extensive database of impressively high quality but also some new methodological procedures. One important outcome of these initiatives was a better understanding of the intrinsic spatial relationships between series of different types (indicators of levels, growth rates, ratios, etc.) that were incorporated in much cross-tabulation, economic modeling, and graphic analysis. UNRISD research also drew attention to problems of transformation, cardinal scaling, and aggregation. Later, UNRISD's social concerns expanded to embrace questions of civil conflict, social instability, and issues of governance.

One thing most researchers seemed to agree about was the need for an appropriate "social context" in which numbers could be understood. In other words, in the absence of a defining social theory, what sort of framework would convey most meaning? UNSO followed the OECD idea of approaching these questions by identifying different categories of social concern such as education, health, and crime. This required categorizing a set of indicators that, while independent, jointly illustrated the progress (or lack of progress) toward certain social goals. The achievement of progress in each respective social field might not necessarily be linear or sequential, but the statistical measures and indicators most often proposed to monitor this transformation possessed relatively limited scaling properties. Many series suffered from the drawback that they often reflected only relatively well-defined administrative actions. They thus represented the manifestations of official regulatory control and other supervisory or advisory decisions. How countries report crime and measure morbidity are good examples. Administrative series were sometimes at variance with similar indicators, which supposedly reflected the same phenomena, because they were drawn from different sources. Each source has different coverage and perspective. For example, school enrollments and attendance data culled independently from household surveys or even population censuses rather than from regular official files and school records consistently show a relatively poorer achievement in providing education. On balance, the social analysts would prefer to take the household data as more accurate, but they are not available on a regular basis.

UNSO and its various expert technical groups thought long and hard about developing an overall integrated framework for social indicators, but in the end it kept its general classification framework. UNRISD, on the other hand, came up with composite and synthetic sets of development indicators that served a different but important purpose. Their derivation of an overall indicator of social development proved to be a solution with which many analysts profoundly disagreed. While everyone acknowledged the importance of integrating social data sets, few felt that any overall measure could be devised to serve the needs of both a social overview (with appropriate aggregation) and social connectivity (illustrating motives and incentives). Although UNRISD's composite indicator of development was technically sophisticated, it was dismissed by observers and UNSO as too complex and insufficiently transparent. No one knew what it measured or felt that what it measured was very interesting or useful. It was not clear how changes in the index should influence policy and how, in any case, these changes could be regarded as reflecting policy. No one knew what steps to take, practically, to move the index significantly in an appropriate direction. By contrast, the UNDP's human development index, which first appeared at the end of the 1980s, obtained immediate political (if not professional) approval.

The preoccupation of UNSO and UNRISD with comprehensive measures and social data systems seems curiously misplaced now. UNSO's concern was primarily with creating the statistical concepts and the appropriate general classifications to process new social data, while UNRISD was more intent on generating composite social profiles using already available data. Both focused on national datasets. UNSO was set up mainly to advise government statistical offices on these matters, whereas UNRISD felt it could call in a wider group of users and producers to determine what was needed to provide a proper social perspective and give expression to these needs. UNRISD's primary interest in research was to explore how different levels of development, in their broadest sense, could be related to a series of "correspondence points" across a range of indicators. Eventually, in its composite indicator of development, which required international comparability, UNRISD boiled down its index to a core set of eighteen variables that provided the most comprehensive common coverage across countries about the general well-being of their societies. The core set of measures was determined by a matrix of cross-correlations between the various social variables. The agency experimented with many other combinations and produced a wide variety of indicators, some of which had an even more extensive coverage of social conditions (but, correspondingly, a less comprehensive country coverage).

There were two basic ideas in the UNRISD approach. One was to see whether progress in a particular chosen field in a given country measured up to the level that should have been attained by a country at some defined stage of development (according to scores achieved by other countries in the "correspondence" chart or equivalence scale). The second was to ascertain how much a particular economic or social profile gave rise to some assessment of development progress in general. This idea presupposed that economic and social inputs were primarily interactive and did not work against beneficial and desired social outcomes. The procedure was designed mainly to test if economic development gave rise to uniform social progress, as many politicians would have liked to have claimed it did. It was not an independent assessment of social progress. The analysis of particular countries highlighted some interesting observations. Iran's strong economic profile in the 1970s and early 1980s appeared to give rise to a level of social progress along a wide range of fronts for the population at large, which was lower than might be expected. Studies of Sri Lanka and of subnational states such as Kerala, on the other hand, showed unmistakably that social achievement could be obtained even if remarkably little attention was paid to economic inputs and progress as these concepts were conventionally defined. How social achievement subsequently fed into economic goals and then influenced the pattern of progress was not pursued analytically by either UNRISD or UNSO.

Some considered UNRISD to be the enfant terrible within the UN system. Although its activities were submitted to an advisory board, it enjoyed the luxury of independence and pursued certain special interests in its own way with little apparent external supervision or control. When the rest of the Social Development Division (which, in theory, it was expected to serve) was moved from New York to Vienna, UNRISD put its roots down in Geneva, removing itself still farther from any unwelcome bureaucratic intrusion in its research programs and routine supervision of its regular operations. This gave rise, in due course, to some political and administrative dissent when its pursuit of certain other paths of investigation of civil conflict was eventually called in to question. UNRISD's ideas and experiments were important and its approach was innovative; it pushed the envelope of social measurement. It was essential that these approaches be explored to improve general understanding about development.

Social Indicators

The social indicator movement, which began in the late 1960s, developed quite separately from the official postwar interest of governments in the regulatory side of statistical monitoring. The primary purpose of such measures was to supervise the distribution of public services and various transfers of household benefits provided under the newly established welfare-state programs introduced across Europe. The scope and limitations of what the state took on as a responsibility was the constraining factor on what was measured. Early studies focused heavily on monitoring food and nutrition intakes (reflecting the continuing legacy of rationing in countries such as the UK), especially of children and nursing mothers. Naturally, because of the extensive damage to private property caused by the war, there was also a concern throughout Europe to provide housing—a task that fell mostly to the government rather than the private market, although private contractors were extensively involved in the actual construction of social housing projects.

Certain social (and economic) indicators of progress were also compiled internationally—at the ECE, for example. These produced—by indirect means—comparative estimates of GNP and measures of development progress in the socialist states of Eastern and Central Europe. Such estimates were not generated officially by the Council for Mutual Economic Cooperation (Comecon) countries behind the Iron Curtain. These states produced quite different estimates of "national income" that corresponded to their own notion of social production. This early emphasis on proxy measures had an influence on how the first UN working groups—which drew in specialists in particular fields from different countries in Europe—approached the question of social statistics and reviewed the choice of indicators and ways to use them.

The renewed interest in social indicators emerged from the increased awareness of the limited capability of the national accounts to quantify welfare, particularly in nonmarket circumstances. Issues such as satisfaction, fulfillment, social participation, happiness, comfort, and security remain elusive and subjective. They are not readily amenable to objective, reliable, and robust quantification and comparative assessment. Countries nevertheless recognized that the various circumstances and conditions that generally contribute to certain desirable and identifiable states of well-being—such as adequate shelter, good health, sound education, effective policing, clean water, efficient solid waste disposal, and an unpolluted atmosphere—could be assessed more directly using both cardinal and ordinal scaling procedures. These measures could thus represent proxies for certain phenomena and serve as indicators of those changes in circumstances that were not directly observable and measurable in themselves.

In the process of developing indicators, the first thing that was done was to monitor overall social progress at the country level. It was argued that social indicators such as infant mortality or life expectancy, which were founded on a standardized population base that implicitly treated everyone with equal importance, were more "equitable" and less misleading as a standard of progress. Normalizing by population rather than a common currency unit meant the indicators were not subject to the bias toward higher-income groups inherent in GDP and other indices that weight total expenditure. Thus, social measures were deemed to be fairer and more balanced indicators of "delivered" development progress. It was subsequently realized, however, that this was not necessarily true in the case of population and that income, too, could have socially desirable consequences.

Taken by themselves, average national measures of social condition can similarly conceal wide discrepancies in actual social attainment. This is because national averages take little account of other important issues such as access to and availability of social resources. These features could discriminate against certain groups and restrict people's use of supposedly freely available nonmarket collective goods and services such as health or education. Regional disparities in social resources also affect household well-being. More recently, therefore, agencies such as UNICEF have begun to develop more informative cross-sectional "social panoramas." Under its own specific mandate, UNICEF has been working in association with several UN regional commissions such as the Economic Commission for Latin America and the Caribbean (ECLAC) and with local UNDP offices to add a socioeconomic dimension to a range of policy-relevant social measures it uses to monitor the provision of health, education, and other communal services by governments. These disaggregations are intended to give a better idea of the spread and impact of social benefits and the corresponding progress in well-being across different population groups. The data tend to show that in areas where, theoretically, people can enjoy public education and health services equally, poor families get a raw deal and end up at the bottom of the pile or at the end of long waiting lists; the per capita value of the services the poor receive is consistently less than other groups. Agencies such as the World Bank which are concerned with allocating resources to support development in the poorer countries of the world and who traditionally fund programs and projects have also started to devote attention to the social impact of their policies and, quite specifically, their effect on the poor.

Several of the recently recommended indicator lists are policy related. These include indicators for the OECD's Shaping the Twenty-First Century initiative,[22] which were absorbed into the UN's indicators for the Millennium Development Goals initiative. The intention of these indicator lists, which cover a broad spectrum of issues, is to keep track of what is happening regarding poverty in its broadest sense. The main focus is on low-income countries that receive donor support. UNSO, taking for its part a more general view, had earlier proposed a Minimum National Social Data Set (MNSDS), which consisted of a core group of indicators drawn up by a team of experts whose objective was to achieve the widest country coverage of social issues. In this list an attempt was made to incorporate all the more pertinent development goals defined by a succession of global summits. UNSO has also lent strong support to the UN Development Assistance Framework (UNDAF) and United Nations Fund for Population Activities (UNFPA) initiatives on indicator construction. An array of measures has been suggested to assess the varying needs and capacities of developing countries to take advantage of different UNDP program initiatives. The UNDAF measures are designed to help countries and their donor partners make development assessments that are common across countries and thus more readily define their respective development programming needs and priorities. Sustainability is a matter of primary concern in these appraisals.

Quite apart from these efforts, the UNDP Human Development Office set out to compile its own Human Development Index (HDI) in its first report in 1990. Although its exact format has undergone significant changes, the HDI is a simple composite index designed to measure development progress.[23] The index, which bears a strong resemblance to the earlier Physical Quality of Life Index (PQLI), gives relevant weight to social progress as reflected in education achievement and health status. This is then combined with comparative per capita income to assess the capabilities of individuals to achieve personal material goals. The HDI has suggested a path of progress somewhat different from that indicated by the traditional measure of annual GNP (or GDP) per capita. It has affected perceptions of the rankings of countries in terms of development, and the HDI has undoubtedly made a political impact as an advocacy tool.

Other than some intervening work related to the role of women that UNSO carried out in association with United Nations International Research and Training Institute for the Advancement of Women (INSTRAW), most of the work on establishing a social framework and compiling social indicators at the New York headquarters was sidelined in the latter half of the 1980s. In hindsight (although the question was raised at the time), this meant that the UN had little or no evidence with which to counteract the concerted pressure from the Bretton Woods institutions to implement, at some social cost, structural adjustment policies to turn around the economies of poorly performing developing countries. Later data compilation conducted alongside the preparation of the first report on *The World's Women* in 1991 was one of the earliest UNSO efforts to adopt a methodology of trend analysis and to use derived statistics.[24] This marked a departure from the more conventional UN presentations of raw data in tabular format. In the mid- to late 1990s, the issue of monitoring social progress, particularly poverty and its gender characteristics, assumed a new policy priority not just for aid donors and agencies but for the global community in general. This renewed emphasis was driven by a series of high-profile social and topically specific global summits.[25] UNSO then began to reassert some influence on these questions. Initially, however, its engagement was not strictly on matters of substance. It was more concerned with the purpose of bringing order and control to what it perceived was an unnecessary burgeoning of social measures. UNSO wanted to control the proliferation of indicator lists, mainly because it feared that if they were to be officially mandated, these requirements would place an undue burden on the statistical community.

Elsewhere in UNICEF and the UNDP, the development of social indicators continued to move on apace. This area of work also took off in the World Bank with the publication in 1987 of what subsequently became an annual report on *Social Indicators of Development* (SID). The original SID report created two-page spreads for each member country depicting the broad progress each had made along a number of key social fronts, taking a long-term (15–25 year), medium-term (5–10 year), and relatively short time period and current perspective. But even earlier still, in 1978, under the initiative of the president of the Bank at the time, Robert McNamara, the World Bank had launched its first annual *World Development Report,* which included an array of (mostly economic) indicators in a separate statistical annex. Eventually, this annex itself grew into a distinct World Bank publication and, in incorporating the SID data and amplifying the format with data drawn from a wide variety of sources, it took center stage in 1997 as the annual *World Development Indicators* report. This report contains separate statistical sections covering people, the environment, the economy, the state (and markets), and indicators of governance.

Tools of Inquiry: Surveys and Sampling

An important part of what the world understands as "truth" or reality has been gained from carefully designed statistical observations of circumstances and events that note and explore the relationships that surround them and analyze their significance. What looks like abstract statistical ideas and theoretical concepts with no obvious relevance to many social and economic issues emerge as important tools of discovery in most primary fields of empirical inquiry. Well-chosen statistical methods establish the appropriate framework for testing hypotheses and provide the numerical alchemy required to facilitate a more profound understanding of what is being observed. Nowhere are such investigative techniques more important than in the area of survey design and sampling procedures. While most survey methods cross the boundaries between the economic and social, the topic is seen as a means to investigate human-related social questions.

Scientific sampling methods allow analysts to go beyond the straightforward question of "Can it be figured out?" and to ask, "What degree of confidence can potential users have in the reliability of the derived results?" In other words, "How precise is a particular survey estimate?" Statistics thus move beyond the scope of descriptive method to that of inferential analysis. This provides the essential link between specific propositions and hypotheses based on selective data that relate to perceived or observed phenomena, characteristics, and relationships and a more definitive judgment about the "truth" and the general validity of such observed conditions to the statistical universe concerned. Statistics thereby contribute to a more rigorous and integrated knowledge structure. In addition, by taking smaller and more selective scientifically designed samples, the use of statistics reduces the total costs in time and resources of taking complete counts. Such samples are not only more detailed but also, invariably, more interpretative, revealing, and insightful. Often, too, their results are more relevant and accurate.

UNSO's interest and involvement in the development of the interconnected topics of sampling and survey methods as they have been applied to different fields of official inquiry has followed a somewhat checkered and spasmodic path. An initial enthusiasm and keen interest in these techniques was expressed by the Statistical Commission in 1946. Before the war, sampling methods had been only occasionally applied, especially in matters of economic and social investigation. When UNSO was set up, more conventional and pedestrian modes of data collection were common. The Statistical Commission felt clearly that sampling was one of the main priorities for statistical development, and the topic appeared regularly on the early agendas of the commission. Strongly influenced by the authority of P. C. Mahalanobis and others, who saw considerable technical and financial merit in pursuing this path of statistical inquiry and data compilation, the commission encouraged UN member countries to adopt sample survey methods more extensively. Members of the commission thought that in most fields of inquiry sampling would prove to be a less expensive and less time-consuming means of general data collection. The appropriateness of the technique to the poorer and mostly agriculturally based developing countries, which possessed fewer statistical resources and had minimal finances at their disposal, was clearly recognized. The approach seemed especially relevant to the compilation of information about crop production where estimates of total output (a phenomenon that, for the most part, was not directly measurable) could be obtained indirectly through separately collected data on plot yields and total crop areas.

Soon after UNSO was established, a number of seminal academic texts dealing with sampling methods appeared. Most of these were theoretical and somewhat mathematical and technical in character and were mostly applicable to agriculture.[26] UNSO felt that a more user-friendly manual dealing with sampling procedures was required to move the topic out of a clinical laboratory context into the area of practical operations. Nevertheless, in preparing this manual, the UN turned to several of the authors who had published these seminal texts for their guidance and advice. It sought their help in devising a program to illustrate the various applications of sampling methods to actual surveys. What UNSO got was not, in the ultimate analysis, a text that proved as useful as expected for managing and conducting surveys, particularly in samples of households and enterprises.[27] Instead, the UNSO document represented a more simplified treatise on the merits of alternative sampling procedures. The manual weighed the various pros and cons of each sampling method, but it tended to pay greater attention to the theoretical and technical choices presented than to the practical questions and operational relevance of a particular sampling design and the survey approach required to assess a specific problem. The manual made little or no reference to the nature of the universe (or population) and the adequacy of the sampling frame. The procedures were applied to a series of examples using the results of a hypothetical agricultural survey. Other types of surveys and areas of inquiry for which a different sampling approach might be appropriate were hardly mentioned, let alone discussed in any detail. The common problem of nonresponse and how to cope with it and other common problems of survey organization were not mentioned.

Nevertheless, *A Short Manual on Sampling* was published by the UN in 1960 and went into widespread use.[28] A second volume, which would have contained a useful compendium of actual surveys and descriptions of the sampling techniques used, was never completed and published. It was thus left to national statistical offices, along with some UN specialized agencies such as the FAO, the ILO, and UNICEF and certain regional commissions, to sort out the complications of sample selection. These organizations experimented with questionnaire designs, survey management and organization, enumeration procedures, and so on. They had to decide on such matters as crop-cutting experiments, method of inquiry, household interviews, and enterprise questionnaires. Those involved did much to promote this area of statistical work, and in many cases they were able to implement initiatives that have now become common practice in survey design. Some of these initiatives included the introduction of a continuous rotating sample design, area sampling, integrated multitopic surveys with specified modules, panel sampling and in-depth subsampling, and post-enumeration surveys.

Volume I of the *Manual* was divided into two parts. Part I was aptly entitled "Theory," and Part II, "Sample Process, Formulae and Examples." The introduction contained a preliminary note on mathematical notation, which set the general technical tone for the rest of the report. The authors of the manual appeared to have struggled hard to reconcile their declared aim of providing a simple guideline for official survey practitioners with an equally serious academic concern of ensuring a reasonable degree of rigor of expression. The latter was necessary, it was argued, because even in the basic elements of sampling, there were inherent complexities that could not be resolved without some recourse to mathematics. For local survey organizers and field staff, the manual proved to be of limited use, but for generations of students sitting for university exams and applying for professional qualifications in applied statistics, the manual (and its theoretical part in particular) served as an essential text.

Part II, despite its forbidding title, actually turned out to be more practical. It provided simple examples drawn mostly from the area of agricultural surveys that were designed to illustrate a variety of sampling processes. Each was prefaced by a note about the appropriate formula to be used for estimation purposes. But sampling inanimate and immobile objects such as plots of land and standing crops poses fewer problems than sampling households or firms. The manual admits that some of the examples chosen might not have been typical, even of crop and livestock sampling. The case studies were limited, therefore; they only characterized agricultural survey methodology in general. Part II was primarily intended to show how the various calculations should be performed once the data had been collected. It referred only incidentally to the potentially wide range of sampling procedures in practice and to the fact that, in agricultural surveys especially, these procedures might be dictated by the nature of the terrain and physical logistics. Readers had to work this out for themselves because there would be variations in the results obtained as a result of applying different sampling procedures. The manual gave little consideration to the need for local adaptations to take account of limited local statistical capacity, unsophisticated administrative arrangements, unknown populations, and so forth. The manual did not pursue practical discussions about the general conduct of a statistical inquiry, the scope of survey training (for interviewers and their supervisors), and the organization of data and the processing of results, including the treatment of nonresponses and problems of coverage. A particular omission was any detailed overview of nonsampling errors which, because of the unsatisfactory sampling frames available in many developing countries, was a genuinely serious problem, restricting the use of the manual as a working handbook.

The first draft of the manual was prepared in house in the UNSO. This was subsequently and significantly amended by a team of experts that included, inter alia, Tore Dalenius, Edwards Deming, Morris Hansen, Walter Hendricks, and P. D. Thionet. Each of these experts had authored a well-known theoretical text, which is referred to in the manual's brief bibliography. The influence of the standard works of W. G. Cochrane, P. V. Sukhatme (who was later to head the FAO office in Rome), and Frank Yates is also clearly apparent, particularly in the choice of examples drawn from agricultural statistics. But too few people with practical survey experience were involved; as a result, the manual is an interesting illustration of technical overkill. It lacks the critical step-by-step instructions that local officers in the field in places such as Malawi or Uganda needed to guide their actions and survey planning. The fact that they actually got surveys going in these and other countries is due, in no small measure, to the high quality, practical skills, dedication, and effort of local staff and to the professional expertise of the experts who were hired as technical advisors.

The main problem with the manual, paradoxically, was its excellence as a text and theoretical workbook. Because it did not include practical survey advice, some official statisticians were forced to come to grips with the need to adapt the recommendations to practical circumstances in order to fit their particular survey requirements and meet budgets. The manual would have benefited from a much fuller exploration of the relationship between the objectives of a proposed survey and its organization. A discussion of the nature of different inquiries based around different sampling units and a review of questions of sample and survey design and their cost would have been helpful. At the time it was published there were, sadly, few examples of best practice in the case of household income and expenditure surveys, housing unit surveys, industrial inquiries, small-scale enterprise surveys, employment and wage inquiries, informal sector studies, and so on. Few people had much experience with how differently shops and farms that were owned by households might be covered in a survey, for example.

This lack of direction and guidance was especially pertinent in the case of the developing countries, where, for the most part, there was a marked absence of up-to-date sampling frames. The way these fundamental constraints determined the choice of the basic unit of observation was crucial. It led sometimes not to the most desirable or most appropriate unit of inquiry for the declared policy objectives. A particular selection could give rise to misleading results and could create some tension. For example, many social service provisions and support programs are geared to the nuclear family or to the head of the family and are related especially to the size of the family and the age and sex composition of its members. Most survey data, however, refer to the broader notion of a "household," which may relate to an identifiable dwelling or housing unit rather than to a family unit. This is because the housing unit forms the "defined collection unit" that is readily locatable from a census map. The physical unit constitutes the easiest way of finding respondents from an available population frame and represents a convenient source for collecting and reporting data on households.

The practical focus and application of the sampling methods described in the manual is agriculture. This is neither surprising nor inappropriate, given the importance of that sector. At the time the manual was written, in 1960, the overwhelming proportion of people in the world still lived in rural areas. Most of them were engaged in some form of agricultural activity. Furthermore, a large proportion of the population, even those who lived in towns, remained dependent on the agricultural sector. Successful agricultural production was crucial to the essential survival of some populations. It was also an important element in the process of economic (and social) transformation and permitted necessary structural change, releasing resources tied to the land for more productive use in manufacturing. The individuals who served as consultants on the manual had a special interest and experience in this area. This meant, however, that some other important areas of application that demanded a somewhat different approach were overlooked, leaving gaps in knowledge, particularly about the plight of the poor. The absence of suitable practical recommendations for other areas of inquiry, such as industrial surveys and business inquiries, is noticeable. National statistical offices often had to find new survey approaches and adapt existing methods in the field. In the newly independent and emerging developing countries, which were only just beginning to establish benchmark data measures, it was invariably necessary to call upon the services of expatriate experts in survey methods to provide technical assistance. Those managing such work had to confront many practical problems that arose as much from the nature of the country and field of inquiry as from the lack of national survey experience. This was especially the case in those areas of data gathering where errors and problems of data processing frequently arose. It was crucial to minimize these survey management problems. Concerns about overall survey efficiency, managing and balancing the demands of staff and budget, overseeing safety, controlling costs, and organizing the day-to-day logistics of data collection were frequently given far less attention than determining the efficiency of the technical sampling design. It became quickly apparent that the local capacity to conduct and implement data collection and to carry through a survey to an appropriate conclusion that resulted in the publication of a detailed survey report was often lacking. The full results of such inquiries were rarely published and a comprehensive analysis was not always undertaken. This problem of analysis and dissemination was one that UNSO believed it had some responsibility to address.

In the 1970s, UNSO launched the National Household Survey Capability Program (NHSCP), which recognized that it was desirable that all national statistical offices possess an ongoing in-house survey capability. The NHSCP was developed because UNSO was haunted, on the one hand, by the enormous resources required to carry out national surveys that sometimes yielded less than what was planned, and, on the other, by the reasonable success of the World Fertility Survey (WFS), which was conducted under the auspices of the International Statistical Institute (ISI). The NHSCP was originally intended to support the operation of national household surveys and to place them within the broader context of a routine (continuous) and integrated survey program. In the end, the program also embraced surveys that were not really national, that were quite topic specific, and that were only loosely connected to household inquiries. The idea broadened into an understanding of common survey techniques that were applicable to any area and the importance of sharing survey experiences. The management and direction of the survey program was housed in UNSO, but it was funded, initially, by a substantial contribution from the World Bank. The NHSCP was full of all the right ideas and intentions, but it lapsed into an excessive concern with narrow technical issues. It paid too little attention to genuinely useful applications, the need for simple and straightforward procedures, the sharing of effective practices, the external coverage of the survey results, and the importance of making sure that good-quality results were produced that were operationally useful and reasonably timely. The poverty of the follow-up analysis of the surveys themselves and of the (usually less-than-comprehensive) results obtained and the eventual limited publication of results left much to be desired.[29]

The NHSCP was established against the background of the success of two integrated national survey programs, one in Nigeria and the other in Kenya. UNSO felt, quite rightly, that this experience should be widely shared. The example programs were designed to provide topically organized and integrated sample surveys that could be conducted sequentially or with different rotating and interchangeable modules of topical interest. The Kenya survey program, in particular, was an integrated continuous survey of rural households. While it received important financial and technical professional inputs from the FAO and UNICEF, the program was managed locally. It could be viewed as a model for many subsequent approaches to survey design and effective organization. By its evident success, it demonstrated that not only were more complex multifaceted programs feasible but also that they could be efficiently carried out in developing countries. The Kenya surveys generated information within an Integrated Rural Household Survey program. The subcomponent studies were immediately relevant, and the surveys generated an array of results that offered considerable scope for conducting more detailed policy reviews and specific research analysis. The results of the Kenya surveys were used in a number of contexts, including the Social Life Profile Analysis conducted by the OECD Development Center.

By contrast, the NHSCP provided little guidance about possible results and outcomes. It remained essentially neutral with respect to survey content and rarely referred specifically to the policy areas and concerns or objectives that the results were intended to address. There was only a vague, wide-ranging intention to produce data for development planning. Such planning was a process of economic and social resource allocation that was already beginning to fall from favor in many low-income countries. This was especially the case where IMF and World Bank influence was brought to bear and the effects of their policies urging countries to free prices and liberalize markets became more clear.

The real emphasis of the NHSCP was on strengthening the basic statistical infrastructure of government. The establishment of a better survey capability that was specifically centered on the household enabled governments to shift their policy emphasis away from production, growth, and objects and to give more attention to local people and their needs. But while this more people- and community-focused approach was clearly laudable, the idea of having better information to underpin a more efficient planning and allocation mechanism was not seen as politically desirable. The NHSCP prospectus failed to indicate clearly how the planned survey results would be related to the declared policy objectives of government. The program outline was light on local commitment, detailed outcomes, and relevant analytical potential. The apparent lack of thought given to downstream effectiveness, perhaps because the expected outcomes were simply taken for granted by the program's developers, undermined the attractiveness of this survey process to possible users and policymakers. This feeling was strengthened by the evident inability actually to produce results that were sufficient to provide a first initial round of analysis, even in those countries that embraced the NHSCP philosophy. Where results were obtained, countries were often not able to produce them in a sufficiently timely manner to be of any relevance to policy. The process of public dissemination was even more deplorable.

A consequence of this excessive concern with methodology and of paying too little attention to outcomes was the withdrawal by the World Bank of the significant financial support it gave to the program. The Bank concluded that the NHSCP was not an appropriate tool for giving policy guidance, for evaluating and monitoring development projects, for advising programs, and for assessing the impact of various government interventions on household well-being, and it decided to embark on its own country-level survey program, the Living Standards Measurement Studies (LSMS). These resource-consuming surveys were to become a significant source of conflict within the international statistical community as arguments about arm's-length involvement, the capacity of the country to conduct and maintain a program, and statistical policy distortions and diversions of resources for statistical work in developing countries came to the forefront of debate. Another source of concern was the World Bank's Social Dimensions of Adjustment Program, which initiated and supported a number of surveys in sub-Saharan Africa.[30]

The LSMS program is still in place, albeit in a slightly different guise and with local ownership of procedures. It was designed from the outset to provide insights into household behavior and the work activities of its members and to see how these could be related to the different socioeconomic characteristics of people and their well-being. The World Bank's need for policy-relevant information for its lending programs and project evaluations drove the move to become independent and to get out from under the UN survey umbrella. Many felt that this move was ill advised because the Bank itself did not have the technical survey capability or hands-on experience to organize and conduct such an ambitious program of surveys. This showed up in several of the early studies and in the inability of statistical analysts to conduct robust comparisons of LSMS data with data from other surveys. In leaving the UN's NHSCP, the Bank chose to ignore many of the important lessons of survey management and sample design that had been learned the hard way in actual field experience. The Bank was also interested in particular problems and thus looked at specific focus groups it knew were disadvantaged and at risk. From the outset, it made two significant mistakes. One, it overdesigned the scope of each survey, producing excessively long, complicated, and essentially unmanageable questionnaires that contained virtually unprocessible information about interrelationships. Just like the NHSCP, the results were typically incomplete, were not robust, and did not include extensive analysis. Second, many LSMS surveys did not provide for a random and nationally representative sample of households because they concentrated on specific target groups and populations deemed to be at risk. The results could not be aggregated to form national totals of relevance to macrolevel policy. The early surveys proved to be very expensive, yet one of the reasons the Bank disassociated its initiative from the UN's efforts was to achieve greater savings by covering many objectives under the same survey process.

The layering of inquiries and overloading of issues created new problems of processing and interpretation. This led to difficult questions about how observed sample estimates should be appropriately weighted to provide meaningful statistical population measures. In many cases, the survey results could not be applied to the country as a whole or compared with other countries. The establishment of consistent comparisons over time on the basis of repeated surveys also proved difficult because the same survey procedures were not replicated.

Statistics on Women and Men

> A lack of concrete knowledge about the activities of women has been a major impediment to the formulation of policies and programmes, at both the national and international levels, to achieve equality.
> —UN Secretary-General Boutros Boutros-Ghali
> in his introduction to *The World's Women 1995*

The first UN report on *The World's Women 1991* marked a watershed in the compilation of statistics relating to women. It gathered in one place, more or less for the first time, an extensive collection of statistics culled from various files that related to the reported condition of women over the previous two decades. The real breakthrough on women's statistics, however, came with the publication of the report of *The World's Women 1995*, which was prepared for the 1995 World Conference on Women in Beijing, because this document explicitly recognized that much of the official historical data on women reflected a particular institutional perception of women and their role in society and the economy. The report thus drew attention to the need to adopt new instruments of inquiry and different methods of investigation, especially surveys of time use and a reorientation of enumeration procedures. Even this was not enough because a true understanding could come only from a cultural change that altered entrenched perceptions about the status of women, even among women themselves.

Over the years, the UN responded by updating the guidelines on census-taking and revising the handbooks on census methods and the manuals on the conduct of surveys. These actions were all designed to take into account the previous oversights in evaluating the position and status of women. Although these were important contributions to a better understanding of the social and demographic circumstances of women, the following discussion relates primarily to the evolving procedures through which the work of women and their contributions to both the social well-being of society and to the economic status of the household are more comprehensively taken into account.

To be pertinent and have a bearing on issues of public concern, statistics need to be current not only in their timelines but also in their capacity to keep up with social changes and important shifts in social conduct. This often demands new approaches and alternative methodologies that pose a direct challenge to the traditional ways of doing quite basic things in statistics, such as collecting raw data. A move to any new data agenda inevitably raises fundamental questions about the importance of continuity in promoting understanding and facilitating interpretative analysis, especially about the factors influencing change. The need for continuity has to be balanced against a desire to increase general awareness of an issue by drawing attention to crucial new evidence about its importance.

Perhaps nowhere is this dilemma more apparent than in the introduction of the dimension of gender across a wide spectrum of social and economic statistics. This is clearly indicative of the desire of officials to properly quantify the role of women in the whole range of activities in which they are involved.

A key advance in the development of gender statistics has been a review of the concepts and methods of data collection. Most governments now ensure that statistics related to individuals are collected, compiled, analyzed, and presented by sex and age. They compile data that relate to problems, issues, and questions that affect women and men in society in different ways. The 1995 Beijing conference called for the development of new methodologies to compile and disseminate information on women. The development of the Women's Indicators and Statistical Database (Wistat) is part of this important initiative; it covers all UN member countries and nonmember states with populations greater than 100,000. The Wistat database was designed and used for the *World's Women* reports in 1991, 1995, and 2000. These reports contain an important and unique set of social indicators relating to the respective roles of women (and men) in society.[31]

From as early as 1980, an UNSO post was specifically allocated to the compilation of statistics on women, but the work became subsumed within the more general area of social and demographic statistics. Social development did not emerge as a priority until later the same decade, and even then some governments continued to resist the notion that social factors could play an important role in enhancing economic progress. Others believed that improved social well-being, per se, was not the only desirable outcome of economic policy.[32] Personal prosperity, with the expanded sovereignty over consumption choices and the material culture this implied, was considered no less important. Prompted by the concerns expressed by women from all walks of life, who came together in conferences of NGOs, governments, special agencies, and academia, that official statistics mostly held up a mirror to current cultural and social attitudes about the role of women in society, a renewed effort was made to examine how statistics on women and men were structured and how corresponding data about them was generated. These women's groups argued strongly that the lack of information about the substantial contributions women made to the well-being of their families and the support they gave to their communities meant that these activities were dismissed as unimportant, which reinforced the firmly held beliefs of the (predominantly male) decision makers. Eventually this critique led to a review of how data on women were collected, particularly in the censuses of population and labor forces. The issue was not just about separating existing aggregates to provide a gender dimension; the goal was to ascertain why women did not count in any broader socioeconomic assessment. The data problem often started from the very fundamental circumstance that in most developing countries, the census or survey enumerator was a male who collected information from a single primary respondent, the head of the household, who was usually also male. The consequent lack of recognition that what women did at home and on the farm had any importance, simply because it was not paid work, was inevitable.

The first report on the world's women in 1991 covered trends and statistics on women over the previous two decades, 1970–1990, and presented the most comprehensive and authoritative compilation of global indicators on the status of women until then available. *The World's Women 1995* represented a significant advance over the first UN study. It provided evidence of significant changes in the international mindset and official attitudes and the greater availability of data relating to women in key areas of life. It also clearly reflected the fuller participation of women in the economy and society in general, as had been observed by the ILO. The second global report was prepared as a general reference document with the Fourth World Conference on Women (Beijing 1995) in mind. The way the data were organized established new guidelines for the work of other UN specialized agencies, which, in turn, have influenced how information about women's activities are now presented and understood. Those involved in these pioneering data initiatives contributed at the same time to related efforts to modify existing concepts and methods in the important fields of census organization and survey activities. Modifications to the compilation methodologies of the national accounts were introduced to make sure such inquiries yielded less biased results and were better able to inform policy debate about women's roles in producing goods and services.

Generally, the local influence of culture on statistical methods, particularly in this area of gender characteristics, has been significant. For example, in Pakistan and many other countries, male enumerators survey male heads of households. A household that is headed by a female is judged to be an unusual and extreme case. This assumption invariably generates erroneous and incomplete results, even in an area of simple people counts by sex and age. The official undercounting and undervaluation of the female's role in the household and her contribution to economic activity remains a serious issue.

Data help effect change, and change, in turn, affects data by expanding choices, changing options, and influencing outcomes. Because of the initiatives taken in the UN to compile data about women and men, the world now knows much more than it did only a few decades ago about how they differ in social, political, and economic life. Statistics can now show the participation of women and men in their respective activities and their corresponding contributions to well-being. An important aspect of this methodology is that it is now possible to track the different causes of death for women and men, their different patterns of morbidity, their mobility, and, not least, their different needs from and uses of health services. This suggests one reason why far more attention has been given in recent years to female reproductive health and why the lack of common privileges among women is viewed, increasingly, as a human rights issue in many parts of the world. One important explanation for the gender differences observed can be found in the reported discrepancies between girls and boys in literacy and school enrollment rates above the primary level. Such differences raise further concerns about the respective rights of women and men in their access to education. Where women have obtained a better education and have taken over more control of their lives, they have falling birth rates and fertility rates; the lower net reproduction rates benefit the entire society.

In principle, although the problems with measuring the contributions of women to the economy and of defining accompanying concepts such as "the household" or "household head" were resolved in the 1993 SNA, in practice, a number of difficulties remain. There are still widely held but incorrect perceptions that what is seen, traditionally, as "women's work" has zero value. Assessing the relative importance of the efforts of women and men across the range of economic activities in which both are involved in the household, such as livestock tending and harvesting, is difficult, but that difficulty pales into insignificance when attempts are made to put a value on women's domestic activities in the home. Women's inputs into agriculture and the service sector tend to be underestimated when their values are estimated. Moreover, for legal and regulatory reasons, the extent of women's involvement in many branches of manufacturing—particularly in the case of girls and young women—is often underreported. It is interesting to note that the concern in the 1960s and 1970s with "manpower" planning in developing countries was often simply just that. Such planning tended to have very little to do with expanding the range of career possibilities for women beyond the traditional occupations of nurse and schoolteacher.

In agriculture, women's activities in the field are mostly unremunerated either in cash or in kind. Their contribution to GDP through subsistence farming activities (rural household production for own consumption) is valued far lower in monetary terms than the true value of their labor in contributing to the food security and basic survival of their families. In addition, they often perform other tasks at the same time, such as child minding. In the household, the activities of collecting fuel, carrying water, cleaning, and processing food form elements of a "second shift"[33] that is not well quantified. In some cases of domestic service, such as child care and looking after aged relatives, the value of time spent in these activities is not recognized and is actually discounted in the SNA, despite the enhanced family welfare these activities obviously provide. The judgment is that "traditional" women's activities such as food preparation are common across all countries and that time spent in them cannot be adequately assessed in value terms. Furthermore, it is argued that such time, because it only represents labor "inputs," does not represent individual productivity in generating outputs.

3.4. Women and the Informal Sector

The 1993 SNA, however, departs from previous tradition and gives a great deal more emphasis to the production as well as consumption activities of the household sector. Perhaps just as significant, it sees the informal sector as an important source for female engagement in the economy. Informal-sector activities can be performed anywhere, but they often take place in the home or in the house of the coordinator or overseer and the outputs are distributed from there. Typically, the work is carried out at low levels of organization where the traditional divisions between capital, labor, and enterprise are indistinct and the process of remuneration is blurred. Often pay is related to piecework or to a specific commission or percentage of sales. There may be an initial expense to buy into the business, purchase a franchise, or pay rent, ensuring the seller a decrease in expenses without exposure to any market risks. The activities of the sector are unregistered and are usually mobile and diverse. They generally involve relatively low levels of technology, but in some cases they may demand considerable skill and manual dexterity, such as in small-engine repair, carpet weaving, and pottery production. While such industries are a source of employment, employment can be irregular and directly dependent on demand. The wage rewards, consequently, can be highly variable. In many low-income countries, the informal sector embraces almost all branches of economic activity through to medical and transportation services and entertainment. It thus represents a parallel system to the formally established economy and its comparatively well-organized and well-regulated markets.

The issues of gender-related development and gender imbalance and apparent inequality in matters of economic progress are very relevant to social policy. The data about women's contribution to economic activity and their burden of housework is now being reviewed more extensively. Another volume in this series, *Women Enrich the United Nations and Development,* by Devaki Jain, will draw attention to the cultural and economic reasons why females have been treated differently and unfairly with regard to access to education and thus to opportunities to pursue lives and careers of their own choosing.

When and how statistics on women—beyond those already established in the areas of population and demographic analysis and, of course, health—became an important issue within the UN system not only illustrates the sociopolitical changes of the time but also the development of new measurement instruments and redesign of methodologies. Individual initiatives and institutional interventions by NGOs and research centers have assumed an important role on a par with that of international agencies. International recommendations have emerged from work at global summits to define goals and have helped to get such data work underway. The work of women's groups in academic institutions and other NGO research studies in the field have raised awareness of the importance of gender in statistics. These groups have emphasized the incongruity of conventional social measures and aggregation procedures used in the construction of national accounts.

However, from the very beginning UNSO was alert to the need to bring to the attention of the world the special position and role of women in society and their contribution to economic activities. Although UNRISD briefly explored the question of gender while pursuing its research in developing measures of levels of living in the late 1960s and early 1970s, it quickly concluded that it would not be feasible to calculate separate level-of-living indicators for males and females on the basis of the indicator information at its disposal, at least for most variables and the majority of countries. A decade or more later, at UNSO itself, the issue of gender would reenergize the whole field of social statistics and give it fresh focus. Concerns about women emerge—somewhat tentatively—in the areas of employment and production in the 1980s. During World War II, women not only joined in the workforce in increasing numbers but they also entered professions and acquired skills in such areas as engineering and shipbuilding that were long thought to be the exclusive province of men.

Certain special provisions of employment (related to physical effort and conditions of work, for example) were laid down to afford some measure of protection, but generally these regulations were probably recognized only in their breach. Anecdotal evidence suggests that under wartime conditions, women "mucked in" with the rest, laboring equally alongside men in both agricultural and industrial production. It was the ILO, therefore, with its concern for hours of work and rates of pay, that first recognized the importance of quantifying more appropriately the contribution of women's work to the national production effort. The issue was to assume added importance when the UN System of National Accounts established from the beginning that household production activities on own account—mostly for consumption, but also for construction and land improvement—should be appropriately counted in the GDP. The SNA accounting conventions were designed to ensure greater comparability of GDP, both over time as economies became more monetarized and across countries so that all nations covered the same scope of production activity and all were placed on the same basis of valuation, regardless of the stage of development they had reached.

In the late 1950s and 1960s, as the techniques of national accounting spread to all corners of the world, especially with the process of decolonization and the establishment of political independence (and hence self-government), statisticians were confronted with major questions of how to impute for undefined economic activity. They became more aware of the need to count in the role of women and value women's efforts in subsistence production.[34] This work received an added boost with the growing interest in monitoring the nature and scope of the informal sector following the ILO employment missions to Colombia, Sri Lanka, and particularly Kenya. It is at this stage that analysts such as Luisella Clermont-Goldschmidt and Ann Chadeau began thinking about how best to value the contribution of women's work to national production and in the household and how to decide by what principles imputations for women's wages in unpaid activity should be properly calculated.[35]

In the 1993 SNA revision, the production boundary for economic activity was expanded further to include all household output of goods for own use and not just goods made from primary products. In addition, a much clearer emphasis was placed on the household sector, and the activities of the household as both a producer and consumer are more fully recognized. Although the net effect takes into greater account women's economic activities in the home, the new rules do not help to distinguish what these are. Furthermore, many services performed by women within the household for its members, such as cooking, cleaning, sewing, and child minding, still remain outside the formal production boundary. In this area, the developed and developing countries are much more alike, although more and more often in the richer countries, many services such as preschool childcare, laundries, meals, and housecleaning are outsourced and paid for. Less frequently, perhaps, a full-time domestic service employee might be engaged to perform these and other housekeeping functions while also living within the household. This underlines the point that since the range of activities performed by the employee and family member is very similar, both should be treated equally in the national accounts whether they are explicitly paid for their services or not.

In December 2000, UNSO took on a special project, "Gender Issues in the Measurement of Paid and Unpaid Work"; it drew its mandate from recommendations of the Platform for Action adopted by the Fourth World Conference on Women and the United Nations Statistical Commission.[36] The Platform for Action called on national, regional, and international statistical services and relevant governmental and United Nations agencies in cooperation with research and documentation organizations to:

- Improve data collection on the full contribution of women and men to the economy, including their participation in the informal sector
- Develop a more comprehensive knowledge of all forms of work and employment
- Develop an international classification of activities for time-use statistics that is sensitive to the differences between women and men in remunerated and unremunerated work
- Collect data disaggregated by sex

From the statistics side, the legislative mandate comes from the twenty-eighth session of the Statistical Commission, which emphasized the value of time-use statistics for a range of national and international socioeconomic statistics, including gender statistics. It asked that UNSO prepare a draft classification of time-use activities as a basis for further research and special studies.

In March 1998, an expert group meeting on gender issues in labor-force statistics was convened to review a range of problems and issues which needed to be addressed to improve statistics on paid and unpaid work. The meeting was organized by the Gender in Development Program (GIDP) and the Human Development Report Office (HDRO) of the UNDP and UNSO in cooperation with the ILO. The meeting agreed on three broad areas of statistical work for consideration as project objectives:

- Promote the collection of time-use data (see below), particularly in developing countries, through methodological work and other means
- Compile statistics on difficult-to-measure sectors of the economy, including the informal sector, home-based work, and subsistence agriculture
- Improve the measurement of paid and unpaid work in labor-force statistics

In July 1999, the primary focus of the project was further identified by the Project Steering Committee, consisting of representatives from GIDP, HDRO, and UNSD:

- The promotion and evaluation of ongoing activities on national time-use surveys in countries with the objective of developing guidelines and methodologies for national work and an international classification of activities for time use for both developing and developed countries
- Improvement of statistics on women's participation in difficult-to-measure sectors of the labor market such as home workers, street vendors, and the informal sector

A project implementation plan was subsequently formulated which identified and prioritized activities in accordance with these objectives.

At its thirty-first session in March 2000, the Statistical Commission reviewed a report on the implementation plan and recognized the importance of the work by the Secretariat on the measurement of paid and unpaid work. It noted that additional work was being carried out by various countries and agencies, particularly on time-use surveys.[37]

The identification and implementation of the project's activities were to be guided by two interrelated strategies: first, outputs were to be mainstreamed in the work of national and international statistical services, and second, the ongoing efforts related to project objectives in countries as well as regional and international organizations were to be built upon.

To promote mainstreaming into official statistics, the project implementation plan was presented to the Statistical Commission in 1999 at its thirtieth session and a follow-up report on progress made was presented at the thirty-second session of the commission in March 2001. Working with the statistics offices of countries was another aspect of mainstreaming. Project support to countries was based on the existence of ongoing efforts on time-use surveys and a clear commitment of the country to the development and integration of time-use methodology to improve the measurement of paid and unpaid work.[38]

Until recently, time-use data were not part of the regular data-collection programs of national statistics offices in developing countries. Following the Fourth World Conference on Women, data-collection activities on time use were initiated in twenty-four developing countries, fourteen of which completed national data collection on time use. These surveys generated statistics on the time spent by both women and men in paid and unpaid work.

The UN project on paid and unpaid work has been closely involved with this developing field. It backstopped several of the activities and promoted the development of others. Most important, it consolidated experiences from what were initially ad hoc activities and drew out the lessons to be learned. It further facilitated the exchange of information and promoted discussion on suitable methodology and classifications. In doing so, the project provided a timely impetus for the development of international guidelines for time-use statistics and laid substantive groundwork for a guide to the production of statistics on time use for measuring paid and unpaid work to be issued as a publication in the methodological series of the UNSD.

Time-use survey data provided the essential groundwork for measuring women's role in national production and helped to develop the necessary methods and classification system for this procedure. Having a time-use perspective improves the general understanding of women's place in the labor force and provides data on unpaid housework which is not counted by other means. It also improves estimates of goods and services that are mainly produced by women and are undercounted in national accounts. Identifying the subgroups of people working at home and street vendors is also relevant to an understanding of the status of informal-sector workers.

The relative importance of the various functions performed within the household cannot be properly assessed without time-use surveys. These studies are still few and far between because they are expensive, demand a great deal of resources, and are difficult to supervise and manage. But such surveys remain essential to the construction of more realistic household accounts because they distinguish between inputs of labor and intermediate consumption, on the one hand, and outputs of the household, on the other. They also reveal the main means of distinguishing the separate contributions of males and females to total household economic activity. Time-budget surveys have made evident what previously could be only implied; namely, that women make an enormous contribution to the output of the country and to the general well-being of the household. Because unremunerated household activities are not subject to the labor market, they have been rarely recognized as economic contributions. Even in the latest round of population censuses (2000–2001), voluntary and charitable activities as unpaid work have been dismissed as not contributing to any economic value in the country.

One of the problems of gendering activities is that data-collection and compilation procedures have been so well institutionalized in a neutral, best-statistical-practice sense that it is difficult for investigators to break out of the established mold of statistical inquiry. The issue of gender statistics is not merely one of disaggregating the actual data results; it goes much deeper than that. Gender bias is embedded, unwittingly, in the methods of data collection and in the basic sources of information. It is a question of changing administrative filing procedures and the established bureaucratic rules of the game, which are designed only to make sure that the procedures laid down for reporting are followed. The process needs to become more representative and relevant to reality. Similarly, approaches to conducting surveys and samples must be kept sufficiently flexible to capture all the pertinent dimensions, particularly gender issues, relevant to the questions under investigation. There are several aspects to this question of which tools and instruments to use. In the case of administrative filing, the procedures in place are unlikely to change unless ministerial policies change or there is a public service review; it seems unlikely that policies will change unless new information is made available. This is a catch-22 situation where the role and rights of women are concerned. The formal procedures of inquiry for surveys and censuses, especially those based on the household but also those that use the holding or farm or enterprise as the unit of analysis, often preclude any direct firsthand feedback from females (of all ages). This is because such studies are geared toward recording responses from the "head of household." For cultural and technical reasons, even when a woman is the de facto head of household, the enumerator usually defers to the most senior male in the family, such as the matrilineal or patrilineal father or an uncle or elder brother if the husband is not present.[39] It would be an interesting piece of survey research to investigate what bias exists here and whether a female head of household is reported primarily when there is no obvious male around. The predominant use of male enumerators as interviewers in some very poor developing countries aggravates this problem. It clearly accentuates the tendency to underrate the importance of female activities. A handful of village case studies in India and Latin America that were not conducted by official agencies as well as other labor-related surveys in Asia and

Central Europe have alluded to some of these issues.[40] Gradually, policymakers have become more aware that "women hold up half of the sky" (according to an old Chinese proverb). But there are still many difficulties to overcome and many gaps in our knowledge in quantifying women's real contribution to the world, both socially and economically.

A few specific examples indicate directions for further research. The first is the need for a more comprehensive review of the context in which certain female conditions, their status, and their contributions are reported. For example, time-use surveys indicate that a considerable portion of the day of most women in developing countries is assigned to the preparation of food, including the collection of firewood and water and maintenance of the fire. Where most of these activities physically occur within the house, it is clear that the tasks of cooking and boiling water over the open fire often expose women to the health problems associated with smoke pollution and the use of certain fuels. Other situational characteristics associated with the burden of daily duties that frequently involve physical exertion and stress may also have an important impact on reproductive health. It is not sufficient, therefore, to collect gender-related data about the specific status of women (disease, injury, literacy, etc.) without going beyond the immediate situation to look at the broader community- and household-related aspects of their family's socioeconomic circumstances.

There is a continuous interplay not only between what goes on in the UN system and what goes on in countries but also between new methods of inquiries taken up in the countries and those adopted in the UN. In this area, the UNDP's *Human Development Report* and its increasing range of country-level reports as well UNICEF's regional-based "social panoramas" of different countries are perhaps the best examples of studies where gender-related statistics have been collected on a more regular and systematic basis. In the early 1980s, INSTRAW sought UNSO's assistance in producing data explicitly on women; this initiative first raised the profile of this question and gave impetus to the issue of gender in the field of social statistics. Like other social indicators, measurements of well-being on the basis of gender raised concerns in certain countries that publication of survey results would be used politically to judge the adequacy of their political systems and human rights record.

Another early interest in the conditions of women was linked to their eating habits and nutritional status. It was long believed that women required significantly fewer calories than men for their survival, mostly because of their smaller physical stature and assumed lower level of physical exertion. In developing countries, this assumption appeared to be confirmed by direct observation of women's calorie intake, measured by what they actually ate from the plate and in the kitchen. Two different and confounding influences worked to reinforce this misconception. The first failed to recognize that in many instances—especially in rural households—women were exerting a proportionately higher work effort than men. They thus expended more energy and actually required a proportionally greater daily calorie intake in relation to their body weight to sustain their well-being and a satisfactory health status.[41] The need for protein and vitamins was even more evident in the case of pregnant and nursing working mothers. The second factor was that when they observed actual dietary intakes, observers invariably failed to take into proper account the cultural aspects and priorities of household feeding habits. Thus, the way the female members of many households were required to hold back until after the main male members of the family had eaten and to be satisfied with what was left over was not usually taken into account. This inequality within the household with respect to food consumption is now well recognized. But the early assumptions of statisticians appeared to be justified by a self-fulfilling data-observation process conducted by enumerators who were not trained to detect such cultural sources of potential bias.

Understanding the different gender-related indicators often requires a more in-depth review of the cohort characteristics. Progress (and the lack of achievement) is sometimes masked by the way changes happen and are observed for different age groups. Issues such as employment, education, and literacy, particularly among older people, are preconditioned by what has transpired in the past and present attitudes and patterns of behavior. For example, adult illiteracy rates tend to decrease as the impact of improved primary school enrollment rates gradually takes effect. Adult female illiteracy has much more to do with gender bias in primary education than to differences in the application of adult literacy programs. Furthermore, the apparent prejudice against appointing women to senior-level positions in companies and to the civil service often has less to do with the so-called glass ceiling than it does to the fact that three or more decades earlier, fewer women had access to higher levels of learning and specific forms of professional and technical training. Some professions such as law, architecture, and engineering were not open to women in many countries, or as easy to enter, in the past. Consequently, women were not able to secure an early foothold on the career ladder. The lower rates of participation for women, therefore, may have little to do with present prejudices and gender preference but are perhaps more often the legacy of discriminatory practices exercised in the past that now no longer exist. Some of this emerges from the demographic life profiles and social life chances studies carried out in the late 1970s under the auspices of the UK Institute of Development Studies (IDS) and the OECD Development Center. Studies conducted in Kenya found that differences between urban and rural people were more important in determining individual living conditions and social status with respect to education, health, risk of crime, and so forth than differences in gender. Consistently across all age groups, however, the familiar gender differences existed and, not surprisingly, the differences appeared to be more marked in the urban areas, reflecting the greater variation and extent of inequalities in the large towns in Kenya.

The problem with quantifying the extent of female participation in society, perhaps especially in developing countries, is that even where the activities of women are measured—as, say, in their engagement in the labor force and employment—their contribution is poorly identified. This, again, raises important questions not only about what definitions and classification systems have been used but also about the different ways that survey interviewers and administrators (in effect, the front line of bureaucrats people encounter) have approached their subjects and treated respondents. Fear, intimidation, curiosity, a desire to please authority (on both sides), deception, and so forth are among a host of different culturally determined emotions (or nonsampling factors) that influence survey responses. Low nonresponse rates to survey inquiries in developing countries are evidence of a basic willingness on the part of citizens to help and cooperate, but while this desire to give information is a necessary first step, it is not sufficient to ensure that the information provided is accurate.[42]

Historically, one of the biggest criticisms of methods of data collection about economic activity has centered on a belief that the household activities of women, such as in animal husbandry, food processing, child minding, and routine home maintenance, were deemed to constitute part of women's normal duties inseparable from their roles as "housewives." Therefore, they could not be considered "economic" activities of any real value or constitute part of what surveyors considered to be "paid employment" in the ILO or SNA sense of the term. Many functions performed by women constitute basic services and are essential to the day-to-day survival of the family, even though they take place mostly outside the market and often entirely within the household unit. This led the ILO to propose different subcategories of the labor force to cover the different circumstances of unpaid labor and other eventualities that might apply to women's work, such as the seasonal nature of much work. The proposed new categories included the paid labor force (and concepts related to the market-oriented labor force), the standard labor force, and an extended labor force. This scheme included workers at progressively higher levels but at somewhat weaker degrees of engagement in economic activity.

Measures that provide a different perspective of the various levels of composition of the labor force by age and sex could prove helpful in guiding official policy in several areas. So far, however, such a categorization of activity has not been implemented. Recognition of this deficiency in the data, however, has given rise to the implementation of more relevant statistical procedures in general inquiries of official surveys, with the result that data users now have access to better information on activity and participation rates.

Another important lesson to learn from this UN data-gathering experience is that "women's issues" per se are not simply women's issues as statisticians first recognized them and thus set out to measure them. A gendered approach that measures the range of economic activities that women do is necessary. Indeed, it is somewhat surprising that the traditional methods of labor force surveys that were recommended and supported by the ILO for many years did not develop sooner into general activity surveys. As noted earlier, little attention was paid to (admittedly resource-intensive) time-use studies to supplement the findings that had been reached. Similar issues exist in the evaluation of health and education issues by gender.[43]

The ideas that precipitated changes in the way women's roles in society were measured fused the influences of statistical method with specific social concerns. It was recognized that the scientific methods of survey inquiry, which purported to be independent and neutral, contained an inherent bias in practice. In some instances, this might even have been aggravated by the way the population universe was defined and the associated sampling frame was chosen. Few surveys are now carried out without first seeking expert advice on all these issues. Now a variety of community representatives are canvassed early in the planning stages of a survey about questionnaire design and sample selection. This process can only enhance the scientific quality of a survey's conduct.

The Measurement of Population

At its most basic level, quantifying the world requires three minimum but essential data elements: a knowledge about land and its geographical distribution; information about economic resources, production in particular; and statistics on world population classified according to countries. At the root of the UN's mandate lay the task of building a better world. This meant creating a richer (and more peaceful) life for the world's peoples. This objective hinges on population characteristics, its distribution around the globe, its ethnic composition, and the fundamental dynamics of demographic change. The universal desire to improve people's health and enhance the human intellect as well as an individual's natural abilities to create a more productive and well-paid workforce are closely related to population features. The UN has always been concerned to achieve a better balance between population and economic resources. The success of such UN agencies as the WHO and the FAO in the areas of health improvement, nutrition, and food production contributed, at least initially, to an intensification of the problem of resource imbalance because these changes led to a rapid expansion in the world's population, particularly in the poorer areas. More people survived infancy and childhood and those who survived lived much longer. Eventually, but only very slowly, fertility has begun to fall as economic conditions have improved and better education has become more widely available. The activities of many UN agencies are now beginning to have an effect on the positive side of the resource equation, although the population will continue to grow as more children enter childbearing age and more people live longer. These factors will tend to partially counterbalance the slower growth in fertility rates.

Population statistics is one area of data development where the UN has taken a strong lead. The UN not only produces reasonably current person counts throughout the world on a regular basis, but it has done so by establishing the appropriate procedures by which actual baseline population counts (censuses) are taken. It has also laid down the definitions and methodologies for collecting information about vital demographic events and migration. The dynamics of population change by sex and age group have been tracked by means of relevant cohort analysis. While there is no general theory of population, the availability of demographic data provides researchers with a way to examine the validity of certain assumed relationships between population growth and economic status both within countries over time and between different countries. Statisticians and policymakers are coming to understand that the changing age and sex composition of the population exerts an impact on economic policy directly, as in the way household expenditures are structured and have influenced the well-recognized nature of consumer price indices (CPI) in the developed world.[44] More directly, of course, governments with strong commitments to broad-based social programs have long been interested in such issues as aging and the impact of changing dependency ratios. Recently, there has been a growing interest in the population momentum and capacity of a population to reproduce itself and the effects the changing composition of an age group might have in expanding the labor force and strengthening the economy. This analysis links a particular population group with known saving and spending characteristics to the process of economic change. As the group passes through the demographic profile of a country over the space of several decades, it affects a number of core economic parameters that may have little direct relationship to current market circumstances.

Demographic data focus, from a UN perspective, on democratic concerns. They are related to people and are not concerned with things (such as commodities) or processes (production) or their related transactions (exchange and trade). Monetary phenomena form the main matter of interest of other statistical series and are value laden. Demographic data, especially when disaggregated by region, bring individual relevance, context, and content to broader economic issues. Used as a denominator, they tend to "normalize" general economic features and facilitate comparisons. They provide a step toward understanding the real meaning of events, phenomena, and monetary aggregates to individual people and households.

While a simple aggregate approach does not really get close enough to differentiate between the concepts of value and money, it helps to establish the appropriate benchmarks against which performance can be measured. Transactions, stocks, flows, and so forth expressed in money terms demonstrate magnitude but only hint at the importance of economic activity to people's lives and well-being. On their own, such money sums do not provide information on how many people are involved or who these people are. Not only is the activity measured in money units, but each money unit has different significance in the hands of different people. A dollar does not hold the same real value in the hands of a rich person as it does for a poor person. It also has more or less purchasing power depending upon where it is spent. If the demographic data can be used to separate out the various social groups and where they are located, the resulting statistics can convey even more meaning. The economic power, or sovereignty, a specific sum of money accords over goods and services will also differ depending on the actual prices people have to pay. Evidence suggests that poor people pay more for the same goods and services that are acquired by richer families and that large families benefit from economies of scale in their purchases. An individual's capacity to exercise choice may also be constrained by a variety of factors. The ability to categorize aggregates by population groups and their geographical location can provide a significant aid to understanding individual well-being and help in specifying remedial actions.

The importance of the population count is that each person represents an individual "vote" that is not weighted by any explicit money values and, hence, by a person's economic, social, or political status. In aggregate, people's votes send a key message to governments about resource needs and priorities. They represent a collective response to any assessment of the government's provision of public goals. They indicate the direction in which policy should be oriented; whether a government should focus its policy efforts on the young or old, on certain disadvantaged groups, or on people who belong to a particular region or ethnic group. Purely demographic data indicate whether greater or lesser emphasis should be given to schooling instead of hospitals, to secondary schools or universities and tertiary training instead of primary schools, and to health clinics and day-care facilities for old people instead of hospitals or crèches and where all these amenities and services should be located. Since most censuses contain interrelated general information not only about the socioeconomic status of households and individuals but also where people live, they provide an objective demographic basis for deciding about the most effective delivery of public nonmarket goods and services.

In countries where statutory provisions exist to distribute benefits to the poor or indigent and to provide transfers to those with certain disabilities, it is critical that the population counts be conducted accurately and completely. The recent concern in a number of countries about population undercounts relates to worries that minorities, people in remote locations or without permanent shelter, immigrants and asylum seekers, and large families that are poor or have female heads of household are not properly accounted for in the census. This means that legal entitlements may not be fully budgeted and schemes and programs to help the disadvantaged may be underfunded or misdirected. Scientific attempts to adjust and correct for the known undercount are often bitterly opposed politically and are considered in some countries to be not only unconstitutional but also unscientific.

The UN Population Division was created within the UN Secretariat in October 1946 to service the Population Commission, which was set up at the same time by a special resolution of ECOSOC. The Population Division was required to provide expert analysis and advise on population matters to the commission. The commission was charged, in turn, to advise and assist on those matters that both affected and were affected by population changes. Population was not really a new international concern. Although the formal precedents were more modest and limited, the League of Nations had previously played a part in improving population statistics. It had also commissioned work before 1946 on the population issues likely to arise in postwar Europe. From the outset, though it was set up as a representative body of nation-states (twelve in all), the Population Commission itself was composed of some internationally distinguished demographers.[45] It also allowed representatives of other UN Commissions to participate in the Population Commission's meetings as nonvoting observers, particularly the Statistical Commission and the Social Commission; the ILO, the FAO, UNESCO, the WHO, and other UN specialized agencies; and the American Federation of Labor.

The Population Division of the UN was charged with the primary task of estimating the global population and quantifying its demographic composition and dynamic characteristics. In 1946, there was more concern about declining populations and birth rates in the industrialized world than there was anxiety about the enormous pressures building up for population expansion in the larger, heavily populated developing countries. Little was known about the population dynamics in some of the largest countries, such as China, Brazil, Nigeria, and Indonesia. The total population was roughly known but the detailed demographic characteristics were less clear. Much of the indigenous population of Africa remained unquantified. The Population Division was required to serve as the secretariat to the Commission and to report separately from UNSO to ECOSOC, which was composed of a group of mostly Western countries. The Population Commission (and hence its composition and concerns) was not subject to the same questions and tensions that seemed to vex the Statistical Commission. Its activities, and which nations would be represented on it, it was unanimously agreed, would be decided by the member countries to which it was responsible. This made sense because it was accepted that the Population Division, as the commission's agent, would need to work closely with and through countries to fulfill its mandate. In many ways, the issues the Population Division confronted were more technically straightforward, descriptive, and reportorial than political. Although wider moral issues were later raised by virtue of the estimates that emerged, value judgments per se did not form any part of the division's terms of reference. The impact of the failure of national policies to react to certain population conditions, nevertheless, was felt and was reflected in the subsequent estimates and projections.

In its early years, the division was empowered to undertake special demographic studies, an activity it has continued to pursue to the present day. It benefited considerably from the technical expertise of consultants and the ready advice it received from internationally distinguished demographers such as David Glass, Bill Brass, and Philip Hauser. It could also call on a range of technical experts not only for help in compiling its reports but also in carrying out fieldwork overseas, particularly in directing census operations. Early agreement was reached on which demographic measures to use (and why), but other connected issues and definitions proved more difficult to establish; for example, an internationally comparable measure of urban and rural, the definition of a stay, or identifying someone as a migrant or a refugee as opposed to a visitor. More recently, the division has faced some of the philosophical questions about what constitutes a death (or birth) in the registration records of different countries and when and where such events occur.

Many population questions are bound up in national cultures, local laws and customs, religion, and even languages; each of these factors affects the technical measurement of populations. Civil law may also intervene in the definition of citizenship and residence. Being born in a particular country provides absolutely no guarantee that a person will be recognized as a citizen of that country. Demographic statistics, however neutral they may be in any auditing or accounting sense, are invariably political in the wider meaning of the term. The early heads of the Population Division, especially Mr. J. Rippert, were anxious to put the stamp of universal authority on its work and to establish the gold standard for independent technical and scientific work in the area of demographic analysis. The aim was to produce intercountry and intertemporal estimates that were consistent and robust and that would be recognized universally. The division supported extensive work on model life tables and advanced the in-depth exploration of demographic transition and the population explosion. More recently, the division has drawn attention to the significance (for economic development) of the population momentum and of aging and the demographic consequences of HIV/AIDS for those populations most at risk.

The division has always kept extensive files on the size and characteristics of national populations and has shown considerable interest in the main determinants and consequences of population change. These demographic issues have been related to other important and relevant questions about the adequacy of food supply and stocks, emergency reserves, health, the environment, and housing (shelter). Mapping migratory movements between countries has proved more difficult. This has usually been regarded as the province of the respective ministries of the interior (police/immigration) in each country. The dynamics of migration are related more to local protective laws and cultures than to demographic factors, although historically population pressure has been an important influence on movements. The matter of migration and refugee movements in recent years and assessments of their importance has fallen mainly to the task of international relief agencies active across national boundaries.

Over its life span, the Population Division has hired many experts to provide technical assistance in demographic statistics and to assist in the global dissemination of best practice in the area of demographics. Most of its ideas and recommendations about estimation procedures, the conduct of population and housing censuses, the construction of life tables, and so forth have been fully elaborated in various UN manuals and journal articles. Training at the national level and assistance in the conduct of demographic inquiries and the management and conduct of population censuses continue to be important concerns of the division.

The Population Division played a key role in setting up the UN Fund for Population Activities (UNFPA). This was a trust that was initially created in the Population Division in conjunction with the conduct and financing of the World Fertility Survey. It gained the support of the Johnson administration in the U.S. for population activities which were channeled through the United States Agency for International Development (USAID). The Demographic Health Surveys program was one such activity that came under this heading. UNFPA subsequently departed from the main line of the Population Division by focusing on women and adopting a distinct advocacy role in its dealings with the UNDP and other potential supporters. Most recently, UNFPA has been concerned to promote female reproductive health, which has important implications for child spacing and total family size. This, it has been argued, is the only politically acceptable approach to more effective population control.

Although its work has raised issues and opened debates on issues such as migration, abortion, aging, sustainability, and so forth, the Population Division has tried to stand aside from any well-defined political stance and disputes on morality, in particular with respect to human rights (and rights to life) championed by religious groups. Even the more specific questions of anonymity and confidentiality have to be handled with considerable care.[46] Recent research by the former head of UNSO provides clear evidence that population information has been used inappropriately (and illegally) to identify the whereabouts of certain (mostly minority) population groups in order to single them out for discriminatory policy treatment.[47] This may include restrictions on employment, the sequestration of property, forced repatriation, imprisonment, containment, temporary internment. In rare cases, unfortunately, such information has been sought in policies to preserve racial purity and conduct ethnic cleansing. In a few well-known cases, it has led even to attempts to exterminate particular populations. The importance of adequate safeguards to protect the release of population information cannot be underestimated.

The UN has always seen the population problem as a major obstacle to progress, not only in terms of the familiar dismal Malthusian dimension it presented but also because of the low life expectancy of more than half of the world's peoples. These and other challenges continue to pose huge problems for international policy. Although improvements in health contribute to population survival and longevity, in the long run, they are seen to be desirable for containing population expansion. But policy initiatives specific to population sectors need to be backed up by strategic decisions by the UN to strengthen human security in many political, economic, and social fields.

While the techniques of demographic accounting follow rather formal auditing procedures that are bounded by various age and sex profile parameters, the quality of the estimates depends on the reliability of the basic assumptions countries and agencies make about their demographic dynamics. Many of these are associated with particular fertility assumptions and the specific life table a country without adequate registration data chooses as its model for estimating its population. For this reason, the UN Population Division, when making its projections, draws up a number of alternative scenarios based on different fertility, mortality, and migration assumptions.

The latest global population estimates give projections to the year 2050; these include the current estimate for 2000. These projections (published 28 February 2001)[48] show the population of the poorest countries rising fastest; three-quarters of the increase is occurring in just six countries. The questions of global imbalance between population growth and the world's resources, and regional distribution of those resources, remain among the most important problems confronting the world's community. Their solution raises even more complex questions about redistribution and the environment. These questions are all the more pressing if, as is hoped and targeted, the number of poor in the world is to be halved by 2015.

The Measurement of Education

The merits of education have never been in doubt, despite the old adage that a little learning is a dangerous thing.[49] In terms of national strategies, however, the debate has turned on whether education is important as a social leveler and as a significant factor in bringing about a better distribution of income and wealth in society or is mainly a way to satisfy the skills and occupational requirements of economic enterprise. Is education a way of restoring dignity to the disadvantaged or the means to build up a country's human capital? More generally, education is regarded as the key process that helps to create a knowledge-based society. It is regarded as an essential element in the establishment and maintenance of a smooth-functioning democracy. The technological progress that drives economic advance is as dependent on invention and the skills acquired in education as it is on the management of ideas.

Current data are needed to inform educational policy and to test the relative significance of each of these core features about the role of education. Those making decisions must be able to distinguish between statements based on empirical evidence and those that have no more foundation in substance than a personal supposition resting on an ideological belief about the merits of different types of education. Education processes are sequential and closely correlated with age and the institutional characteristics of the system itself. Education is also a cumulative process, conditional on previous states and on pupil performance and the ability of those pupils to traverse well-defined thresholds such as examinations, end-of-term assessments and, sometimes, subjective evaluations by teachers. The satisfactory conventional functioning of an educational system is not enough, however, because individual educational status is also dependent on a variety of external conditions, including family circumstances, cultural attitudes, and the physical location of individual households. The age and sex composition of the family and the level and continuity of its income are as critical in determining the degree of education family members enjoy as innate ability and intelligence and availability of facilities. Existing international statistics on education relate only to the institutional features and administrative workings of the system. Data compiled at the national level only rarely take into account some of the more instrumental and socially determined features of the formal educational process. They also say very little about why and how informal education structures operate and what they contribute to knowledge capital.

Compared with UNESCO's original high priesthood on education and culture, public concerns about education generally have to do with the comprehensiveness (universality) of the coverage and the availability of education services to all children. At a more fundamental level, these concerns are about social justice and equality of opportunity in their broadest sense. Countries which have achieved an essential universality, whether or not this extends beyond primary education to secondary schooling and into tertiary education, focus more intensively on questions of quality—skills of teachers, range of subjects taught, relevant curricula, availability of materials (especially books and writing equipment), and school buildings. UNESCO and the various national education departments that tend to supply it with school data on an annual basis have concentrated their attention on these official administrative censuses as the main means to compile information. This applies to both the traditional decennial (and quinennial) census of population and to annual school censuses designed to collect comprehensive data on the number of enrollments in different grades at the beginning of each school year. Most population counts incorporate at least one question on completed years of education, current or past schooling status, vocational or professional qualifications, and occupation (which will necessarily correspond with a person's current employment status). Schools surveys also usually collect information about dropouts and repeaters. Although every school keeps attendance registers, only a few countries also gather data relating to actual attendance. Annual average attendance data necessarily relate to the previous school year and not to the current period or to initial registration. At the beginning of the school year, enrollments are at their highest. Even if they do not have adequate resources, school administrators generally encourage the maximum possible class enrollment because pupil head counts frequently determine the budget and resources made available to them by the government or local authorities. Families are clearly aware of the benefits of education, and in all developing countries parents work hard to save (and often borrow) to put their children in school. But through the year, the numbers actually attending school usually decline, mostly because parents cannot afford the unavoidable fees and extra expenses that are associated with admission to "free" education. School fees fall due in the first month or so of the school year and are often accompanied by other compulsory charges and special outlays for books, writing materials, transport, uniforms, use of sports equipment, meals, and so forth. From the family's point of view, especially those in rural areas, a child in school is the loss of a potential income earner, carer, or minder. Over and above the real expense of schooling there is an important opportunity cost that rural families face, particularly when seasonal harvest activities in the field, lambing, and other tasks are at their peak.

Enrollment data are thus mainly a measure of potential opportunity. They relate as much to the number of schools and places available and the number of classrooms at different levels as they do to the number of children who want to receive education. Educational information about grades, skills, and occupational qualifications has been developed to facilitate the cross-over applications of such data to "manpower" considerations. In the 1960s and 1970s, labor force needs and "manpower" determination at various skill levels were much in vogue in planning macroeconomic policy, especially in newly independent countries. In many of these developing countries, the state engaged directly in identifying capacity constraints. It gave quite detailed direction to education policy—to the point of specifying teacher requirements, courses, overseas scholarships, and training programs. The core parameters and political imperatives driving these processes were rarely subjected to question or criticism until a generation later. Much less was done to link the education and "manpower" structures to any analysis of other factors such as fertility, maternal mortality, and reproductive health that, irrevocably, determine a country's current (and future) conditions of educational need.

The significance of the potential statistical links of such "human capital" studies to the World Fertility Survey (WFS) conducted by the ISI in the 1970s, and ongoing Demographic and Health Surveys initiated by the U.S. government also seem to have been little utilized at the time or, if recognized, not pursued as a consistent policy. Perhaps this was simply because global data gathering for the WFS was undertaken by independent external agencies out-side UN direct authority that used different classifications. Perhaps the practical scope for integration and close coordination of population data from different sources was more limited. In any case, the "manpower" approach took note mainly of the formal supply aspects of the labor market, identifying on the demand side the registered and licensed activities of enterprises that offered opportunities for employment to those with a recognized formal education. Some sort of diploma or certificate of schooling completed that gave an indication of the specific course followed and, hence, of the skills it was assumed had been acquired was necessary to demonstrate eligibility for these opportunities. Outside the formal education sector, however, lay a much larger informal sector that consisted of generally small, often mobile and flexible operational units that employed labor on an unprotected and semi-casual basis. The workers these units absorbed were mostly unqualified and uneducated, but they had other skills such as dexterity that their employers valued.

The Measurement of Health

Individual Ailments

The World Health Organization (WHO) has published a manual on the *International Statistical Classification of Diseases and Related Health Problems* (ICD-10) that is an important contribution to the understanding of people's health status.[50] This document serves as a valuable guide for the categorization of different diseases (morbidity) and causes of mortality by gender and age in various countries. It also provides information on physical infrastructure and health personnel by selected categories; for example, the number of pharmacies, nurses, physicians, dentists, and midwives per 100,000 population. Perhaps it is not surprising that the WHO has concentrated more on the incidence of illness rather than on conditions for good health.

In 1977, the Thirtieth World Health Assembly declared that the main social goal of the WHO and member nations in the coming decades would be the attainment of Health for All by the Year 2000 (HFA 2000).[51] To realize the goal of HFA 2000 and to facilitate effective public provision of health care, the most immediate requirement was to acquire knowledge about the economic and social characteristics of the patient population. Classifications of health data that would extend well beyond simple records of age and gender of patients and type of disease or cause of death were required. It was important to collect additional information on the socioeconomic characteristics not only of the patients but also of the populations at risk. Because it is increasingly recognized that sickness is not accidental, data relating to health status by region, occupation, income, education, and other factors need to be recorded. None of this shows up in the existing classifications that relate to illness and reported morbidity rather than to health.

In brief, the existing data system provides information on health that relates only to morbidity and mortality. It says little or nothing about who these patients are, what income category or social status they belong to, what occupation they follow, and where and how they live. Governments and other health agencies are less readily able to assess comprehensively the resource implications of policy interventions to improve the health status of the population. The data guide only loosely describes actions officials must take to ensure "health for all."

In the absence of universal health care, people's access to medical services and the rates at which patients use different health services are determined by financial, physical, legal, locational, cultural, and institutional factors. In developing countries, decisions about who gets what type of medical facilities and when may not necessarily be based on need, and the value of the service poorer people receive is often proportionally worse than others. Ensuring more effective delivery of public and government health services calls for statistics, not only on ailments but also how available different types of medical facilities and services are and how easily people can get access to them according to their socioeconomic status and other relevant individual and household characteristics. To ensure efficient and cost-effective delivery of services, particularly public services, information should also be gathered on the distance of different health facilities from users, time and costs of transportation, medical and hospital fees, and the utilization rates of health centers by different socioeconomic groups. Such data help to determine priorities even if problems of exclusivity and discrimination in access to health entitlements in some countries cannot readily be removed. Even the dismantling of barriers may not be sufficient. Equal utilization rates reported across socioeconomic classes or income groups may conceal the fact that the cost of the type of health services that are provided by the public sector "free" or below market prices is much greater for the better-placed income groups than it is for those at the lower end of the scale. Detailed classification of access by socioeconomic status may be necessary to monitor the fairness of publicly provided services and ensure that they reach those for whom they are intended. Until this classification is done, traditional rules and institutional customs will continue to prevail and to exclude poorer groups of the community from proper treatment. While precise information and precise comparative measures are not available in most countries, empirical observations suggest that poorer people have a significantly lower life expectancy than those in the higher income brackets but measures of actual longevity can only be obtained from calculations of average age at death.

Clean Water and Sanitation

Additional factors that have an important bearing on the level of health are access to clean or safe water and sanitation. Many developing countries suffer from an extremely deficient basic infrastructure for providing clean water and sanitation. This is identified as one of the principal causes for the outbreak and spread of diseases. In this instance, access has as much to do with habitat, the location of personal shelter, and housing density as it has with the features of health and social status that are specific to individuals, although such features often determine where a household is forced to live and hence the health of its members. Public health facilities by their nature are fixed and not as flexible as other health services. Many believe that in late-nineteenth-century Europe, the great municipal water supply schemes, sewage disposal works, and refuse collection activities contributed more to the better health of the urban working class than any new medical discovery. Soap proved more effective than medicine in keeping most children healthy.

Nutrition

Similarly, the serious question of adequate and appropriate nutrition is relevant to almost all poor households, particularly to women and young children. This is an issue that significantly impacts individual health status, particularly at young ages, and affects lifetime resilience to disease. Researchers recognize that culture and tradition also play a role in determining nutritional status. Nutrition classifications are broad and there is no agreed-upon definition or classification scheme between the agencies; nor is there inter-agency acceptance of a specific calorie intake norm to determine whether someone is malnourished. UNICEF, the FAO, and the WHO work jointly under the Inter-Agency Food and Nutrition Surveillance Programme (IFNS) to reach a common perspective and take a coordinated approach to this question. Each organization encourages governments to report on a few common indicators in a standardized and timely fashion so that decision makers can be more aware of emerging problems and take appropriate actions to resolve crises. Such indicators need to be founded on common sources, comparable classifications, and standard definitions of the basic units being observed.

Various countries report on the nutrition status of their children (defined as those under 15 years of age) and pregnant or lactating women. Food consumption surveys are conducted to provide statistics on average nutritional intake—measured in kcals and grams of protein—by sex and age across different regions. In addition, anthropometric measures related to weight and age, height and age, and weight and height are used to calculate the incidence of stunting and wasting and to provide indicators of malnutrition by sex and age (in months) of children by region. These classifications are also of considerable value (when read as a whole) in assessing overall child and maternal health status as well as in measuring the adequacy of nutritional intake. They are widely used as markers to monitor the normal physical growth of children across age groups.

Compared with the classification systems used to monitor health and education, nutrition classifications are not comprehensive, but they are better designed to reflect the underlying socioeconomic structure of the nutritional status. Even so, the nutrition classification system tends to be unidimensional when it is aligned to the question of poverty assessment as expressed in terms of daily calorie requirements. It is incomplete insofar as it does not provide information on the occupation and income or resources of the individual or parent. Similarly, in the case of childhood malnutrition, the birth order of a child and the size of family it belongs to are often very important. This is a limiting factor for policymakers, since the costs of government and public intervention are hard to assess.

UNICEF has traditionally supported the provision of dietary supplements of vitamins and minerals to women and children, especially vitamin A, iron, and iodine. UNICEF has also conducted widespread immunization programs and oral rehydration therapy for children and infants, often at the same time that food is distributed. But in the absence of statistical classifications and related indicators pertaining to social and income status, the benefits of publicly provided nutritional supplements cannot be readily monitored to ensure that they reach those for whom support is intended. The important point here, however, is that simple and effective ideas and advances made in medical knowledge have been brought directly into the scales and standards of statistical measures.

UNDP Human Development Index

In 1990, the UN system, through the UNDP, made an important foray into the global statistical arena with the publication of the first *Human Development Report* (HDR), a document that has since been published on an annual basis. Each year the HDR dwells on a different, usually politically current, theme of human development. In addressing important concerns, the HDR has rapidly become an influential policy document with a clear impact upon national and international strategy and development thinking. The HDR has an extensive outreach. It receives far wider circulation than any other report with similar statistical coverage issued by other international agencies. It is published in eleven UN languages and is widely read, and not merely by the development community. It helps to fulfill one of the UN's most important mandates: to spread information and knowledge and to promote human development throughout all nations of the world. The HDR has focused on both the successes and failures of policy. It has critically reviewed the overriding ideologies such as the Washington Consensus that have guided government action and international intervention, and, as a result, it has sometimes been subject to strong official criticism.[52]

The first HDR introduced what has become a politically important and widely used simple composite index of progress known as the Human Development Index (HDI). The HDI combines indices of economic and social achievement along the dimensions of income, education, and health. These components are designed to reflect human capabilities to acquire an improved level of living. Several ideas lie behind the original concept of a Human Development Index, which is intended to unite concerns of deprivation with those of capability. The first is that policymakers with a more sophisticated understanding of development want an index of national progress that makes practical sense and goes beyond pure economic achievement as expressed by GNP per capita and its growth. Second, it recognizes that good health and improved personal knowledge are essential factors to improving quality of life. Third, agencies and governments need a simple summary measure whose calculation and message are reasonably transparent. The HDI thus combines, in a straightforward unweighted average, a long and healthy life, as measured by an index of life expectancy related to a maximum (average) potential life span; knowledge, reflected in equally weighted education indices of adult literacy and the overall school enrollment rate; and a decent standard of living, which is estimated by an adjusted (log) measure of GDP per capita to take account of price-level differences between countries. The first modification reflects the fact that those with very high income levels do not secure living standards that are markedly different for themselves. Although calculated at a national level, the aim of the HDI is to draw attention to individual status and to indicate each person's possibilities, on average, of making human progress.

In many ways, the UNDP, faced with the necessity of confronting development issues directly in trying to implement its country programs in the field, was the appropriate institution to launch an annual evaluation of human development progress in its member countries. In so doing, it stole a march on some of its UN sister agencies. But at the same time, it also became immersed in the technical complexities of maintaining rigorous control over the quality, consistency, and comparability of statistics emanating from different sources in the countries from which the specially set up Human Development Report Office (HDRO) has had to draw its data. The HDRO diverted from customary UN practice in three main ways:

1. In the selective use of data, often drawing on extreme cases to underline polarized situations or highlight a particular point (rather than choosing the whole range of data to examine or review a general hypothesis).

2. In resorting to new and different statistical measures, officials were hesitant to try to capture the essence of a given phenomena such as "marginalization," "human rights," or "governance."

3. In its introduction of the Human Development Index (and, later, other composite indicators) to quantify progress and deprivation and to give scale to crucial socioeconomic phenomena that were not directly identifiable and measurable in themselves. Related indices devised by the HDRO have been designed to provide a perspective on critical questions relating to poverty and gender equality.

The HDR was a bold departure from the data traditions of the UN; it challenged political ideologies and entered into what previously had been forbidden measurement territory. It invaded the political comfort zone of many national leaders and their governments and orthodox statisticians. Such a role demands that very careful attention be paid to the political tightrope the report and its supporting statistical base must walk.[53] The HDR must balance a desire to disseminate as much relevant information as possible in the interests of improving transparency with an equally important concern for development advocacy. At the same time, this advocacy must be recognized as being based on internationally respectable evidence in order to serve as catalyst for action.

There is no doubt that the original aims of the HDR were entirely worthy. Some of the ideas floated in its successive reports—and the attempts to measure them—have been important, innovative, and thought provoking. Since the beginning, the human development reports have aroused considerable discussion and debate. They have also encouraged cooperation and technical interaction among involved actors, none of which has been a bad thing. The HDR ran into problems when questions about statistical accuracy and use of poor-quality and inconsistent data arose.

Several countries and agencies took issue with the HDR on the question of the fitness for purpose of the data it published. The matter was drawn to the attention of the Statistical Commission and resulted in the setting up of an independent group of experts to conduct a thorough review of the statistical content of the HDR. This unprecedented concern with the data in a UN document was, at least in part, a reflection of the success of the HDR in using information creatively and was evidence of its power to influence and inspire national development strategies and thinking. The HDR is not (by its own admission) primarily a statistical document, although it employs data extensively in support of its text. The inquiry was called for because of what the professional statistical community considered to be an inappropriate, selective, and biased treatment of data to support positions and its unclear statistical definition of terms such as marginalization. The readership of the HDR is not, by and large, composed of technical data experts and so the information it presented, the commission argued, had to be taken on trust. This clearly placed an unusual responsibility on the HDR's authors to present good-quality data in their attempt to reach out to the report's ever-expanding audience with new ideas and concerns about development issues.

Apart from the extensive criticism of the HDR's use of data in arguing about global inequality, deprivation, and marginalization, the other idea to encounter controversy was the Human Development Index itself. The HDI is simplistic, but no more so than any other composite index in which the issues of appropriate weighting and scale transformation are unavoidable questions of judgment. The transformation procedures used in the index are logical, and the choice of component indices, if they are statistically sound internationally, is quite reasonable for the purposes identified. The main question centers on the aggregation formula, which must necessarily remain a political rather than a statistical choice. The essential raison d'être for the HDI, to get closer to a more reasonable indicator of human progress and to move away from the purely monetary assessment of GNP per capita, is popularly motivated and certainly in line with the prevailing development philosophy. The conclusion must be that the index is not meant to be a statistically precise instrument but a tool for advocacy and for illustrating the desperate plight of the populations of particularly poor countries.

4

The Environmental Dimension

- **The Role of UNSO**
- **Accounting for Environmental Change**
- **The Environmental Impact of Socioeconomic Change**
- **Integrated Environmental and Economic Accounting**
- **Environmental Costs and Prices**
- **Environmental Indicators**

Only in the last few decades has the important intersection between the economy and the environment been studied in any detail. For much of the past century and even before it, the resources that nature provides were treated as free goods. Although natural resources have been used to benefit humankind (or particular privileged sections of it), they have also been used indiscriminately and avariciously in many instances. This occurred because users possessed neither a good sense of the true value of these assets nor any recognition that such resources might be needed by future generations. Similarly, the capacity of the environment to dispose of waste (the so-called sink function) has been liberally exploited in an often-unregulated manner by almost every community and economic agent, irrespective of level of development. Over the years, the earth's limited natural resources have been significantly depleted (some would say plundered) by economic entities that have not had to pay appropriately for their extraction. Consumption has taken place irrespective of whether the resources in question are exhaustible and nonrenewable (such as subsoil mineral deposits) or potentially renewable (such as natural forests and marine fish stocks). The irresponsible use of resources has also applied to less tangible precious natural assets such as clean air and water.

In most cases, a more balanced and proper use of these resources is manageable, or at least negotiable, but this depends on appropriate evaluation and monitoring. Sometimes, however, the full range of functions of existing natural assets is virtually irreplaceable. Certainly the complete restoration of natural assets to their original state, or even the stabilization of their use in their present state, demands sacrifices, even embargos, and takes time. The implementation of clean air legislation and bans on certain types of fishing are examples of conservationist actions. Other actions are taken to protect rare species. Because of the current expectations of rewards from economic activity and the adverse impact of such controls on specific communities, the costs of these restraining actions may be deemed excessive and unacceptable to a particular political constituency. A nation might find moves to preserve certain resource stocks unsupportable because many small enterprises would be driven to the wall. Trying to undo past environmental mistakes while trying to implement more sustainable activity undoubtedly imposes a heavier burden than the pursuit of a more consistent and circumspect strategy that encourages the careful stewardship of the planet's finite and precious resources. Unfortunately, how to identify all the issues and assess the implicit and explicit costs associated with degradation has been a bone of contention between environmentalists and economists.

A number of economists have proposed approaches that attempt to account more effectively for identified environmental changes.[1] The seminal work of Peter Bartelmus, Jan van Tongeren, and Carsten Stahmer was developed within the UN system.[2] It uses the SNA as its core framework. This provides the outer bounds of resource use as defined by the availability and capacity of existing assets and defines a level of consumption consistent with the economic notion of income, the basis of which is founded on a sustainability concept of capital.[3] The SNA provides standard concepts and definitions to consolidate such data about natural resources according to a consistent weighing pattern. It also sets out to make the data comparable across countries and over time. Nevertheless, to fully incorporate depletion of environmental capital in an economic set of accounts, observers felt it desirable to elaborate the existing SNA to provide an additional accounting entry for the using up of natural capital in the economic process. Such consumption was initially viewed as analogous to the consumption of fixed (productive) capital, more commonly referred to as depreciation. This type of accounting would appear appropriate, even if the environmental assets concerned—although they are used in the economic production process—are not themselves generated by that production but are an endowment of nature.

Maintaining the natural asset base of production, whether the asset consists of an intermediate product (such as coal, oil, iron ore, and chemical compounds) or is a piece of natural capital (pristine beaches and fertile soil), is essential for the generation of future income. The manner in which resources are exploited and the real cost of such use influences parallel developments in technological progress and affects the search for new resources. At the same time, people's lifestyles are affected by specific resource use.

The System of Environmental and Economic Accounts (SEEA) draws attention to the availability and maintenance of different environmental services that natural assets provide both to the community and to the economy sustaining that community. The reason it is important to make monetary calculations of environmental change is that such assessments draw attention to the need to incorporate concerns about resource use into the realm of economic and other policy decisions. The SEEA was developed to create a comprehensive set of physical accounts on which to base subsequent valuation assumptions, but physical accounts and indicators have only a limited capacity, even politically, to highlight the importance of particular problems of environmental deterioration. Monetary accounts are also required to assess the cost of compliance with independently (scientifically determined) physical standards that define "acceptable" tolerance limits and maximum resource use consistent with some accepted notion of sustainability.

Box 4.1. Significant Events in Environmental Politics

1972   United Nations Conference on the Human Environment, Stockholm
1972   Publication of the *Limits to Growth: A Report for the Club of Rome's Project on the Predicament of Mankind* (Donella H. Meadows, Dennis L. Meadows, Jorgen Randers, William W. Behrens III)
1982   United Nations Convention on the Law of the Sea (went into effect in 1994)
1985   Vienna Convention for the Protection of the Ozone Layer
1987   The Montreal Protocol on Substances that Deplete the Ozone Layer
1987   *Our Common Future,* Brundtland Report from the World Commission on Environment and Development
1990   First Assessment Report of the Intergovernmental Panel on Climate Change (IPCC)
1992   Convention on Biological Diversity
1992   The United Nations Framework Convention on Climate Change
1992   United Nations Conference on Environment and Development (Earth Summit), Rio de Janeiro
1992   *Policy Implications of Greenhouse Warming: Mitigation, Adaptation, and the Science Base* (publication of panel by the National Academy of Sciences)
1994   International Conference on Population and Development, Cairo
1994   United Nations Convention to Combat Desertification in Countries Experiencing Serious Drought and/or Desertification, Particularly in Africa
1995   Second Assessment Report of the IPCC
1997   Kyoto Protocol to the United Nations Framework Convention on Climate Change
2001   Third Assessment Report of the IPCC
2001   *Climate Change Science: An Analysis of Some Key Questions* (National Research Council)

Despite all the international political initiatives being taken at the time, it was pressure to place the proposals into a comprehensive national accounting framework—that is, a domestic context—that came to the fore. This came from two main sources. The first was institutional and was linked directly to the gathering momentum for a revision of the 1968 SNA. The initial draft of the SEEA was very much based conceptually around an input-output framework. This was logical, given the prevailing pressure-state-response (PSR) philosophy at the time. The World Bank also pursued this approach in its own statistical research activities in this area. This conventional fixed-parameter approach centered on an interindustry analysis of throughputs and all outputs, including waste products. Outside research went even beyond this framework to more fluid interactive models to determine the dynamic processes of change. Later, the standard input-output approach was simplified and oriented more to the valuation and calculation of environmentally adjusted macroeconomic aggregates.

The second source of influence posed a stronger conceptual challenge. The well-respected World Resources Institute was beginning to highlight the need to calculate an environmentally adjusted GDP in its various reports, which were based on actual country case studies.[4] NGOs such as the World Wildlife Fund (WWF), pressed even harder for the specific calculation of a "green GDP."[5] At the political level, there was strident support for these views. Early work in this area of environmental adjustments to the national accounts had clearly stressed the importance of distinguishing between the generation of true income from productive activity and net revenues from the gradual running down and sale of nonrenewable resources assets (capital) in the calculation of value added.[6] The progressive mining of known reserves of mineral resources[7] as a source of income was unsustainable in the long run.[8] More generally, the innovative study by William Nordhaus and James Tobin[9] to assess net welfare rather than total net output when deriving macromeasures of well-being and similar pioneering work by the Economic Planning Agency in Japan leading to adjustments (downward) in GDP to account for the unavoidable "bads" in the economy were highly influential in steering the UN in this particular direction.

Ideas about how to measure the way people and civilizations affect the environment have moved to the forefront of attention over the past two decades. A historical preoccupation with how the environment has impacted on people and their cultures—in such areas as maritime defense works, land conservation, and hurricane protection—has shifted into the background. Early classical economists such as Adam Smith and David Ricardo and later neoclassicals such as Alfred Marshall gave considerable thought to the environment, especially to the question of land and its value. They stressed the importance of preserving both the quantity and quality of natural assets, especially the "indestructible qualities of the soil." But their economic ideas dealt mainly with steady-state systems and marginal changes in these static states. They shared the same primary concern, however, with sustainability. They always emphasized the importance of adequate replacement, renewal, and reproduction to the preservation of the level of well-being. This is what one economist has recently referred to as the continued satisfactory functioning of "a provisioning system."[10] The comparative inaction and slowness of policymakers to recognize the growing extent and magnitude of environmental degradation can be attributed in part to the powerful influence and economic thinking of Harold Hotelling and his belief that the price mechanism would handle the problem of the world's shrinking resources.[11] The unwillingness of corporations to shoulder the full costs of their productive efforts in previous eras and the ability of companies to persuade their political masters that any enforcement of restrictions that might limit their free hand would have undesirable economic consequences meant that little was done.[12]

Confronted throughout the nineteenth and twentieth centuries with the unprecedented growth in industrial production and overall consumption that has created an exponential escalation in the use of global resources, economists and ecologists have become increasingly alarmed about the rate of depletion and degradation of the world's natural assets—a process that has been encouraged by free-market sentiments. The evident despoliation of the environment has raised questions about how to control the worst effects of human production and consumption activity, which is destroying and degrading the world's resources and reducing the inherent capacity of those resources to sustain successive generations. Governments are now anxious to know what policies to institute in the future and whether they should be predominantly regulatory or whether they should be part of an overall economic strategy that takes account of the full costs of production-related activity. This implies paying more attention to the complex and thorny scientific issue of environmental measurement and to the development of an environmental accounting system that can put a price on natural damage and the loss of the earth's limited resources. Initially, this question of environmental resource use was seen as a classical cost-benefit evaluation matter, but later it was realized a more sophisticated approach was necessary to capture the many externalities involved in making a full assessment of the gains and losses.

At the global level, a strong influence was exerted by the systems dynamics modeling approach of the 1972 book *The Limits to Growth*, which was developed by Donella Meadows and others under the auspices of the Club of Rome. This approach brought to the surface all the latent worries about environmental deterioration and population expansion.[13] But people recognized that the review's conclusions depended very much on the use of exponential growth rates and other assumptions about key parameters in the model. Nevertheless, in resurrecting old Malthusian fears of inevitable resource exhaustion that was inexorably linked to economic progress, the report of the Club of Rome met with considerable acclaim and received widespread recognition in the arena of political advocacy. It aroused intergovernmental concern and underlined the relevance of exploring environmental issues in a more inclusive, cooperative, comprehensive, and integrated way. The authors believed that their findings could have practical application and, thus, operational relevance at the domestic level. But the study failed to provide a convincing or practical basis for national policy review and direction.

The Role of UNSO

UNSO's important role in opening up the technical debate on environmental impact costs was influenced by both external pressure and a series of fortuitous circumstances. These also demonstrated the leadership's ability and willingness to tap into the small and specialized independent groups of researchers and practitioners in this highly technical field. UNSO built up a network of experts in quantitative analysis that consisted of a select group of scientists, economists, ecologists, and statisticians who were available to address some core features of environmental concern. After the 1972 United Nations Conference on the Human Environment in Stockholm,[14] Simon Goldberg, then director of UNSO and a former senior officer in the Canadian statistical service, established an environmental evaluation team in New York. Robert Ayres, a leading figure in the area of commodity balances and energy use, who was attached to the UN in Geneva, was seconded to Statistics Canada to work on input-output tables.[15] At the same time, an internationally recognized researcher on environmental issues, Tony Friend, was transferred to UNSO in New York from Statistics Canada to work on environmental statistics. Friend had been previously engaged with the OECD in developing this area of research and analysis and is noted for his introduction of the pressure-state-response approach to environmental monitoring. His task was to implement a program of environmental measurement. Friend had already played an important role in setting up the group that wrote and serviced the *State of the Environment Report* to parallel annual *State of the Economy Report* at the OECD. At the time, the intention of UNSO in New York was to produce a similar global environmental study to supplement the *World Economic Reports*. Friend brought his expertise to bear on the direction of this work and assisted in the recruitment and staffing strategies of UNSO in this area. An ecological economist was hired and the advice of experts in various specialized environmental fields such as Roefie Hueting, David Pearce, and Robert Goodland was sought. Much later, another leading researcher from the Federal Statistics Office of Germany, Carsten Stahmer, was recruited to help build up the early environmental accounting initiative. These all liaised with the chief of the Energy and Environment Section of UNSO, Peter Bartelmus, who was originally hired from the UN Environmental Program Office in Nairobi to work on the development of a framework for environmental statistics.[16] This work led first to the establishment of technical procedures for the compilation of natural resource statistics. Later, Bartelmus, Jan van Tongeren, the chief of the National Accounts Division in UNSO, and Stahmer jointly produced the first handbook to describe a prototype set of environmental accounts. From the beginning, the methodological framework and data activities were centered on the national accounts because these reflected the assumed interaction between production, consumption, and the environment. The national accounts also provided the asset balances from beginning and end periods that were necessary to establish overall control. Their basic economic structure and macroeconomic focus to the analytical approach was what observers felt was most meaningful in linking human activity to environmental change. The original intention in the UN was to develop environmental accounts primarily as a satellite system because the issue merged noncongruent questions of valuation and quantity change—especially in the assessment of externalities—that did not appear to be readily compatible with the intrinsic price basis of the national accounts.

Because of these crucial relationships to the core socioeconomic system and its measurement, UNSO found itself uniquely placed as an international organization able to make an important contribution to the field of environmental statistics. It did so through the happy coincidence of having, at the outset, the staff with the right ideas to make a difference. It subsequently engaged various leading environmental economists to coordinate with the respective UN authorities on this issue and thus firmly establish the work on the basis of a system of environmental accounts. Although they were from different branches in UNSO and had different backgrounds, the UN experts worked closely together, consulting regularly with several national and international authorities and with other UN statistical officers to establish an initial trial accounts structure for environmental statistics. This structure was later strengthened to produce the foundations for the first fully comprehensive and integrated system of environmental and economic accounts (the SEEA). This early initiative constituted a major breakthrough in understanding environmental questions and represented an important, conscious, and relevant attempt to address an emerging international policy concern. Other institutions such as the OECD, the Arab Development Fund, and the World Resources Institute had already published studies that were concerned specifically with the impact of resource depletion on economic sustainability.[17] These reports raised alarm bells about how the uncontrolled exploitation of subsoil assets and antisocial economic behavior impacted adversely on resource use. But most fell short of taking a more holistic environmental perspective that embraced the totality of the earth's natural resources. UNSO was the first to incorporate *all* elements of environmental degradation (including new discoveries) into a comprehensive accounting framework that describes the main flows and balance sheets. The approach challenged commonly held notions about economic growth as well as the very meaning of conventional measures of GNP.

Accounting for Environmental Change

Environmental accounting has mainly to do with assessing the impact of human activity on the environment. On the one hand is the damage due to the degradation, depletion, and deterioration of a country's resources; on the other, the improvements reflected in state parks, wilderness preservation, reclamation, and the discovery of new resources.[18] All economic behavior has some influence on environmental conditions, and clearly, the more humans who inhabit planet Earth, the bigger their impact will be on an ultimately limited environment.[19] For a long time the poor were blamed for creating pollution and unsanitary conditions, but research has shown that actually rich people consume more and generate more waste. The level of personal income is not the only relevant factor in this situation; the distribution of income is also important. These critical factors change the magnitude of environmental costs and alter the relative importance of different environmental changes. In general, it is the unrestrained consumerism of the rich that puts the most pressure on the earth's limited natural resources and has increased the cost of putting things right. In most cases, when incomes enter into the equation, environmental decisions are dominated by a willingness to pay. When individuals also have to pay some of the real costs of using a particular environmental resource, they are likely to take more care in how they use that resource. But when such costs are borne by global society as a whole and not by specific users, as in the case of the unavoidable expenses created by global warming and ozone depletion, it is not easy to settle the questions of who should pay and of how to appropriately distribute environmental charges.

Depletion and Degradation

Serious work on monitoring environmental change did not commence in most countries until after the 1972 Conference on the Human Environment in Stockholm. This work followed the adoption of a resolution at the summit that recommended that all countries begin collecting environmental statistics. As already mentioned, early data initiatives were taken in the OECD. These were founded on the material energy balances approach, which had moved into favor following the 1973 oil crisis. There was a parallel focus, however, on some clearly evident environmental concerns related to the publicly visible pollution and deterioration in ambient air and water quality. Measurement of these effects followed a conventional and simple assessment that measured individual media one at a time. Others went beyond this single-dimensional and distinctly physiocratic approach to draw attention to the externalities, interactions, and multiple layering of issues and dysfunctional elements within an integrated system.[20] These forces were seen to be degrading and ultimately capable of destroying the essential flow of environmental services provided by natural capital. Such services had been always taken for granted and were assumed to be a free gift of nature. Opponents argued that the real costs of environmental deterioration should be internalized; that is, paid for by someone and thus deducted from a country's GDP. This gave rise to a belief in principle of "the polluter pays." Despite the apparent logic of this approach, analysts faced some genuine dilemmas in resolving the question of who should pay because consumers, through their demands for material goods and services, seemed as much to blame for the pollution problem as the producers.

There is a dichotomy between how physical scientists or ecologists value the loss of environmental assets and their services and how economists approach the same question. Ecologists do not think it is possible, in a multifaceted system, to reduce the reporting of the environment to a single (monetary) measure. For policymakers, however, it is an issue of what matters most and where the priorities lie. This point of view translates into a question of what affects future sustainability; how the weighing of actual costs with the opportunity costs and benefits that have been permanently foregone is performed.[21] The assessment of environmental damage thus still demands a cost-benefit appraisal that balances the advantages of doing certain things for the present generation against the possible costs (some of which are cumulative) for those in the future. If the system is to be measured in some sort of economic sense, then environmental losses ought to be consistently deducted from GDP to estimate the net progress that has been achieved. These economic costs would include the expense of cleaning up the environment and undoing past damage as well as (even if under regulation) all those specific charges incurred by firms to avoid further environmental deterioration and slow down the rate of degradation. Deducting all such costs from GDP or GNP, however, would then prove misleading because those countries that made most efforts and incurred the greatest expense to repair past and present environmental damage and to avoid such problems in the future—which would hence contribute, in principle, to a higher real "green GNP"—would actually generate by conventional methods a lower estimate of "green GNP." By the rules of national accounting, if all such activity was conducted or paid for by the government, the costs incurred would contribute to a higher GDP. But if private enterprises assumed these costs, they would deduct them from their operating surpluses, which would lead, in contrast, to a lower GDP. All this refers to environmental protection expenditures, commonly referred to as "defensive expenditures" when deducted from GDP.[22] The idea of costing environmental degradation in this way has not attracted many followers, which is why the maintenance cost approach, which extends to estimating costs that are not actually incurred (but deemed necessary to avoid further environmental deterioration), has found more support.

Estimates of perceived environmental damage, however, have to be related to both the direct and indirect effects of environmental deterioration and decay. The global socioeconomic system is interrelated, and certain features of the environment are more interdependent than others. Many effects are difficult to identify and quantify and difficult to predict without some recourse to a comprehensive integrated data framework based on an interactive dynamic model. The internationalization of environmental costs and thus the possible effects on the national economy are not taken into account in the static maintenance cost approach, which is why an estimate of a "greened economy" GDP has to be the outcome of various modeling assumptions rather than a clearly determined statistical calculation.[23]

An alternative is to take a sector-specific or thematic approach to an environmental question, but any approach that looks at a single resource such as land or air or water is often too simple, and the outcomes can be misleading for policy advice. The environmental system is like a recursive model; it is riddled with complex feedback mechanisms in all areas. The various flows incorporate not only the outcomes of different human activity and policy incentives (past and present) but also the dynamic functions of a constantly adjusting ecological system.[24] The ordinary bureaucratic actions of government itself, in consciously or unconsciously creating different economic incentives and outcomes through its fiscal and monetary policies, can be equally unfriendly to the environment. Some forms of subsidy, for example, have proved disastrous for the environment; precious resources have been overused. A complex holistic framework is required to handle all these issues. At present, the most sophisticated policy frameworks available, such as the National Accounting Matrix including Environmental Accounts (NAMEA), which was developed by the Dutch, are still essentially economic at their core. Because these systems are linked to a detailed economic input-output system with social parameters, they can take into account the more important externalities and thus offer clearer choices for politicians. The NAMEA represents a hybrid physical and monetary set of accounts that is nonetheless intimately related to the SEEA.[25]

Renewable versus Nonrenewable Resource Use

Recently, ecological economists, recognizing that the massive economic growth (in quantitative terms) of the past two centuries must have come from somewhere (in physical terms), have argued persuasively for the greater replenishment of resources through increased renewal and recycling. Similarly, but often in some alternative form, they realize that waste disappears elsewhere down some different "sink." The physical outcomes of growth together with the waste and pollution generated from a continuous production process and an unabated consumerism must also end up in a specific place within the same closed system. Economists, consequently, draw a clear distinction between the respective importance of reproductive and nonreproductive activities as well as between resources that are intrinsically renewable and those that are not.

Environmental argument has recently shifted away from a conventional emphasis on the significance of the irretrievable loss of nonrenewable resources and moved to an even greater concern with maintaining the renewable (sustainable) elements of the system. This has again focused attention on the cycle and processes of regeneration, some of which may evolve over several epochs rather than take just generations to complete. The problem of nonrenewable resource use has been examined carefully for several decades. In the absence of obsolescence and accompanying technological advances, it has always been assumed that the so-called Hotelling rules apply.[26] These rules argue that scarce resources will be used in the most economically efficient and careful manner even as the resources get closer to the point of exhaustion. This is because as the assets become more scarce, their prices will rise proportionately, thus helping to curtail demand and restrict wasteful usage. Ultimately, however, the assets disappear and replacements must be found. What has happened historically is that improvements in technology have made it economical to exploit resources that were previously thought to be unusable and too expensive.[27] The stock of proven reserves of most strategic resources has remained constant even though consumption has risen.

The recent shift in attention to the renewable features of the system acknowledges the growing concern for the health and sustainability of a provisioning environment. This aspect of sustainability is, in turn, dependent for its effective functioning on the quantity and quality of the circulating capital available.[28] As a consequence of this relatively new bifurcation of approach and the variety of different time scales involved to regenerate particular resources—or indeed to lose them and their services completely—some argue that two different implicit price systems must be involved in making any environmental cost assessments. One of these is related most visibly to the cost and impact of using nonrenewable resources and the other to the cost of provisioning the ecosystem on a regular basis by maintaining the throughput of circulating and sustaining capital. This is not easy; some environmental phenomena cannot be measured in economic terms because meaningful prices do not exist. In most cases, these would not be consistent with the market-based valuation assumptions embedded in the SNA.

Most of these alternative approaches and valuation questions recognize that nature does not function optimally in economic terms and that, fortunately for human society, the environmental system continues to include, for the time being, an extensive array of redundancies. These allow human beings (or at least past and present generations) to get away with their own less-than-optimal behavior in terms of securing the future survival of their offspring. While keeping track of the effects on the quality of the environment may mean resorting more to physical indicators rather than monetary valuation, the latter underlines the cost of making provisions for the future.

Three decades ago, *The Limits to Growth* may have got it wrong with its too-simplistic systems dynamics model and inappropriate estimates of the parameters driving changes in global characteristics, but there is increasing recognition of the existence of an upper environmental ceiling. Any solution to the development problem that includes a reduction in global poverty cannot be obtained without incurring some major global environmental costs and making changes in how resources are distributed. This might involve more than voluntary curtailment of excessive or unnecessary and socially undesirable consumption, restricting nonessential production, and implementing a working international agreement on redistribution, which transfers resources and savings from the rich to the poor. Without some future sacrifices, and if current demographic and economic trends continue, the global system is likely to implode and fail.

The Environmental Impact of Socioeconomic Change

The highly interdependent nature of the whole environmental and economic complex is beyond debate. One hundred years ago in Europe and North America, rubbish, or solid waste, was virtually nonexistent. Food refuse was recycled for animal consumption or dumped in a location where it could biodegrade. Old clothing and papers were collected by rag-and-bone men for recycling, and metal and porcelain objects were either repaired, resold on secondhand markets, or melted down or crushed into aggregate. It is only since the turn of the last century, and particularly over the past fifty years, with mass consumerism and extensive presale packaging, plastics containers and materials, throwaway culture, fashion trends, planned obsolescence, and genuine technological development, that "trash" has become a serious increasing concern.[29] The problem has been aggravated by uninhibited and unrestrained advertising.[30]

The most sophisticated input-output– and impact-output–based systems now used to track environmental pressure/stress-response reactions arising from both human action and nature itself trace their origins back to the early work of Wassily Leontief.[31] Indeed, some would argue they go back as far as François Quesnay and the eighteenth century; in his *Tableau Économique*, the focus of Quesnay's analysis was on agriculture and the use of land resources to produce output. The core of these frameworks, however, is founded in the more encompassing and coherent input-output work of Wassily Leontief and, later, Richard Stone and his immediate colleagues who were associated with the Cambridge Growth Project at the Department of Applied Economies in Cambridge in the 1960s and early 1970s.[32]

It was logical that the input-output approach would be used to undertake some trial mappings of environmental issues. Stone himself used the framework to evaluate the impact of pollution on the use and allocation of resources.[33] Others experimented with the sequential conditional probabilities involved in moving from one state into (chronologically) the next to explore potential resource needs (especially of energy). Generating the Markov chains that were linked to the relevant transitional matrices illustrated this conditionally dependent process very well. The methodology proved somewhat too complicated for most practicing statisticians to apply, but it was elegant and straightforward in defining the appropriate data-collection methods and applications to use.

The 1968 SNA framework, which was centered on a core input-output industry-commodity structure, proved especially appropriate for exploring the nature of different environmental interlinkages associated with the economic change. Stone's original ideas were as much concerned with national accounts as they were with the implementation of a systematic methodological approach to resolving the different socioeconomic problems facing a society in constant change. Although it lacked the ability to measure technological change, the methodology embodied the capacity to provide the interrelated dynamic analysis of economic activity. In introducing price endogeneity into the system, Stone also showed that such analysis could be performed irrespective of any economic philosophy, because it worked with actual observations and measured outcomes. In the area of environmental assessments, it was thus possible to test whether socialist systems possessed an equal capacity to pollute and degrade as capitalist ones. There is no record that Eastern and Central European countries similarly used their preferred Material Product System for this purpose.

Integrated Environmental and Economic Accounting

The UN statisticians recognized the need for an environmental data system consisting of an accounting framework that could provide policymakers with a basis for weighing alternative strategies within an overall context of sustainability even in the context of distorted value systems that focused on market prices to the exclusion of all else.

The UN SEEA framework, being linked to the national accounts in a comprehensive and consistent manner, related the type of use and consumption (or using up) of resources to recorded changes in asset balances between the beginning and end of each respective accounting period.[34] The SNA provided the conceptual framework, integral consistency, comparability, international authority, and universal recognition of the accounting approach. The defined intersectoral relationships helped to determine the impact of human activity on the nature of output, and hence on the environment, that were consequent on the achievement of various socioeconomic policy goals. The SNA also established the common categories of policy interest that provided a meaningful context in which interpretative analysis could be carried out. The SEEA initially emphasized the deterioration of natural and economic assets, broadly defined, and advanced the notion that degradation in the environment could be interpreted as closely paralleling the accepted economic concept of the depreciation—or, more accurately, current consumption—of productive fixed capital. The SEEA recognized natural capital, in addition to produced capital, as an economic factor and an important component of the wealth of a nation. More and more analysts began to see the accounts as a way to assess the costs and benefits of pursuing different policy actions and of evaluating the impact of these actions on both the environment and the economy.

The SEEA marked a watershed in promoting a wider and more rational understanding of environmental change. It provided an integrated way of thinking about environmental issues, moving policymakers away from a more simple and mutually exclusive thematic problem-solving approach. Its success in developing a broader awareness of the interaction between economic policy and the environment is evidenced by the debate and discussions to which it has given rise. The SEEA represents a concerted desire by government statisticians and academics to make environmental accounting more accessible to the public.[35] Unfortunately, to date, with some key exceptions, it has proved difficult to arouse much direct policy interest in the SEEA, perhaps because it forces governments or, rather, political parties to take a longer-term strategic perspective than that which generally falls within their immediate political time frame. This is despite the fact that the framework gives analysts the means to review and address:

- Environmental problems
- How environmental concerns can be better managed and controlled
- The primary economic consequences of environmental damage and its relative cost
- Questions underpinning future sustainability (through modeling and simulation)
- The analysis of related sectoral concerns, as characterized by the World Bank's measure of genuine savings and consequent derivation of an ecological or environmentally adjusted GDP[36]

These functions are useful for policymaking because they endow the accounts with both analytical and political power. Although the derived outcomes may be more indicative than definitive, the SEEA emphasizes their relevance and improves communication between policymakers and agents. The system gives people a better understanding of both general and media-specific environmental issues. The SEEA also underlines the fact that the traditional thematic or project-based cost-benefit approach to decision making cannot be used, by itself, to assess overall environmental questions. Most environmental questions are not resolved by calculating conventional net economic returns. The SEEA forces analysts to take a more comprehensive look at broader questions of welfare and sustainability in order to assess the size and potential impact of all the externalities. In contrast, a purely economic approach would deny that incomes and levels of well-being could also significantly affect choices about the best use of environmental assets. This is readily evident from the acceptance of an apparent economic logic that argues for dumping hazardous waste in low-income countries (in denial of any higher morality) because it costs less. Any first-hand observation of the actual living conditions surrounding the poor (urban decay, accumulated refuse, etc.), even of those living in rich countries, provides clear evidence of the inextricable interrelationships between poverty and the environment.

The relative importance of the SEEA to a particular country clearly depends on how much that country relies on its own natural resources, including clean air and safe water supplies, for future sustainability.[37] Most countries find it useful to compile energy and emission accounts. To what extent the sales of naturally endowed economic resources (particularly if they are nonrenewable) yield savings that can be transformed into other types of (reproducible) productive capital is another key factor. The concepts of market value and net present value, applied to those economic and natural assets that are embedded in the SEEA framework, are necessarily based on a national accounting system oriented toward observed market transactions. This approach tends to attach importance to the permanent loss in the ability to generate income associated with the extraction and one-time sale of a given resource. Such a focus emphasizes the importance of maintaining the economic benefits—that is, the flow of services—of the environment rather than maintaining the assets. It underlines the distinction between the notions of weak and strong sustainability. Proponents of strong sustainability argue that what is important is the total flow of real environmental services that arises from the existing disposition of resources. They suggest that there is a need for the preservation and full restitution of present assets. Proponents of weak sustainability argue that an ossification of existing asset structures is both impractical and unrealistic in a modern dynamic economy and that the best policymakers can do is strive to preserve an equivalent flow of economic service values from the use of assets. Part of the returns can then be transformed into other assets that reflect society's current preferences and priorities. This position recognizes that despite the welfare, psychological, and aesthetic grounds for going along with strong sustainability,[38] there is a far more compelling economic rationale for reallocating available resources to places where they can be used to best advantage. Many indeed would argue that by transferring the service value of these assets to other groups and locations where the real returns are greater, the world gains from an allegedly improved economic efficiency. In the longer term, however, the gains might not be so impressive, and the issue turns on the question of the choice of starting point and knowing what present value should be attached to the environmental losses already sustained.[39]

The above arguments do not address the more fundamental question of what happens if the whole ecosystem is lost. The SEEA framework may be suitable for evaluating economic and environmental concerns within defined national or territorial boundaries—even for assessing the extent of the import and export of undesirable environmental externalities such as forest smoke and acid rain to other regions. But because it is a national system, the

SEEA cannot satisfactorily handle the broader global issues of ozone depletion, variations in biodiversity, greenhouse gas emissions, and global warming. The extent to which global warming, for example, is occurring and whether it is the consequence of unpredicted changes in the solar system, the cumulative effect of human production activity over the past two centuries, or the outcome of the present behavior of a greatly enlarged global population (or all three factors) is difficult to unravel and impossible to monitor using the SEEA and simple aggregations of national environmental assessments. All of these transnational questions arise from the combined and complex interactive effects of individual actions and national policies.

While none of these environmental "bads" observe any explicit territorial boundaries, the SEEA may be able to help assign responsibilities to different countries for their respective contribution to global degradation. The SEEA, unfortunately, does not satisfactorily measure the extent of the environmental debt already inherited from past generations, as evidenced by the deterioration in environmental conditions that has taken place through time. Some of this legacy may be over and above the planet's intrinsic carrying capacity or absorption ability. In many cases, this debt will merely be passed on to future generations, progressively raising the costs of its eventual redemption as the environment's various "sink" functions dry up or are used up less and less effectively.[40]

Environmental Costs and Prices

No one, so far, has been able to quantify this broader class of intercountry and intergenerational questions and answer them properly using existing statistics and tools. These are issues where there is no simple either/or trade-off. The effects of environmental change, of degradation, and of permanent site damage are difficult to isolate. They are hard to identify and quantify in a specific manner. It is even more problematic to put an appropriate price on this environmental damage since every price system is related to a set of particular (and mostly nationally defined) circumstances.

Quantifying the Physical Effects

Certain environmental changes (improvements as well as deteriorations) may be directly observable; state parks and flood-protection works are seen as environmental "goods," whereas forest depletion, open-cast mining, waste tips, and water pollution are obvious "bads." Some environmental changes, however, may be only indirectly observable, such as improved air quality from clean air legislation or worse pollution from higher carbon dioxide or nitrogen oxide emissions resulting from increased traffic congestion and heavy-industry production in certain locations. But many of the more serious global environmental concerns, such as the depletion of the ozone layer, acid rain, or increased greenhouse gas effects are essentially invisible. Using conventional means, they are undetectable. Indeed, these problems were almost unheard of twenty-five years ago, and it took the investigative efforts and deductive analysis of a devoted group of scientists to draw the attention of policymakers to them. Without a common scientific understanding and agreement it would be almost impossible to obtain any political agreement about the need for uniform environmental regulations across countries such as is embodied in the 1997 Kyoto Protocol.

Although much of this exploratory work on the environment and experimentation in measurement has been carried out in institutions and laboratories outside the UN system, it has filtered through to UN thinking through the setting up of ad hoc review bodies. Furthermore, institutions such as the World Wildlife Fund (WWF) and other conservation bodies such as the International Union for the Conservation of Nature (IUCN) clearly carry the banner for a particular cause and pursue a specific line of advocacy. This is not to deny the importance of any given stance, because each has been able to draw attention to particular concerns, whether they are related to rare species, biodiversity, or dams. The WWF also took a wider perspective that was particularly innovative and demonstrated a deeper communal commitment to the broader political agenda. It helped focus special attention on the desirability of developing measures of "green" GDP. But the main concern of the WWF is to preserve rare species in the wild and conserve pristine habitats. The actual resolution of some of these problems may well require a separate international agency with appropriate legal authority and powers. It will not work unless it possesses the stature and potential influence of the UN. Backed up with relevant data, a more permanent institution—rather than the occasional global summit—may be able to secure global agreement on concerted national action. Questions currently being faced have more to do with measuring *what* has happened than with *why* they have happened, and in this respect, politicians must reexamine their whole fundamental ideology and see their responsibilities extending beyond current sentiment.

Patterns of behavior that have important environmental effects need to be properly monitored. It is already well recognized that, just as in the case of social progress, economic growth and higher income levels will not automatically result in improvements to the environment. The conditions of life for many people might change for the better, but the downside effects of growth could be extensive. Changes in attitudes and actual patterns of behavior (such as the recycling of many types of household waste) take place only after informed discussion and education of the public. The subsequent expression of public (i.e., collective private) preferences and the effect of these on political decisions and public (government) actions can only help raise the profile of environment questions and strengthen the role of data collection and analysis as a basis for policymaking.[41]

Objective environmental data may also be required to counter pressure groups that resist regulatory policies because they believe that official intervention will harm their current and future commercial interests. Data are needed to point the way toward innovation and increased productivity and efficiency among private partners. This would demonstrate that the inevitable outcome of codes and rules is not necessarily increased costs, lower output, and slower growth but new and more efficient ways of doing things. Abatement measures that work hand in hand with adaptation proposals and other feasible alternatives, especially in the case of nonexcludable public goods (where the respective burdens of costs and dispersion of benefits to various groups are differentially felt) can often be shown to be economically advantageous in a broader context. The SEEA is a tool for assessing changes in behavior (consumption and production patterns) and structural effects within the economy since these change the burden on the environment. Indeed, the enforced abatement strategies introduced through international cooperative agreements that relate to the unsustainable overextraction of stocks of fish and forests, overgrazing, and so forth have worked. These international agreements acknowledge the need for regulation and replacement for the good of all, and regulations must be guided by data. Other examples can be seen in such clearly defined areas as ocean whaling, herring and cod fishing in and around the North Atlantic and the North Sea, and salmon fishing in the Northern Pacific estuaries.

It has been a much more difficult task to reach agreement on such matters as the 1992 UN Framework Convention on Climate Change in Rio de Janeiro or the 1997 Kyoto Protocol.[42] In these cases, the statistical evidence was not as clear and unambiguous as it should have been, and its capacity to guide policy and shape political stances was compromised. Because the issues are so large, it has been relatively easy for some powerful interests to dismiss critical statistical evidence, as in the case of national carbon dioxide emissions, as "stylized facts."

Assessing the Cost of Environmental Changes

In the early years of debate about what should be the appropriate basis for evaluating the cost of environmental degradation within the SEEA, UNSO reviewed the different conceptual bases underlying the notions of avoidance costs, defensive costs, damage costs, elimination costs, and maintenance costs.[43] Seeing that most were forms of maintenance costs, UNSO first settled on this approach, although eventually it looked into both cost-based and damage-based evaluations. The various objective functions and policy perspectives governments pursue, however, clearly have a bearing on the valuation basis they choose to answer certain policy questions. There are advantages and disadvantages to each approach for specific contexts. Maintenance costs provide answers to questions such as how much it would cost to avoid or significantly reduce the level of current emissions or other waste products to achieve certain standards or meet given regulations. It is based on the accepted principle of "the polluter pays" and the desirability of maintaining capital in its broader physical and natural meaning. Damage-based methods are related to the cost of bearing the current level of pollution, restoring assets to their pristine states, and dealing with all the adverse health and corrosive impacts. UNSO has also explored the notion that true environmental costs (and a willingness to sustain outlays) are reflected in a delicate balance between the reasoned judgments of elected politicians concerning cost (because they are assumed to represent both the subjective value systems and collective policy choices of their electorate) and the wisdom of scientific experts. The latter are held responsible for determining and advising on "safe" or satisfactory (and not just adequate—that is, minimal) environmental standards. This procedure is not so far-fetched as it appears to be and is not without some economic justification. This quasi-scientific feasibility approach has already been adopted by the Dutch government and by certain state authorities in the United States. It has received serious consideration in the UK, where the methodology of identifying the full costs of reaching a certain predefined environmental standard has been applied to issues such as clean air, temperature levels, and water quality.

Although maintenance costs are quite hypothetical, they represented UNSO's first choice for estimating the assumed costs of environmental deterioration arising from the use of economic assets. In this approach, the costs that arise from pursuing a given course of action are related to the adoption of a net present value basis for valuing all relevant natural assets in place. The desire to maintain the real value of all productive assets over time is the underlying principle of the maintenance-cost approach. Maintenance costs are related to questions of full restitution and the costs of introducing into any production process the most economically and environmentally efficient machinery and equipment presently available. The idea is to avoid further environmental deterioration. The drawback to this approach is that it assumes that the current structure of assets and production in place, on which the valuation is based, provides the most appropriate benchmark. The existing levels of assets, nevertheless, may be less than optimal, and current uses of these assets could be leading, in the long term, to environmental deterioration. The methodology also ignores the legacy of any environmental debt that may have been passed on to the present population from the past use of assets by previous generations. This is well illustrated, for example, by the massive 20-year cleanup operation of Tokyo Bay in Japan, where damage costs were incurred but maintenance costs implied huge restitution costs.

The World Bank has a preference for assessing observed damage costs. This is because the Bank feels that they represent the most robust measure of the real economic costs that have actually been sustained and so better reflect true opportunity costs. But as a practical measure, the approach fares little better as an all-encompassing basis of valuation because of the problems of valuing the damage to air quality, for example. The methodology's ability to provide practical computations and provide prescriptive policy guidelines is limited. However, it is important to note that this was the approach the early "depletion" researchers took, and it fueled an interest in the broader notion of genuine savings and deficits in investment strategies. It revealed how financial savings, as evidenced in the national accounts, can be quickly offset by continued natural capital and resource losses. This calculation seriously affects considerations of available savings and investment requirements, which comes back to the original issue that first troubled those looking at the impact of resource depletion: the need to distinguish between true income and the depletion of wealth. It again focuses attention on a country's inability to live off its fixed natural capital indefinitely.

One of the main problems with these valuation procedures is that they are inevitably related to an existing price system (including exchange rates) that has not been modified to any sufficient extent by the environmental costs that have taken place and are continuing to be sustained by the economy.

Environmental Indicators

More generally, UNSO, in association with UNEP and the UN Commission for Sustainable Development (as well as other agencies such as the World Bank) has come up with an array of indicators that use various methodologies and benchmarks to depict different environmental situations. The FAO also compiles indicators for specific natural resources. For simplicity, many of these are topic related in order to allow more direct cross-country comparisons. The measures are mostly national, although they invariably deal with broad topics such as water or air quality that transcend national boundaries. Others are more location and situation specific; for example, urban water or rural lakes or forested areas. For many of the proposed indicators, however, the absence of relevant measurement instruments and of appropriate standard benchmarks (and the consequent lack of consistent and reliable data) has precluded their regular compilation and operational use in a large number of countries. This may often indicate, in turn, that the proper institutional and legal structures are not yet in place to collect the appropriate information or to oversee regulations concerning the environment and the use of its resources. Quite a few environmental indicators are limited because they are based on census of population and housing questionnaires and on geological surveys, which are updated only occasionally and at regular decennial intervals at best. Other measures are drawn from household surveys, which are similarly conducted at irregular and infrequent periods and sometimes cover different socioeconomic groups. Very rarely are the household survey classifications fully compatible with their corresponding census definitions. Unfortunately, for a variety of operational reasons, most surveys are not strictly comparable with each other over time within the same country even when they cover the same topics. The collection of relevant administrative data also sometimes raises questions about responsibility and presents problems of coordination. There are greater problems when data are compared with other countries. It has thus proved difficult to observe and relate environmental concerns to their impact on households in different locations.

Under various different international initiatives such as the Millennium Development Goals, 2000: A Better World for All,[44] Shaping the Twenty-First Century, and so forth, UNSO has prepared a subset of some seventy indicators relating to the environment. Many, such as energy efficiency, clean water, and air quality, are replicated or overlap across various programs. Indeed, as one observer has noted, there are more proposed indicators than the number of data variables that are currently measured in most countries.[45] The idea behind such approaches is not to give a composite view of some amorphous notion of environmental change but to provide a comprehensive perspective, taken from various thematic angles, on what a particular goal or issue (such as sustainability or poverty reduction) actually implies. This use of indicators is intended to define the underlying logic by which a problem can be tackled. The indicators are also performance related and are intended to monitor improvement or deterioration.

Each of the above international initiatives has the eminently desirable objective of bringing all interrelated environmental, social, and economic issues to the attention of the broader public and thereby opening a proper policy dialogue about environmental problems that includes all of those who are

affected by them. In this respect, indicators derived from a broader accounting system have the potential for greater in-depth analysis because they tend
to be more consistent across subject areas and over time than do standard
measures. By these means, UNSO, in advising the UN Secretariat and global
community at large, wants to ensure that there is greater transparency and
accountability in policymaking on major environmental questions.

In the area of environmental measurement, UNSO remains in line with
the latest thinking in other international institutions and national agencies
around the globe. It brings its technical knowledge to expert group meetings
and conferences and especially to the London Group on Environmental Accounting. UNSO has done much through training programs and awareness
seminars and by providing overseas technical assistance to publicize international efforts that are being conducted alongside its own initiatives to quantify environmental changes. It has drawn attention to the potential risks that
might lie in store for governments that ignore the environment. In this important field, UNSO has gone beyond supporting statements of general principle. It has produced statistics that are more than "stylized facts" and has
provided an approach that offers a sounder basis for analysis and discussion.
Its continued aim is to provide more relevant and operationally meaningful
environmental measures. These are intended to be useful in guiding specific
policy action on topical (sectoral) environmental concerns at both the national and global levels. They are designed to help countries inform their electorate about international agreements on global problems and so dispel doubts
about the government's ability to promote development without damaging
the environment. The potential strategies have important ramifications for
the private business sector, and a broad public awareness of the choices to be
faced is essential. Collaboration, not just coordination, is the keynote to future progress in this area and seems more likely to see success than regulatory
action by governments.

5

Other Statistical Dimensions

- Classifications and Conventions
- Statistics on Governance under Global Influence
- Measuring the Role of Government
- The City Groups: Turning Over the Stones
- Global Indicators: The Missing Calculus
- Human Rights, Security, and Individual Welfare
- Technical Cooperation

There are as many unanswered questions as there are unquestioned answers related to the coverage of data activities by the UN system and UNSO in particular. The reason for this is part conceptual, part political, and part budgetary. This chapter is mostly about what ground has not been tilled by UNSO and proposes some topics for its pending agenda.

Box 5.1. A Classification That Changed the Understanding of the World

In 1815, William Smith, a self-taught blacksmith's son from Oxfordshire who became a canal engineer, single-handedly and without any financial support or professional direction completed the first geological map of England and Wales. Smith identified, classified, and named all the various layers of rock he discovered as he dug canals and journeyed the length and breadth of the country. He then transferred his findings to a huge eight-by-six–foot hand-painted map that he spent almost twenty years painstakingly preparing. His work of carefully delineating, locating, and classifying rocks transformed the way people understood the world around them. The map represented a critical step in the development of geology as a modern science. This remarkable achievement paved the way for the exploration and discovery and subsequent exploitation of various precious metals and many other subsoil resources, including oil, and changed the face of the world.

Source: Simon Winchester, *The Map That Changed the World: The Tale of William Smith and the Birth of a Science* (London: Viking, 2001).

The early work of the UN statistical system has had a lasting impact on how analysts perceive the world. Much of this work has been to good effect, but some has been undesirable. It led indirectly to the acceptance of economic philosophies and the adoption of policies that over the past half-century have failed to alleviate human suffering from material deprivation in the poor parts of the world. Initially, the ideas and corresponding statistical frameworks that were advanced strengthened the role of government and encouraged central oversight and direction. They focused particularly on output, investment, and the creation of jobs, which reflected an interest in economic growth and an unqualified belief in the universal efficacy of Keynesian policy. While this may have been relevant to the relatively diversified and economically advanced countries of Europe and the U.S., it gave rise to problems of interpretation and conflicts of policy interest in the poorer developing countries of the world. In these nations, the disparities between those engaged in the formal economic system and those outside that system are more marked and are only marginally narrowed by redistributive tax transfers. At a time when most industrial countries were beginning slowly to dismantle the excessive involvement of the state in all aspects of socioeconomic policymaking, government involvement was increasing in countries with inefficient bureaucracies and weaker institutions. This has had disastrous longer-term consequences for democracy and effective governance.

Several observers have argued strongly that actions by the West to support such regimes underpinned the existing pattern of control and concentration of power and suppressed alternative solutions.[1] The transfer of resources to countries facing food shortages and other emergencies in combination with external collateral finance for "convenience haven" right of use[2] for logistical and strategic purposes may have, in some instances, obstructed the proper maturation of democracy. Such external support has tended to reinforce existing regimes and protect certain governments from their own domestic policy mistakes. In some situations, generous but ill-conceived food-supply programs may have also undermined the determined efforts of local farmers and entrepreneurs while bolstering existing electoral advantage. The very provision of aid has helped mitigate domestic policy mistakes and strengthened the positions of local politicians in place.

The concentration on growth (and to a lesser extent on promoting structural change) has been viewed as being synonymous with development, irrespective of the fact that monetary growth invariably favors those already reasonably well off and has thus aggravated problems of income distribution.[3] This has had implications in many emerging countries for the pattern of consumption expenditure, the propensity to import, the low-level of spending power, the structure of housing demand, and private international capital transfers. Poorer people commonly have reduced access to the goods they use and may often have to pay more to buy them.

The underlying data model similarly leans heavily in the direction of economic growth and the market and, hence, toward measuring capitalist enterprise and ownership of private property. Revealed demand remains confused in the minds of policymakers with real needs, prompting analysts in developing countries to question why the system does not provide the basic necessities of life for the larger number of poor people in their populations. Traditionally, data about poverty has been generated "back to front," from predefined calorie standards and minimum food baskets to the identification of those at risk from undernutrition. Historical estimates of poverty have rarely been made by direct observation of its multidimensional characteristics and a perceived relationship to an essentially unquantifiable status associated with the absence of individual rights and restricted access to human security has not been defined.[4]

Household surveys, either by design or for reasons of cost, have often deliberately or implicitly ignored collecting data about the poorest in the community. The identification of the very poor has come from a hypothetical determination of minimum human needs. This has been narrowly defined in terms of the fulfillment of some basic calorie requirement that could then be translated into a poverty line. From this calculation, an estimate of the number of poor—but not any description of their real characteristics—could be obtained. The required balance of commodity flows and equations of food intake were produced within the framework of the national accounts and tables on the supply and use of food items. But these calculations have done little to dispel misrepresentations of the capacity of the economic system to secure genuine development progress for those who are less well off, particularly in light of the more conventional estimations of rural production for own consumption. This again draws attention to the unavoidable fact that the conceptual model shapes the compilation of statistics and the question of whether data describe reality or merely offer a perception of reality. Historical experience does not always provide the most appropriate guide to how different groups of people and societies in various states will react to a policy change.

In general, adjusted for other minimum needs, the traditional food-basket approach to measuring poverty and social well-being does not appear inconsistent with the Universal Declaration of Human Rights that was first put forward more than fifty years ago. This laid down that everyone had "the right to a standard of living adequate for the health and well-being of himself and his family, including food, clothing, housing, medical care and necessary social services."[5]

Policymakers should be able to examine in detail the multiple dimensions of well-being that correspond to this standard and identify how they are experienced by different social groups in the country. How well market and nonmarket goods and services serve to sustain individual well-being should be indicated by statisticians. An examination of how demographic characteristics such as age, birth order, gender, family size, and socioeconomic status affect minimum consumption needs and purchasing patterns is also relevant. All this may call for more extensive research on the relationship between household behavior and household characteristics beyond the conventional reporting of measured outputs, purchases, and other outlays at the household level.

The following sections first consider the overall context of measurement and then identify in more detail some of the paths not taken—those lines of enquiry that, so far, have not been officially taken up by the UN organization. These pertain to the UN's human rights agenda and the choices before it with regard to moving the world community closer toward achieving commonly held goals for human development in a democratic environment. They serve as a touchstone for considering UNSO's future activities and for refining its role. First, however, it is necessary to look at the way current thinking is framed within existing data frameworks.

Classifications and Conventions

When an investigator reaches a clear understanding of a problem, he or she has gone a long way toward finding the solution. The ability to quantify the world well lies in a common understanding of the statistical procedures that provide analysts with clear insights into the nature and composition of the universe and how it operates. The creation of a relevant taxonomy is an essential step in any scientific endeavor to dispel ignorance and replace it with knowledge. Clear and meaningful classifications (and their associated definitions) lie at the very root of statistical analysis by introducing a rational structure to disparate information. They define what can and cannot be reasonably understood and concluded when interpreting data that are grouped in various ways. A classification provides the fundamental framework and method for summarizing, describing, and reporting statistics. It is the outward manifestation of a model that represents a certain conceptual understanding of how the world works. Yet the very establishment of a classification also creates its potential nemesis. A good framework employed in a dynamic context should indicate how that model may need to be refined or modified in the light of changing circumstances. Simply subdividing or consolidating existing headings is not usually the most logical way to develop a responsive classification structure. The process of observation and experience and the resulting application of data to policy will either help to strengthen a model's explanatory powers or make it less valid with the passage of time.

Classifications, while they are predetermined and appropriately defined to facilitate the ordering and processing of data, also influence significantly how the raw data are collected in the first instance. The core structure of a classification represents the basic assumptions made by analysts and users about the nature of the observations needed to produce the information desired. It forms the primary element in the statistical compilation process. To understand the meaning of the data, therefore, it is first necessary to understand the nature and institutional features of a classification system. Because classifications are prepared by various administrators and official users to serve different purposes, the resulting methodology that is adopted to blend theory with practice may simply represent a compromise solution that is as much the outcome of negotiation as it is of basic design.

Most classifications consist of two primary components:

1. A basic and immutable core component that initially categorizes observed phenomena (as represented by the data to be collected) into coherent, identifiable, and unambiguous fundamental dimensions such as location, reference period, and standard compositional features. This component requires data to be organized by administrative or political regions such as the state (national and provincial) and geographical location, by time and date (to provide a specified period or single point of reference), and by gender and age group (to define the scope of population coverage). These are the uniform identifiers across the international spectrum. They fix all other aspects of the data to a clear, common, and defined set of reference points in a basic framework that is assumed to be relevant to all countries and the chosen time period.

2. A variable component that tracks the distinct characteristics of the different phenomena under investigation. These dimensions define the potential links to other variables and to the core identifiers. They refer to such matters as the size, ownership, and type of activities of enterprises and establishments; the extent and relative magnitude of household expenditures; the scale and characteristics of production; the state of health, educational status, employment characteristics and types of occupation, sources and levels of income of the population, and so on.

Some characteristics of "variable" components are easier to define and separate into clear, mutually exclusive categories than others. This is not just an issue of the distinction between what is widely assumed to be hard economic data that is based objectively on identifiable phenomena and real counts and soft, sometimes subjective, social information. As the world becomes more complex and sophisticated, definitional boundaries and the activities associated with them are becoming more blurred and often overlap. Goods purchased in the market incorporate a growing proportion of services. People take on two jobs, one of which may be only part-time or even on a volunteer basis; each may require quite different skills. Different pay packets or compensation flows probably will be associated with these activities. The frequently assumed one-to-one relationship between a job and an individual person, or the relationship that is implied in the corresponding aggregates that link a particular skill or occupation to a person, is thus obfuscated. Information about employment and the sources of household incomes also tends to become confused with the expansion and increasing complexity of people's capabilities and individual activity. Difficulties with data interpretation ensue when trying to understand whether an increase in employment, represented as either the number of jobs filled or number of engaged persons, represents a corresponding change in unemployment or a doubling up of jobs. Does the real rise in average household incomes observed get enjoyed only by "double dippers" and dual-income households or by households generally? These ambiguities are less the fault of the classification scheme than they are a feature of the complexity and changing nature of the economic circumstances (in this example, the more flexible labor market) under investigation. Recent official information releases have drawn attention to this problem. They underline the misunderstanding that can arise from the uneducated interpretation of data carved out of specific inquiries.[6] Confusion arises especially where different sources and thus different classification systems and definitions are used in the collection of raw data. Paradoxically, this problem arises because the desire to improve the frequency of information and broaden the perspective on a problem sometimes necessitates drawing on data from different supplementary sources.[7]

International classification systems must necessarily obey some rules of stability and consistency. These are indispensable virtues that permit comparisons across countries and regions and allow the monitoring of variables over time. Institutions, and not just statistical agencies, strongly resist major changes in classification schemes. This is particularly the case where a classification scheme is linked not simply to data organization within statistics offices but to administrative procedures and policy decisions adopted by government generally. Proposed changes usually call for different reporting and recording methods and sometimes imply the reorganization of filing systems, significant alterations in computational procedures, and modifications to how work is conducted and results are presented. This may upset established managerial practice and the sequence of data processes. Consequently, in the interests of continuity, there has been a general tendency over time to extend existing classifications simply by adding extra elements and modules and by disaggregating already-existing standard headings to accommodate new features and characteristics. Sometimes, however, it is necessary to re-think the essential philosophy of the overall classification. Features such as the growing importance of the services industry (including financial services) in many economies, changes in the distribution structure for marketing goods and increasing incorporation of service components into those marketed goods, and the dramatic emergence of a new and dynamic high-technology sector have had to be handled within classification systems that were formulated in the 1950s or even earlier. In such cases, a more appropriate treatment of the modern economy might have been called for. To paraphrase the famous Solow Paradox: productivity existed everywhere except in the productivity statistics.[8] The question here is more about how goods are produced (and what their embodied properties are) than it is about identifying the external characteristics of production and the physical nature of products.

Classifications play such a key role in the interpretation and understanding of observed phenomena that it is important to keep them under constant surveillance. This ensures that they will continue to have the capacity to capture the significant changes taking place in society. The perpetual dilemma between continuity and keeping current complicates the interpretation of history. Past changes influence thinking and have a major impact on present cultures. The consequent interaction and interdependence between ideas and experience poses cogent questions for present policy that cannot always be captured in formal data-reporting systems. Measures relating to the performance of the economy must clearly be kept relevant and up to date. Investigations into the desirability of introducing new classifications rather than developing extensions to existing ones need to be regularly undertaken when an important new dimension, such as time use (which provides a different perspective to the apparent problem of the overlapping "duality" of states referred to above) or changes in conjugal or physical living arrangements, arises. The report of the UN Sub-Group on Social Classifications recommended in May 1995 that a special body within the UN system be appointed to provide continuing oversight of all UN international classifications.[9] Not only should classifications be kept current but they should also be made more compatible with each other to ensure the maximum scope for integrated, harmonized analysis. Such an objective is undoubtedly difficult to achieve but it would help reduce further complications and thus avoid the need to add extra elements to each separate classification system that are already identified and in other coding dimensions; for example, adding educational attainment (or skill levels) to characteristics of employment and wages and occupation. This is not to deny that such issues are important, but classifications also need to recognize the capability of respondents to provide the data required and identify what the appropriate reporting units are.

Among all the data agencies, UNSO—through the Administrative Coordination Committee Sub-Committee on Statistical Activities—takes the initiative in this area because a large number of classifications fall under the separate responsibilities of the individual specialized UN agencies. These agencies deal respectively with agricultural activities, employment, occupations and wages, education, health status, and so on. The key to closer coordination lies in identifying some common building blocks and basic units of inquiry and laying out the most important links between them.

Early statistical classifications in the UN were developed around the economic activities of production and exchange. Goods were distinguished according to their observable physical characteristics and were arrayed by their main material of final composition or the basic raw material used in their fabrication. The output of a firm and the industry to which an establishment belonged was correspondingly defined by its principal product. The approach was simple, observable, and verifiable. It was a relatively easy task for mostly untrained data clerks to perform a viable coding procedure. The classification worked well when firms were generally quite small, single establishments that were not engaged in producing more than one or two main products, most of which used the same materials and used a similar production technology. The majority of such firms could probably be allocated to an identifiable principal line of business. Classification difficulties began to arise when technologies changed, firms grew bigger and more diverse, and a wider range of products and an accompanying array of services to satisfy different markets were developed. Even breaking down larger firms and enterprises into separate constituent establishments could not satisfactorily resolve this problem, not least because nonmanufacturing activities such as storage and distribution became functions that were directly incorporated into the activities of the establishment. When the intrinsic coherence of a classification is challenged, it is difficult to retain true historical and international consistency in statistical series.

Standard industrial classifications did not permit the development of equally plausible and economically meaningful parallel industry classifications related to, for example, the scale and type of technology or energy used in the transformation process. Although more complex, a technological classification would have been relevant to a clearer understanding of the changing relationship of the employment of workers and technology to output. The economic importance of the size and managerial structure of firms and the ownership of businesses cannot be well captured in conventional mappings. Such features are also of significance to employment and investment questions, payments of capital and labor, and output strategies. Nevertheless, coding goods primarily according to their nature rather than, say, by their functions or end use clearly made it easier to monitor transactions and to codify international output and trade.[10] It made the incidence of the application of tariffs and commodity taxes more clear but it also made less clear questions of local industry protection and whether goods or technologies were being protected. Even here, SITC has given way to a harmonized (tariff-related) classification structure, and the ISIC, as the conventional way of classifying industrial output, is currently under critical review by international experts.[11]

The adoption of a classification and aggregation of a material-based procedure, however, has made it more difficult to identify the various agents engaged in production and trade, to assess their relative economic importance, and to evaluate their respective contributions to production and trade activities.[12] Analysts have had to carry out special research studies using original source documents. Which firms were the major importers? How much did they contribute to exports or to domestic production, as opposed to local sales? In official statistics, why and how certain things happen has been accorded less importance (mainly because it has proved more difficult to measure) than what can be reported as having actually taken place. This inability to slice the economic cake in different ways has inhibited valuable policy analysis and econometric research.

Statistics on Governance under Global Influence

Many believe that what should be of increasing concern to international agencies such as the UN is the inherent tension between government policy and the alleged threat to national authority from globally determined actions. Governance has to do with sensible, evenhanded official management of domestic affairs and how governments are selected and behave. It is also about how individual officials and party politicians can be held accountable for managing national resources efficiently, effectively, and fairly through a nonpartisan civil service and the expression of interest by the public at large. But the independence of domestic policy is threatened by external forces and pressures. One of the primary characteristics of globalization is the diffusion of an international economic system that inevitably reduces the influence of national governments and transfers power to an international corporate capitalist culture. Good governance also has to do with how national governments can use these external influences to the maximum advantage of their own countries.

While seeking legal authority and protection for their operations, many global enterprises probably prefer to have as little official intervention in their activities as possible. Indeed, most entrepreneurs around the world would like to see the role of government shrink. Their argument is based on the popular belief that the market offers the general public the greatest freedom to exercise and expand their range of choices at the lowest cost. This philosophy applies to both hiring workers and making products. Many believe that the market best supports what people would popularly understand as a working democracy that delivers what the public most wants.[13] But this thinking can undermine the implementation of good governance and the role of a local civil society in reaching more equitable and desirable outcomes. The inhabitants of some countries fear that foreign influence will gradually alter and reshape the way they live and think. They worry that existing lifestyles and traditional cultures will disappear, as has happened already in America in the uniform shopping malls and chain stores billboards across the continent. In addition, people are concerned that global enterprises are fickle and mobile and that greater corporate power will lead to more direct foreign intervention in political and even public (civil) service decisions. The fear is that this could lead to the corruption of local officials. Means must be found to track these undesirable elements of globalization, democracy, and corruption.

The private capture of the process of government through direct lobbying is widely believed to be a genuine risk when major corporate interests are placed on the line. Over the past two decades, the citizens of developing countries have witnessed how even the international agencies, especially the IMF and the World Bank, have used strategies of financial stabilization and structural adjustment to exert a strong measure of influence and control over national policies. Countries have very little say in the priorities of the international institutions, even if those priorities enhance efficiency by paving the way to achieve more open markets and improve liquidity. Some countries have adopted open economic policies such as minimal taxes and tariffs, the removal of subsidies, and special investment incentives to bring about lower prices in order to encourage foreign business to relocate on their soil, but such policies have also had the effect of facilitating a footloose style of corporate operation. The geographical separation by enterprises of their production activities from their markets (manufacturing in locations of lowest cost what can be sold elsewhere at highest prices) is a characteristic feature of recent economic trends and of the corporate strategy underpinning increasing globalization. It is important to maintain the structural integrity of a political economy and to preserve national and cultural characteristics, but it is also important to identify the institutional causes of apparent failure to implement good governance. It is clear that continued surveillance of the public sector that goes well beyond the existing scope of government financial statistics is necessary.

Effective monitoring of policy demands the implementation of now commonly recognized performance indicators related to both official outcomes and processes and with the introduction of more directly related diagnostic measures of governance. The former might show, for example, not only how many people are treated in public hospitals and health centers but just what proportion of them were poor and how much of the public budget was spent on each social group. The latter might refer to perceived levels of official corruption encountered by local firms and to subjective evaluations of reforms in procedures for filling civil service appointments. In areas where corruption is well known, the methods for purchasing goods and services and disbursing and delivering those goods should be subject to closer public monitoring.

Measuring the Role of Government

With the passage of time, the traditional struggles between the people and the state, between the church and the state, between crown and parliament or the president and the executive, and between dominant groups and minorities have tended to shade the conventional distinction between "left" and "right" (represented by radical and conservative) in politics. The influence of these two powerful opposing dogmas, the revolutionary and the reactionary, nevertheless, has had a marked bearing on how the role of government is perceived and how its authority is exercised. Furthermore, public expressions of concern about the steady growth of government at the expense of the individual and the replacement of private initiative and plans by state actions require investigation. The task of measuring official actions involving the formulation, orchestration, and coordination and eventual implementation of policy is difficult, not least because the specific services provided by governments are invariably imprecise.

The Effectiveness of Government

The essential role of good government is to improve the efficiency of the economic and social system. A good government works to make markets and other delivery systems work effectively, controls monopoly, enforces the law, addresses externalities such as pollution and congestion, and provides the necessary infrastructure and social overheads to ensure flexible and basic services to maintain human security, health, and opportunity. But in the field of government statistics there is an undeclared tension between those who believe that governments have a natural tendency to become more bureaucratic and conservative (or bound by regulations that encourage inertia) and lean inexorably toward profligacy and those who see government as the primary agent for ensuring greater distributive social justice and maintaining the satisfactory functioning of civil society. Over the years, the former view has tended to prevail; because bureaucracies are deemed to be synonymous with poor management, inefficiency, and waste, the service-specific indicators that quantify government performance have been implicitly judgmental. The collectivist idea of empowering governments with greater economic and social control is believed fraught with potential danger.

Performance inevitably must be assessed in some comparative context of space or time and be related to norms (averages), benchmarks, or desirable targets. Invariably, the emphasis in practice has fallen more on identifying underperformance in the delivery of various public services than on determining the proper focus and direction of official policy. The danger is always that the raw numerical targets themselves will become the criteria of efficiency and thus come to represent the object of policy. Until a proper social dimension can be added to national-level indicators that represent the activities and functions of government, notions about how well governments perform and views about what is good will remain embedded in prejudice, superstition, ritualistic thinking, and unsubstantiated political folklore. While they are politically beguiling, indicators can only become appropriate tools for prioritizing policy goals if they allow crucial statistical bridges to be constructed across classes that can differentiate which groups are in need and at risk, and those that are vulnerable and dispossessed in respect of the receipt of official services. Such information is essential to the foundation of a socially just and properly functioning democracy.

Democracy and Government

The existence of a democratic system is now regarded as a fundamental prerequisite for comprehensive development. Democracy is government of the people, by the people, and for the people. But the democracy of Parliament or the U.S. Constitution or the UN mandate may not be acknowledged in all official institutions or in regular statistics. In many cases, the prevailing rules of the game determine how people's lives are made subject to authority on a daily basis. The danger in reducing the size of governments because of profligacy is that the bureaucracy will serve primarily the interests of a largely unrepresentative and privileged elite. Less government means less governance and a greater risk that issues of public concern that cannot be resolved politically will be left to the market and to the whims of the price mechanism and caprices of demand. As has been seen in different parts of the world, many important social goods may be allowed to fall by the wayside of privatization and a "liberalizing" ideology because they are deemed too expensive to be provided from the public purse, irrespective of their social value. In areas where nonmarket goods and services from the public sector provide disadvantaged people with a significant element of their regular well-being, good governance helps ensure that questions of need assume priority over expressions of individual demand in the market. The latter reflects only the priorities and preferences of those who already possess the economic power to exercise their choices through their willingness to pay for what they want. In the gray areas where goods are supplied at below-market cost, the availability of independent, neutral, and scientifically objective data is essential to ensure a balanced perspective and assessment of individual well-being and persistent need. This is clearly an important emerging area for official statistical development and one in which human security, social justice, and equity are considerations to be taken into account.

In the above instances, through protocols, formal agreements, and legislation, international (including regional) and national governments have an important role to play in improving the conditions of individuals.[14] On the surface, democracy's trappings of free speech, free press, open government, no detention without trial, and so forth appear to be relatively uncomplicated concepts to quantify, although many measures may need to be nonparametric and attributional, subjective rather than objective, and more ordinal than cardinal. Determining the share of eligible voters on the electoral register in the relevant population cohort, looking at the percentage of those eligible who cast a vote at parliamentary elections (i.e., situations where there is more than one legitimate party with the potential ability to form a government), counting the number of candidates put up by different parties, and so forth have all been recognized as ways to assess the degree of a nation's political maturity. But numbers alone merely reflect the letter of the law and convey little information about the outcomes and quality of democratic institutions. They do not register more than a general message about the nature of governance or how well governments perform as democratic agents for good in society.

This issue requires independent evaluation of the outcomes of government actions combined with an assessment of the resources used (real and financial) to achieve them. Open government calls for an array of indicators to measure the performance of officials, particularly those in sectors such as health and education for which government often holds primary responsibility either as a supervisor or as an involved provider and operator directly running hospitals and schools. To do this properly, open government must necessarily observe publicly verifiable principles of transparency and accountability because normal market circumstances are not in place to help ensure that some of these conditions are adhered to automatically.

Probably the most important line of information available to monitor officialdom relates to the different functions of government, conventionally expressed in cost terms in the public accounts (budget). These represent the outlays made by general government in supplying those collective, household, and individual goods and services that the market is not able to provide on customary basis of one-to-one transactions (or is only able to offer to a limited extent). Apart from military defense and protection from crime, judiciary services, and official administration, these services include street lighting, roads, educational institutions, and health services. Over the last decade of the twentieth century, particularly in the area of the individual consumption of public services, governments tried to privatize many of these functions and to sell off their stake in various operations. They also outsourced traditional responsibilities to private agents. This represented an important ideological shift toward alleged greater efficiency. But these changes took place at the expense of equity and overall societal well-being in some cases. The move has driven institutional and organizational change and has had significant implications for policy oversight and control. It is clearly important for statisticians to understand what is going on in order to enable analysts to determine the positive and negative effects of such a major political transformation. Information is required to access whether the assumed benefits have universal application and to ascertain whether the alleged efficiency gains are passed on and outweigh the social losses; indeed, if the new services properly benefit the less privileged.

Performance Measurement

Clearly, the necessary procedures for obtaining sufficient data coverage of this area must be strengthened. This is because recognized outcome measures that have been adopted as performance indicators, particularly in poor countries, are becoming increasingly important for determining the level and extent of international support for the policies of governments of developing countries. Whether or not the Millennium Development Goals can be achieved by the year 2015 will depend heavily on the ability of each respective government to meet their defined targets. Defending policy by simply spending more in any specific social sector may not be enough; it is easy to allay potential criticism and opposition by paying higher salaries to senior officials in social departments. That the amount of government spending on education goes up as a share of total government spending or as a share of GDP may say little other than that the government finds it expedient to buy off politically active teachers by justifying substantial salary increases in response to acceptance of a vaguely defined productivity deal. What people really want to know is whether there are more teachers in specific subjects and geographical areas. Higher spending for education may also reflect only an elitist decision to switch resources into tertiary education, perhaps at the expense of the primary or preschool education that many feel is a higher priority. For long periods in many least-developed countries, real government salaries were so inadequate that civil servants were forced to find alternative sources of income or to work on their own plots of land in order to feed their families. This clearly affected the quality of services across the whole range of government activity, not just in education or provision of health care. For example, it had an immediate and obvious impact on the quality and coverage of statistics.

These are all serious matters that indicate that close attention should be paid to how official funds are allocated. Beneath the level of aggregate disbursements, there lies a more profound political agenda that impacts significantly on social class and status. In this area, the UN should be taking a lead, not only going beyond the standard classification of the functions of government (COFOG) but delving into greater depth to learn how national numbers have been derived. Sadly, for some population groups, most current indicators and data series are too general and aggregated to serve as more refined measures of service delivery defined by location and class (that is, socio-economic status however identified). This gap exists because the primary institution for generating numbers about government operations is the IMF. The IMF's particular mandate for fiscal stability requires that financial data be collected; its singular concern is with the traditional problems of bureaucratic efficiency and overspending and official debt. The framework it has established primarily reflects an interest in matters of accountability and transparency. The size and nature of a country's reserves and of the government's deficit (or occasional surplus) is of key concern to the IMF because of its explicit responsibility for and agenda to restore or maintain domestic stability, preserve conservative economic management, ensure adequate liquidity and reserves, and encourage sound fiscal and monetary policies. The IMF's over-whelming interest is in a government's financial standing, not in its social prac-tices. The harmonization and integration of the official accounts with the balance of payments, money and banking data, and the system of national accounts fall naturally into this context of economic oversight by the IMF.

The City Groups: Turning Over the Stones

The city groups were a manifestation of UNSO's failing ability to provide appropriate leadership and direction on newly emerging statistical questions. They evolved initially as informal and ad hoc meetings not held under UN auspices, at which national statistical experts shared specific concerns of policy relevance. For some issues there was little history of statistical work in the area of interest. There was no central budget for such discussions, and the brainstorming and individual involvement had to be financed by the partici-pants themselves or their respective institutions. The work was usually prompted by the need for an early resolution of a significant statistical prob-lem for which there was little or no international guidance. Although the groups were unstructured and relatively free-wheeling, each group had an agenda and ideas about the end objective and how to reach it. People were invited to join a group in their own right as recognized statistical authorities on the particular topic under investigation. The groups thus normally con-sisted of senior people of professional standing who possessed an authority (direct or indirect) to gather support for whatever recommendations were deemed appropriate and workable and to carry through the agreed-upon de-cisions in their respective countries.[15] From a country's point of view, each member's presence clearly had to be acknowledged and supported by his or her respective government or institutions, indicating thereby its interest in the question.

The first real city group meeting grew out of a discussion on classifica-tions. This first group was concerned with the structure and development of business registers and how to handle the question of services in the proposed new code for industries (ISIC, Rev. 3). Specifically, it was set up to tackle how to identify services and deal directly with the products of the service sector in an international industrial classification. Out of this emerged the so-called Voorburg Group (on service statistics), so named because the first meeting was convened in Voorburg, The Netherlands in 1987 (at the invitation of the director of the Centraal Bureau voor de Statistiek). This established the nam-ing pattern adopted in subsequent city groups. All were charged with specific statistical tasks.[16]

Box 5.2. The City Groups

As statistical problems became increasingly complex, the international statistical community of national experts, particularly in the OECD countries, recognized that networks of informal consultative groups were an effective and efficient way to reach agreements on new methodologies and determine common international standards on certain critical problems in economic statistics. This bypassed the need to work through a single international conduit that oversaw all these questions and the avoided inevitable bureaucratic conditions that such a procedure could imply. The establishment of the city groups was explicit recognition that technical expertise and direct practical experience in the resolution of policy-related data problems resided primarily in national statistical offices rather than in UNSO.

The following city groups have been set up. Most of them remain active, sometimes in pursuit of issues that are extensions of their original main focus. They are listed in alphabetical rather than chronological order.

City Group	Primary Area of Interest
Canberra (I)	household income statistics
Canberra (II)	capital stocks; now covers technology and issues relative to measuring the "new economy" and intangible capital
Delhi (I)	informal-sector statistics (data on the unobserved and unrecorded economy)
Delhi (II)	intangibles (software, intellectual property, etc.)
London	environmental accounts
Ottawa	price statistics
Paris	labor and compensation data
Rio de Janeiro	poverty statistics
Sienna	social statistics and social monitoring
Voorburg	service statistics

Setting up these special groups drew attention to the absence of a similar initiative by UNSO, whose authority seemed threatened. Despite some early opposition from UNSO, which did not welcome the trend and felt the process was disruptive, this new approach was widely accepted, particularly by the developed countries. UNSO, for its part, worried about how the outcomes and recommendations of these discussion groups of mostly advanced countries were to be implemented internationally. The Statistical Commission was also less than enthusiastic about the development. However, the city groups provided a successful formula for getting around time-consuming local and international bureaucratic procedures. Their ability to come to grips with pressing statistical issues quickly was readily recognized and thus adopted in several subject fields that were problem areas. Eleven city groups were set up with the participation of statistical experts drawn predominantly from national statistical agencies. Many remain in existence, but for some, the focus of interest has been modified or expanded as new issues have come to the surface. Formal reports with accompanying recommendations have been published in several cases. Each group annually reports, by agreement, to the Statistical Commission.

The international community has found this innovative arrangement for obtaining consensus on the resolution of emerging statistical questions to be beneficial. The work of the city groups has contributed significantly, through their broad consultative process and networking links, to the clarification and refinement of new workable international definitions, standards, and approaches. The arrangement has proved successful in handling changing concepts and situations. On a number of critical statistical issues, the city groups have been an important source of new ideas.

Inevitably, the establishment of other international centers of statistical expertise and excellence outside UNSO has caused tensions. Each city group, as such, had no formal legitimacy because members served in their personal capacity, contributing their own time and technical expertise. UNSO was first skeptical as to their influence. Its own image, of course, had been severely battered in the eyes of its national professional counterparts. But UNSO found that it could exercise little control either over the process or the separate agendas each pursued. It assumed, incorrectly as it turned out, that because country resources were used, the city groups would represent certain national or regional positions and interests. Furthermore, because the resources that were required to support the involvement of a particular national expert were considerable, UNSO thought that the city groups would exclude inputs from developing countries and would produce solutions applicable primarily to countries in the richer developed world. The poorer developing countries invariably lacked the necessary capacity to participate in these technical discussions, and the UN justifiably wanted their viewpoints to be considered and fully taken into account. A compromise was reached by which a convener would be selected who would set a working agenda that recognized the precise terms of reference for each group. These terms would then be submitted to the Statistical Commission for approval. It was agreed among the statistical community at large to have a regular review of the work of each group at the annual Statistical Commission meetings in New York. The voluntary participation and informal nature of discussion and debates within the groups was essentially preserved, but the discipline of a more formal external reporting procedure, including the setting of specific milestones and deadlines for the achievement of predefined objectives, including a closure position, was introduced. In the end, to the benefit of both the city groups and UNSO, professional staff of UNSO also began to take part in the city group deliberations. The ideas emerging have also fed directly into recommended international practice, though with little input from the developing countries constrained by financial circumstances.

Global Indicators: The Missing Calculus

The measurement of global phenomena is another area where the coverage and comprehensiveness of data related to emerging problems is deficient. In the context of global assessments, there is a distinct difference between truly global concepts and international measures and world totals. World totals are simply that; straightforward additions of national measures relating to the phenomenon concerned; for example, world population or world production of coal or steel. International measures relate to situations where a representative (that is, appropriately weighted) figure is needed and a common standard, often a common currency unit such as the U.S. dollar, is applied to allow comparisons and aggregations that transcend national territorial boundaries. These measures are international, but they do not necessarily represent world totals or the real global situation. A global measure relates to a global phenomenon. It may be more (or less) than the aggregation of national-level characteristics because it is affected by exogenous and autonomous dynamic global characteristics that prevail beyond the domestic context of the nation-state. Global inflation and global corporate profits are two phenomena that fall into this category. Global concerns about trade inequality and terms of trade or resource depletion, for example, can no longer be treated as if they are simply questions related to the international aggregation of separate national conditions and activities.

Given the inadequacies of some official statistical systems and gaps in data, straightforward aggregation processes also have to be adjusted for the inevitable missing observations in a given time period to ensure that figures are consistent, up to date, and comprehensive. These features are best preserved by the proper matching and mapping of data to reduce errors of coverage. But the lacunae remain. As is well demonstrated in producing regional and international aggregates, many measures miss the essential characteristics of cross-border linkages and transactions and fail to take account of undefined externalities. Indeed, at the national level, some of these characteristics may be embedded in individual and corporate actions that net out in important flows or are not considered to be transnational or "arms-length" operations. In the compilation of national data, only exchanges and agents deemed to have a bearing on *national* interests and concerns—those whose activities are conducted mostly within the administrative boundaries of the country in question—are considered to be statistically relevant. For several reasons, some of which are logistical while others have to do with accounting procedures, there may not be a complete overlap between administrative, political, and geographical boundaries used in the legal and financial regulations that define how business is conducted in different parts of the world.

Such distinctions are drawn out more clearly when consideration is given to how a country puts together its national data compared with how multinational or transnational global corporations prepare their own commercial "national" accounts. Business organizations use reporting mechanisms that are global. They define global and national operations according to the various company holding arrangements they use. They can partition activities and transactions between political boundaries and regions while also retaining evidence of core corporate management "dues" and cross-border linkages. This makes it easy for them to post charges from the head office for administrative and technical overheads, franchising fees, leasing arrangements, consultancy work, and other management service costs and transfers to different countries according to a variety of benchmark indicators such as respective asset values, turnover, numbers employed, and so forth. A global company takes a global (business) perspective; countries take a national (political) one. An example of these differences emerges when looking at traditional IMF documentation related to international service transactions as embodied in the balance of payments manual compared with the new General Agreement on Trade in Services recommendations. The latter takes a far more comprehensive view of the extent of the global economic system and how components, especially features of labor service, are interlinked with international transactions. To take another example, because of international migration flows, the world population cannot be obtained by simply adding up reported national population totals.[17]

Global indicators should not be confused with indicators of globalization. The latter has to do with the degree to which large corporate entities are controlling world trade and production. (The flip side of this question is expressed in the growing concern with the marginalization of poorer countries, economic polarization, and the disappearance of weaker organizations and local firms that have been squeezed out by international businesses.) Globalization measures are being currently developed by the OECD (Science and Technology Directorate) and UNCTAD. These agencies are attempting to draw an important distinction between corporate influence and corporate control. Their intention is to determine the extent of international domination of local markets and the way production activities located in different countries are separately controlled (and how labor and capital engaged in this production process are managed) in generating global corporate output. The proposed globalization indicators focus on the extent to which foreign countries contribute to national production and on the proportion of output under foreign control in host countries. For the moment, these indicators mostly respond to a more limited interest in identifying physical volumes of trade and production that are controlled by international companies. The measures that have so far been advanced provide a much weaker representation of financial and management involvement and how this relates back to ownership. Direct investment, the acquisitions of portfolios, and management service contracts that originate overseas are more difficult to disentangle from the nominally "exporting" countries and actual sources.

At present, it still seems unclear whether globalization of markets is concerned with the geographical outreach of some international companies or the domination of certain sectors by their trademark products and production technologies, broadly defined. It also remains debatable whether a rise in a chosen globalization indicator should be considered a bad or good thing and, if bad what the particular policy response from host governments should be.[18] Many issues are closely interrelated and cannot be viewed as independent national concerns; for example, the movement of "dirty" production into lower-wage areas where environmental codes are less rigorously enforced. This practice may be linked to the corresponding decline in employment in higher-wage locations or to waste-dumping in poor countries and serious health problems. The UN has tackled this global responsibility less forcefully and has not yet developed suitable data mechanisms for monitoring these and other issues that are the subject of serious public concern. As electronic communications advance along their exponential growth path, it becomes even more difficult to quantify the reality of highly mobile, rapidly expanding, borderless international commercial activity.

There is a remarkable lack of indicators that are truly global. This is surprising given the present public disquiet about the perceived undesirable aspects of global phenomena and change and growing anxiety about the domino effects of politico-economic instability in different parts of an increasingly interconnected world. There is a considerable degree of political concern about how global development affects the fate of the planet and those who inhabit it. Basic numbers about world population and the rate of growth of output have been produced for well over a century, and more recently, rather less tangible statistics on global warming have become available, but there are very few other global socioeconomic measures in existence that purport to possess a universal coverage. Most aggregate measures and indicators remain essentially international rather than global. They represent the accommodation of existing data into a global framework and the accumulation across states of national-level statistics that conform to rather specific ideas about coverage and timing. While physical estimates of production exist, there are no robust measures of global output (especially by sector) and no official estimates of critical issues such as global inflation or global inequality and global resource depletion. Even estimates of the volume of global merchandise trade remain incomplete and demonstrate irreconcilable inconsistencies both in total and across countries. Observed differences depend on whether one is looking at the data from the perspective of a producer/provider or user/receiver and what currencies are used to settle payments. The timing and valuation of transactions also cause statistical problems. That the official numbers are inadequate as indicators of cross-border transnational trade and unsatisfactory as indicators of international transactions is generally overlooked. More and more often, trade data fail to capture the increasingly dominant and expanding "full service" component of international trade. The important role of these invisibles in the global market is an example of why compiling global measures using traditional perspectives, definitions, and classifications is difficult and ultimately misleading for policymaking.

Measures of Global Trends and Progress

Among global issues, few topics have aroused greater concern in recent years or have been the subject of more contentious debate than globalization. In part, this is because the issues are ill defined and poorly specified. It is curious that the statistical treatment should be so obscure for a topic of such obvious importance to social well-being. The traditional concentration on measurable outcomes and the relative neglect in identifying agency involvement and transnational institutional relationships has bedeviled more robust research in this area. Governments still need to identify which features of globalization are positive from an economic perspective and which are considered negative. Over and above this, the social, political, and cultural consequences of globalization must be assessed. The adoption of appropriate measures can better inform policy and provide evidence to support international agreements to control the less desirable aspects of globalization while simultaneously encouraging its positive aspects.

Many smaller economies are worried about the way private enterprises are extending the tentacles of global economic influence. They fear that they may be unable to counteract external intrusions into important areas of domestic policy. Aspects of their policies, they suspect, may no longer remain under their rightful provenance as sovereign national states. Because national identity seems at stake, some countries believe that the UN should assume a more overarching international responsibility and authority for monitoring these processes and analyzing their effects. Clearly, such authority cannot be exercised without relevant knowledge and pertinent intelligence about the global ownership of the means of production.

Although globalization is multifaceted, it is not the only issue in the global arena subject to pressing public concern: atmospheric pollution, global warming and climate change, transnational environmental degradation, the international distribution of income, global poverty, world population dynamics, international migration and the distribution of people between urban and rural areas, world production, international finance, the distribution of debt, and global inflation (or deflation) are all serious issues that impinge on each other in many ways. A handful of global problems do command international attention, and in these cases, a degree of coordinated action has already been exercised: global disease control, international migration, air traffic control, and criminal extradition are some important examples. Within the UN system, however, most global issues are evaluated statistically as an aggregation of national rather than truly interactive global concerns with significant externalities. This reflects the fact that the international statistical system is founded on data that is separately compiled at the national level by individual countries. The domestic sources of these national data are often quite varied and sometimes overlap. At an official level, totals frequently include data not only from national statistical offices but also from central banks, ministries, and research institutions. Such data, generally, are compiled according to national objectives and institutional priorities. They reflect local measurement procedures and terms of reference.

Differences in data-collection methods and local circumstances are most apparent where value measures expressed in current domestic prices and national currencies are used. These represent local price structures that are the outcome of expressed consumer preferences, national cultures, domestic market logistics, local topography and so on. The use of local prices poses a more complex aggregation question that goes beyond the UN's standardized classifications and its concern to coordinate national statistical initiatives to assure greater cross-country comparability. A special initiative, the International Comparisons Program (originally referred to as the International Comparisons Project; see Chapter 2), was taken to provide appropriate currency conversions for economic transactions based on a uniquely determined set of average international prices for a given year. The results of this exercise are essential to the conduct of any global comparisons or aggregations of real economic values.

The task of preserving and strengthening global economic and financial stability has been the central role of the IMF. The Fund also shares a mandate with the World Bank to fight the war against global poverty. Both organizations, like the UN, approach these tasks on a state-by-state basis. The rationale is both political and practical; the state is not only where the relevant data can be found but also where the basic decisions are made. The Bretton Woods institutions implicitly observe the traditional theory of value in pursuing a common strategic agenda that is applied at the national level. They have the means and resources to tackle many global issues directly, but their approach is influenced by the assumed economic philosophy of well-functioning markets in an international environment. At the global level, however, some countries believe they are no longer, for the most part, the principal agents and transactors in the economic arrangements that most affect them.

The successive international financial crises of the 1990s, first in Mexico, then across Southeast Asia, and later in Turkey, Brazil, and, most recently, Argentina, make it abundantly clear that global market developments and their financial repercussions overshadow domestic and even international institutional interventions. This has contributed to continued monetary instability and uncertainty that affects even relatively rich and apparently financially stable countries such as Korea and Japan. Countries, as state entities, contribute little directly to global production or to the real international terms of trade. Ill-conceived national policies, however, may well subvert international stability and aggravate an incipient global inflation that erodes the well-being of individuals, especially those forced to survive on small fixed incomes. Financial imprudence may also serve to undermine the welfare of the poor by contributing to the erosion of the basis of national wealth. The ruthlessness of combative market strategies and the restrictive nature of regionally applied protectionist policies are liable to inflict serious damage to living standards in the economically weaker countries.

This is not necessarily to argue for putting back the clock and giving a greater say to government, but the alleged perfection of the international market is an acknowledged myth. Governments only defer to the market when they wish to be let off the hook in making some difficult social and budgetary choices. The strength of the market mechanism cannot be justified on the basis of the observed failure of central planning or alleged weakness of mixed economic systems. Differences in apparent macroeconomic performance should not be the ultimate arbiter of the success or failure of different politico-economic systems. The historical inadequacy of command-and-control mechanisms to allocate resources does not constitute a proper justification for rejecting the necessity for some form of coordinated direction to compensate for the social inadequacy of the market.

The organization of an economic system by means of the market pays heed to those with the capacity to pay and who make their wishes known. It ignores those with genuine and persistent need who are too poor to make their needs felt and their plight recognized. It is clearly possible (and quite probably simpler) to operate a well-functioning economic system by means of the market, but given the forces behind the often wasteful, duplicative, and diversionary competitive dynamics, open markets may simply perpetuate inequalities and encourage socially inappropriate resource use. There has been growing evidence in recent years that existing market systems have aggravated extreme disparities and encouraged income polarization. Private ownership of productive property and moves toward the increased privatization of capital do not provide the only answer to development. The problem is made more complex by the fact that governments do not have the adequate or complete information they need to pursue other strategies. As Keynes once asked when challenged about some inconsistency in his argument, "When I get new information, I change my opinions. What do you do?" In the global context, logic suggests that any international strategy should be informed by global evidence. The essential nature of many global phenomena such as global inflation and real international terms of trade is quite different from synthetic notions of global price change derived from the simple aggregation of national characteristics. The existence of an apparently inexorable autonomous increase in prices embedded in all countries' own experiences of inflation that can be attributed to an undefined "stochastic" element of global inflation is an issue that clamors for investigation.

In matters of global concern, the important objective is to properly identify and define the nature of the problem at hand. This involves examining the evidence rather than relying on ideological assumptions or the accepted conventional wisdom. The primary objective in every global inquiry should be to pursue all reasonable avenues of empirical research and only then resort to variously designed algorithms for consolidating and aggregating data at their appropriate levels.

Global Inequality and Poverty

Poverty, both relative and absolute, can be viewed from two angles: as it exists within a country and as it exists between countries. In a global context, both types of poverty are merged through a comprehensive perspective of inequality that is translated into a more tangible reality depicted by the global distribution of individual income. While this is far from complete as a representation of the multidimensional nature of poverty and as a way to estimate the actual number who are poor (and the extent of their poverty), such an overall income measure probably profiles the problem quite well. Statistically, strong correlations can be found between deficiencies in income and the various dimensions of poverty. The UN paid some passing attention in the 1980s to the measurement of the distribution of income, consumption, and accumulation, but it looked only at factor allocations (the respective rewards to capital and labor) and never came to grips with the more thorny political issue of interhousehold (or individual) income distribution. No international agency has formally endorsed any inquiry into the global distribution of income.

The reason appears to be political; this probably accounts for why the data relating to what some consider to be the most important socioeconomic problem facing the world are so weak. The issue of measuring household income and its distribution was taken up by a city group, the Canberra Group, which recently published their report in *Measures of Household Income and Its Distribution*.[19] However, the Canberra Group only lightly brushed upon the methodological problems of determining the *global* distribution of income. The question of global inequalities has been addressed by the Human Development Report Office of UNDP in all of its reports since 2000 and most recently by the World Development Report 2003 (but mainly by reference to national per capita income levels). It has been left to a handful of individual researchers (some of whose pioneering work was not formally supported and recognized by the institutions they worked for) to draw the world's attention to this problem.[20] Not surprisingly, the different methodological procedures adopted have produced different outcomes and thus alternative opinions about how inequality evolved and changed over various periods. The basic message of gross inequality in the world, however, is clear.

The World Bank has now assumed the responsibility for reporting the number of poor in the world. It has devised its own unique methodology (which is income driven) to determine the statistics. The method the Bank uses is not without its critics.[21] At a regional level, UNICEF, in cooperation with ECLAC, produces operationally useful poverty and income distribution statistics and the FAO continues to estimate poverty primarily according to nutritional status.[22] The UNICEF/ECLAC data present evidence of a corresponding impact on socioeconomic well-being, social status, and ease of access to amenities and services. But no other international organization has become involved in conducting inquiries on this basis across all countries. The UNDP remains the only international agency that formally looks at development polarization and marginalization and tries regularly to assess human progress at the national level. The UN, perhaps uniquely, has the authority and holds the national trust, independent status, and recognized authority to conduct inquiries on poverty and inequality despite their political nature.

Human Rights, Security, and Individual Welfare

In the Security Council and in the General Assembly, the UN regularly pronounces on human rights. But politically it appears to be unable to exert any specific influence over any of its member states in which the fundamental rights of individuals are violated. National recognition of any internationally designated and ratified basic human rights measures means acknowledging certain limitations on the exercise of domestic political sovereignty. In this context, "rights" are seen as universal, inherent, unchanging, and inseparable from "entitlements," which vary according to both political sentiment and available funding. UNSO's preliminary attempt to quantify certain human rights is concerned only with the narrower question of whether the basic necessities for human survival are satisfied. Certain additional prerequisites for sustaining social progress may also need to be regularly monitored.

At various times in the past different NGOs and private researchers have suggested indicators to evaluate and monitor freedom, democracy, and human rights,[23] but the question did not receive any high-profile international interest until the IAOS conference sponsored by the Swiss government and the International Red Cross in Montreux in September 2000.[24] At the conference there was a clear divergence of opinion between the core UN administrative position and the stance taken by the UNDP, but an important advance was made in identifying those areas where human progress could be assessed in a fairly acceptable and unambiguous (and reasonably uncontroversial) manner. The minimum welfare/basic needs fulfillment approach was offered as a first step in the direction of establishing what the fundamental material needs for survival are. This standard adds to the consumption benefits derived from the direct receipt of income and own production those benefits obtained from government and NGO distribution of nonmarket goods and services. Assessments can then be made about whether, together, these resources are sufficient to provide a minimum sustainable way of life for a family or household. This represents a slightly different twist to the traditional basic needs approach so strongly advocated from the mid-1970s to the late 1980s. It clearly raises deeper questions about consumer sovereignty in particular price regimes and issues of entitlement, access, and social exclusion, particularly for the poorest sections of the community.

The approach has since been taken considerably farther by Lars Osberg, who views social progress in an enabling sense.[25] Osberg argues that in order for individuals to choose freely what they want in life they need basic human rights and specific legally enforceable covenants. Human rights covenants recognize the interdependence of social, economic, political, and legal rights that are clearly difficult to quantify, especially because such covenants tend to concentrate on rights rather than observed outcomes. The approach nevertheless argues that it is only necessary to legislate for their observation and monitor this observance. Prior social and sociological changes appear to be essential before much progress can be made, but these changes can perhaps be accelerated both directly and indirectly by economic growth interacting through selective social policy expenditures. Greater national prosperity allows a redistribution that can favor the majority of the population, and not just a select upper echelon of people, if the right cultural conditions and political will exist.

In any appeal to conventional consumer demand theory, needs can be viewed as a subset of a broader set of wants that must be met before other, less urgent, requirements can be satisfied. The statistical objective then is to derive a standard measure of human well-being that can prioritize wants and stand as a proxy for assessing whether needs are met and basic human rights are satisfied or not. The list of basic wants may not be comprehensive. Nor will it apply universally, but with locational and sociocultural values superimposed on the standard metrics, it should prove possible to identify which groups—religious and ethnic minorities, refugees and immigrants, the young or aged, and so forth—find themselves placed at some disadvantage with respect to the satisfaction of their needs, perhaps because of their citizenship or residency status. Such a crude measure would permit statisticians to advise on an established criterion of distributive social justice. Such a criterion could relate to a redistributive transfer in which overall welfare is improved, or apply to measures that recognize the basic principles of justice expounded by John Rawls.[26] Measuring human rights in this limited way, however, may only indicate the outcomes of personal economic and political choices. More meaningful measures should be intended to show whether the essential preconditions for effective free and informed individual choice have been met. Other modern social philosophers have attempted to establish an array of fundamental human capabilities, freedoms, and rights as preconditions for individual autonomy.[27] Somewhat more vaguely, these capabilities have been translated into recognizable concepts of rights.

The concept of social democracy rests on a popular belief that the state has an unconditional obligation to ensure the welfare and security of its citizens and to provide relief from destitution and ease the burden of infirmity. In a democracy, rights and privileges carry responsibilities. This idea has been recently nuanced by governments who have passed on the message that individuals cannot abdicate from assuming some measure of personal responsibility for their own well-being, including the willingness to take a job as well as pay taxes. This applies equally to the rich and to those dependent on state philanthropy.

Political expediency may dictate that issues of labor flexibility and competitive pricing override principles of social democracy; this provides a loophole for those with an interest in controlling market demand to turn a blind eye to consumer rights and accurate product description. Misleading advertising and product misrepresentation, for example, sometimes distort markets because they permit wide and unacceptable variations in service quality to be imposed on consumers who are rarely able to address this problem except through a formal complaints procedure.

How the rich and powerful exercise their responsibilities largely determines the fate of the rest of society, but the well-being and security of the population should not be based on voluntary goodwill and individual sentiment about social obligation, as it was for much of the era before the twentieth century. A social system where the rich retain the rights and the poor bear all the responsibilities is not sustainable. The state has to intervene on behalf of the poorer community to counterbalance the basic animal spirits of the free market.

Certain "rights," such as the right to a long and healthy life, access to knowledge, and a decent standard of living, have become enshrined in the UNDP's Human Development Index. The *Human Development Report 2002* nevertheless points out quite forcibly that human rights do not mean much where poor people receive little justice and where a continuing gender bias consistently subverts evenhanded legal processes.[28]

Most progress, perhaps, has been made in recognizing the rights of women. But here too, even in the more advanced economies, when all known factors accounting for observed gender differences have been taken into account, some form of sexual discrimination seems to remain. Similar findings apply to the situation of immigrants versus citizens. Unfortunately, basic legal rights are more difficult to measure and cannot be easily incorporated into a general index of social well-being. The denial of rights is clearly difficult to identify if the police and other officials conspire of their own accord to pervert the true course of justice and wrongfully claim a person's freedom by preempting judgment.

The present statistical situation is unsatisfactory but there are means to measure deprivation in relation to budget standards, housing, fair wage sufficiency, health, and so forth, and to quantify social progress in terms of securing entitlements. Some of these standards are laid down by statute and thus provide benchmarks within a particular social and political setting. The failure to meet the data challenge and take a first constructive step toward regular measurement of basic rights fulfillment allows many in authority to continue to violate already limited covenants of citizenship and human rights without being called to account.

Technical Cooperation

An important part of quantifying the world involves sharing information and imparting knowledge about what methods, definitions, and classifications to use in preparing statistics and in deciding what systems to follow and various measures to calculate. Over the years, international technical cooperation (TC) has played a critical part in reinforcing UNSO's role as both an innovator and an implementation agency encouraging the spread of new statistical ideas and procedures. It was always implicitly assumed that statistical methodologies are fundamentally value neutral and equally valid across all countries. But even more important, international agencies have invariably assumed that statistical best practice represents good country practice. The common ideology over the years behind UN support of TC has been the desire to build and enhance local capacity. This was seen as the way to speed the catch-up process and cover the evident and often critical data gaps in countries with a weak statistical infrastructure that limited policy capability. Similarly, it was also presumed that statistical TC that was provided by UNSO and mostly from the West represented leading-edge thinking and recommended practice in official data work.

As the principal purveyor of official international statistics, UNSO's wish to produce uniformly consistent and standardized data across the globe is entirely understandable, if not commendable. But historically, despite the disparate nature of countries, many officials never questioned whether "best practice" statistics was instead "one of a kind" statistics and whether the chosen methodology was appropriate to every situation.[29] Most practitioners encountered quite different situations in countries at different stages of development. Some adapted and simplified the recommended procedures to fit local conditions, and often these procedures better reflected domestic institutional arrangements and socioeconomic imbalances. UNSO clearly believed that TC activities in support of national capacity building in statistics was one of its more important responsibilities. Coming to a common data standard established the unity of national understanding through the uniformity of their data systems.

The UN achieved considerable success in the early years in its ability to recruit international experts, often on a long-term basis, to help build statistical systems, run surveys, and construct particular data series in its member countries. Its technical assistance experts were employed extensively throughout Africa and Latin America and, to a lesser extent, in parts of Asia and the Pacific. They conducted censuses, managed surveys, and strengthened the organization of local statistical offices, helping to improve data-collection capabilities and bringing in computers to speed their efforts. This support extended to a wide range of statistical activities, from national accounts, sampling design, and index numbers to data processing, statistical organization and management, and technical training.

In addition, in large parts of Africa, and in parts of Southeast Asia and the Pacific, France took charge of providing technical assistance in statistics to the Francophone countries under its immediate jurisdiction or administrative control. Elsewhere, the English, Dutch, Norwegians, and Swedes made major contributions through their own technical assistance programs in statistics. The urgent need for such intensive support, particularly for national accounts, grew in the 1960s as many former colonies sought and gained their political independence. Independence was invariably accompanied by the desire to construct national development plans. These demanded a comprehensive framework for defining economic structures and determining paths of sectoral growth. The framework needed to incorporate a sound system of government accounts and knowledge of external economic relations. The resulting data models gave guidance on what was (and was not) feasible in terms of proposed investment plans, import requirements, budgeting government expenditures on health and education, and so forth. Development plans were usually of five years' duration and provided some basic guidelines (rather than a precise map or blueprint) for macrolevel policy, within the strict limitations imposed by preexisting resource constraints, potential aid flows, and external financial obligations. As time went by, some became converted into "rolling plans" that were updated as new situations presented themselves and goals changed.

During the 1980s and 1990s, the traditional forms of statistical support began to fade and assistance took on a more limited focus that was often specifically related to the main interest of the source of funding. Long-term contracts gave way to shorter-term assignments and eventually to specialized workshops. Despite the UN requirement that assistance should be provided only in response to a government's request, in practice, much of the support given to statistical capacity building (from all types of agencies) was either implicitly or explicitly driven by supply factors rather than a response to national initiatives, demands, and priorities.[30]

In recent years, there has been a significant decline in UNSO's TC activities and a shift in the primary focus of this work. Only a small proportion of its advisory services would now address what UNSO itself considers to be of the highest priority. The overwhelming emphasis of support has been heavily concentrated on population and housing census activities and related demographic work. Much of this is cyclical and is coordinated to the successive decennial phases of the population census program. However, there has been a distinct unbundling of TC activities such that various UN entities have specific responsibilities for different components. Furthermore, following the restructuring of the UN Secretariat in 1993, there was a separation of the technical execution functions from agency implementation tasks. In the end, this has come down to a question of who holds the funds and whether there are relevant personnel in house to conduct specific assignments and, if available, whether staff could be spared to take on a TC assignment. The reallocation of responsibilities has also required UNSO to carry out its own oversight and supervision of projects and programs in statistics; this means that UNSO now performs administrative support functions that were previously undertaken by the former UN Department of Technical Cooperation for Development. As a technical division, UNSO is not really equipped to perform the whole range of these administrative functions.

Over the past fifteen years or more, UNSO has been involved in the execution of 162 country projects with total expenditures exceeding US$100 million. About two-thirds of this support went to Africa; just over a quarter went to Asia. Similarly, around 70 percent of the projects dealt with population and demographic statistics and a little over 25 percent were concerned with strengthening national statistical systems, national accounts, and other economic statistics. These topics represent very traditional areas of statistical assistance, perhaps to the neglect of other important subjects. A very small proportion of this work has been devoted to the development of software packages to process and analyze data across a wide spectrum of statistical concerns. Nonstatistical tasks and problems of organizing survey work have taken up another small component of total TC support. As UNSO's commitment to TC activities declines, this means that its essentially innovative role in statistics will disappear and new ideas will take much longer to trickle down and sink in.[31]

The decline in the demand from developing countries for UNSO help in particular statistical areas reflects both a shift in perceived statistical authority (and thus of the need to observe certain data priorities) and the corresponding greater availability of funds and resources from other international institutions (and, specifically, the IMF) to bankroll new data demands and standards.[32] At the same time, agencies that have traditionally supported UNSO's TC activity, such as the UNDP and the UNFPA, have begun to show a greater reluctance to fund statistics as opposed to other assistance activities. Despite the recent millennium round of decennial censuses when, more than ever, a groundbreaking demographic benchmark was needed, far fewer resources were made available to UNSO to support this important area of technical assistance.

Compared with Eurostat and the OECD and the resources devoted by the IMF and the World Bank, UNSO played only a minor role in dealing with the statistical issues facing the countries of the former Soviet Union during transition. Both international external assistance and UN support was required for the unique, one-time task of reorganizing the institutional structure and data-collection methods of the former Soviet Union and Central and Eastern Europe. It was also necessary to provide assistance to other socialist states that relied heavily on a central planning system linked to a command-and-control economic mechanism. Although most of this work was undertaken by international agencies with a more direct policy objective and a broader development interest in these countries, UNSO recognized that many statistical offices in those nations had skilled technicians and an institutional and administrative capacity to collect data directly from basic reporting units. Some of the basic reporting units, however, were disappearing and others no longer saw their own self-interest being served by providing such information to the new official establishments. A further source of great contention and debate was the possible degree to which the raw data might have been corrupted by institutional practices that were established during the planning and performance assessment process of the previous regimes. The old regimes were clearly capable of inflicting punishment and imposing penalties on reporting units when official statistics revealed that official objectives had not been met. In the past, this was an invitation to fudge the reported data. Moving data operations away from central control in order to serve the transformed nature of the economy and to reflect the rule of the market in place of the state did not prove as simple and straightforward as most observers had believed. In this field, more than most, the influence of long-held fears and beliefs linked to the forces and expectations that affect human behavior—areas usually deemed to be outside the purview and responsibilities of statisticians—appeared far more complex than many people would have imagined. The new ideas and methodologies have been recognized by the transitional countries, but traditional approaches to information provision and organizational intransigence have still sometimes conspired to impede the smooth practical implementation of market-oriented data-collection procedures.

This seems to pose a more general dilemma. When they are faced with an open book and presented with a clean page, governments are usually quite prepared to adopt new ideas. But when a process has already been established and its data operations have been institutionalized, then it is far more difficult to change, or simply modify, existing statistical procedures.[33]

Epilogue: Success, Missed Opportunities, and the Continuing Agenda in Statistics

- **Statistics in the Greater Scheme of Things**
- **Ideas, Theory, and Evidence**
- **Strengthening the Effectiveness of Government**
- **The Enduring Importance of Statistics**

The main concern of the previous chapters has been how statistics have helped people to understand the vital questions and powerful ideas that have influenced intellectual tradition in the social sciences. This book has reviewed some of the main ideas that have mattered in the realm of measuring human progress. Space and time have not permitted a thorough documentation of all the ideas adopted and actions taken by the UN statistical system. The search for a conceptual framework bounded by theory depends on the ability to fuse the development of relevant hypotheses and associated theories that have not yet been tested and confirmed by empirical inquiry. Since ideas represent how people view the world and are mostly the outcome of a particular way of thinking, the generation of statistics tends to be strongly influenced by contemporary thought and debate. Statistics have therefore shaped, on both the national and global scale, codes of conduct and socioeconomic understanding. They shed light on how people behave and how they have reacted to technology and "progress." They are essential to any attempt to track the manner in which societies have evolved and behavior has changed in the contemporary world.[1]

On the surface, the task of quantifying the world is an apparently unambiguous question of measurement. But this is not the case. Data-compilation frameworks and their associated classifications are predetermined according to recognized concepts and principles, which tend to be driven by particular ideologies and the institutional demands of decision-makers. In addition, many aspects of human activity can be separately assessed only from an organized structural point of view. But it is also important to approach issues from a less readily quantifiable and broader standpoint of human rights, equity, justice, institutional culture, and the quality of governance.

In terms of UN objectives, however, this has not been the logical or comprehensive process by which the issue of measuring development progress has been addressed in the fields of economic, social, or environmental policy. The way statistical ideas have evolved to deal with the important concerns that policymakers and analysts, historically, have felt should be quantified has tended to be material and easily identifiable. The various procedures and solutions developed within UNSO in its role as the lead data agency in the UN statistical system have paved the way for data compilation in these areas. UNSO has performed well to set the international standards within this recognized but limited framework. Although the way that such statistical methods should be applied in common use has been left primarily to individual countries, most have gone along with the international conventions proposed by UNSO over the years. Judgments about how far these practices are sufficient and are relevant to contemporary concerns may not equally survive the test of time.

These chapters have only briefly reviewed the place of statistics in a broader historical and topical context. Each has tried to examine the role of the UN in defining what data should be collected internationally. Each has also described how recommendations and guidelines produced by UNSO have had a major impact on statistical policy and thinking. UN statistics have influenced general perceptions not only about economic and social progress but also about environmental issues. More pragmatically, the extensive adoption by member governments of standard statistical methods to pursue objective analysis and the use of statistics to refine national policies and their implementation has contributed significantly, in most instances, to more considered and careful official actions. Data have also enabled people to take a wider interest in matters and decisions that affect their lives. Statistics have been an important tool in the quest for greater participation and the general pursuit of a higher quality of life. They have contributed to the conceptual intellectual architecture that, in many operational applications, provides the foundation for modern thinking about the forces for good in promoting human progress. The resolution of those problems and dilemmas that continually confront today's political leaders constitute important areas where data remain essential in guiding objective assessments.

Statistics have usually little to say about the individual motives and beliefs that affect the way people behave. But when taken together, as a group, data can broadly map common behavior patterns and relate them to the demographic and social structure of the group under investigation. Statistics support the analysis of the basis for the revealed, and assumed rational, engagement of people in economic, social, and political affairs. Data may even draw attention to the origins and purposes of human activity and challenge traditional notions about values and inherited virtues.

The compilation of statistics, however, tends to underpin the processes of central control and official planning and the conventional hierarchy of authority. Thus, it is all the more important to make sure that the scope of information produced is shared and made transparent. All official statistics are essentially public property, if not always public goods, and most government data should be made freely available to encourage greater individual participation and community involvement in matters of personal and social consequence.

Statistics in the Greater Scheme of Things

Statistics and ideas are in some ways an anathema to each other, yet both play a key role in developing common themes of thought and acceptable schemes of analysis. Ideas do not come out of the blue but are usually the outcome of an unending voyage of exploration and discovery. Statistics represent a key element in the scientific process of investigation, providing the results of quantitative observation and associated explanations about how things work in "the real world." Statistical method belongs to a body of exploratory techniques that define an approach to a question and determine the method of inquiry. On the one hand, it is directed observation related to inference and hypothesis testing; namely, the ability, with a certain defined level of probability, to test if a given finding is false, to advance knowledge. On the other hand, it applies inductive reasoning in identifying, classifying, and describing exemplary cases. Statistical inquiry proceeds on the basis of observing abstracts of universal phenomena in its efforts to reach conclusions that have a general application. At the very least, these approaches are attempts to gain an intelligent account of how the world behaves from records of what is observed about the way things happen. This focus on recorded reality is a reflection of an Aristotelian logic and philosophy of common sense.

In the world of official statistics, the statistical approach can be considered consistent with a liberal Benthamite view of the world. This sees the key role of the state as an agent for good in helping to bring about the greatest happiness to the greatest number (and the avoidance of pain among those less advantaged). Bentham and Aristotle both lay claim to the similar belief that happiness and not pleasure, real well-being and not personal material belongings are the true goals in life. Yet, when it is translated into measurable indicators of progress toward the achievement of such an elusive goal, happiness cannot be quantified. This ultimate goal can only be defined economically in terms of a higher sense of individual well-being that is assumed to come from greater material wealth. Socially, well-being is derived from the improved facilities and services provided by various agencies of the state that are intended for individual, household, and collective use to enhance "welfare." The conventional assumption of Western society is that having more of some material possession, artifact, or service must necessarily yield greater individual satisfaction and hence "happiness" than having less of such resources. While it is qualified by the law of diminishing marginal utility,[2] this principle, historically, has underlined the measurement of development and individual well-being.

What is exposed in this logic, however, is the inherent contradiction between seeking to maximize pleasure through the market, as reflected in the preferences revealed in actual acquisitions and other individual choices, and securing personal happiness and social harmony. There is little place for voluntary consent or moral responsibility and, by extension, basic human rights and individual security in the specific context of markets. However, if statistics form an essential component of information and knowledge and if knowledge (according to Socratic thinking) can be seen as the same as virtue, then it can be argued that knowing what is right should result in doing what is right. Assigning to the state the power to apply such important judgments is always risky, which is why democracy and allowing people to express their own wishes is, in the long run, essential to development. In an authoritarian rather than democratic structure, what is considered right is the matter of opinion of a few people only. Being vested with knowledge and state information, especially when it is not shared, conveys political power to them. This emphasizes the importance of good governance in affecting people's lives and their happiness. But governance has not been given much consideration until very recently. It is now increasingly recognized that state actions should be kept under regular and, as far as possible, independent surveillance to make sure that they do not intrude on individual rights and basic freedoms. Measuring this is undeniably difficult. What emerges is a difference between realism and idealism. The difference has been the cause of much conflict and debate, particularly concerning the capacity of the state to be a force for good and a government's ability to pursue policies of virtue that have beneficial consequences for all, especially for the disadvantaged members of the community.[3]

The compilation of statistics, through both administrative procedures and specially designed social surveys, involves the gathering of data and monitoring of relationships of individuals within a given society. This has affected the relationship between people and the state as well as the relationship between individuals and society. But, with some notable exceptions, it seems less obvious that statistics have been able to track or influence the basic connection between individual freedoms and social and political authority as exercised by the state. There are no implicit or inherent checks to say whether the use of statistics is for good or ill. This is quite fundamental because such a weakness reinforces the contention that "state-istics," or quantitative information pertaining to the state (that is, relating to its operation and characteristics), is merely a reflection of state control and an instrument of its organization.

In principle, information enables the state to exercise power over peoples' lives by taking specific direct action or, indeed, by doing nothing. There is, however, a hidden selectivity in data-driven policy processes. By the ordinary administrative procedures of inclusion in its broadest sense (which facilitate access to entitlements) and by specific institutional exclusion (on account of race, religion, citizenship, employment status, place of abode, location, etc.) human beings are not treated equally. The state is bounded by political and administrative regulations that are determined by resource limitations. Intrinsically, it does not possess any moral authority.[4] Nevertheless, even if official statistics place a greater emphasis on outcomes than on conventional processes or mechanisms, they can still provide a rational basis for more optimal decisions. Because there is no ideal state or utopia, casual observation suggests that in an open democratic environment, people-focused policies regarding social participation work better than income-driven, cost-effective strategies driven by the free-market process.

Ideas, Theory, and Evidence

The heart of rigorous analysis is the construction of logical argument from a set of axioms based on relevant observation and experiments. Standard approaches to evidence cannot always do proper justice to real life and events. Within the philosophy of science, the interplay between argument and evidence depends significantly on the strength of the evidence and its source, and on the timing and observation of events. In the social sciences, the outcome of such observations is important to economic and social policy and the legislative action required to support that policy.

In the social sciences, objective and subjective surveys that are conducted to obtain information about the attributes and variables surrounding phenomena and that are designed to assess attitudes and their importance take the place of genuine (laboratory controlled) experiments. But the ability to replicate and predict results remains essential, and the necessity of creating counterfactuals[5] and use benchmarks and control groups is fundamental in testing actual outcomes. There is, however, a recognized asymmetry between observations that support a theory or particular hypothesis and those that falsify it. Statistically, the strongest comment statistical analysts can ever make draws attention only to the fact that at a certain level of probability there is no evidence to disprove a certain hypothesis. The process, as is well recognized, can still give rise to either Type I or Type II errors, which lead analysts to reject a situation that turns out to be true or to accept one that is false. This can result in consequences that could be financially and socially disastrous. Cross-disciplinary communication and reference to historical experience can circumvent such a tendency and thus avert the rush to incorrect judgment. But false conclusions may simply result from incomplete and inappropriate data or the pursuit of myth and, hence, insufficient and selective observation of "the truth."

Strengthening the Effectiveness of Government

Two important themes are now emerging out of current development policy thinking concerning the positive role governments can play in low-income countries. Each is designed to make governments more effective in delivering public services and responding to human needs. The first is the belief that greater local participation in the process of decision making helps to ensure that governments become more responsive and transparent in the actions they take and will be more fully accountable for them. The second is that any assumption of greater responsibility (to the public) by the state requires better and more precise information about how nonmarket goods and services (whether they are collective or are destined for individual or household use) are distributed to different socioeconomic groups. Local expressions of need and an emphasis on the point of delivery of government goods and services both imply the generation of new sets of data relating to the decentralization of institutions and the types of decisions associated with them. They also require more integrated data series that link decisions on outlays with their impact on households of different socioeconomic status according to where they live in various locations and regions in a country. None of this smaller defined area and group analysis is well developed, even in industrially advanced countries, and new data methodologies need to be put in place to advance this approach. In general, governments do not report on what they do not do. Nor, in fact, do they always report adequately on what they are doing or have done and its impact on various sections of society.

Ronald Reagan and Margaret Thatcher gave almost unprecedented consent to market capitalism in the 1980s and early 1990s. Their actions were powerful evidence of a paradigmatic shift in official development ideology that had sweeping and often negative implications, especially in developing countries. Nevertheless, the era witnessed a simultaneous emphasis on the importance of democracy and freedom of individual choice as a means of ensuring the smooth working of the market economy. These ideas formed a key plank in what became widely referred to as the "Washington Consensus," which enshrined policies deemed necessary to achieve declared development objectives (not yet translated into specific targets). The World Bank embraced democracy as a development goal; its president, James Wolfensohn, publicly underscored the integral role of good governance in the development process.[6] Quoting the analogy of Kim Dae-Jung, president of the Republic of South Korea, of democracy and the market economy as being "two wheels of a cart ... that must move together and depend on each other for forward motion," Wolfensohn interpreted forward motion as the pursuit of fair and equitable growth.[7] This progress could be achieved only by a more holistic, participatory, and inclusive approach to development. For Amartya Sen, the 1999 Nobel Prize winner in economics, the spread of democracy has been the crowning achievement of the twentieth century. Many share his view that the importance of democracy is the way it empowers the weak and accords attention to individuals and their ideas, helping to correct the inherent plutocratic bias in market economics that is imparted by unequal incomes and spending power.

Although democracy is desirable and real rather than abstract, it is an intangible phenomenon and clearly difficult to quantify. Various necessary, although not sufficient, aspects and attributes of democracy such as multiparty elections, the majority vote, the uncensored distribution of news and information, free availability of statistics, and legal enactments to protect people's rights can be measured or at least documented and counted. But other equally essential features cannot, such as the protection of civil liberties and individual freedoms and personal property, the respect and recognition of legal entitlements, and the power of the courts to uphold justice. Official statistics will inevitably reflect the intrinsic values of those societies, whether that system is a democracy that embraces the ideals of the free market or a socialist society that upholds a philosophy of an equitable distribution of goods and services. The quantification of democracy should not be neglected simply because it is difficult to measure directly.

Logical as it may seem to relate the workings of the market economy to democracy in the twentieth century and to relate ideas of laissez-faire economics to the notion of social Darwinism in the previous century, equating democracy with a philosophy that holds that life chances are based on the survival of the fittest poses a serious challenge to the intellect. Natural and economic evolution under this principle is patently reductionist.[8] The balance between the good and bad of democracy in strengthening individual well-being depends largely on the extent to which people not only exercise their rights but also assume collective responsibility for preserving socially desired features of the system. This draws attention to the need to ensure that greater emphasis is placed on cooperation and concordance rather than on competition. In the present global economy, survival should not be an unpredictable event that is dependent on chance and the happy coincidence of random favorable factors. Data are needed to guide appropriate strategies.

Unfortunately, to date, economists have been unable to provide plausible, let alone incontrovertible, proof of a clear correlation between development and democracy. This may be as much a criticism of the use of growth rates as a proxy for development and of the present weakness and unreliability of indicators to measure democracy as it is conclusive evidence of the lack of any relationship. Although democracy enriches people's lives by offering them more freedom and choice and providing everyone with the same political and civil rights (if, sometimes, only temporarily), it also tends to strengthen the hand of powerful interests and the influence of behind-the-scenes political lobbyists that represent them.

How different the international statistical system might have been and how the development of socioeconomic thinking would have evolved without the UN is difficult to say. Certainly if the process had occurred in a different era of history, there would have been marked departures from the present system. Some might add that the more appropriate question to ask is whose interests have been best served by the existence of the UN and the direction it has given since 1946 to statistical policy. The initial dilemma was whether statistics should reflect the overall commonality of the "united nations" with a uniform system of collecting data or if the independent sovereignty of the individual nation-state should be preserved by a country's own choice of its data system that would be guided, nevertheless, by broader terms of reference and recommendations laid down by the UN. The emerging role of the UN itself and its perceived place in world politics had some bearing on the national outcome of these basic questions.

In the later period of UNSO's history, as the world grew more diverse, complex, and sophisticated and governance moved toward an ever-greater number of policy requirements, UNSO has played a less important role in initiating and creating new ideas. For the most part, other agencies and academic researchers working in their own respective specialized areas have taken up such matters. The flow of ideas is not so much the result of strategic vision and creativity as it is of contemporary responses to emerging concerns and challenges and to existing authority and mandates.

UNSO, nevertheless, has been quick to pick up on developments occurring in this wider realm. Its track record on innovation, represented by the process of transforming an idea into good practice and integrating it into existing processes, has been good. But passing on this wisdom and knowledge to others and adapting accompanying information systems, particularly to the poorer and less statistically advanced developing countries, has been more haphazard and ad hoc in the last two decades. In part this is a question of budget, but it is also a reflection of the different priorities of development funding agencies, which, at least historically, have attached minimal significance to statistical development and training. But mostly it is a question of the availability of personnel and resources in the early twenty-first century. There is a need not only to harness and foster creativity but also to apply and cultivate the best and most useful ideas on a more general and universal basis, although it will continue to be necessary to adapt procedures to meet special situations and local conditions.

One of the weaknesses of UNSO is its comparatively small capacity to undertake independent research. Within UNSO, there has been almost no pursuit of cross-cutting studies to explore, for example, the relationship across countries of health and education to income levels or occupational status and residence. In other words, there has been no effort to examine the links between observed behavior and response in the context of prevailing social conditions and a household's or individual's economic status. This would have led, undoubtedly, to improved data quality. In the FAO, the linking of farm output to living standards and more specifically to food production and nutrition was an important issue from the early years of the organization. In the ILO, likewise, the adequacy of the working man's average wage to buy a presumed minimal essential basket of goods was always an important consideration. These approaches can be traced back to medieval religious thinking and the teachings of Thomas Aquinas and notions of a "just" wage and "just" price.

Is quantifying the world as it is viewed now enough? And do conventional statistics produced under the UN umbrella for universal use and understanding continue to have an important part to play in the decision-making process and public perceptions in the world of seductive sound bites, virtual reality, marketing ploys, and political "spin"? Despite their narrow and prejudicial nature, the instant and often vibrant visual images and catchy phrases used by the media have an immediate and apparently significant impact on people's attitudes simply because they are more focused. Selective information "bites," while often biased, have a powerful capacity to influence policy and create lasting impressions in people's minds. They tend to carry considerably more weight than a balanced statistical assessment. Has the UN's international statistical mandate therefore concentrated on some of the wrong issues, pursuing broad generalized structures of evaluation and universalism rather than focusing on specific questions and concerns? Has pedantry in recommended data-collection methods encouraged postmortem autopsies rather than thorough analysis and proper diagnosis by national governments? Even in its sphere of economic statistics, have the rigorous standards originally set by UNSO and their inevitable fixity emphasized what may now seem to be misplaced and irrelevant questions for much of the contemporary world? More important, has UNSO adequately picked up on emerging matters of interest and concern in what were the traditional areas of international trade (especially the growing importance of trade in services and labor), industrial production, innovation and technological development, environmental degradation, investment, corporate control, financial stability, and national indebtedness? Has it, in other words, come to grips with some of the more serious statistical questions raised by globalization? Should UNSO now recognize that it is no longer sufficient to classify some activities solely within a geographically defined framework? Nation-states continue to report on their constituent elements while sometimes having limited control over them.

What then is the future role for the UN in the area of international statistical development? How do present international systems support longer-term strategic planning in countries where processes are changing rapidly? All these questions pose important issues that are not easy to answer.

The emergence of new institutions and expert groups raises the basic question of whether the UN can continue to provide the intellectual leadership and methodological guidance required to meet the increasing demands for data in the growing and increasingly complex sphere of international statistical reporting. For similar reasons, the changing nature of global politics, in which major corporations and financial conglomerates may play a more influential role than nation-states, the same problem confronts even the Bretton Woods institutions and challenges their capacity to provide meaningful data in crucial areas.

The Enduring Importance of Statistics

The real strength of statistics lies in the ability of numbers to cast an independent but insightful investigative eye over the shifting sociopolitical landscape of economic progress. The use of statistics to challenge received wisdom and to pursue an objective search for truth is eloquent testimony to the critical role data can play in exposing a regime's public deceit or its patronage of an unfair political agenda. To believe in an unbiased set of figures is to believe in reason and rational explanation. Data gathered without prejudice, deliberate distortion, and political bias undoubtedly help take independent observers closer to where the secrets are hidden and the truth lies. Statistics are important to democracy because they allow the ordinary citizen to confront myths, challenge conventional wisdom, and understand what is, perhaps, an unacceptable reality. They provide analysts with the right data pieces to fit together to form an integrated mosaic from which a clearer and more complete picture of actual living conditions can emerge. Each simple, unpretentious bit of data helps to strengthen those core ideas that influence policy. Eventually, this picture leads to actions that, in turn, define and govern people's destinies. Such data hold up a mirror to society, shaping the very essence of the culture being observed and reflecting people's socioeconomic behavior in official statistics. In their pursuit of knowledge, the empirical inquiries of statisticians sometimes lead them down strange paths and dark alleyways in order to poke an inquisitive head into the remoter corners of human existence and behavior. But many human problems are thought to be universal, and countries will still turn to the UN for technical guidance as well as moral leadership in tackling the complexity—and multiplicity—of measurement issues confronting them.

The concluding chapters have attempted to identify some of these more pressing areas of data inquiry. Many issues are likely to be of lasting concern, such as reducing poverty and strengthening the ability of policy to ensure financial stability. For other, and perhaps no less important, areas of investigation, the path of advance remains unclear. Some of the problems that continue to concern policymakers relate to areas of inquiry that defy ready quantification. These include human rights and personal security, governance, corruption, social equity, and the importance of civil society in preventing or limiting the extent of social exclusion. In these areas, being able to determine the role of government as an agent for good in society in fairly distributing nonmarket public goods and services is a key element. This involves more than simply providing these goods collectively to the community and individually to citizens; it also involves ensuring that facilities and services are offered and distributed at least equally to all echelons of society, irrespective of class, creed, or income level. The need for "fairness" is well borne out by the experience of many developing countries over the past half-century. The social upheavals accompanying the economic transformation associated with the transition of the centrally planned economies of the former Soviet Union to market-oriented economies provide a case in point. Social stability comes only with evenhanded treatment and equitable conditions; the process is dependent on information about discrimination in all its various guises.

Paradoxically, in following the path of development, some governments have been institutionally shackled by the range of controls and potential power at their disposal. Others have tended to use that power solely to secure their own advantage. Corruption thus superimposes its own layer of unacceptable influence over bureaucratic inefficiency. This only adds to the suffering and plight of the least-well-positioned inhabitants of a country, who have little say in the social allocation process. The main problems facing countries, by their very nature, are shared globally and remain cross-cultural and universal in their significance.

UNSO must continue to declare an earnest sense of mission in delivering truth in numbers. It should be encouraged to provide a realistic vision of future policy demands to strengthen international statistical resolve and reestablish its traditional authority. The UN itself and its articles of faith have laid down the foundations for deciding on appropriate direction. UNSO can make fair headway by determining what needs to be done to achieve development progress. By adhering to a paradigm that enshrines universal notions of equity and fairness at its core, and by declaring openly the nature of the fundamental moral and definitional issues that should underpin data compilation and reported statistics, it can assert true leadership.

Appendix: ILO Special Topics

Measurement of Wage Differentials and Job Segregations

The relative wage disadvantage of women in the labor market is a key characteristic that has received the attention of governments, scholars, and international organizations. The evident disadvantage might be explained by various productivity-related factors (such as age, hours worked, experience, education, training), but when the data are normalized for such effects it also appears that such differentials are due to gender discrimination. Identifying the causes of women's wage disadvantage or explaining its pattern of change is one of the responsibilities of the ILO Bureau of Statistics. In reviewing equality for women in employment, the bureau has examined various methodologies to determine statistically the extent of gender wage-related differentials with the objective of defining "model" procedures that are simple to understand and easy to apply. These methodologies, so far, have not been explicitly described. A proposed technical manual on wages measurement designed to contain practical examples and case studies in this area has yet to be published but is eagerly awaited.

Status of Children and Child Labor

The world economic model not only overlooks the needs of women but also the plight of children and the aged who are cared for by them. An important outcome of the World Summit for Children held in New York in September 1990 was recognition of the need to establish a proper database from which to monitor progress toward the achievement of the various international development goals declared. UNICEF thus set out to transform and improve the way the world collected and processed information on children (and women). It took steps to strengthen the vital database relating to their demographic characteristics to serve as a standard baseline for chronicling progress. UNICEF began to support new survey approaches and encourage specific efforts by governments to improve existing administrative reporting mechanisms. A Multiple Indicator Cluster Survey (MICS) approach was developed for use in conjunction with existing demographic and health surveys (DHS) in developing countries. These methods of inquiry have transformed the ability of many countries to capture what is happening to the social and economic condition of their women and children and to target their policies accordingly.

These approaches, nevertheless, cannot identify all the various social and cultural factors that give rise to disparities in people's well-being and to differences in their potential vulnerability to adverse circumstances. Their individual vulnerability to undesirable social conditions may be a legacy inherited from some past status or inexorably related to a personal characteristic such as caste or religion. The disaggregation of national averages relating to previously underrecorded local conditions associated with infection, bad sanitation, impure water supply, inadequate shelter, and poor maternal care remains a statistical priority for policy makers. With such information governments will be better able to target specific groups and regions in special need of assistance. Despite an improved understanding of the issues, good policy is still inhibited by persistent gaps in knowledge governing the well-being of children and their families. One important area over which questions still hang in many low-income developing countries refers to the prevalence of mortality for children under the age of 5 classified by cause of death. This is because most countries' vital registration systems either do not record such important information or because the children die from a combination of causes that usually include malnutrition as a fundamental factor. Often the real cause is not known or simply not diagnosed. The situation is similar in the case of reporting morbidity among young children, a difficult task in any circumstance, especially without recourse to proper diagnostic testing. In the case of both the death of young children and the diseases they possibly suffer from, cultural factors may intervene, especially perhaps among less well-educated rural populations, to conceal the real truth about a condition or to prevent the reporting of how a child was "taken" from its family or the community.

Elsewhere, the ILO has announced that the collection and dissemination of detailed statistics on child labor at the national, regional, and global levels will be kept on a special database and updated regularly as fresh statistical information becomes available. The idea is to use the data for in-depth analyses and studies relating to the nature and extent of child labor. Initially, what limited labor data that was available for children younger than 15 years of age were evaluated. Subsequently, through a special questionnaire addressed to more than 200 countries and territories, the ILO embarked on an official exercise to gather statistical information on this age group. Based on these sources and also on the most recent ILO estimates and projections of the economically active population, statistical tables relating to the employment status of children under 15 years of age have now been produced by sex and age for most countries. Data have also been compiled by main industry division, major occupation groups, and broad employment status for some seventy countries. The series for 1980, 1986, and 1990 and selected tables, together with an article, appeared in the *Bulletin of Labour Statistics* in 1993 (second quarter). In addition, comprehensive prototype methodological sample surveys were tested in four selected countries of Africa and Asia. These were designed to try out, experimentally, how to obtain statistical measures for as many variables as possible relating to the demographic, social, and economic characteristics of child labor. There have been questions raised, however, about the confidence that can be placed in the results of any formal inquiry dealing with such an emotional sociopolitical issue as children's employment despite the high public interest in and widespread concern about the issue.

Occupational Injuries and Diseases

An indispensable tool for policy formulation and action in the field of safety and health at work is the availability of accurate data. Up-to-date and relevant guidelines are required to establish a code of practice for the notification of the incidence of occupational injuries. These are required for administrative reasons related to beneficiary support, supervisory control, worker's compensation, and factory legislation purposes. During the 1980s, the need for better national data on health in the workplace and for more internationally comparable statistics on this topic was emphasized by the ILO governing council. Information on occupational injuries and diseases is one of the basic set of labor statistics at the heart of the Labor Statistics Convention 1985 (No. 160), and information about national practices was collected, by means of special questionnaires, at the end of 1992. On the basis of the analysis of this information, methodological descriptions are being prepared for publication in the proposed eighth volume of the ILO's Sources and Methods series. These will be supplemented by data on absenteeism.

Employment in the Informal Sector

Issues relating to the operations of the informal sector have become incorporated into the core of development thinking since the concept was first identified some three decades ago in the ILO employment mission to Kenya in 1972. For some years earlier, urban underemployment had been widely observed as a painful economic reality in quite different parts of the world. It seemed particularly evident in urban slum areas, but its crucial relationship to demographic factors and development policies went largely unrecognized. For the ILO, the informal sector is of central concern, along with conditions of low pay and excessive hours associated with continued labor exploitation, to its mandate of social justice. As in the case of the well-delineated specific responsibilities taken up by other specialized UN agencies, the ILO assumed responsibility for "organizing" and monitoring the informal sector question. Several leading development research agencies such as the Institute of Development Studies at Sussex that had been associated with the ILO's work to promote employment also became actively interested in the phenomenon and its characteristics.

The informal sector emerged in part because of the asymmetric demographic profile of developing countries and the heavy concentration of persons in the younger age groups. It occurred because, even under the most optimistic projections of economic expansion and growth, the number of jobs that could be created in the formal sector necessarily always fell far short of the expected demand for work. Those that did not get jobs, given the added pressure from the migration of many young people from traditional farming areas to the towns in search of paid employment and their reluctance to remain at home or to return to their rural communities to work on the land, had to resort to picking up casual and ad hoc work wherever they could find it. The official hope of the early development planners was that, ultimately, an improved economic performance would lead to the absorption of many of these people into full-time paid employment in the formal organized sector. This was not to be the case, as savings and investment flows could not even begin to match up to the amounts required to sustain such employment levels. The size of the informal economy thus showed a marked tendency to grow and to become the dominant and most obvious feature of the majority of undiversified low-income economies.

Conventional data-collection methods for a long time overlooked the very large numbers of men, women, and children engaged daily in these economic activities that, for the most part, were unregistered and unreported. A resolution concerning statistics of employment in the informal sector was adopted by the Fifteenth International Conference of Labor Statisticians (1993). This was the first time that international standards were adopted for monitoring the informal economy. The informal sector is characterized by units engaged in the production of goods or services that typically operate at a low level of organization, on a small scale, and with labor relations that are mostly based on casual or ad hoc contracts of employment. Those employed in this manner may not necessarily be working illegally or engaged in producing unlawful products. The assets used by most informal enterprises (and labor is the most valuable) do not belong to the production units as independent operations but to their owners. Expenditure for production purposes is often indistinguishable from other household expenditure. The units, as such, do not engage in readily identifiable transactions or enter into contracts with other units, nor do they incur liabilities. Two basic criteria (household or unincorporated enterprise) and two supplementary criteria may be used alone or in combination (size of the unit, registration of the unit, or the number of its employees) to distinguish the nature of these units. The ILO recommends that the data-collection program consist of integration into the regular national statistical operations encompassing household surveys, establishment surveys, and mixed household and enterprise surveys. The important concern is to get some quantifiable expression of the different types of activity that help sustain the livelihoods of a large section of the population.

Economically Active Population

A distinct change has occurred over the past fifty years in the way women have become engaged in the labor force. A critical initiative taken by the ILO in the area of both international and "global" measurement relates to the identification of work patterns according to age groups and gender. Data referring to the economically active population capture the major trends in labor-force activity over generations. These trends are driven by more fundamental longer-term social forces and economic conditions than those that affect the current level of business. They reflect how education and changing patterns of gender discrimination combine to alter the essential structure of economic activity and composition of employment, both part-time and full-time. No longer is the male the real (or even apparent) sole breadwinner in the family in many regions of the world. The ILO's approach to measuring economic activity rates, seen initially from a relevant country-study level, has assumed wider importance when viewed in relationship to observed global change.

The ILO provides global estimates and projections of the economically active population according to sex by five-year age groups over the 10–64 age range and 65 years and over for the period 1950–1990. Separate information is available for manufacturing industry for the years 1980 and 1990. The data refer to all 178 countries and territories of the world that had 200,000 inhabitants or more in 1990. The data are also aggregated into regions within major areas and totals are generated for the world.

Data on the labor force are drawn from population censuses and are updated and extended on the basis of more detailed sample surveys of the economically active population. The data are adjusted, where necessary, to conform to a standard concept of economically active population. This includes all employed and unemployed persons and refers to the same age distribution, reference period, and date of census or household or enterprise survey. The definition of the economically active population corresponds to a subset of the labor force that is capable of taking on work. The results concerning activity rates by sex and age group show that over the past several decades, activity patterns around the world have undergone fundamental change, and these trends are projected to continue into the future. Activity rates by age group are given by the percent of the economically active population in that age group to the total population in the age group. Economic activity rates by sex and age group for the whole world indicate that the profile of women's activity rates is moving closer to that of men, although female levels still remain considerably lower than those of males. The activity rates for adult women (20–60 years old) are increasing, while male activity rates (all age groups) are declining. Young men and women are postponing their entry into the labor market, and older workers are retiring earlier. These trends are the result of changing social and economic conditions. Activity rates among younger workers are declining because many are remaining longer in the educational system and some young people are discouraged about seeking work. This is because they think no suitable work is available to fit their skills or simply that no jobs are available.

The activity rates for older workers are declining because of earlier access to retirement benefits and unemployment at the end of a career. Older-age unemployment is reinforced by insufficient education and retraining arrangements for the changing jobs available. Older workers cease seeking work because they become discouraged and decide to quit the labor force. For older women, the lower participation rates now being observed are partly due to cohort effects. When these women were younger, they looked after their families and they participated far less in the economy than women in their comparable age groups do now.

The increasing participation of adult women in the labor force is due to changes in the family pattern (the decline of fertility rates, the increasing incidence of single-parent families, an increase in divorce rates, and the development of part-time work). It also reflects improved statistics that better capture women's activities in the labor market. Modern surveys now inquire directly about women's activities during the reference period instead of asking them for their profession or occupation. The evolution in the female participation rates is reinforced by a generation effect; older generations are progressively replaced by younger groups who have a broader range of skills and career objectives and a higher level of labor-force participation.

In North America, Europe, and Oceania, the profile of women's activity rates by age group has changed and become quite similar to that of men. The increases in female participation rates have caused the gradual disappearance of the bimodal shape characteristic of the female life-cycle profile seen to be uniformly prevalent across these countries in the 1950s. This "M" shape was the result of women leaving the work force around the age of 25 years to have children and then a small proportion subsequently returning to work when they were about 35 years old. The bimodal shape of activity rates by age group that were prevalent historically in the developed regions does not apply to developing countries, where women who enter the work force tend to continue working for basic economic reasons.

Real Wage Measures

From its earliest days, the ILO was concerned about the relationship between food prices and the wages of workers and the hours they worked. In 1924, it began publishing such data with the main objective of making international comparisons of real wages and of determining in each country the food-purchasing power of wages. The idea was to ascertain whether the ordinary worker's wage, for a standard working period, was sufficient to buy the basic staples of life normally consumed by the average worker and his or her immediate family.[1] This was a matter of sometimes urgent concern but one where official interest was only lukewarm.

A major objective was to compare the wages of similar groups of workers across regions and countries to assess their real standard of living. The first inquiry in 1924 collected prices for fifteen basic food items. Wages were obtained for eighteen occupations in four industries for twelve capital cities in Europe plus the capitals in Canada and the U.S. Five years later, the number of items in the basket was increased to thirty-four and a handful of nonfood necessities was added. Until 1930, real-wage indices were calculated for each occupation for all the capital cities involved, using London as a base. The consumption patterns of six groups of countries were used as weights for the food items. In 1950, the list was expanded to forty-one food and nonfood items.

In 1953, however, the real food-purchasing inquiry was disbanded because the data lacked comparability. It was argued the food items no longer reflected the consumption habits of workers and their families. Policywise, this was probably a mistake. The abandonment of such an important and operationally relevant exercise on account of an apparent inability to confront data-collection issues and overcome what was clearly not an insuperable statistical problem must be judged unfortunate, reflecting weak policy awareness or a lack of commitment on the part of the ILO.

The significant weakness of the ILO data on item prices remains their inaccuracy and unreliability. Useful compilations of national and regional indices of the price ratios of selected food items to the price of rice over successive years have tended to illustrate this point. Thus, what had been an important

and innovative initiative designed to enhance a general understanding of labor markets and the capacity of workers to acquire a minimal standard of
living appears to have been set to one side because of the inability or political
unwillingness at the time to tackle some basic statistical questions.

The ILO has continued with its regular price-collection exercise, and in
1985, although the number of items priced had more than doubled to ninety-
three, the list was once again restricted to food and drinks. The ILO took an
important step to define each food item in more specific detail. By the year
2000, the *October Enquiry,* now an annual rather than a monthly or quarterly
survey as it was in the early days, had been extended (in theory) to cover 159
occupations in around 200 countries.[2] The coverage was no longer limited to
single wage-earners but expanded to include all households. Unfortunately,
the overall response rate was poor and it was felt that limitations on the number of countries covered could give rise to some misconceptions.

Very recently, with the more extensive data available from its latest inquiries, the ILO decided to revisit this key question of living standards and work
efforts by commissioning a *Report to Compare Standards of Living across Occupations and Countries using the ILO October Enquiry.*[3] The authors calculated the working time required by different types of labor in various countries
to enable low-income workers to acquire certain basic staples thought to be
representative to their region.[4] Not unexpectedly, the results revealed significant differences between classes of workers and also between countries in the
time it took to buy, as a result of their labor, a given quantity of a specified
staple relevant to their respective food intakes (as determined by the FAO).
This information is clearly relevant to a better understanding of poverty, living standards generally, and inequalities of income that appear to be brought
about by patterns (and distortions) in the labor market in various countries.
It remains an important element of economic and social quantification in
understanding the world and is a concern for analysts of globalization.

Notes

Disclaimer: The publisher has endeavored to ensure that the URLs for external Web sites referred to in this book are correct and active at the time of going to press. However, the publisher has no responsibility for the Web sites and can make no guarantee that a site will remain live or that the content is or will remain germane.

Foreword

1. Dudley Seers, *The Political Economy of Nationalism* (Oxford: Oxford University Press, 1983), p. 130.

2. The Bretton Woods institutions, in this respect, are far ahead. The World Bank published two massive histories—one on the occasion of its twenty-fifth anniversary and the other (two volumes and more than 2,000 pages) on its fiftieth. The International Monetary Fund has an in-house historian who ensures the capture of its place in history with regular publications.

3. Louis Emmerij, Richard Jolly, and Thomas G. Weiss, *Ahead of the Curve? UN Ideas and Global Challenges* (Bloomington: Indiana University Press, 2001), p. xi.

Prologue

1. Emma Rothschild, *Economic Sentiments: Adam Smith, Condorcet and the Enlightenment* (Cambridge, Mass.: Harvard University Press, 2001).

2. Graham Pyatt and Michael Ward, eds., *Identifying the Poor: Papers on Measuring Poverty to Celebrate the Bicentenary of the Publication in 1797 of "The State of the Poor" by Sir Frederick Morton Eden* (Washington, D.C.: IOS Press, 1999).

3. For an excellent review of how individual quantitatively oriented humanitarians played a significant role in generating knowledge about poverty and living conditions, see Richard Stone, *Some British Empiricists in the Social Sciences, 1650–1900* (Cambridge: Cambridge University Press, 1997). For an assessment of living standards at the time, see Arthur Taylor, ed., *The Standard of Living in Britain in the Industrial Revolution* (London: Methuen, 1975).

4. T. Griffin, "The Beginnings of the International Co-operation on Statistical Matters," paper to mark the fiftieth anniversary of the Conference of European Statisticians (CES), Paris, June 2002.

5. Orwell noted that in order to control the future, it is necessary to understand the past. Statistics make an important contribution to the continuing process of discovery and to an understanding of historical change. In making information available and issues more transparent, statistics support debate, encourage a more balanced dissent, and help expose reality.

6. T. S. Ashton, *The Industrial Revolution, 1760–1830* (Oxford: Oxford University Press, 1948).

7. F. Morton Eden, *The State of the Poor*, 3 vols. (London: J. Davis, 1797); see also Pyatt and Ward, *Identifying the Poor.*

8. Karl Marx applauded Eden's work as the only example in which the nature of poverty was documented and understood.

9. Eliot Asinof, *1919: America's Loss of Innocence* (New York: D. I. Fine, 1990). Asinof provides a sweeping evaluation of four significant events in the crucial interwar years that had a profound effect in shaping the American psyche; these included the domestic defeat of President Woodrow Wilson's dream of a world peace secured through American support of the League of Nations and the insidious profiling of suspected Communists in America staged by Attorney General A. Mitchell Palmer, a practice later infamously associated with Senator Joseph McCarthy, an acolyte of Palmer.

10. In practice, while the system was advantageous to many primary producing countries, the principal beneficiary was Britain itself, which could buy its raw materials cheap and sell its manufactured products more competitively on the international market. For a similar reason, the Americans were reluctant to react positively to Britain's requests for help in debt repayments because the former were concerned that the funds might be used to buy back investments previously sold in order to support the war effort.

11. It is interesting that the U.S. seemed rather less worried about French colonial interests in Southeast Asia, perhaps because the subtle, interwoven, often-opaque cultural intricacies of France's overseas empire were more difficult to unravel and understand.

12. The work of the social Darwinists in the nineteenth century, specifically Herbert Spencer's coining of the phrase "the survival of the fittest," underlined a way of thinking that believed that the whole context of life was determined by winning and losing and belied the existence of compassion. Just as Darwinism, which held great sway among many economic philosophers and social observers, was reviled by the church as a threat to an established "religious" view of life, so classical economic theory was seen as a challenge to long-cherished human values and a traditional sense of community that was founded on mutual reliance rather than individual competition. Adam Smith's much earlier prescient notion of the invisible hand nevertheless envisaged economic processes working ultimately for the benefit of all.

13. UN Department of Economic and Social Affairs, "Use of Macro Accounts in Policy Analyses," *Handbook of National Accounting*, Series F, No. 81 (New York: United

Nations, 2002). See, in particular, Section II.B, "The Foundations of Macroeconomics," pp. 12–29.

14. Jack E. Triplett, "Escalation Measures: What Is the Answer? What Is the Question?" in *Price Level Measurement,* ed. W. Erwin Diewert and C. Monmarquette (Ottawa: Minister of Supply and Services Canada), pp. 457–482.

15. Friends of the Chair (of the Statistical Commission), "Report on the Global ICP program," presented at the thirty-first session of the UN Statistical Commission, UN Headquarters, New York, 20 February–3 March 2000.

16. Zvi Griliches and Michael D. Intriligator, *Handbook of Econometrics,* 5 vols. (New York: Elsevier Science Publishing Company, 1983).

17. Jeremy Bentham, the renowned nineteenth-century utilitarian and moral philosopher, defining one of the critical conditions for good policy, argued that actions taken should provide "the greatest happiness to the greatest number." This sits well with the economist's notion of Pareto optimality, which simply states that one situation is an improvement over another if some people come out better off and no one else gets worse off. It is interesting that Bentham was also concerned with "the avoidance of pain," a philosophy fundamental to the Buddhist way of life. A focus on the latter principle would have led people to think more about poverty alleviation than in terms of the imperative to achieve individual economic success.

18. See Yves Berthelot, ed., *Unity and Diversity in Development Ideas: Perspectives from the UN Regional Commissions* (Bloomington: Indiana University Press, 2004), particularly Chapter 1 regarding Prebisch's pathbreaking role in the ECLA's 1949 *Economic Survey of Latin America.*

19. Questions of governance and human rights are clearly important, but they have not been addressed in any comprehensive way by international statistics. Some of these concerns are returned to in the final chapter.

20. In part, this is because "growth," as statistically measured, quantifies mainly what is happening to the reported incomes of the better-off sections of the community.

21. As some might argue, the Bretton Woods institutions laid down conventions and conditions—relating to strategies for balancing external payments, for example—that consigned many low-income countries to an inevitable path of economic dependency and unsustainability.

22. The term "sustainability," while less definite, is used in preference to the words "conservation" or "preservation," which are more restrictive and imply strategies that are not necessarily optimal.

23. C. P. Snow, *Strangers and Brothers* (London: Macmillan, 1959).

24. See Martin Rees, *Before the Beginning: Our Universe and Others* (Cambridge: Perseus Books, 1997).

25. Bjørn Lomberg, *The Skeptical Environmentalist: Measuring the Real State of the World* (Cambridge: Cambridge University Press, 2001). Lomberg damns the cavalier use of statistics in support of political viewpoints on environmental degradation that cannot be substantiated.

1. Ideas and Statistics

1. A. Maxwell Stamp, *Josiah Stamp and the Limitations of Economics* (London: Athlone Press, 1970). In his Stamp Memorial Lecture of that year, he referred not only to Lord Kelvin's famous dictum, "We do not begin to know anything about a subject until we learn to measure it" (10) but also to the economist's inability to measure critically important issues such as the erosion of the purchasing power of money or the standard of living.

2. The incomplete nature of the UN archives in this area, particularly in explaining why certain decisions were taken (as opposed to simply to reporting them), has hampered such investigations.

3. Michael Ward, "Are Codes of Conduct and Professional Ethics Enough?" paper presented to the IAOS Conference on Official Statistics and the New Economy, London, 27–29 August 2002. Available online at http://www.statistics.gov.uk/iaoslondon2002/contributed_papers/downloads/IP_Ward.doc. Just as people have come to accept the triumph of objective information over political rhetoric and concerted propaganda, the principle of evidence-based policy has encountered some recent high-profile setbacks that have undermined public trust in official data. People have come to recognize that media synthesis and packaging of some political decisions often reflects a particular interpretation and understanding that decision makers wish to project. The desire for an independent perspective is a manifestation of a wider appeal for objectivity in reporting. It is part of the search for a better-informed insight that will enhance understanding. How far the moral perspective in formulating policy can be enhanced and the existing ideology better guided by the empirical authority of numbers ought not to be left to chance or to political conjecture as to the true nature of evidence.

4. See especially IMF SDDS (Special Data Dissemination Standards), GDDS (General Data Dissemination System), and DQAF (Data Quality Assurance Framework). For further information go to the IMF Dissemination Standards Bulletin Board at http://dsbb.imf.org/Applications/web/dsbbhome.

5. One of the UN's earliest aims was to counterbalance certain national power structures that it felt could potentially destabilize peaceful international relations and prejudice universal discourse. See the UN Charter, available online at http://www.un.org/aboutun/charter/index.html.

6. Kris Inwood, "Economic Growth and Global Inequality in Long Run Perspective," a review of *The World Economy: A Millennial Perspective* by Angus Maddison (2001), *Review of Income and Wealth*, ser. 48, no. 4 (2002): note 28.

7. Thus, little is known in detail about the real conditions of poverty in a rapidly urbanizing industrial Europe in the late eighteenth and early nineteenth centuries because such records are few and far between and what is known has been strongly influenced by the writings of contemporary novelists and social observers, such as Charles Dickens and Victor Hugo.

8. This problem is recognized by Maddison, one of a handful of economic historians who has traced the processes of economic development and structural

change over the long time periods when different trade and business cycles have exerted a major impact in disturbing trends. See Angus Maddison, *Phases of Capitalist Development* (Oxford: Oxford University Press, 1982); *Economic Growth in the West* (New York: Twentieth Century Fund, 1964); and *The World Economy: A Millennial Perspective* (Paris: OECD, 2001).

9. Fred Hoyle's description of a chance event as "the assembly of a jumbo 747 by a tornado in a junk yard" is used in discussion to underline the likely significance of "design" versus random occurrence and the correlation of concordant events in science and nature.

10. The International Conference on Financing for Development was held on 18–22 March 2002 in Monterrey, N.L., Mexico. Information about the conference can be found at http://www.un.org/esa/ffd.

11. Minutes of the first meeting of the Nuclear Statistical Commission, 1–14 May 1946, which was held at Hunter College, New York, can be found in UNSD archives.

12. The time seems ripe for a comprehensive treatise on "the political economy of numbers." See Dudley Seers, "The Political Economy of National Accounting," in *Employment, Income Distribution, and Development Strategy: Problems of the Developing Countries: Essays in Honour of H. W. Singer,* edited by Hans Singer, Alec Cairncross, and Mohinder Puri (London: Macmillan, 1976) for an early recognition of the importance of this question. Also see Seers, "The Neutrality of Numbers," *IDS Bulletin* 7 no. 3 (October 1975).

13. "[Heinz] Arndt labored long and imaginatively to gather primary information on bank holdings, consumer credit and the sources of public and private investment, all of which nowadays are the subjects of official published statistics." Peter Drake writing in the Royal Economic Society *Newsletter* 118 (July 2002): 12. The extensive historical statistical work of Angus Maddison in *The World Economy: A Millennial Perspective* (Paris: OECD, 2001), for example, bears ample testimony to this problem.

14. H. W. Arndt, *The Economic Lessons of the Nineteen Thirties* (London: Oxford University Press, 1944) was one attempt to evaluate the policy experience of countries in the interwar period. See also Colin Clark, *The Conditions of Economic Progress* (London: Macmillan, 1940).

15. Stone's pioneering work on modern national income accounting later had wider dissemination through his famous succinct publication with James Meade, *National Income and Expenditure* (London: Bowes and Bowes, 1944).

16. Minutes of the first meeting of the nuclear Statistical Commission. Available from UNSD private archives on the Statistical Commission.

On 29 April 1946, the Czechoslovak delegation to the United Nations submitted to the Secretary General document E/STAT/2 containing a proposal for consideration by the Statistical Commission that had been prepared earlier on 4 February 1946 by the Czechoslovak government-in-exile in London. Document number 201/46 read:

Sir, I have the honor to suggest that the following questions should be included on the agenda of the Statistical Commission of the Economic and

Social Council; the establishment of a special information and statistical service which would collect and analyze reports of the members of the UN on the position and activities of women in the social, economic and cultural life of the various countries. Reports would be given on the basis of questionnaires and would deal with these issues.

1.   Status of women, their opportunities for education and training and their right to enter industries and the professions.

2.   Working conditions of women, social services for mother and child and for working women, participation of women in political life, women's activities in the sphere of arts, sciences and education.

The obtained information would serve as a source of research and especially as basis for the work of Commissions of the Economic and Social Council. The collected documents completed in regular intervals, would form the foundations of an international archive on the position and activities of women.

Regrettably, no evidence could be found about how the first commission actually dealt with this prescient, far-seeing proposal but it is clear the issue was dropped from the program for the new UNSO. It probably would have been seen by the members of the commission as being of peripheral importance in the context of the top priority given at the time to postwar economic reconstruction and full employment. It would be more than a quarter of a century before the matter of statistics on the question of the role and status of women in society and the economy would appear again on the UNSO agenda.

17. W. W. Rostow, *The Stages of Economic Growth: A Non-Communist Manifesto* (Cambridge: Cambridge University Press, 1960).

18. The question of time preference has never been adequately addressed in official statistics.

19. United Nations Statistical Office, *A System of National Accounts and Supporting Tables* (New York: United Nations, 1953).

20. The 1968 and 1993 editions of the *System of National Accounts* are United Nations documents ST/STAT/ser. F/2/Rev.3 and ST/STAT/SER.F/2/Rev.4, respectively.

21. See William Seltzer, "Five Decades of the Statistical Commission: Five Results from a Systematic Sample," paper presented at the twenty-eighth session of the Statistical Commission, UN Headquarters, New York, 27 February–3 March 1995, to commemorate the fiftieth anniversary of international statistical work in the United Nations system.

22. The World Fertility Survey was a collection of internationally comparable surveys of human fertility conducted in forty-one developing countries in the late 1970s and early 1980s. This project was conducted by the ISI (International Statistical Institute) with funding from USAID and UNFPA. This survey was subsumed by the Demographic Health Survey.

23. IMF, *Direction of Trade Statistics* (Washington, D.C.: IMF, 1981–). This is an annual publication by the IMF. United Nations Statistical Office, *A Short Manual on Sampling* (New York: UN, 1960).

24. For simplicity, the term "UNSO" is generally preferred in the text, except where "UNSD" is referred to specifically in a time-relevant context.

25. The WTO is not within the UN system but is intimately involved in tariffs, trade issues, negotiations on trade in services, agreements, and so forth, and their resulting issues of measurement.

26. Other international organizations such as the IMF are responsible for producing manuals on the balance of payments, money and banking, and government financial statistics.

27. Information about the Millennium Development Project can be found at http://www.unmillenniumproject.org.

28. Jack Triplett, "The Solow Productivity Paradox: What Do Computers Do to Productivity?" *Canadian Journal of Economics* (April 1999); available online at http://www.brook.edu/views/articles/triplett/199904.htm. See also Dale Jorgenson, *Productivity and U.S. Economic Growth* (Cambridge, Mass.: Harvard University Press, 1987), and "Whatever Happened to Productivity Growth?" in *New Developments in Productivity Analysis,* edited by C. R. Hulten, E. R. Deau, and M. J. Harper (Chicago: University of Chicago Press, 2001), pp. 205–246.

29. This is not to say that classification systems and even elemental data frameworks have not been modified or amended but that the assumed rationale for preserving certain systems and procedures has shifted. The inability, even by the turn of the century, to recognize the importance of trade in services, what this is, and its significance to the balance of payments is just one example.

30. William Seltzer, "Statistical Standards and National, Regional, and Global Requirements and Capabilities," paper presented at the Joint Statistical Meetings, Chicago, Illinois, 4–8 August 1996.

31. An instance of Francis Bacon's notion of an observed result representing only a "fingerpost at the crossroads."

32. The problem is the interrelationship between changing weights and prices over long time spans and the Gerschenkron effect. This is a widely acknowledged but unquantified phenomenon that is related to how the component structure of prices and quantities interact within a reported expenditure outlay when the economic distance, as seen either over time or as between two countries with dramatically different economies, affects the statistical interpretation of recorded output or expenditure outlays. If price and quantity structures change significantly between two observations—as would have occurred in most industrial countries in the composition of output, say, between the year 1900 and the year 2003—then measured changes in the underlying real output derived from applying a price index over this same period to deflate the reported current values would not accurately represent the true changes that had taken place. Exactly the same problem arises when trying to apply a spatial price index to compare the output of the U.S. or Japan with the output of Laos or Burundi. This has mostly to

do with substitution effects as prices rise (or fall) and how, in an exogenous way, new technology brings about often-unforeseen obsolescence and significantly affects the relative structure of the factors of production used to generate output.

2. The Economic Dimension

1. Thomas Kuhn, *The Structure of Scientific Revolutions* (Chicago: University of Chicago Press, 1996).

2. Dudley Seers, "The Limitations of the Special Case," *Bulletin of the Institute of Economics and Statistics* 25, no. 2 (May 1963).

3. Established data methodologies and definitions generally do not allow observers to test the validity of new theories.

4. Respectively, Friedrich A. Hayek, *The Road to Serfdom* (London: G. Routledge & Sons, 1944); and John Maynard Keynes, *The General Theory of Employment, Interest, and Money* (New York: Harcourt, Brace, 1936) and *How to Pay for the War: A Radical Plan for the Chancellor of the Exchequer* (London: Macmillan and Co., 1940).

5. Max Weber, *The Protestant Ethic and the Spirit of Capitalism* (New York: Scribner, 1930); R. H. Tawney, *Religion and the Rise of Capitalism* (London: J. Murray, 1926).

6. In a contribution to a series of recollections of distinguished economists, Angus Maddison, who was born and brought up in northeast England before the war in an area heavily dependent on coal mining and shipbuilding, recounts how members of his family were unemployed for lengthy periods of time and how they were not only poor but also became despondent and depressed. He describes their children as "sickly and tubercular." He recalls that in Gateshead, he saw "nowhere so depressing until visiting Calcutta some thirty years later." ("Confessions of a Chiffrephile," *Banca Nazionale di Lavoro Quarterly Review* [June 1994]: 123–185.) Unemployment involving prolonged periods of no work, resource misuse, and underutilization were the burning issues that challenged economists from all political persuasions. It is why "full employment" became the watchword of postwar policy. Definitions of unemployment, however, differed considerably across countries and have changed over time. Moreover, the monitoring of unemployment (as the obverse of employment) has been manipulated by various governments to disguise labor slack during periods of comparatively high and politically unacceptable levels of unemployment, underemployment, and significant job losses in OECD countries.

7. An interesting case in point is corporate strategy and how ideas of social (and environmentally friendly) accounting are also taking hold in the private sector.

8. For example, if a chief executive officer is offered a remuneration package that is heavily weighted by a personal (short-term) share-option component and his or her compensation is related to annual or share-price profit performance, then the priorities of company managers and their policies may be influenced. A conflict of interest must undoubtedly arise because major shareholder interest will now reflect management interest directly. The interests of other staff employees (and their status in the enter-

prise), those of clients, and those of the public at large, in order of perceived importance, are often compromised. All could be affected by the pursuit of short-term goals that have often involved sweeping institutional restructuring and unsustainable changes.

9. Douglass North, *Institutions, Institutional Change and Economic Performance* (Cambridge: Cambridge University Press, 1990).

10. In the short term, this may not necessarily include making "profits."

11. United Nations, *Links between Business Accounting and National Accounting* (New York: United Nations Statistical Division, 2000).

12. *Inland Revenue Report on National Income, 1929*, with an introduction by Richard Stone (Cambridge: Department of Applied Economics, University of Cambridge, 1977). This important report, produced in the year before the world entered the Great Depression, was not published until almost fifty years afterward, much to Stone's lament, because it would have initiated an official series of national income estimates.

13. John Maynard Keynes, *General Theory on Employment, Interest, and Money* (New York: Harcourt, Brace, 1936). Keynes showed that aggregate spending power supported the economy. If this fell off because people became unemployed, then output would decline further.

14. A. C. Pigou, *The Theory of Unemployment* (New York: A. M. Kelley, 1933).

15. John Maynard Keynes, *How to Pay for the War: A Radical Plan for the Chancellor of the Exchequer* (London: Macmillan and Co., 1940).

16. Charles Kindleberger was another distinguished economist who was involved in devising the Marshall Plan. Kindleberger also exerted a strong intellectual influence on matters of trade measurement. He worked for a time under Alvin Hansen, an early champion of Keynes in the United States.

17. To find out more about W. Edwards Deming and his work, visit the W. Edwards Deming Institute's Web site at http://www.deming.org.

18. But note the pioneering work of the UK Inland Revenue Service (see note 12 in this chapter).

19. For an important and interesting discussion of the issues, see Gyorgy Szylagyi's recent review of Utz-Peter Reich's book *National Accounts and Economic Values—Study in Concepts* in "What Is the Theory Behind?" *Review of Income and Wealth*, Series 49, no. 2 (June 2003).

20. In 1929, the Inland Revenue Department in Great Britain produced a detailed set of national accounts that foreshadowed subsequent developments.

21. Later it was recognized that issues of personal safety, environmental degradation, and so forth were equally important to well-being. The only real concession to concerns of social policy was a brief but eventually inconsequential flirtation in the early 1970s with the System of Social and Demographic Statistics (SSDS) and somewhat more successful social accounting matrices (SAMs). The latter were seen as a way to bring in the essential element of household preferences and consumption behavior into the national accounts. Both these approaches were, for the most part, the brainchild of Richard Stone. Stone was not only one of the primary authors of the original SNA (and

a recognized international authority on demand equations and linear expenditure systems) but also the dominant figure in the substantive revision of the system in 1968. The SSDS and the SAMs were intimately linked to the 1968 SNA in an all-embracing conceptual model that envisioned social progress as a direct primary outcome of the successful implementation of economic policy.

22. Derek Blades, *History of the System of National Accounts* (Paris: OECD, 2001).

23. Organisation for European Economic Cooperation, *A Standardized System of National Accounts* (Paris: OEEC, 1952).

24. James Meade and Richard Stone, *National Income and Expenditure* (London: Bowes and Bowes, 1944); updated in 1966 by Richard Stone and Giovanna Stone. For an insightful and personal view of Stone's life and his association with the UN, see M. H. Pesaran, "An Interview with Professor Sir Richard Stone," *Econometric Theory* 7 (1991): 85–123. See also the annex to Keynes's *How to Pay for the War,* note 14.

25. There are some notable seventeenth-century precursors of this work, inter alia: William Petty (1623–1687) in *The Economic Writings of Sir William Petty,* edited by Henry Charles Hall (Cambridge: Cambridge University Press, 1899); Gregory King, "Natural and Political Observations and Conclusions upon the State and Condition of England 1696," in *Earliest Classics,* edited by Peter Laslett, John Graunt, and Gregory King (Farnborough, UK: Gregg International, 1973); and François Quesnay, *Quesnay's Tableau Économique,* edited by Ronald Meek et al. (London: Macmillan, 1972). More recent work is associated with Arthur Bowley and Josiah Stamp, *National Income 1924* (Oxford: Clarendon Press, 1927); and Bowley's edited work, *Studies in the National Income, 1924–1938* (Cambridge: Cambridge University Press, 1944). Earlier, Colin Clark had produced his own estimates in *The National Income, 1924–1931* (London: Macmillan, 1932). For an overview of national income development in the U.S., see Carol Carson, "The History of the United States National Income and Product Accounts: The Development of an Analytical Tool," *Review of Income and Wealth,* ser. 21, no. 2 (1975): 153–181.

26. Wassily Leontief, *The Structure of American Economy, 1919–1939,* 2nd ed. (New York: Oxford University Press, 1951). See also Hollis Chenery and Paul Clark, *Interindustry Economics* (New York: Wiley, 1959).

27. Eurostat, *Material Flow Accounting: Experience of Statistical Institutes in Europe* (Luxembourg: Eurostat, 1997); United Nations, *Comparisons of the System of National Accounts and the System of Balances of the National Economy* (New York: UNSO, 1977).

28. C. A. Bochove and H. K. Van Tuinen, "Flexibility in the Next *SNA:* The Case for an Institutional Core," *Review of Income and Wealth,* ser. 32, no. 2 (1986): 127–154.

29. Nancy Ruggles, "Comment" on papers on the structure of the SNA, *Review of Income and Wealth,* series 32, no. 2 (1986): 213–216.

30. André Vanoli, *Une histoire de la compatibilité nationale* (Paris: Découverte, 2002).

31. International Monetary Fund, *International Financial Statistics: Supplement on Government Finance,* International Financial Statistics Supplement Series No. 11

(Washington, D.C.: IMF, 1986), 30; International Monetary Fund, *Balance of Payments Manual* (Washington, D.C.: IMF, 1948).

32. Cambridge University, Department of Applied Economics, *A Programme for Growth*, vols. I–XII (Cambridge: Chapman and Hall, 1962–1974). The most influential volumes in this twelve-volume monograph serial are the first three: Richard Stone and Alan Andrew Brown, *A Computable Model of Economic Growth* (Cambridge: Chapman and Hall, 1962); University of Cambridge, *A Social Accounting Matrix for 1960* (Cambridge: Chapman and Hall, 1962); and University of Cambridge, *Input-Output Relationships, 1954–1966* (Cambridge: Chapman and Hall, 1963).

33. Graham Pyatt and Eric Thorbecke, *Planning Techniques for a Better Future* (Geneva: ILO, 1976); and Graham Pyatt and J. I. Round, eds., *Social Accounting Matrices: A Basis for Planning* (Washington, D.C.: World Bank, 1985).

34. Transcript of interview with Lawrence R. Klein, 4 January 2002, United Nations Intellectual History Project, The Graduate Center, The City University of New York.

35. Edmond Malinvaud, *Statistical Methods of Econometrics,* 3rd rev. ed. (Amsterdam: North Holland Pub. Co., 1980).

36. Seers, "The Limitations of the Special Case"; and "An Accounting System for a Specialized Exporter of Primary Products," Yale Economic Growth Center paper, 1963.

37. Inwood, "Economic Growth and Global Inequality in Long Run Perspective."

38. Utz-Peter Reich, *National Accounts and Economic Value: A Study in Concepts* (New York: Palgrave, 2001). While the conceptual macroeconomic basis of the national accounts is clear, the formal relationship of the accounts with a longer-standing traditional theory of economic value is more controversial and less evident. Reich, for example, argues that the theory of value embodied in the national accounts is different from the traditional macroeconomic model. The matter turns on how a set of descriptive accounting balances described in monetary terms should be interpreted as representing an economic value system in some more dynamic interrelated micro sense. Observed values in the national accounts depend on a multiplicity of revealed intersections of prices with quantities (and qualities) in the market that may not necessarily reflect utilities viewed overall. In part this is because the fundamental emphasis in the accounts is on production and on the incomes such economic activity generates and not on expenditures and the preferences these outlays represent. See Szylagyi's review of Reich's *National Accounts and Economic Values—A Study in Concepts* in "What Is the Theory Behind?"

39. Seers, "The Limitations of the Special Case," note 2.

40. The methodology and procedures and these practical applications were subsequently written up by Ward in *Review of Income and Wealth,* ser. 18, no. 3 (September 1972).

41. It is interesting that Seers advocated the consolidation of vertically integrated processes into a single industry (even if they were identified separately in the ISIC) to define the sugar industry, for example, as the planting and harvesting of sugar cane, the transportation and processing of the raw cane, and the production of raw sugar.

42. Thus, the sugar industry, the main industrial sector in Fiji, was taken to be a combination of agriculture (cane farming), manufacturing (sugar crushing and processing), transportation and distribution (since the milling company owned its own vehicles, a railway line, and ships), and the retailing of raw sugar. See Dudley Seers, "The Statistical Needs for Development with Special Reference to National Accounting," *IDS Communication* 120 (1977).

43. For several countries, the World Bank also produced its own midyear population estimates.

44. The Atlas method was a procedure of averaging the current actual exchange rate with projected exchange rates for the same period going back over the past three years. For a methodological description of the Atlas procedure, see the technical notes in the annex to any World Bank *World Development Indicators* publication.

45. Lance Taylor, "A Three-Gap Model," in *Problems of Developing Countries in the 1990s*, edited by F. D. McCarthy (Washington, D.C.: World Bank, 1990), pp. 55–90.

46. And which could be viewed also as countries falling into a UNDP special category of support according to the same standards.

47. These are, broadly, the "real economy," the monetary sector, government, and the external sector. For the GDDS, it also reviews the methods of compiling social and demographic statistics.

48. In the short run, there is no theoretical reason in standard neo-classical and endogenous growth models to expect the ICOR (incremental capital-output ratio) to be a measure of investment quality, to be the derivative of growth with respect to investment, or to be constant during transitions. See William Easterly, "The Ghost of the Financing Gap: How the Harrod-Domar Model Still Haunts Development Economics," *Journal of Development Economics* 60, no. 2 (December 1999): 423–438. Easterly further asserts that the "financing gap" model has little empirical validity.

49. The magnitude of this missing element depends on how porous a country's borders are; while long, landlocked borders create difficulties for frontier surveillance, the biggest problems tend to be associated with corrupt and inefficient customs control.

50. In the early 1950s, trade data were mostly compiled by hand according to the original SITC. In 1962, an IBM mainframe was acquired and a system of punched cards transferred to magnetic tapes was introduced. In 1979, some 10,000 magnetic tapes were moved to disc storage using a highly compressed format to produce what became widely accepted as "Comtrade." In 1981, an interactive user interface to Comtrade was further developed and in June 2002, plans were made to launch the system on the Internet. Over the years, UN trade data have been effectively marketed through the media of hard-copy publications, selected data on diskettes, and CD-ROMs.

51. Comtrade got its name from its inventor, Jerzy (George) Rozanski, a Polish citizen working at the ICC who was transferred to the UNSO in Geneva specifically to develop the system. In those years, the computerized system was literally referred to as "Comp.Trade" but eventually, since George was always affectionately greeted as "Comrade," it became better known as "Comtrade."

52. Questions about whether catching fish in open seas constitutes trade (or production) and how to record petroleum held in ship's bunkers on the high seas still concern some analysts.

53. It was decided from the beginning that trade related to the movement of merchandise goods and not to who were the traders. This is perhaps surprising, given the earlier age of mercantilism, the importance of the Hanseatic League, and the power of the large trading companies such as The East India Company and the Hudson's Bay Company. In terms of the policies and direction of trade and the process of development associated with economic awakening, knowledge about who was involved in trade, the value of this involvement in terms of particular commodities (spices, tea, coffee, sugar, rubber, and various minerals), and the extent to which different companies play a dominant role in a country's trade are of crucial significance. Even now, and even in quite complex economies, the extent to which a handful of major national producers (and exporters) are, in effect, also important importers is a significant piece of information that remains unobtainable. Such an analysis of trade transactions by individual economic entities, though feasible on the basis of the basic trade documentation submitted by agents, cannot be pursued because of the rules relating to confidentiality. This is one of many arguments to replace current regulations about confidentiality with those that refer only to anonymity, a procedure that would still preserve the spirit of the law.

54. United Nations Statistical Division, Standard International Trade Classification, Rev.3 (Series M, No.34, Rev.3), 1996. Available online at http://unstats.un.org/unsd/cr/registry/regcst.asp?Cl=14.

55. I am indebted to Soonhwa Yi of the Trade Unit of the Organization of American States in Washington, D.C., and to Jacob Ryten, formerly of Statistics Canada and a prime moving force in setting up the Voorburg Group on Service Statistics for their generous help and advice in preparing this section on trade in services.

56. Soonhwa Yi, "The Missing Element in Trade in Services," paper presented at the fifty-third conference of the International Statistical Institute, Seoul, South Korea, 22–29 August 2001.

57. It is not so much that the BOP manual does not cover trade in services but that its guidelines are designed to serve a somewhat different purpose. Thus, different aspects of international services transactions are classified under alternate headings relating not only to services but to property-income flows and transfers.

58. William Cave, "Measuring International Trade in Services and New Demands on the Family of Classifications," paper presented at the IAOS Conference on Official Statistics and the New Economy, London, 27–29 August 2002.

59. Soonhwa Yi, "Trade in Services and Income Distribution," paper presented at the fifth annual conference on Globalization Growth and (In)Equality, University of Warwick, UK, 15–17 March 2002.

60. W. W. Rostow, *The Stages of Economic Growth: A Non-Communist Manifesto* (Cambridge: Cambridge University Press, 1960).

61. Organisation for Economic Cooperation and Development, *Services Statistics on Value Added and Employment 2000* (Paris: OECD, 2000).

62. Some contemporary economists also identify knowledge and communication as production factors, but these are embedded in the quality of human and physical capital, respectively. The factor of entrepreneurship is important and relevant, but it presupposes a particular (that is, market) economic system. Energy, another supposed factor, is not a real factor but an input that is related to production levels by the technology in place.

63. The market system is driven by demand backed up by a willingness to pay *in aggregate*. This means that it may not respond adequately to people's needs on an individual basis. Much depends on the pattern of income distribution and how this impacts on the structure of production. In many so-called market systems, people's basic needs are not met and have to be provided by other means, usually by way of charity or the public sector.

64. Productivity is related to the amount of output, not its usefulness. See R. Turvey, *Developments in International Labour Statistics* (London: Pinter, 1990) for a clear and comprehensive discussion of these distinctions and their significance. Most analysts now recognize that producing goods faster and more efficiently (i.e., in relation to the amount and cost of inputs used) is not very productive if no one wants the goods concerned.

65. It is a paradox, at least perhaps in the eyes of neoclassical economists, that the welfare state helped strengthen the forces contributing to economic growth. As Maddison points out, it legitimized capitalist perspectives on property relations and the "free" operation of the market. By protecting the weak and providing a fallback position to those who fell through the economic system, it created a cushion for those economic actors in society who did not make it. In doing so, the welfare state "removed many of the grievances which motivated proponents of the socialist alternative, relieving pressure to reduce the amount of social distance between classes." See Angus Maddison, *Economic Growth and Standards of Living in the Twentieth Century* (Groningen, The Netherlands: Groningen Growth and Development Centre, 1994).

66. Often, however, this was a matter of deciding how externally determined production targets would be achieved.

67. The "Big Four" signatories of the Versailles Treaty (1919)—President Woodrow Wilson (U.S.), President Georges Clemenceau (France), Prime Minister David Lloyd George (Britain), and President Vittorio Orlando (Italy)—endorsed the need to have an organization concerned with the international adjustment of conditions of industrial life and labor.

68. The more cynical have seen the creation of the ILO as a bastion against the (then) encroaching influence of communism. But for some, the ILO stood as a trade union rather than a labor organization.

69. ILO, "75 Years of Labor Statistics," in *ILO Labor Statistics 1995* (Geneva: ILO, 1995).

70. International Labour Office (ILO), *Employment, Incomes and Equity: A Strategy for Increasing Productive Employment in Kenya* (Geneva: ILO, 1972).

71. There was here, perhaps, a hidden agenda to combat communism.

72. Paul E. Bangasser, "The ILO and the Informal Sector: An Institutional History," ILO Employment Paper 2000/9, International Labour Office, Geneva, Switzerland.

73. ILO Convention Concerning Labor Statistics (no. 160) was adopted by the International Labor Conference at Geneva on 25 June 1985.

74. The fact that PPP indices are mostly based on expenditure outlays and not on actual output measures is recognized as a drawback. The ILO had previously flirted with some selected binary country comparisons back in the late 1920s, using a technique that takes the geometric mean of each country's prices for a given basket of consumption goods weighted by the other country's respective expenditure weights.

75. "The imputation of market wages to non-market productive time according to the 'opportunity cost of time' method is not compatible with national accounting procedures. . . . [T]he imputation of other market wages (equivalent function in market enterprises and 'substitute household worker' methods) produces valuations which do not provide the necessary information for economic analysis purposes; households' productive time should be valued in relation to the imputed market value of the product." L. Goldschmidt-Clermont, "Monetary Valuation of Non-Market Productive Time: Methodological Considerations," paper presented to the twenty-second general conference of the International Association for Research in Income and Wealth (IARIW), Flims, Switzerland, 30 August–5 September 1992.

76. Marie Lavigne, *The Economics of Transition: From Socialist Economy to Market Economy* (New York: St. Martin's Press, 1995).

77. Some researchers in the field have argued that the ILO's approach was far too heavy-handed, formal, and procedural in evaluating the significance of the informal sector and that it tended to underestimate its extent and importance. They stressed the importance of using informal survey methods to capture the informal workings of this labor market. In 1992, the ILO initiated a worldwide series of harmonized surveys on the informal sector.

78. Ann Chadeau, "Measuring Household Activities: Some International Comparisons," *Review of Income and Wealth*, ser. 31, no. 3 (September 1985): 237–254.

79. Professor Klein won the Nobel Prize in economics in 1980.

80. Apart from the loans and transfers that formed part of the resumption of responsibilities of the original "colonial" powers, the U.S. PL480 shipment of grain represented one of the first major food aid programs to developing countries.

81. Opening remarks by Sir John Boyd Orr, director general of the FAO (1945–1948).

82. The true nature of livestock output and its coverage, however, raises a number of quite distinct conceptual and measurement issues, and in some countries these areas were ignored or not handled effectively.

83. See reference to Molly Orshansky in Jessie Willis, "How We Measure Poverty: A History and Brief Overview" (February 2000) available online at http://www.ocpp.org/poverty/how.htm.

84. In matters of measurement, "indigence" refers to situations where individuals have insufficient food to sustain themselves (that is, to keep body and soul together),

and "poverty" relates to conditions where minimum basic needs, including shelter, fuel, and clothing, are not met.

85. Timothy Marchant, Christopher Scott, and Veejay Verma, paper presented at the forty-seventh session of the International Statistical Institute, Paris, 29 August–6 September 1989.

86. National Agricultural Census Office of China, *Abstract of the First National Agricultural Census in China* (Beijing: China Statistics Press, 1999); National Bureau of Statistics, *International Seminar on China Agricultural Census Results, 19–22 September 2000: Summary Report* (Beijing, China: National Bureau of Statistics, 8 December 2000).

87. Dennis Casley and Krishna Kumar, *Project Monitoring and Evaluation in Agriculture* (Baltimore: Johns Hopkins University Press, 1987).

88. While the World Bank contributed significantly to the early financing of the ICP (and has recently taken on the global coordination of the latest round of inquiries) and the IMF has contributed to more recent phases of the program, the Bretton Woods organizations never fully embraced the concept the program presented. They preferred to see the exercise as a piece of research. In large part this was because the initial emphasis of these studies seemed to suggest that the calculation of PPPs, in line with the writings of Gustav Cassel, would enable policymakers to explore the extent of observed deviations in countries' official exchange rates from the derived PPPs, which some assumed reflected a notion of an "equilibrium" rate of exchange. Such a line of approach challenged the IMF's basic mandate on exchange-rate maintenance and was fundamentally inconsistent with the institutional management imperatives of the Bank, which applied the exchange-rate methodology of the Atlas method to help determine its operational guidelines in devising its lending programs to member countries. That the ICP is essentially the spatial analogue to well-established temporal price index measurement and analysis and is thus about the determination of differences in price levels across countries and between major expenditure categories was less well recognized.

89. John Edelman, who joined them as a researcher a few years later, did so because his U.S. academic appointment was blocked politically.

90. For the European Community (EC), Eurostat's results have an important prescribed political importance. For the OECD, the outcome had primarily research and analytical significance. Since the number and composition of countries in any comparison affect the PPP results, the EC had to insist on the "fixity" of the derived economic relationships and PPP between EC member countries participating in the OECD comparison to avoid political argument.

91. Sultan Ahmad, "Improving Inter-Spatial and Inter-Temporal Comparability of National Accounts," *Journal of Development Economics* 44 (1994): 53–75.

92. Department of Economic and Social Development, *Handbook of the International Comparison Program* (New York: United Nations, 1992).

93. Ian Castles, *Review of the OECD—Eurostat PPP Program*, OECD document STD/PPP(97)5, available online at http://www1.oecd.org/std/ecastle.pdf; and J. Ryten, *Report on the Evaluation of the International Comparisons Programme* (New York: United Nations, 1999).

3. The Social Dimension

1. Arthur Miller in "*The Crucible* in History," a series of lectures on BBC4 radio that was broadcast in December 2002, describes in vivid detail the Cold War–era U.S. political background behind the metaphor of his famous play about the witches of Salem.

2. "Health" would thus necessarily include enjoying adequate nutritional sustenance and having access to other basic requirements of life. Even from a purely medical perspective, it is easy to see that if health is approximated by the sum of all medical costs and the loss of income due to absence from work on account of illness, it could be equally interpreted as a reduction in sickness (i.e., an improvement in health care) or an increase in ill health if such real costs increase.

3. Statistically, the doctor who saves a life creates a real value (even in purely monetary terms) that is higher than the current value added that would normally be attributable that year as the equivalent labor contribution to the national income for his or her medical services.

4. "You have never had it so good" was the slogan Britain's Conservative Party prime minister Harold Macmillan used in his 1959 electoral campaign. Macmillan was prime minister from 1959 to 1963. For more information, see his online biography at http://politics99.co.uk/people/haroldmacmillan.htm.

5. In ascribing the virtues of a general improvement in living standards to economic growth, those who formulate policy have not paid enough attention to the isolation and alienation that has come about as a consequence of the perception that such gains are unfairly spread among potential recipients. Those who manipulate the economic system play on the basic human characteristics of envy and covetousness and influence the whole social context in which individual incentives are promulgated and encouraged. The reliance of policymakers on rapid economic growth and on the assumption that the benefits will be equally shared across society in a market system has to a large extent precluded proper consideration of alternative policies by which communities share in finding solutions to social problems.

6. Bertrand Russell, *A History of Western Philosophy* (New York: Simon and Schuster, 1945).

7. Richard Stone, "Towards a System of Social and Demographic Statistics," *Studies in Methods*, Series F, No. 18, UN sales no. E.74.XVII.8 (New York: UNSD, 1974).

8. United Nations, *Towards a System of Social and Demographic Statistics* (New York: United Nations, 1975).

9. Angus Maddison, "What Is Education For?" *Lloyds Bank Review*, April 1974. In a general survey of educational objectives, Maddison highlights in his article the difficulties of measuring educational performance and notes the power of interest groups that promote particular ideologies to resist the production of relevant evidence, including the collection of data relating to the cognitive progress of students at different levels over time. Elsewhere, Maddison remarks that in the area of social policy, the empirical (and, hence, analytical) basis of decisions was generally poor; see Angus Maddison, "Confessions of a Chiffrephile," *Banca Nazionale di Lavoro Quarterly Review* (June 1994): 123–185.

10. Some might say they are also quixotic in character, since no one size fits all and each SAM needs to reflect the socioeconomic circumstances peculiar to that particular country.

11. Available online at http://www.developmentgoals.org/index.html.

12. *Social Indicators: Preliminary Guidelines and Illustrative Series* (New York: United Nations, 1978).

13. *International Definition and Measurement of Levels of Living: An Interim Guide* (New York: United Nations, 1961), prepared jointly with the FAO, the ILO, UNESCO, and the WHO.

14. United Nations Research Institute for Social Development, Statistical Unit, *Research Databank of Development Indicators,* 4 vols. (1976; reprint, Geneva: UNRISD, 1987). The 1987 edition was updated and revised.

15. See Charles L. Taylor and David A. Jodice, *World Handbook of Political and Social Indicators III, 1948–1982* (Ann Arbor: Inter-University Consortium for Political and Social Research, 1985).

16. *Social Trends: A Publication of the Government Statistical Service,* annual series (London: HMSO, 1970).

17. The UNDP *Human Development Report,* published annually since 1990, reports an elaborated version of this approach.

18. See Dudley Seers, "A System of Social and Demographic Statistics: A Review Note," *Economic Journal,* no. 76 (1976); "Life Expectancy as an Integrating Concept in Social and Demographic Analysis and Planning," *Review of Income and Wealth* 23, no. 3 (1977); and "Active Life Profiles for Different Social Groups: A Contribution to Demographic Measurement, a Frame for Social Indicators and a Tool of Social and Economic Analysis," in *Economic Structure and Performance: Essays in Honor of Hollis B. Chenery,* edited by Moishe Syrquin, Lance Taylor, and Larry E. Westphal (Orlando: Academic Press, 1984). See also Henry Lucas, *Life Expectancy as an Integrating Concept for Social and Demographic Data* (Paris: OECD Development Center, 1985).

19. UNRISD was a special body set up in 1963. It had, as one of its original principal functions, the task of servicing the UN *Report on the World Social Situation,* a document that received scant attention around the world.

20. Jan Drewnowski, *On Measuring and Planning the Quality of Life* (The Hague: Mouton, 1974), p. 1.

21. Gunnar Myrdal, *Asian Drama: An Inquiry into the Poverty of Nations* (New York: Twentieth Century Fund, 1968).

22. OECD, *Shaping the 21st Century: The Contribution of Development Co-operation* (Paris: OECD, 1996). Information about the Millennium Development Project can be found online at http://www.unmillenniumproject.org.

23. The original version of this index was similar in format to the Physical Quality of Life Index (PQLI) formerly prepared under the auspices of the U.S. Overseas Development Council.

24. UNSO, *The World's Women, 1995: Trends and Statistics* (New York: UN, 1995). Other reports under the same title were published in 1991 and 2000.

25. The most significant being on population (Cairo, 1994), women (Beijing, 1995), the environment (Rio de Janeiro, 1992), and social development (Copenhagen, 1995).

26. See for example, Frank Yates, *Sampling Methods for Censuses and Surveys*, 3rd ed. (New York: Hafner, 1960); P. V. Sukhatme, *Sampling Theory of Surveys with Applications* (Ames: Iowa State College Press, 1954); W. G. Cochran, *Sampling Techniques* (New York: John Wiley and Sons, 1953); and W. E. Deming, *Some Theory of Sampling* (New York: John Wiley and Sons, 1953).

27. In these areas, C. A. Moser and G. Kalton, *Survey Methods in Social Investigation* (New York: Basic Books, 1971) remained for many years the handbook many turned to for questionnaire design and simple sampling matters.

28. United Nations Statistical Office, *A Short Manual on Sampling* (New York: United Nations, 1960).

29. For a comprehensive evaluation of this program, see K. T. de Graft-Johnson, *Review of the National Household Survey Capability Programme (NHSCP) 1979–1992* (New York: UN Statistical Division, 1992).

30. Jean-Luc Dubois, *Think Before Measuring: Methodological Innovations for the Collection and Analysis of Statistical Data*, Social Dimensions of Adjustment in Sub-Saharan Africa Working Paper No. 7 (Washington, D.C.: World Bank, 1992).

31. The report and its contents were modeled after the official UK publication *Social Trends.* (Personal communication with Joann Vanek, one of the two directors of *The World's Women 1995: Trends and Statistics.*)

32. See Richard Jolly, Louis Emmerij, Dharam Ghai, and Frederic Lapayre, *UN Contributions to Development Thinking and Practice* (Bloomington: Indiana University Press, forthcoming); and Yves Berthelot, *Unity and Diversity in Development: Perspectives from the UN Regional Commissions* (Bloomington: Indiana University Press, 2004).

33. Arlie Russel Hochschild and Anne Machung, *The Second Shift: Working Parents and the Revolution at Home* (New York: Viking, 1989).

34. D. Blades, *The Measurement of (Non-Monetary) Subsistence Output* (Paris: OECD Development Centre, 1977).

35. L. Goldschmidt-Clermont, "Monetary Valuation of Non-Market Productive Time: Methodological Considerations," paper presented to the twenty-second general conference of the International Association for Research in Income and Wealth (IARIW), Flims, Switzerland, 30 August–5 September 1992; and Ann Chadeau, "Measuring Household Activities: Some International Comparisons," *Review of Income and Wealth*, ser. 31, no. 3 (September 1985): 237–254.

36. United Nations Statistics Division, *Guide to Producing Statistics on Time-Use for Measuring Paid and Unpaid Work: An Outline*, (ESA/STAT/AC.79/7), 17 October 2000. This source addresses gender issues in the measurement of paid and unpaid work. Available online at http://unstats.un.org/unsd/methods/timeuse/xptgrpmeet/guide.pdf.

37. Minutes from the thirty-first session of the Statistical Commission, held in New York 29 February–3 March 2000, can be found in the UNSD archives.

38. At the outset, it was agreed that the project would not provide full support for a pilot study. This reflected the need to maximize limited project funds available for

country use. It also reflected the importance of national support in building new data-collection efforts, both from advocates and statistical authorities, to ensure their sustainability.

39. Much of the information related to the role of women may thus be collected by proxy and will be seen only through the eyes of a different respondent. In some cases, the respondent may not know in detail about the activities of the women in "his" household.

40. See, for example, Monica S. Fong, *Female Labor Force Participation in a Modernizing Society: Malaya and Singapore, 1921–1957* (Honolulu: East-West Population Institute, 1975); Monica S. Fong and Michael Lokshin, *Child Care and Women's Labor Force Participation in Romania* (Washington, D.C.: World Bank, 2000); Bina Agarwal, *Women, Poverty, and Agricultural Growth in India* (Delhi: Institute of Economic Growth, 1985); and Carmen D. Deere and Magdalena León de Leal, *Rural Women and State Policy: Feminist Perspectives on Latin American Agricultural Development* (Boulder: Westview Press, 1987).

41. Quite possibly, the lower body weight itself was a measure of inadequate calories.

42. Nancy Baster, *The Measurement of Women's Participation in Development: The Use of Census Data* (Brighton, England: Institute of Development Studies, 1981). In *Women's Roles and Population Trends in the Third World* (London: Routledge, 1988), Richard Anker, Mayra Buvinic, and N. H. Youssef point out that the use of the term "job" (which is equated with paid work in most people's minds) as opposed to "work" (which has a broader, more generic, meaning) clearly affects responses. "Job" is also defined elsewhere in the ILO in the sense of "occupation" rather than work.

43. The organizers of the Extended Programs of Immunization supported by the WHO and UNICEF, for example, felt that their aim should be to cover as many children as possible and that little would be served by making any gender distinction because this would simply add cost and extend the time of programs.

44. In developed countries with aging populations, because older people tend to be richer (and have smaller households), the expenditure weights in the CPI are skewed in their direction.

45. Among the internationally recognized members were David Glass (UK), Alfred Sauvy (France), and Philip M. Hauser (U.S.). The first meeting of the commission, which was created on 3 October 1946 by ECOSOC, was held at the temporary UN headquarters at Lake Success, New York, 6–19 February 1947. The first director of the UN Population Division was Frank Notestein (U.S.).

46. These issues have become more pertinent with continuing budgetary con-straints and the increasing pressure on all data agencies to market information. They are also associated with the growing technical capacity to electronically retrieve and repackage personal information for private use.

47. William Seltzer, "Politics and Statistics: Independence, Dependence, or Interac-tion?" Working Paper No. 6, Department of Economic and Social Information and Policy Analysis, United Nations, New York, 1994.

48. Available online at http://www.un.org/esa/population/unpop.htm. Accessed July 2001.

49. Alexander Pope, *An Essay on Criticism, 1711* (London: Lewis, 1970).

50. World Health Organization, *International Statistical Classification of Diseases and Related Health Problems* (ICD-10) (Geneva: WHO, 1992–1994).

51. The conceptual framework of Health for All was defined in 1977, when the thirtieth World Health Assembly (WHA) decided, in resolution WHA30.43, that the main social target of governments and the WHO in the coming decades should be "the attainment by all citizens of the world by the year 2000 of a level of health that would permit them to lead socially and economically productive lives."

52. The Washington Consensus was originally conceived as the common denominator of policy of the Washington institutions providing international assistance to Latin America, but later it assumed the more apt sobriquet of "market fundamentalism."

53. Each HDR has contained a wide range of tables incorporating statistics relating to different aspects of human development in most countries of the world.

4. The Environmental Dimension

1. Henry Peskin, "A Proposed Environmental Accounts Framework," in *Environmental Accounting for Sustainable Development: Selected Papers from the Joint UNEP-World Bank Workshops,* edited by Yusef J. Ahmad, Salah El Serafy, and Ernst Lutz (Washington, D.C.: World Bank, 1989); and Henry Peskin, "Alternative Environmental and Resource Accounting Approaches," in *Ecological Economics,* edited by D. Costanza (New York: Columbia University, 1991).

2. P. Bartelmus, C. Stahmer, and J. van Tongeren, "Integrated Environmental and Economic Accounting: Framework for a SNA Satellite System," *Review of Income and Wealth,* ser. 37, no. 2 (1991): 111–148; and P. Bartelmus, "Environmental Accounting and the System of National Accounts," in Ahmad, El Serafy, and Lutz, eds., *Environmental Accounting for Sustainable Development: Selected Papers from the Joint UNEP-World Bank Workshops* (Washington, D.C.: The World Bank, 1989).

3. Peter Bartelmus, "Whither Economics? From Optimality to Sustainability?" *Environment and Economics* 2 (1997): 323–345.

4. Robert C. Repetto, *Wasting Assets: Natural Resources in the National Income Accounts* (Washington, D.C.: World Resources Institute, 1989).

5. Fulai Sheng, *Real Value for Nature: An Overview of Global Efforts to Achieve True Measures of Economic Progress* (Gland, Switzerland: World Wildlife Fund, 1995); also Wouter Van Dieren, ed., *Taking Nature into Account: A Report to the Club of Rome* (New York: Springer-Verlag, 1995).

6. J. R. Hicks, *Value and Capital,* 2nd ed. (Oxford: Clarendon Press, 1946) defines the essential characteristics of income as the maximum amount of permissible consumption without running down existing capital.

7. U.S. Bureau of Economic Analysis, "Accounting for Mineral Sources: Issues and BEA's Initial Estimates," *Survey of Current Business* (April 1994): 50–72.

8. Salah El Serafy, "The Environment as Capital," in Costanza, ed., *Ecological Economics;* and Salah El Serafy and Ernst Lutz, "Environmental and Resource Accounting: An Overview," in Ahmad, El Serafy, and Lutz, eds., *Environmental Accounting for Sustainable Development,* pp. 1–7. See also M. Ward, *Accounting for the Depletion of Natural Resources in the National Accounts of Developing Countries* (Paris: OECD Development Center, 1982).

9. For a discussion of the measurement of net economic welfare, see William D. Nordhaus and James Tobin, "Is Growth Obsolete?" in *The Measurement of Economic and Social Performance,* edited by Milton Moss. Studies in Income and Wealth Vol. 38 (New York: National Bureau of Economic Research, 1973; distributed by Columbia University Press, 1973), 509–564. See also Net National Welfare Committee, Economic Council of Japan, *Measuring Net National Welfare of Japan: Report of the NNW Measurement Committee* (Tokyo: Ministry of Finance, 1974).

10. Anthony M. Friend and David J. Rapport, "The Evolution of Information Systems for Sustainable Development," IREE Occasional Paper Series No. 1, Institute for Research on Environment and Economy, Ottawa, 1989.

11. Ahmad, El Serafy, and Lutz, eds., *Environmental Accounting for Sustainable Development.*

12. In some countries where resource exploitation is a major economic activity, the government (or at least certain leading politicians) may well be in the pocket of the main corporate players.

13. Donella H. Meadows, *The Limits to Growth: A Report for the Club of Rome's Project on the Predicament of Mankind* (New York: Universe Books, 1972).

14. The "Report of the 1972 United Nations Conference on the Human Environment" can be found at the United Nations Environment Programme Web site at http://www.unep.org/Documents/Default.asp?DocumentID=97.

15. Allen V. Kneese, Robert U. Ayres, and Ralph C. D'Arge, *Economics and the Environment: A Materials Balance Approach* (Baltimore: Resources for the Future, 1970).

16. This resulted in the publication of the Framework for the Development of Environmental Statistics (FDES) in 1984. The FDES followed the same principles of the OECD pressure-state-response (PSR) framework. In the late 1980s, Friend and Bartelmus worked together on a UN technical report, which was published in 1991: UNSO, *Concepts and Methods of Environment Statistics: Statistics of the Natural Environment* (New York: United Nations, 1991).

17. See Bartelmus, "Whither Economics? From Optimality to Sustainability?"; and Sheng, *Real Value for Nature.*

18. Many view past damage as bygones and already-sunk costs, but some countries have made enormous and expensive efforts to return conditions to the more pristine past; for example, Japan's work to clean up Tokyo Bay, U.S. efforts with Chesapeake Bay, and UK efforts with the Thames River.

19. See Hermann Daly, *Beyond Growth: The Economics of Sustainable Development* (Boston: Beacon Press, 1996), and "Toward a Measure of Sustainable Social Net National Product," in Ahmad, El Serafy, and Lutz, eds., *Environmental Accounting for Sustainable Development,* pp. 8–9.

20. Rofie Hueting and P. Bosch, "On the Correction of National Income for Environmental Losses," *Statistical Journal of the United Nations Economic Commission for Europe* 7 (1990): 75–83; Rofie Hueting and Bart de Boer, "Environmental Valuation and Sustainable National Income According to Hueting," in *Economic Growth and Valuation of the Environment: A Debate*, edited by E. C. Ierland, J. van der Straaten, and H. A. J. Vollevergh (Cheltenham: Edward Elgar Publishing, 2001).

21. Any loss (however defined) in the environment has to be assessed in terms of the true total monetary costs and, according to basic logic, set against any gains adduced in the system. Such costs are both real and absolute, and they should also be measured in terms of the lost potential opportunities and progress.

22. Christian Leipert, "SEEA, 1989: National Economic Growth, the Conceptual Side of Defensive Expenditures," *Journal of Economic Issues* 23, no. 3 (1989): 843–856.

23. David W. Pearce, Anil Markandya, and Edward Barbier, *Blueprint for a Green Economy* (London: Earthscan, 1989).

24. The SEEA was not designed to measure the interactions within the environment and ecosystem. Such interrelationships have a time lag that is sometimes very long. Moreover, these effects can be specific to certain geographical areas.

25. S. J. Kuening and M. de Haan, "Netherlands: What's in a NAMEA? Recent Results," in *Environmental Accounting in Theory and Practice*, edited by K. Uno and P. Bartelmus (London: Kluwer Academic Publishers, 1998), 143–156. For a discussion of the LINK model encompassing a set of identities and stochastic equations about economic behavior (GDP related), see UN, *The Use of Macro Accounts in Policy Analysis* (New York: United Nations, 2002), p. 296. Available online at http://unstats.un.org/unsd/nationalaccount/hbnause.pdf.

26. See Harold Hotelling, *A General Mathematical Theory of Depreciation*, reprinted from the *Journal of the American Statistical Association*, September 1925. Hotelling makes the point that as a product with economic value becomes more scarce, its price will rise, thus limiting the rate of its future consumption and encouraging a switch to cheaper substitutes and to alternative technologies.

27. See E. U. Weizsäcker, A. B. Lovins, and L. Hunter Lovins, *Factor Four—Doubling Wealth, Halving Resource Use* (London: Earthscan Publications, 1995) for a discussion on how technological solutions push back environmental deadlines.

28. Friend and Rapport, "The Evolution of Information Systems for Sustainable Development."

29. Susan Strasser, *Waste and Want: A Social History of Trash* (New York: Metropolitan Books, 1999).

30. Vance Packard, *The Waste Makers* (New York: D. McKay, 1960).

31. Wassily Leontief, "Environmental Repercussion and the Economic Structure: An Input-Output Approach," in *Economics of the Environment: Selected Readings*, edited by Robert Dorfman and Nancy S. Dorfman (New York: Norton, 1972), pp. 403–422; and Wassily Leontief, "National Income, Economic Structure and Environmental Externalities," in *The Measurement of Economic and Social Performance*, edited by Milton Moss (New York: National Bureau of Economic Research, 1973), pp. 565–578.

32. The Growth Project team consisted of a very small but brilliant group of scholars who were joined from time to time by different experts from around the world. Many of these applied economists and statisticians would shape the measurement of development on returning to their home countries and institutions. Throughout this period to the mid-1970s, the process of putting the tables together was referred to as "social accounting." This was not simply a chance choice of phrase. Stone saw the system as having societal relevance and influencing decisions and long-term strategy to improve people's well-being and their environment.

33. Richard Stone, "The Evolution of Pollution: Balancing Gains and Losses," *Minerva* 10 (1971).

34. And eventual exhaustion in the case of nonreproducible resources.

35. The work of both the Nairobi Group and the London Group on Environmental Accounting is of particular importance in this respect.

36. World Bank, *Expanding the Measure of Wealth: Indicators of Environmentally Sustainable Development* (Washington, D.C.: World Bank, 1997).

37. Perhaps especially in the case of countries heavily dependent on tourism.

38. For which, in certain specific instances—such as the preservation of virgin forests or conservation of particular plant and animal species and the establishment of national parks and heritage sites—there is considerable public support and, perhaps, an equal willingness to pay.

39. Weak and strong sustainability represent the extremes of a spectrum that considers various possibilities for substitution, from limited to completely absent. Certain forms of capital are of value only when combined with others; for example, harvesting of fish stocks. Other forms of capital provide a service that is unique and essential to the functioning of Earth and its systems; for example, the global atmospheric system and the protection it provides against solar radiation. For these types of services, there is no substitute.

40. The revised SEEA looks at environmental debt as part of the valuation of damages caused by activities that took place in previous years.

41. This indeed is one of the bedrocks on which the approach taken by the Dutch government to environmental questions is founded.

42. To view the texts of the 1992 United Nations Framework Convention on Climate Change, and the 1997 Kyoto Protocol, visit the United Nations Framework Convention on Climate Change Web site at http://unfccc.int.

43. See Peter Bartelmus, "The Value of Nature—Valuation in Environmental Accounting," in *Environmental Accounting in Theory and Practice,* edited by K. Uno and P. Bartelmus (The Netherlands: Kluwer, Dordecht, 1998) for a more elaborate discussion of the pros and cons of different valuations in environmental accounting.

44. Organisation for Economic Cooperation and Development, United Nations, and World Bank Group, *A Better World for All: Progress towards the International Development Goals: 2000* (Washington, D.C.: International Monetary Fund, 2000).

45. Aisha Talib, background paper for 2002 *Human Development Report,* available from UNDP Human Development Report Office, New York.

5. Other Statistical Dimensions

1. Peter Bauer, *Economic Analysis and Policy in Underdeveloped Countries* (London: Routledge, 1965). If mean incomes (GNP per capita) increase rapidly because of improved performance in the formal monetary economy, then the distance between the mean and median income (that earned by the middle person) grows and so too does the gap between the mean income and that received by the majority of people in the country. The conventional way the national accounts are compiled, particularly with respect to imputing household production and own account activities, merely bears out this asymmetry. In reality, the living standards of some poor people could actually fall while the national average income rises.

2. The (purchased) right of powerful military states to use overseas facilities such as storage structures and airfields in foreign countries as strategic bases.

3. Mahbub ul Haq, "Human Development in a Changing World," Human Development Report Office Occasional Paper 1, United Nations, New York, 1992.

4. For a more detailed perspective, see Angus Deaton, *The Analysis of Household Surveys: A Microeconomic Approach to Development Policy* (Baltimore, Md.: Published for the World Bank by Johns Hopkins University Press, 1997); and Angus Deaton, "Counting the World's Poor: Problems and Possible Solutions," *World Bank Research Observer* 16, no. 2 (2001): 126–147. See also Martin Ravallion, Gaurav Datt, and Dominique Van de Walle, "Quantifying Absolute Poverty in the Developing World," *Review of Income and Wealth* 37, no. 4 (December 1991): 345–362; and Sanjay G. Reddy and Thomas W. Pogge, "How *Not* to Count the Poor," paper presented to the twenty-seventh general conference of the International Association for Research in Income and Wealth (IARIW), Djuronaset, Sweden, 18–24 August 2002, available online at www.socialanalysis.org.

5. Universal Declaration of Human Rights, 1948, Article 25. See also Kofi A. Annan, *We, the Peoples: The Role of the United Nations in the 21st Century* (New York: United Nations Department of Public Information, 2000).

6. Willem de Vries, *Meaningful Measures: Indicators on Progress, Progress on Indicators*, November 2000, available from the UN Statistics division.

7. Following the recent release of new crime figures for the year 2002–2003 showing a reported 18 percent rise in violent offenses over the previous year, the UK Home Office stated that new methods introduced by all forty-three police forces in the country made it difficult to interpret the statistics. It went on to assert that "crime has been showing neither a large rise nor a large fall." The Home Office argued that the figures had been inflated by new recording practices and when this was taken into account—by which manner it was not made clear to the public—there was actually a fall of 3 percent in overall crime. On the other hand, crime figures for drug possession and trafficking, which rose by 16 percent, are believed to underestimate the true full extent of the problem. The example illustrates not only how difficult it is to measure trends consistently if sources are changed, definitions amended, and coverage extended but also how discrepancies arise when adding information across different reporting

units. Discussion of the issue on a Web site especially set up by the *Times* of London indicated that people were concerned about the lack of transparency in the numbers and were frankly incredulous of the alleged fall in overall crime. They argued the Home Office needed "to come clean" on the problem and either stop publishing series that were not comparable across time or make clear how it had implemented adjustments to the originally reported figures to give what it believed was a more realistic picture. The episode did much to discredit official statistics and to undermine people's faith in the government's ability to tell the truth on a crucial social issue with which the public was deeply concerned.

8. Prof. Robert Solow of MIT, winner of the 1987 Nobel Prize in economics, is frequently quoted as saying, "You can see the computer age everywhere but in the productivity statistics."

9. *Report of the Special UN Sub-Group on Social Classifications,* 1–3 May 1995, available from the UN Statistics Division; see also *International Economic and Social Classifications Report of the Secretary General* (ECOSOC document E/CN.3/2002/14), 28 December 2000.

10. It is pertinent to note that a useful broad economic end-use cross-classification of imported merchandise was developed quite early by UNSO.

11. In a number of countries, the SITC was used for tariff purposes in the 1950s and 1960s, often replacing national end-use defined-tariff structures which (because the actual use of an import could not be irrevocably determined) were clearly not watertight.

12. Robert M. Pirsig, *Zen and the Art of Motorcycle Maintenance* (New York: Morrow, 1974). The book is about the art of rationality and the search for simplicity in the quest for truth. All the many parts of a motorcycle can be comprehensively identified by their nature (nuts, bolts, springs, etc.), their material composition (steel, chrome, rubber, plastic) and their relationship to different functions (the drive mechanism, the fuel system, electrics and so on), but even the most complete and interrelated classification structure cannot provide a picture of the assembled bike or explain how a motorcycle actually works.

13. In his introduction to the 50th-anniversary edition of Friedrich A. von Hayek's *The Road to Serfdom* (Chicago: University of Chicago Press, 1994), Milton Friedman boldly asserts, "the free market is the only mechanism that has ever been discovered for achieving participatory democracy" (6). But for an alternative view, see Amartya Sen, "The Value of Democracy," *Development Outreach* 1, no. 1 (Summer 1999): "[S]erious harm has resulted in the past from taking the market mechanism . . . as a solution to many problems, whereas it is an instrument that can be used in different ways—with or without vision, with or without social responsibility" (9).

14. William Shawcross, *Deliver Us from Evil: Peacekeepers, Warlords and a World of Endless Conflict* (New York: Simon and Schuster, 2000). In quoting Edmund Burke's "the only thing necessary for the triumph of evil is for good men to do nothing," Shawcross refers to the problems of implementing elections and ensuring that the process supports democracy and human rights. He points to the danger of rebuilding failed states in a Western image.

15. In this respect, they mirrored, nearly a half-century later, the original intentions of the nuclear Statistical Commission for an expert body to lead statistical developments.

16. This symbolizes the EU's habit of naming policies after meetings and conveys the different objectives of specific groups in a succinct reference.

17. For 2000, this simple exercise yields a larger estimate than the true (unknown) figure. This is because most countries count immigrants better than they monitor those who leave the country. At the world level, these international migrant flows should cancel out in reality.

18. The anti-globalization movement has been variously described by some commentators, such as *New York Times* columnist Tom Friedman, as an (ill-advised) coalition that will only help to keep the world's poor people poor.

19. Expert Group on Household Income Statistics, *The Canberra Group, Measures of Household Income and Its Distribution: Final Report and Recommendations* (Ottawa: Statistics Canada, 2001).

20. Branko Milanovic, "True World Income Distribution 1988 and 1993: First Calculations Based on Household Surveys Alone," *The Economic Journal* 112, no. 476 (January 2002): 57–93; Yuri Dikhanov and Michael Ward, "Evolution of the Global Distribution of Income 1970–1999," paper presented to the fifty-third session of the International Statistical Institute, Seoul, South Korea, 22–29 August 2001. Available online at http://www.warwick.ac.uk/fac/soc/CSGR/PDikhanov.pdf.

21. See Reddy and Pogge, "How *Not* to Count the Poor," note 4.

22. UNICEF, *Progress Since the World Summit for Children: A Statistical Review* (New York: UNICEF, 2001) is a model of reporting in a closely related area.

23. Charles Taylor, *Indicator Systems for Political, Economic, and Social Analysis* (Cambridge, Mass.: Oelgeschlager, Gunn & Hain, 1980).

24. The conference of the International Association for Official Statistics (IAOS) on Statistics, Development and Human Rights was held in Montreux, Switzerland, from 4 to 8 September 2000. A complete program can be found at http://www.statistik.admin.ch/about/international.

25. Lars Osberg, "Needs and Wants: What Is Social Progress and How Should It Be Measured?" *Review of Economic and Social Progress* 1 (June 2001): 23–42.

26. John Rawls, *A Theory of Justice* (Cambridge, Mass.: Harvard University Press, 1971).

27. Amartya Sen, *Commodities and Capabilities* (New York: Elsevier Science Pub., 1985); see also *Development as Freedom* (New York: Knopf, 1999).

28. Osberg, "Needs and Wants: What Is Social Progress and How Should It Be Measured?"

29. Performance measures used to define good practice can be seen as part of a policy of conditionality. The developing world has inherited a legacy of suspicion and doubt that sees in conditionality an echo of former colonial bonds and obligations. For the most part, policies imposed under the terms of conditionality are usually unpopular, politically unacceptable, and seldom sustainable in practice. See for example, Joseph Stiglitz, "The Role of Participation in Development," *Development Outreach* 1, no. 1 (Summer 1999): 10–16.

30. Most donors would argue, however, that TC activity reflected common objectives and policy needs.

31. The UN continues to maintain or support a small handful of statistical training centers, probably the most important of which is the Statistical Institute for Asia and the Pacific (SIAP) in Tokyo, to which the government of Japan contributes a significant share of the budget.

32. Here too, of course, the Fund sets the agenda and defines the standards.

33. An interesting analogy can be found in the medical profession, whose foundations rely very heavily on *Gray's Anatomy,* the standard work for mapping the structure of the human body. In the original text, this reference provided its detailed description of the body according to its various functions and distinct characteristics such as the skeletal framework, the bones, muscles, digestive system, intestines, and so forth. The latest revision, however, refocuses the anatomical descriptions on particular regions of the body, such as the lower abdomen, because these are the specific locations where surgeons usually need to operate and physicians have to concentrate much of their attention when diagnosing a patient's condition. In other words, traditional form and structure often needs to give way to the priorities of users to serve a more useful purpose.

Epilogue

1. Well-known astronomer William Herschel (1738–1822) noted "Is it not the same thing whether we live successively to witness the germination, blooming—and wither of a plant, or whether a vast number of specimens, selected from every stage through which time passes, be brought at once to our view?" Quoted in Martin Rees, *Before the Beginning: Our Universe and Others* (Cambridge: Perseus Books, 1997).

2. This law asserts that as people acquire more units of a given item, each successive unit will provide less and less satisfaction and utility than the previous one.

3. Hobbes viewed man as being free but thought that his actions should be controlled by the state and laws of his own making (*Leviathan,* 1660). Two centuries later, Bentham and Mill were advocating principles of liberty in their writings. Even later, Marx saw people in chains who should be free: "The proletarians have nothing to lose but their chains. They have the world to win" (*Manifesto of the Communist Party,* 1848), and in this, he paraphrases Rousseau's well-known observation, "Man is born free; and everywhere he is in chains" (*The Social Contract,* 1762).

4. Henry David Thoreau, *On the Duty of Civil Disobedience* (London: Housmans, 1963).

5. In the social sciences, a counterfactual is what analysts expect would have taken place had no (policy) action been taken. It is a way of representing the method of holding certain things constant as a scientific control measure and assessing the significance of change.

6. James Wolfensohn in his "Welcome" to *Development Outreach* 1, no. 1 (Summer 1999): 1.

7. James Wolfensohn, "Opening Address," Conference on Democracy, Market Economy and Development, sponsored by the Republic of Korea and the World Bank, Seoul, South Korea, 26–27 February 1999.

8. An unrestrained capitalism "red in tooth and claw" clearly has many destructive characteristics.

Appendix

1. The First International Conference of Labor Statisticians, held in 1923, passed a resolution, later approved by the Governing Body of the ILO the following year, stating that:

> In order that the International Labor Office may make tentative comparisons of the level of real wages in the different countries, the competent statistical authorities of each country should furnish the International Labor Office at regular intervals (if possibly monthly) with statements, in a form to be agreed upon, showing for the capital cities of their respective countries:
>
> a)   The time rates of wages and normal weekly hours of labor current in a limited number of typical occupations; and
>
> b)   Information as to the prices of a limited number of those items upon which the income of working-class families in most industrially developed countries is largely spent.

2. In practice, the response rate to the ILO questionnaires has remained quite poor, and only 50 percent of the countries on average reply each year to the inquiry.

3. R. Oostendorp and M. Przybgla, *Report to Compare Standards of Living across Occupations and Countries using the ILO October Enquiry* (Geneva: ILO, 2001).

4. Apart from the fact that this adds another dimension to the difficulty of making robust international comparisons, some might argue that the choice of certain specific staples and their defined level of processing, given the age and sex distribution of the population across urban and rural areas, did not represent the core diet of several countries.

Index

About the Author

Michael Ward graduated with combined honors in economics and statistics from the University of Exeter and with an M.A. from the University of Cambridge. His first appointment was as an official statistician in Central Africa, where he acquired the basics of the craft of data collection in the field. He is past Director of Studies in Economics and Dean of Selwyn College, University of Cambridge, and Principal Economist in both Operations and Policy areas at the World Bank. Mr. Ward has authored many articles and official reports in both applied economics and statistics and has published several books. In 1999, in Helsinki, he was awarded the Henry Methorst Medal of the International Statistical Institute for "outstanding contributions to international statistics." In 2000, he was elected Chair of the International Association for Research in Income and Wealth and currently serves on its Council. He is also on the Statistical Advisory Panel for the Human Development Report.

About the Project

The United Nations Intellectual History Project was launched in mid-1999 to fill a gaping hole in the literature about the world organization. The project is analyzing the origins and evolution of the history of ideas cultivated within the United Nations family of organizations and of their impact on wider thinking and international action. Certain aspects of the UN economic and social activities have of course been the subject of books and articles; but there is no comprehensive intellectual history of the world organization's contributions to setting the past, present, or future international agenda.

This project is examining the evolution of key ideas and concepts about international economic and social development born or nurtured under United Nations auspices. Their origins and the motivations behind them are being traced and their relevance, influence, and impact are being assessed against the backdrop of the socioeconomic situations of individual countries, the global economy, and major international developments. The project will publish fourteen books about human rights and key economic and social ideas central to UN activity. The first volume in the series, *Ahead of the Curve? UN Ideas and Global Challenges,* was published in 2001 by Indiana University Press.

The project also has completed seventy-five in-depth oral history interviews with leading contributors to crucial ideas and concepts within the UN system. A summary of the collection with excerpts will be published in 2004. The project is expected to be completed by the end of 2005.

For further information, the interested reader should contact:

UN Intellectual History Project
Ralph Bunche Institute for International Studies
The CUNY Graduate Center
365 Fifth Avenue, Suite 5203
New York, New York 10016-4309
212-817-1920 Tel
212-817-1565 Fax
UNHistory@gc.cuny.edu
www.unhistory.org